LAURENCE OLIVIER

LAURENCE OLIVIER

A Biography

DONALD SPOTO

HarperCollins*Publishers*

First published in Great Britain in 1991
by HarperCollins Publishers,
77/85 Fulham Palace Road,
Hammersmith, London W6 8JB

9 8 7 6 5 4 3 2 1

Copyright © Donald Spoto 1991

The Author asserts the moral right to be
identified as the author of this work

A CIP catalogue record for this book is available
from the British Library

ISBN 0 00 215857 4

Typeset in Linotron Aldus by
Rowland Phototypesetting Ltd,
Bury St Edmunds, Suffolk
Printed and bound in Great Britain by
HarperCollins Manufacturing, Glasgow

For Douglas Alexander,
whose graceful and benevolent influence
is everywhere evident in this book.

I say that we are wound
By mercy round and round
Gerard Manley Hopkins

CONTENTS

LIST OF ILLUSTRATIONS

31 As Heathcliff, with Merle Oberon as Cathy.
32 At Selznick Studios during the filming of *Rebecca*, with Reginald Denny and Nigel Bruce (1939).
33 Preparing his production of *Romeo and Juliet*, while filming *Pride and Prejudice* (1940).
34 The Rev. Gerard Kerr Olivier.
35 As Darcy, with Greer Garson as Elizabeth in *Pride and Prejudice* (1940).
36 The New York production of *Romeo and Juliet*, with Vivien Leigh (1940).
37 The Oliviers, soon after their marriage in 1940.
38 Preparing his false nose as Nelson in *That Hamilton Woman* (1940).
39 With Vivien as Emma in *That Hamilton Woman* (1940).
40 As Johnnie in *49th Parallel* (1941).
41 Holiday snapshot by Vivien: Olivier falls through a deckchair at Warsash (1941).
42 Training Air Scouts at Worthy Down (1942).
43 In his film of *Henry V* (1943).
44 As Henry (1943).
45 In the Old Vic production of *Arms and the Man*: as Sergius, with Margaret Leighton (1944).
46 As Astrov, with Ralph Richardson as Uncle Vanya, Old Vic (1945).
47 As Hotspur in *Henry IV, Part I*, Old Vic (1945).
48 As Shallow in *Henry IV, Part II*, Old Vic (1945).
49 As Oedipus Rex, with Sybil Thorndike as Jocasta, Old Vic (1945).
50 As Puff in *The Critic*, Old Vic (1945).
51 As Lear, with Alex Guinness as the Fool, Old Vic (1946).
52 Durham Cottage, Christchurch Street, Chelsea.
53 Directing *Hamlet* (1947).
54 Hal Wallis and Ray Milland present Olivier with his Special Oscar for *Henry V* during filming of *Hamlet* (1947).
55 The daring final leap during the filming of *Hamlet*.
56 Notley Abbey.
57 Docking at Tilbury aboard the *Corinthic* after the Australian tour (1948).
58 Backstage with Tarquin, opening night of *Venus Observed* (1950).
59 During production of *Carrie*, with director William Wyler and Vivien, at Paramount Studios (1950).
60 As George Hurstwood, with Jennifer Jones as Carrie (1950).
61 With Danny Kaye at a Hollywood party.
62 Sir Laurence and Lady Olivier at Durham Cottage, 1950.
63 As Mark Antony in *Antony and Cleopatra* (1951).
64 The Oliviers as *Caesar and Cleopatra* (1951).
65 With Maxine Audley and cast members of the two *Cleopatras* (1951).
66 During filming of *The Beggar's Opera* (1952).

He's gentle, never schooled and yet learned, full of noble device, of all sorts enchantingly beloved, and so much in the heart of the world

As You Like It

ACKNOWLEDGMENTS

My litany of saints includes very many generous people in England and America.

Actors who shared the stage with Laurence Olivier provided unique perspectives on production histories. They welcomed me to their homes, to their offices, or backstage at theatres and shared their experiences frankly and in lively detail. For interviews, for opening personal albums and sharing private correspondence I am grateful to: Dame Peggy Ashcroft, Maxine Audley, Claire Bloom, Michael Caine, Alexander Clark, Constance Cummings, Peter Cushing, Denholm Elliott, Douglas Fairbanks, Jr., Gwen Ffrangçon-Davies, Edward Fox, Sir John Gielgud, Sir Alec Guinness, Julie Harris, Rosemary Harris, Katharine Hepburn, Charlton Heston, Georgina Jumel, Harold Kasket, Rachel Kempson (Lady Redgrave), Alexander Knox, Basil Langton, Alec McCowen, Sarah Miles, Sir John and Lady Mills, Helen Mirren, Terence Morgan, Lotta Palfi-Andor, Ronald Pickup, Anthony Quinn, Michael Redington, Mercia Swinburne Relph, Jean Simmons, Maureen Stapleton, Susan Strasberg, Frances Tannehill, Ann Todd, Dorothy Tutin, Robert Wagner, Jeanne Watts.

Writers, directors and producers of stage and screen works collaborated with Olivier in quite different capacities and their viewpoints and impressions, recorded also in personal interviews, greatly complement the narrative. Herewith my thanks to: Robert Anderson, John Badham, Robert Bolt, Don Boyd, Stuart Burge, Alexander H. Cohen, Richard Fleischer, Robert Fryer, William Gaskill, Sir Peter Hall, George Roy Hill, Robert Knights, Euan Lloyd, Alexander MacKendrick, Arthur Miller, Jonathan Miller, John Mortimer, John Osborne, Hildy Parks, Daniel Petrie, Alvin Rakoff, John Schlesinger, Dale Wasserman and Terence Young.

The following friends, colleagues and associates of Laurence Olivier supplied crucial details and rich material, and I am grateful to them, too, for granting important interviews: Mark Amory, R.B. Appleton, Arthur Barbosa, Felix Barker, Ben Benjamin, Diana Boddington, Anthony Crickmay, Elaine Dundy, Leslie Evershed-Martin, Virginia

Fairweather, Angela Fox, Lynda Gilby, Renée Gilmore, John Goodwin, Lawrence Holofcener, Jean Howard, Joyce Howard, Michael Korda, Robert Kreise, Joseph Laitin, Sir Denys Lasdun, Sunny Lash, Evelyn Light, Marcella Markham, J.D. Newhouse, Donald Petrie, Floyd Phelps, Peter Plouviez, Douglas Rae, Pieter Rogers, Carew Wallace, Richard Wyatt and Talli (Mrs William) Wyler.

Various kinds of practical assistance, personal introductions and important creative suggestions were provided by Pierre Barillet, Barry Burnett, Larry Dalzell, Mitch Douglas, Anne Edwards, Sue Edwards, Lewis Falb, Gene Feldman, Stephen Galloway, Stella Heiden, Ruth Anne Henderson, Kay Hutchins, B. Larsson, Seth Lerner, Don Moore, Roland Oberlin, Ivy Pamphilon, Dorothy River, Arnold Sundgaard and Andrew Zeller.

The staffs of major archives, libraries and photographic files and those who supervise private collections were unfailingly attentive and helpful during the course of my research, and I owe very much for the time and assistance provided by: The staff of the British Newspaper Library, Colindale; Mary Corliss, at the Museum of Modern Art's Film Stills Archives; the administrative staff at the Central School of Speech and Drama – Robert Fowler, Stephen Hazell and Linda Cookson; Enid Foster, librarian at the British Theatre Association; Carolyn Grimaldi and Fred Tumas at the Museum of Broadcasting, New York; the staff of the Tyrone Guthrie Memorial Theater, Minneapolis; Stephen Pickles, at the Institute of Education, University of London; Dr C.C.G. Rawll, church warden and archivist at All Saints, Margaret Street, London; Allen Reuben, at Culver Pictures; the personnel at the Billy Rose Theater Collection of the New York Public Library at Lincoln Center; Darleen Rubin, photographer; the staff of St Edward's School, Oxford; the staff at the Research Library of the University of California at Los Angeles; and Ray Whelan, at Globe Photos.

The place of Shakespeare's art in the life of Laurence Olivier cannot be overstated, of course, and I am grateful to Professor Gerald M. Pinciss of the City University of New York, a leading scholar and an author of important books and monographs on Shakespeare. He discussed the plays at length, indicated major points for consideration in both Olivier's performances and directing, read large portions of the first draft of my typescript and made incisive suggestions.

And another close friend, the noted surgeon and oncologist Barry Mann, M.D., answered important medical questions and supplied data relevant to Olivier's major illness.

ACKNOWLEDGMENTS

From the first weeks of research, I was constantly given major assistance and endorsement by Laurence Evans, who was Olivier's close friend for sixty years. In addition, they were professionally associated from the time of their work on an early sound film, through the Hollywood years, their collaboration on the film of *Henry V* and at the Old Vic during and after the war; their professional relationship and personal trust culminated when Laurence Evans eventually became Olivier's agent and trustee. He provided me with incalculably crucial material, submitted to numerous personal interviews and transatlantic telephone enquiries, and facilitated important introductions. Laurence and Mary Evans (whose diaries were indispensable aids in tracing the contours of Olivier's last twenty years) were also attentive and devoted friends to me during the time I lived in London preparing this book, and I am grateful, too, for the many memorable occasions on which I enjoyed their generous hospitality and the warmth of their homes in London and Sussex.

Elaine Markson, my agent, is a wise and trusted friend; her guidance of my career, her abiding affection and leavening humour enrich my life daily in more ways than I can say, and she gives new meaning to the word patience. She and her associates – Geri Thoma, Lisa Callamaro, Karin Beisch and Sally Wofford – are ever buoyant and efficient, and I am grateful to be represented by so honourable and intelligent a team.

Kirtley Thiesmeyer, my attorney, constantly provides the benefits of his prudent counsel and affectionate companionship; no writer could be better served, nor could anyone find a more faithful friend.

In the New York offices of HarperCollins, Gladys Justin Carr, vice president and associate publisher, has been an author's ideal editor – enthusiastic, supportive, and insightful; she and her associate, senior editor Thomas Miller, offered numerous judicious comments and suggestions that improved the text. Their assistant Tracy Devine cheerfully despatched numerous daily tasks, making my work easier.

At HarperCollins in London, I was fortunate to have the amiable and intelligent guidance of Simon King and Carol O'Brien; zealous for this book from the first day, they and editor Robert Lacey offered many important notes and observations.

Finally, a few words about the name on the dedication page. In 1988, Douglas Alexander came to work with me as research and library assistant. I quickly recognised his prodigious creative gifts and so, while he continued to be an invaluable aide in the daily tasks of preparing a book – hunting arcane materials and scrutinising archives – I invited him to collaborate on even more challenging enterprises as my editorial associate (and as my co-author on works for film and television). It was one of the smartest decisions I ever made. With particular regard to this biography, it is impossible for me to detail how much I owe him. He read each chapter and offered substantial, acute critiques that clarified and bettered the text; he then edited the completed first draft, improving it enormously with his keen insights and queries. More important still, I cherish his loyalty to me and my work, his collegial companionship, his humour, gravity and grace. *Laurence Olivier: A Biography* is, therefore, offered to Douglas Alexander with the author's affectionate gratitude.

D.S.
Los Angeles
Ash Wednesday: 13 February 1991

CHAPTER ONE

1907–1920

He has been yonder i' the sun, practising behaviour
to his own shadow, this half-hour.

Maria, in *Twelfth Night*

The town of Dorking in Surrey is recorded as early as the twelfth
century, when it was an isolated market town in the valley of the
River Mole. Much later, after the coming of the railways in Victorian
times, its citizens enjoyed excellent access to larger cities. By 1900,
most of the ten thousand inhabitants laboured at dairy farming and
the cultivation of wheat, oats and barley in the nearby fields, where
gypsies and vagrants often pitched camp.

Twenty miles to the north-east, London in 1907 teemed with new
motor buses, but Dorking's streets still clattered with doorless, hard-
topped and decoratively fringed horsedrawn carriages. One spring
morning that year, such a vehicle was parked on Wathen Road, a few
steps from the High Street. Inside a modest semi-detached house, a
local doctor delivered a son to Agnes and Gerard Olivier.

Like Cooper, Smith or Carpenter in English, Olivier is a French trade
name, identifying one who plants, tends or sells olive trees. The Olivier
family is an old French one, traceable to Laurent de Olivier (for whom
the infant was named), a sixteenth-century citizen of Nay, a village
near the Pyrénées in south-west France. His descendant, the Huguenot
Jourdain Olivier, came to England in 1688 as chaplain to William of
Orange, and the family clerical tradition continued with his son Jerome,
born in London. The lineage is remarkable for a profusion of clergy-
men, and its family emblem expresses the ideal of devout service: the
motto accompanying an olive branch of peace is the eighth verse of
Psalm 52, '*Sicut oliva virens laetor in aede Dei* – Just as the flourishing
olive tree, so do I rejoice in the house of God.'

By 1800, Jerome's grandson, the Reverend Daniel Stephen Olivier, was Established Church rector of Clifton in Bedfordshire. Daniel's son Henry became a lieutenant-colonel in the army, and Henry's children (by Mary Dacres, daughter of a rear admiral) included the Reverend Dacres Olivier, who confirmed the family's venerable status by marrying Emma Eden, daughter of the Primate of the Church of Scotland. Dacres himself was promoted to a rectorship at Wilton and died as a canon at Salisbury Cathedral. Dacres and Emma had ten children, among whom were the Reverend Henry Eden Olivier (who married the daughter of Queen Victoria's chaplain) and the novelist Edith Olivier.

The eldest son of Lieutenant-Colonel Henry Stephen Olivier was the Reverend Henry Arnold Olivier, rector of Poulshot, Wiltshire. In addition to siring six daughters, this Reverend Olivier had four sons. Henry became a career officer. Sydney was Commander-in-Chief of Jamaica and Secretary of State for India during 1924, when a life peerage made him the first Lord Olivier. Herbert became a noted portrait and landscape painter and was Britain's official war artist from 1914 to 1919. The youngest of the four sons was Gerard Kerr Olivier.

Born on 30 April 1869, Gerard was first educated at Winchester. He had a fine singing and speaking voice, and at first intended to follow his father's example and join the ministry. But this idea was derailed after he was sent down from Merton College, Oxford, as a result of his extravagant spending and a wild drinking spree. Rebuked by his parents, Gerard calmly announced that he had abandoned his plans for the priesthood in favour of teaching. He then attended Hatfield College of Durham University, where he completed a degree and was a useful member of the cricket team.

Admired more for his suave manner and attractiveness than any remarkable intelligence, Gerard at twenty cut a tall, handsome and slim figure, with penetrating grey eyes and a wide, expressive mouth. During one term holiday, he readily agreed to appear in a painting by his brother Herbert, for whom he posed as a comely, half-naked Actaeon.

Of his natural assets Gerard was fully aware, and in 1894, aged twenty-five (after some further studies at Heidelberg), he had no difficulty in securing a position as assistant master of a preparatory school in Guildford, Surrey. Alert and confident, he soon attracted the attention of Agnes Louise Crookenden, the headmaster's sister-in-law. Born on 1 December 1871 in Kidbrooke, Kent (where her father Isaac was a minor gas company official), Agnes was an extremely pretty and intelligent young woman with thick chestnut hair, bright brown eyes, alabaster skin and a quick humour.

The engagement extended four years while Gerard and his fiancée saved enough money to marry and open their own school. Soon after their wedding at St James's Church, Kidbrooke, on 30 April 1898 (Gerard's twenty-ninth birthday), they moved into Tower House, Dorking, and welcomed their first students. Gerard was a stern master, as intimidating towards his young charges on the cricket field as in the classroom.

On 26 July 1901, while every town in England was preparing to celebrate the coronation of King Edward VII two weeks later, Agnes gave birth to a girl they named Sybille.

But soon after, the enrolment at Gerard's school, as elsewhere, dropped alarmingly. Because most local children were needed to supplement the family income, there were only twenty-four students beyond the age of fourteen in Surrey's schools in 1901. Simultaneously, Gerard announced to Agnes that he had rediscovered his faith and had decided to become a priest − a decision that caused her no particular joy, for the country curate's life was traditionally frugal, if not downright impecunious. But he insisted that the ministry could provide him with both a wider field for his talents as a persuasive teacher, and with a connection to his revered ecclesiastical past. Over the next two years, Gerard added religious studies to his teaching duties; in 1903 he was ordained in the Church of England.

Gerard Olivier was one of very many who favoured the Roman designation 'Father' over the Anglican 'Reverend' or 'Mister', just as he preferred sung High Masses, incense, gold brocade vestments, wearing a cassock in public and leading pious weekday devotions − elements that had again become popular in the Church of England since the Oxford Movement. Led by John Henry Newman, John Keble and Edward Pusey, the Movement urged (among other things) the adoption of considerable Roman Catholic ceremonial, ritual and vestments as the Oxford scholars sought renewal of the Established Anglo-Catholic Church against 'Low Church' Protestant tendencies. (Some, like Newman, eventually became Roman Catholics.) As one of the Movement's heirs, Father Olivier saw his Christian Englishness as intimately linked to an ancient, hallowed, apostolic tradition.

He had been a stern, aloof schoolmaster with a penchant for stylish dress and somewhat orotund speech, and according to the actress Sybil

3

Thorndike (whose father was to be a priestly colleague a few years later) Gerard quite probably would have liked to be an actor himself, for he was very dramatic in his sermons and elegant in his appearance. He was serious about his parochial duties, and although he seems not to have been a man of especial piety, neither was he a hypocrite. Of his time in Dorking, a local church record simply claimed, 'He was very popular during his several years of persistent and energetic work in the parish.' His brand of religion was socially respectable and ethically sound, but not necessarily mystical; his was a Christianity that glorified the King as God's legate, the bishops as His ambassadors, and patriotism as a sure sign of godliness. This was the spirit that animated his ancestors, and he enjoined it on his own children.

In 1904, Gerard closed the school on Tower Hill, moving his family northward across town to 26 Wathen Road, a red brick house with sitting room and kitchen on the ground floor, two small bedrooms above, and a small garden in the rear. That summer he was appointed curate at the Dorking parish church of St Martin's. A neo-Gothic edifice dominating the village since 1875, St Martin's featured a marble reredos, an ornate crucifixion scene over the choir, elaborate stained-glass windows and an expensive pipe organ – all of which appealed to Gerard Olivier. Its two-hundred-foot-high spire was clearly visible from Wathen Road, just a few hundred yards away.

At the church font, Father Olivier christened his son Gerard Dacres (always called Dickie) soon after his birth on 5 September 1904. And there too he baptised their third and last child, Laurence Kerr Olivier, who was born at Wathen Road on 22 May 1907. The Edwardian era was at its zenith.

Quick to smile and keen on sport, Edward VII was devoted to all kinds of pleasure, including the theatre. The decade of his reign – beginning when he was fifty-nine in 1901 – was marked by an opulent and freewheeling courtly life that welcomed dramatists, actors and music-hall performers as readily as world leaders. 'The modern English stage has been made by King Edward,' said actor-manager Charles Wyndham at the time. 'His Majesty has made the theatre fashionable and respected.' A man of limited intellect but potent charm, the King also infused his native propriety with a fresh, unpatronising regard for the working commoner.

But by 1907 there was greater change in society than a mere shift of monarchical style. Britain was no longer unassailably confident of its eternal primacy among the nations, as Victorian preachers and statesmen had liked to maintain. Edward himself, preferring political realism and compromise, sensed that earlier certainties about class distinctions, economics and the routes to political power were undergoing a slow but irreversible process of erosion and transformation.

In England, the affable sovereign was witnessing the rise of liberalism in politics and the emergence of socialism in a strident labour movement. Despite important reforms to the educational system, schooling was a luxury for the vast majority of English households. Abroad, there were bloody conflicts in South Africa, uneven relations with Germany, problematic accords with Japan and Russia and disputes with China. Glamorous idealism at court clashed with bitter unrest in parliament, and there were increasingly angry complaints about the plight of the overwhelmingly poor majority.

But in fashionable London drawing rooms, certain Victorian traditions were still highly prized, and there were fierce arguments about the replacement of men's frock-coats by the more comfortable lounge suit. Even more hotly debated was the drastic reduction in whalebone corseting for women and the raising of hemlines to two or even three inches above the ankle. For many concerned gentlefolk, these lapses in formality – and the individualism they betokened – heralded the imminent collapse of the Empire.

Nowhere was the decline of uniformity more obvious than in matters of religion. The established and official Church of England orthodoxy and praxis had been severely weakened by the proliferation of freethinkers, the rising divorce rate and the increase of interfaith marriages; by the multiplication of new denominations and the spread of low-church nonconformism; by the gradual integration of Roman Catholics within all aspects of public life (following the Catholic Emancipation Act of 1829, which extended to them civil and political rights); and by the open criticism of traditional doctrines and dogmas by writers, philosophers and politicians.

'Creed sat lightly on the great majority in the middle and upper classes,' as one English historian noted. 'The Bible lost its hold on them, and the volume of outward religious observance shrank steadily [as] the labour and socialist movement poached extensively' on the preserve of the realm's faith. Nevertheless, a clergyman in Edwardian England was a distant member of an extended royal court that counted bishops in the House of Lords and curates at garden parties more numerous than royals at Ascot.

One risk to the integrity of any established national religion is a concomitant polite respectability that is often taken for profound virtue. An established ministry can be a passport to esteem, and a man of no particular spiritual bent but zealous for social approbation can aim to attach himself to an aristocrat, or perhaps even to a member of a royal family. The novels of Jane Austen and Trollope satirically depict the minor clerical gentry who admired the nobility, imitated their speech and sometimes vulgarly affected their mannerisms.

It was to this revered ecclesiastical estate that Gerard Olivier aspired when he decided to exchange an instructor's gown for a priestly cassock, the garb worn by so many of his illustrious forebears. In Gerard Kerr Olivier, the twin devotions to crown and cross fused easily; in his son Laurence the amalgam was further complicated with a strong sense of militaristic pride. If the father was a warder, the son was a yeoman.

When Laurence was two, the Oliviers moved north-east to a larger house they named East Dene (after its district, Deepdene), near the lush forests of Box Hill and closer to the River Mole. In their garden, Agnes cultivated vegetables and flowers, and among her youngest son's first vague memories was the sight of his mother, swathed in a white sunhat and flowing white dress, happily gathering a little harvest while he perched in a pram close by. He was her Larry, or 'Baby', she his 'Mums'.

In 1910 they moved again, this time to London, where Gerard had secured what he hoped would be a more prestigious curacy, at St James's, Notting Hill, and they lived at 86 Elgin Crescent. A four-storey terrace house off Ladbroke Grove, this was the place of Larry's first clear memories. From his rear bedroom window he overlooked a wide, verdant public park separating the houses of Elgin Crescent from those in Blenheim Crescent, and here his mother first taught him the names of flowers and trees, instilling a lifelong love of gardens and gardening. The family situation was not one of genteel poverty, as Olivier later said.

Young Larry was regularly taken to his father's church (in St James's Gardens, off St Ann's Road) for worship, and here he first saw an imposing lifesize crucifix, heard choral music, and caught (as he said later) 'the feeling of a show'. Before his fifth birthday, there was another change – this time due to renovations at St James's. While the work was in progress, the faithful joined the parishioners of St Clement's, a few blocks away. Two parish staffs were unnecessary, and soon Father Olivier and his family moved to 22 Lupus Street, Pimlico, a narrow terrace house diagonally opposite his new post at St Saviour's.

In the new house, two aspects of Larry's young character emerged. He became a proficient liar, and at the same time he made a kind of stage debut.

Common though lying may be among children – perhaps as a way of asserting their own mind and will against parental omniscience – it was a significant enough memory for Olivier to devote a page to this sin in his autobiography *Confessions of an Actor* seventy years later. Apparently the habit was linked to a slyly manipulative personality, for (to his father's dismay) he was much pampered by his mother ('I was the apple of her eye'). But the lying became alarming, and his mother occasionally resorted to a sound beating to correct it.

Lying may also have been an early sign of a vivid fantasy life, as indeed Larry's games of make-believe at Lupus Street indicate. He was also an expert little mimic, imitating his father's religious rituals with a cross, a candle stub and a blanket for liturgical vestment. And he would entertain family friends with a variety of sounds, from birds and dogs to train whistles.

More remarkable was the series of amusements he often staged at home from the age of five or six. He would drag a wooden chest in front of a window, around which he rigged the curtains for a stage effect. He set church candles in cigarette tins for footlights, and in this makeshift playing area he sang, danced and improvised what he thought were excerpts from plays performed at his brother Dickie's school. His audience consisted of his sister, sometimes a visiting relative or a neighbour's child – but always, and most attentively enthusiastic, his mother – 'my heaven, my hope, my entire world, my own worshipped Mummy', as he termed her even in his old age. He played shamelessly to her, and whenever he stumbled she encouraged him, applauding heartily when he got through a scene and hugging him tightly at the finish.

'Mummy was just everything,' according to Sybille.

> She was the most enchanting person. Hair so long she could sit on it. She absolutely made our childhood, and she adored Larry. He was hers. He always amused her very much. He was a complete clown. He'd have the whole lunch table shaking with laughter.

There was, however, no mention by Sybille or Larry of any similar warmth from their father. Quite the contrary, for Larry was terrified of him, referring to him decades later as a frightening Victorian figure who considered his youngest child only a needless expense since he already had a lovely daughter and a male heir. Gerard – ever seeking means of economising – required Larry to bathe in water already used by himself and by Dickie. Forever after, Larry felt that his mother's favouritism for him further antagonised his father, but this may have been as much Agnes's attempt to compensate for Gerard's hostility as the cause of it. Sybille recalled their father's temper as a storming, raging tornado directed almost exclusively at Larry, and rarely at herself or Dickie.

'I was frightened. More than anything else, I was terrified,' Laurence Olivier said many years later, summing up his childhood. And to augment that fear, the man to whom he looked for loving sustenance, and who offered him only a chilly indifference, also represented the ineffable, unimaginable world of God. In the dusty darkness of St Saviour's Church, he watched as parishioners deferred to his father. Garbed in ancient vesture, he saw the autocratic taskmaster conducting mysterious rites, heard him from the pulpit speaking of things transcendent, warning of the risk of damnation.

By the time he began to attend primary school, the tense relationship with his father had brought out another trait, as Larry developed a quiet, sombre demeanour, sometimes sitting wordlessly for long periods at home; at times, there almost seemed something remote and sad about the child. His childhood was a dramatic inconstancy of playroom antics and maternal solace, uneasily counterpoised with dark, imprecating pieties that confused earthly and heavenly fatherhood. The result was a tangle of emotional realms, of youthful frolics surviving in an atmosphere of cool, respectable rigidities. Photographs from this period show a handsome, round-faced boy with tousled hair, his clear brown eyes and gentle half-smile suggesting a slightly fearful uncertainty about just how the adult world perceives him.

In 1914, Larry was sent to a day school in Blackheath, south of the Thames, his brief attendance marked by a tearful homesickness for his mother. Agnes enrolled him for a term at a school in Cliveden Place, Sloane Square, which was much closer and enabled her to deliver and collect her seven-year-old.

But soon there was trauma greater than the emotional adjustment of first schooldays. Since 1066, no foreign power had invaded England's shores, and London had seemed inviolable until June 1915, when the German Zeppelin attacks of the World War began. In August the bombings continued in the East End, and the following month the streets blazed – just when Larry was beginning two terms at the Francis Holland Church of England School in Graham Terrace.

London life became noticeably drabber. The university boat race and cricket Test matches were suspended, and the British Library, the Tate Gallery and most of the Victoria and Albert Museum were shut. Surface transport, which had only recently been widely expanded, was severely curtailed as buses were shipped to the front in France. At the same time, the petrol shortage at home meant cutbacks in both taxis and private use of motorcars. Every class used the underground and trams, thus instituting an unprecedented social mix that outlasted wartime.

Virtually every family in London was affected by the war, either by damage at home or the loss of a loved one abroad. Of eight million Englishmen mobilised, eventually two million were wounded and almost a million died. King George V, who had succeeded his father Edward VII in 1910, roused the people to vigilant sacrifice. Londoners affected a bright and eager patriotism, and every young man expected that he would eventually follow his elders into battle.

By autumn 1916, Agnes and Gerard were informed that nine-year-old Larry, after a vocal audition, had been admitted to the school Dickie already attended – All Saints, in Margaret Street, near Oxford Circus. Following his reception of First Communion and Confirmation, the rollbook recorded Laurence Kerr Olivier's formal entry to the school as the 283rd pupil in All Saints' history.

Since opening in 1848, All Saints had acquired a reputation as one of the most exclusive choir schools in Britain, an ideal place for an English boy to prepare for later entry to public school. Its fourteen boys boarded in a highly disciplined environment. But while it was respected for its academic and musical traditions, All Saints was (like many other schools) a quiet cauldron of incivility, crudeness and petty cruelty. Corporal punishment was frequently administered, and from this the boys took their cue. Dormitory life required a student to be tough and vigilant, for bullies abounded. While it lacked the grisly horrors of Nicholas Nickleby's Dotheboys Hall, neither did it offer the decorum of a Sacred Heart Convent.

When not singing in choir (which required its own liturgical garb of black or red cassock, collar and white surplice), the choristers wore the school uniform of grey trousers, a cerise tie with matching socks, a

9

wide Eton collar and patent-leather shoes with a silver buckle. The cost
of this clothing was included in the annual fee of twenty-four pounds.

For the vicar of All Saints, the redoubtable, humourless H.F.B.
Mackay, the choir school was of special importance. He loved dignity
and protocol, and he was cold and strict. Mackay's choirboys were
somewhat rigid and overdrilled, but there could never, he insisted, be
an excess of perfect manners. The children must move, walk and turn
together in unison, always be neat and precise with their surplices
perfectly starched and ironed. They must show to the worshippers an
image of proper religious deportment and gentlemanly etiquette.

Discipline was demanded especially in the chapel, which had been
designed under the influence of Anglo-Catholicism. The focus was a
single altar, enclosed by a low marble wall. The nave arches, supported
by shafts of Aberdeen red granite, carried the eye forward toward the
sanctuary and the pulpit of multi-coloured inlaid marble. It was the
most solemnly designed church Larry had seen, and he spent at least
two hours here almost daily for over four years. When Father Mackay
preached, his voice resonated, rising and falling in rich cadences –
indulgent one moment and cautionary the next, first gentle and then
severe – and here the young chorister learned that his father was not
the only successful public performer, not the only cynosure of eyes.
The preacher utilised all the actor's rhetorical skills to win the attention
of his congregation.

Like all their classmates, Larry and Dickie returned home only for
one weekend each month. In addition to solemn Masses on Sundays,
they sang at Morning Prayer and Evensong, at seasonal feasts and at
parish weddings and funerals throughout the year. They mastered the
works of Bach, Mozart, Handel and Schubert as well as Tallis, Wesley,
Stainer, Stanford and others of the English choral tradition. In the
classrooms, there were daily lessons in religion, literature, mathematics
and history. Sports were also compulsory.

But the most famous of all their cultural activities apart from the
choir was the dramatic society. In December and January of each year,
under the direction of Father Geoffrey Heald, the students presented
excerpts from plays.

There was also a holiday treat for all the boys that winter of 1916 –
and it was especially important for Larry. Henry Pelham-Clinton, the
Duke of Newcastle, a devout High Churchman and a generous patron
of All Saints, invited the boys and their teachers to be his guests for
the annual Christmas pantomime *Babes in the Wood* at the Strand

Theatre. The show offered a hotchpotch of scenes and skits: a precision children's ballet; a dancer with the unlikely name of Pauline Prim, who mimed a balloon-popping cat; a re-enactment of scenes from the tale of Robin Hood, with a boy and girl cast, respectively, as girl and boy; and brief slapstick acts, topical songs, acrobatics and the always-popular male-female impersonations. Afterwards, the duke escorted them backstage to meet the performers and to see the stage machinery.

In the new year 1917, Larry still did not mix easily with his peers. Slender to the point of delicacy, overprotected by his mother and ignored by his father, he had no natural aptitude for the playing field. 'I was a muddled kind of boy, a weakling,' he remembered. 'As a child I was a shrimp, as a youth I was a weed – a miserably thin creature whose arms hung like wires from my shoulders.' To those who had not seen his precocious performances at home, everything about Larry must have seemed unexceptional. His classmate Laurence Naismith (who also became an actor) remembered him as an ordinary boy with nothing remarkable about him.

The young Olivier was, however, singularly proficient in elocution and recitation. 'The distinction between the various vowel sounds must not become blurred, nor pronunciation indistinct, nor facial expression stiff,' warned the Board of Education's 1912 guidebook, *Suggestions for the Consideration of Teachers*. Informal conversation classes were scheduled – designed to overcome shyness and foster spontaneous conversation. 'Distinct articulation must be required,' the teachers' guide continued. 'In reading aloud, students must be on guard against exaggerated or affected expression and merely mechanical rules such as raising one's voice at a comma. The essential quality is clearness of utterance.' In this, the priests at All Saints were most fervent, for they had themselves been trained for preaching.

Larry's teachers gave particular attention to poetry recitation, and for four years he was required to memorise long passages from Scott, Macaulay, Longfellow and Tennyson. 'Shakespeare is perhaps the most difficult of all authors to handle in school,' cautioned the *Suggestions*, 'but some of his easier plays – like *Henry V* – can be enjoyed by the more advanced children.' Every boy at All Saints was treated like an advanced pupil, and because the teachers refused the expediency of abridged editions or prose summaries, the ten-year-olds were painstakingly led through the thickets of iambic pentameter. Few were to exploit this training so directly and successfully as Laurence Olivier.

11

He had his first opportunity very soon. In the parish hall, Father Heald rehearsed scenes from *Julius Caesar*, and Larry, the youngest and smallest, was cast as one of the citizens; his brother Dickie was Caesar. The boy playing Brutus, however, proved inadequate, and Larry was promoted to that role. Although he was small and thin for the part (and the other boys were older), he had impressed Father Heald with his quick aptitude for rhetoric. Rehearsals were often accompanied by air-raids, but Larry, absorbed in the text, crouched under a table in the crypt and memorised his speeches.

'We embarked on the Roman scenes of *Julius Caesar*,' recalled Geoffrey Heald years later. 'It was the cramped stage space [of the parish hall] which made us take to the Elizabethan method of playing amongst the audience.' Sybil Thorndike considered Heald one of the unsung visionaries of the theatre, his productions more advanced than any of the time, as he used the entire auditorium, including the aisles, for the action of his productions.

To the performance came not only parents and parishioners, but also Sybil Thorndike with her father, who was a friend of Gerard and a priest at St James's, Pimlico, and the great Ellen Terry routinely attended the respected productions at All Saints. Years later, Sybil Thorndike recalled that Larry gave a remarkable performance. Another member of the audience was Evelyn Light, who also came from a clerical family; she was dancing instructor for the boys at All Saints.

> After the performance, everyone was praising the Caesar and the Antony, but Ellen Terry, putting aside the paper bag of boiled sweets she munched constantly, said, 'No.' And there was silence, I shall never forget it. 'The boy who played Brutus,' she said. 'The dark little boy – he is a born actor.'

(When told of Miss Terry's endorsement, Larry asked, 'Who is she?') The complimentary remarks by Thorndike, Terry and others were of course made many years later, and it is easy to detect the wisdom of hindsight. Larry's playing may well have been astonishing in light of his youth and inexperience – admirable from a child, but hardly the performance of a seasoned adult professional.

Larry soon announced to Father Heald that he wanted to be an actor. In that case, the priest replied, he must read Dickens, and he would never lack for a characterisation.

*

It was natural in 1917 for families like the Oliviers, the Thorndikes and the Lights to be as enthusiastic for the theatre as the priests of All Saints. Following the Reformation's rejection of the medieval mysteries and the subsequent Puritan reaction against licentious Restoration plays and their notorious actresses, there had until recently been a long tradition of religious hostility to the theatre. Preachers regularly attacked the drama and its exponents, and as late as 1900 the Church Pastoral Aid Society called on vicars to regard local theatrical performances as a serious menace to the spiritual influence of the Church. After Queen Victoria knighted Henry Irving in 1895, however, and in light of her son Edward's subsequent attraction to the theatre and its people, the acting profession enjoyed official court approval.

This did not mean automatic ecclesiastical approbation, but by 1900 there flourished in London the vigorous Actors' Church Union, founded by the Reverend Donald Hole (who some years earlier had supported a defunct 'Church and Stage Guild' led by his old friend, the Reverend Stewart Headlam). Hole's wife was a touring actress, and his Actors' Church Union was established not to proselytise, but 'to organise the work of the clergy more easily within the reach of the theatrical profession, whose lives are spent in travelling from place to place'. They became chaplains to sick actors on tour, and they also took to helping players find lodgings. Even for actors with minimal religious or spiritual interests, the Union was a helpful and caring influence in their lives. Many prominent actors joined – Cyril Maude, Ben Greet, George Alexander, Johnston Forbes-Robertson, Lilian Braithwaite, Ellen Terry, Charles Wyndham, Irene Vanbrugh and the Thorndikes.

Soon there were twelve national ACU centres where clerics either ministered to or simply maintained social contact with local theatres. (One former actor was by this time Dean of Rochester Cathedral, and he persuaded his bishop to endorse the Union officially.) In all their activities, the Union emphasised social, professional and practical assistance for needy actors – it was in no sense a moral police, much less an agency to gain converts. In 1914 there were over 900 actor members and 350 chaplains at over 250 centres, and the Union could proudly claim that 'the atmosphere of suspicion and misunderstanding which once existed between the Clergy and the Actor is now almost entirely a thing of the past.' Accordingly, anti-Puritans influenced by the Oxford Movement – High Churchmen like Fathers Mackay (whose brother Gayer Mackay was an actor) and Heald (whose virtual avocation was directing and acting), and Fathers Olivier and Thorndike – naturally gravitated to the theatre. It was at last a respectable interest for clergy-men as well as princes.

The school year continued, and lessons now included a course in British history and recitations of suitable poems (Macaulay's 'Spanish Armada' was on the list, along with selections from Sir Walter Scott), and classes on the lives of heroic men and women (Socrates, Hannibal, Marcus Aurelius, Charlemagne, Francis of Assisi, Joan of Arc and Henry IV of France). 'Stress should be laid,' urged the Board of Education's *Suggestions*, 'on the personal qualities of the heroes of the stories, and the pictorial illustrations . . . should be bold and dramatic.' No teacher would have failed to refer to the men fighting for England in the trenches; no schoolboy, with these recitations interrupted by war news and air-raid warnings, would have been unmoved by the implied canons of heroism. This association between great lives and the nobility of patriotism would be always linked for Larry and would inform much of his later achievement.

The gentlemen of the theatre were unlikely to be forgotten in this honour roll, for they were among the most noted patriots, both as fighting men and propagandists for victory. Actors like Basil Rathbone and Lewis Casson (who was married to Sybil Thorndike) were serving with distinction on the Continent and were awarded the Military Cross, and their colleagues Godfrey Tearle, Ivor Novello, Ben Travers and Cedric Hardwicke were also at war. Actors were frequently heard on variety stages, in Hyde Park and at concerts, making patriotic speeches or recitations, and Sir Frank Benson began a tradition when he selected passages from Shakespeare for a rousing programme of patriotic pieces.

That autumn, Larry was still rather slight of build – the perfect choice when Father Heald needed a convincing Maria for his Christmas production of scenes from *Twelfth Night*. 'The smallest wren of nine,' Maria has to look diminutive but wily, and Larry eagerly took on the role, scampering about the stage in the plot to fool Malvolio with the forged letter. (The sudden indisposition of the boy cast as Sir Toby Belch led to a last-minute appearance by a churchwarden's daughter named Ethel McGlinchy; she was later to become famous as an actress with the more impressive name Fabia Drake.) Again, there were theatre notables in the audience, led by the enthusiastic Ellen Terry.

In 1918, Gerard Olivier secured a rectorship at St Mary's in Letchworth, Hertfordshire. He and Agnes took up residence at a large Queen Anne parsonage there, and the same year Sybille went to London for studies in voice and drama, which she soon abandoned for an office job. Nobody wanted to act more than Sybille, Olivier said years later. 'She had all the aspirations on earth but was absolutely no good, poor darling.' Dickie left All Saints for Radley, where Larry hoped to join him.

While he remained at All Saints, Larry's academic achievements were resoundingly average. Easily bored by most subjects except poetry and a few classes in botany and history, he did not distinguish himself in his examinations. He enjoyed the religious rituals, the choirboy's responsibilities and the drama of the solemn liturgy. Most of all he coveted the role of thurifer, the boy who carried the chain-suspended thurible, carefully but grandly swinging it in wide arcs to cloud the sanctuary and nave with billows of pungent incense.

Larry seems also to have affected a kind of cockiness that belied his sensitivity, perhaps to compensate for his still immature appearance at twelve. On Saturday evenings, when there was no prep, he often entertained his classmates with impromptu impersonations of (as class-mate John Freebairn-Smith recalled) the organist, the kitchen staff and film actors such as Charles Chaplin. Sometimes Larry was overconfident, and forever after he recalled a day in choir when, assigned a solo part, he calmly closed the music book, convinced he knew everything perfectly. Gazing upward, ignoring the score as if only a rank amateur would need it, he was overcome with guilt for his superior attitude. Suddenly short of breath, his voice cracked and he missed his cue. Olivier always remembered this embarrassing moment as a punishment for his pride.

In the spring of 1920, Larry first saw his family's friend Sybil Thorn-dike onstage, when she invited the Oliviers to a performance of Gaston Leroux's *The Mystery of the Yellow Room*. Sybil and Larry chattered happily away backstage after the final curtain, the pleasure of the evening marred only by the absence of Agnes Olivier, who was feeling ill. Throughout the previous autumn, Agnes had occasionally com-plained of headaches and suffered several fainting spells. During Larry's monthly visits from school she hid her increasing discomfort from him, but by winter she was experiencing frequent bouts of nausea and occasional blurred vision. In early March a doctor was consulted, and soon there was a bleak diagnosis. Agnes was suffering from glioblastoma, a particularly fast-growing, inoperable and lethal tumour within the brain cells. With admirable calm and, it seemed, concern solely for the future of her youngest child, Agnes prepared herself and her family as best she could. Larry was told only that his mother required rest, that she had been ill, but that all the resources of medicine and prayer were being summoned.

One Sunday in mid-March, he was preparing to return to school from a weekend at home. Agnes, by this time partially paralysed, called him to her bedside, as Sybille recalled. Their mother seemed much older than her forty-eight years and very weary as she whispered to him, 'Goodbye, my darling.' They embraced for a moment, and Larry stood briefly in the doorway, wearing his shabby winter coat, his school cap in his hands. He never saw her again. Two weeks later, on Saturday evening, 27 March 1920, Father Heald came to Larry after choir practice and told him that his mother had gone to God.

CHAPTER TWO

1920–1926

And those things do best please me
That befall preposterously.

Puck, in *A Midsummer Night's Dream*

For twelve-year-old Larry Olivier, for whom his mother's devotion and endorsement were crucial, her death was frightful indeed. Her sudden absence produced a sense of desertion and abandonment, a rude introduction to adolescent independence and, perhaps, the suspicion that any loving relationship in life could be suddenly and capriciously terminated. 'I don't think I ever got over it,' he said in later years. 'She was marvellous to me. I was the baby, she was the world to me, and I belonged to her. I didn't know my father. When she died it was the most shattering thing imaginable.'

Unfailingly encouraging of her son's interests, Agnes Olivier had been a genially energetic, fun-loving woman with a bright sense of humour, and Larry had absorbed her spirit as well as the dark, detached, ecclesiastical formality of his father. In his mother he had seen an amused, amusing and contented middle-class citizen; in his father, a man longing for social position and influence, and apparently fulfilled by the genteel life of an aristocrat *manqué*. Later, the mature Laurence Olivier could be alternately an affable companion without social pretence and a celebrity with the grave air of a venerable nobleman.

Whether or not the word 'sin' is ever mentioned, an unprepared child very often feels guilty for the death of a loving parent. The matter of sinfulness had been a recurring theme in the moral injunctions Larry had heard from infancy: he had first heard about evil in his father's sermons, and then it was discussed more elaborately in the admonitions of his priestly teachers at All Saints. Disrespect, rowdiness, lying,

17

laziness, the ordinary sexual curiosity of children – all these Victorian-Edwardian society in general and the Church in particular routinely classified as worthy of divine displeasure and punishment.

Since his mother's death could not be regarded as punishment for *her* sins, it would have been natural for him to see it as at least partially caused by *his* – for having been somehow disobedient, for having displeased God by displeasing his father. For the rest of his life, in conversation and in writing, guilt and sin were astonishingly frequent terms in Laurence Olivier's vocabulary, and he constantly reproached himself for actions and omissions for which he felt guilty. 'Bless me, Reader, for I have sinned' appears at the opening of his memoirs. 'Since my last confession, which was more than fifty years ago, I have committed the following sins . . .' The identification of one's own life history with a catalogue of moral failures is an odd one, perhaps more the trait of a scrupulous choirboy than of a mature man.

Except for weekends and school holidays, Larry had not lived at home for three years, and had longed for Agnes's occasional visits to school events and for his monthly sojourns to her; his relationship with Gerard, on the other hand, always bore a suggestion of mutual caution. The children never mentioned her death to each other, as Sybille remembered years later; it was simply too dreadful to discuss.

Sybil Thorndike's children tried to console Larry, who said only that he was 'very very sad' and for weeks wore a black mourning band on his sleeve. Comfort was offered by his Uncle Herbert Olivier (the painter) and his Aunt Margaret, who welcomed him to their grand Victorian house at Airlie Gardens, Kensington. Here he was cosseted and entertained, and he enjoyed pumping the huge bellows of their pipe organ while Herbert led the family in an afternoon of merry tunes refreshingly different from the staid strains of 'Oh, for the Wings of a Dove' and the dour patriotism of 'For Thee, Oh Dear, Dear Country', both regularly sung at school.

In the autumn of 1920, Larry began his final year at All Saints. He developed a taste for serious lyrics, memorising among others a poem of Yeats to perfect his enunciation:

> Had I the heavens' embroidered cloths,
> Enwrought with golden and silver light,
> The blue and the dim and the dark cloths
> Of night and light and the half-light,

I would spread the cloths under your feet:
But I, being poor, have only my dreams;
I have spread my dreams under your feet;
Tread softly because you tread on my dreams.

Visiting him once at school, Sybille detected a sombre side. She noticed that he sat for a long time not saying anything at all, as though he was working everything out in his mind before he spoke.

At Christmas time, Father Heald presented *The Taming of the Shrew*, casting Larry as Katharine and evoking a lively characterisation that delighted the audience. Classmate Laurence Naismith recalled that in a dark wig, elaborate hat, colourful gown and impressive make-up, Larry was a credibly unruly little girl, and Ellen Terry thought he played the shrew better than anyone except Ada Rehan and gave 'an idea of what the boy-actors [who played the women's roles] in Shakespeare's time were like'. Sybil Thorndike also judged his portrayal as just right, 'a perfect little bitch – he could play the girls beautifully'. And Theodore Komisarjevsky, who had recently arrived in England and was soon to be one of the most influential theatrical designer-producers, wrote to Father Mackay praising the sincerity and seriousness of the cast led by an especially impressive Katharine. After the performance, Larry was complimented on both his womanly grace and the frown he had painted on and removed later in the play. 'That was my own frown!' he declared emphatically. The feminine gestures may well have been inspired by his mother, the frown by his father.

In autumn 1921, it was time to move on to higher classes, and Larry entered St Edward's School, Oxford, with twenty-nine other new pupils; the register identifies him as the 1885th boy to enter since the founding in 1863. There were 213 boys at the school that year, most of them clergymen's sons, admitted at the half-tuition of sixty pounds per year. St Edward's, not considered an institution of remarkable distinction, consisted of buildings constructed around a central quadrangle, imitating the design of Oxford's colleges. A Romanesque chapel joined classrooms and library to the dining hall and the residence of the warden (or headmaster); there were also residence halls, shops, a small theatre and a cricket ground and pavilion. The school was a model of High Church practice and decorum – an extension of life at All Saints, without mandatory choir, but with compulsory Morning and Evening Prayer every day, in addition to Sunday Mass. Another new boy, Richard F. Wyatt, arrived at St Edward's at the same time. He recalled that Larry started appearing in school plays at once and with great success. But like other classmates, Wyatt remembered that Larry seems not to have had a gift for friendship. He kept rather to himself at school, recalled J.D. Newhouse, and no one thought he was very remarkable until he acted in a school play.

'I was ostracised,' Olivier wrote later. 'I was a flirt [who] sang like an angel and was as pretty as was needed to attract the worst in certain males,' by which he meant not only older bullies but also those repressed homosexual teachers who vented their frustrations by sadistic beatings of desired but forbidden boys. 'In any case, I was generally disliked. My manner was florid, and I was girlish and a bit sissy.' These characteristics made him a ripe target for the sexual advances of older boys, with whom (as he later freely confided to friends) he blithely cavorted throughout his school years. Such adventures, blessedly free for Larry of any subsequent neurotic guilt, were typical of the English boarding school tradition, and are not unknown elsewhere.

There was considerable respect for Larry's recitation and acting, and his abilities were becoming ever more developed. Classmate Carew Wallace recalled that the young Olivier could often be found alone in the basement washroom, loudly practising speeches from Shakespeare and modifying his volume and intonation. His acting was also, perhaps, a comforting escape from his solitude and unpopularity, and a refuge from the sting of his mother's death. By losing himself in a role, he found not only pleasurable fantasies but also the approval of others, just as he had once earned Agnes's applause after his little shows at home.

Larry's success with the role of Katharine in *The Taming of the Shrew* was still fresh in the minds of Fathers Mackay and Heald when All Saints was asked to participate in a birthday tribute to Shakespeare at the Memorial Theatre, Stratford, in the spring of 1922; they invited Larry to return, therefore, as an honoured old boy at the age of fifteen.

And so on Thursday, 27 April, Larry joined the priests and choristers on a private train provided by the Great Western Railway to take them and their huge wardrobe baskets from London to Stratford.

At half past twelve the All Saints visitors, in full choir habit, arrived at Holy Trinity Church, Shakespeare's burial place. Father Mackay wrote a privately circulated account of the visit, identifying boys only by first names (a custom designed – like the omission of players' names from school dramatic programmes – to avoid the pride of celebrity).

> Up the great lime walk to the Porch came the procession of choristers
> and their Precentor [Heald], the choristers in their rose-coloured caps
> and cassocks, and . . . in the midst Larry [Olivier] carrying the poet's
> wreath of bays bound with Roman purple . . . When the choristers
> were grouped about the grave [i.e., the stone marker on the church
> floor, beneath which the poet is buried], Larry knelt and laid their
> wreath.

The boys sang the dirge 'Fear no more the heat o' the sun' (from the
fourth act of *Cymbeline*), set to music by W.S. Vale, choirmaster and
organist of All Saints.

A formal luncheon at their hotel was followed by a guided tour of
Shakespeare's birthplace and the important sights of Stratford. The
American actor James K. Hackett was rehearsing his *Othello* at the
Memorial Theatre, and he welcomed the boys, explaining details of
scenic design and stagecraft between scenes with his Iago (Baliol Hollo-
way) and his Desdemona (Hackett's wife, Beatrice Beckley).

The performance of *The Shrew* was given on Friday afternoon, and
although his name was absent from the programme and the subsequent
reviews, this production earned Laurence Olivier his first public notices.
'Katharine has [a] fire of her own,' wrote the correspondent for *The
Times*. 'You feel that if an apple were thrown to this Katharine she
would instinctively try to catch it in her lap, and if apples give her
pleasure we hope with all gratitude that someone will make the experiment.' The reviewer for the *Daily Telegraph* was also at Stratford:
'The boy who took the part of Kate made a fine, bold, black-eyed hussy,
badly in need of taming, and I cannot remember seeing any actress in
the part who looked it better.' The *Birmingham Post* critic praised the
boy's portrait as 'boldly and vigorously played, with dark flashing eyes
and a spiteful voice', and even the *Stratford Herald* – usually reserved
when considering student performances of Shakespeare – singled
out Larry's final speech, 'as delightful a rendering of the lines as
could be imagined . . . not one of the traits [of the character] was
missing.'

Larry returned to St Edward's with a new self-assurance, and that
spring he tried out successfully for the rowing crew. But there was still
an adolescent awkwardness and untidiness that would take years to
correct. Comb and brush were apparently unknown to him, his meagre
wardrobe was invariably ill-fitting and unpressed, and his manners
were graceless.

Like All Saints, St Edward's had an enthusiastic drama coach.

W.H.A. Cowell, who taught English and Classics, had been directing pupils in scenes from Shakespeare since 1882, and for Christmas 1923 – the sixtieth anniversary of the school – a fully staged production of *A Midsummer Night's Dream* was presented. After a weekend of football, solemn chapel services, long dinners and longer speeches, the play began on the afternoon of Monday 11 December. The role of Puck, so the programme noted, was assigned to L.K. Olivier, who executed the mischief-maker's little songs and dances with wiry agility. Strapping torches round his chest to illuminate his face, he sprinted gaily onstage and off, scampered through the audience, dashed back and forth through the auditorium doorways in what Cowell called his 'open stage production'.

But after the challenges of Brutus, Maria and Kate, Larry felt that the manipulative Puck was beneath him: 'this wretched part', as he described it, 'this utterly hopeless, so-called opportunity'. Such an attitude affected his performance, which was apparently condescending towards his fellow performers and slightly hysterical in its attempts to impress the audience. 'The boy who played Puck,' commented a local reporter, 'although he had a potent stage presence, emoted with frantic and altogether unnecessary effect, as though playing a joke on his fellow cast members instead of the audience.' And a senior boy named R.C. Mortimer (later Bishop of Exeter) described Larry's performance as 'by far the most notable, [if] a little too robust and jovial . . . but he gave a consistent rendering, and showed by his gestures and movements that he has a knowledge of acting and a good mastery of technique'.

During the winter holiday of 1923–24, Larry's brother Dickie, now aged nineteen, sailed for India to work on a rubber plantation. Because this was his last year at St Edward's and because he had not the remotest idea about his own future, Larry asked his father when he could make the voyage out to join his brother. The reply was immediate: 'Don't be such a fool. You're not going to India, you're going on the stage.' So often did Olivier recount this statement in later years that it had the mythic quality of a great epiphany – the unexpected, transforming moment that altered his destiny. The remote, indifferent father he could never please had, he claimed, suggested his future career.

According to Olivier, the discussion occurred at Letchworth, as he was sitting in the lukewarm bath Gerard had left behind, still insisting that Larry avoid the extravagance of fresh hot water. But like this humble setting, the father's pronouncement is perhaps too dramatically neat, too tidily composed to be credible. The words Larry reported may, on the other hand, have represented what he wanted to hear his father say – both in 1924 and especially in the difficult years ahead, before his success was assured.

Up to this time, there is no evidence that Gerard took much interest in Larry's talent or future, nor afterwards did he seem very impressed by the progress of his son's career or his eventual celebrity and achievements. On the contrary, Gerard Olivier's concerns were invariably financial; for this reason he had urged Dickie on his exotic voyage because there was work in India. In addition, the stage was (then as now) among the most parlous of careers – unreliable as a source of income and not guaranteed to bring about a stable or polite life (despite the Thorndikes, whose successes onstage and as models of a Christian family Gerard did not consider typical).

On the other hand, Agnes had encouraged Larry's acting at home and at school; it was she whose approbation buoyed him. At sixteen, he was comfortable onstage, and obviously pleased his directors and his audiences. No other career excited him, and it was crucial that he enlist Gerard's support. The neat little bathroom scene has the air of a dramatic reconstruction. And because it tells us something about a son's wish to please his father (even retrospectively), it contains a truth deeper than any a stenographer might have recorded that evening.

Serious training was the first objective. Because young men were desperately needed to complement the mostly female enrolment at the Central School of Speech and Drama in London, scholarships and bursaries to cover living expenses were routinely available to them – so much they learned from Sybille, who had overcome a minor speech defect by studying briefly with the renowned and redoubtable Elsie Fogerty, the Central's director. Larry applied to her and was told to complete his final term at St Edward's before coming to London for an audition in late spring. She also directed him to a touring company in Letchworth, where he appeared in a performance of *Macbeth* (his smallest role so far, that of Lennox), and where he learned the duties of assistant stage manager (preparing actors for their entrances, giving cues and serving as general factotum).

While Larry concluded his studies at St Edward's, his father was preparing to assume the leadership of a small parish at Addington, Buckinghamshire. Gerard was also courting Isobel Buchanan

Ronaldson, whom he married on 27 June 1924; at forty-five, she was ten years his junior. But Larry resented his mother's replacement; by the time of his audition at the Central School that same month, he was glad of the opportunity to be living on his own, in a tiny London garret in Castellain Road, Paddington.

The founding of the Academy of Dramatic Art in 1904 (granted Royal status in 1920) and the Central School of Speech and Drama in 1906 helped to legitimise acting by associating it with education. Until recently, actors had been regarded as 'rogues and vagabonds', as they were during the Elizabethan era. The daughter of the great actor-manager Samuel Phelps was expelled from school in the 1850s when it was learned that her father was an actor; the wife of Henry Irving so ridiculed him about the shame of his profession that they separated, and their grandson was condemned as the 'son of a dirty actor'; and as recently as 1889 – when she was on the verge of international fame – Mrs Patrick Campbell received a letter from her Aunt Kate calling her a 'poor unfortunate child . . . yet to learn the shame, the humiliation of seeing yourself despised by decent people' as an actress.

Early in her reign, Queen Victoria herself had been a discerning playgoer and had brought performances to Windsor Castle. Although she denied herself this pleasure for twenty years after the death of her husband Albert, she later regularly attended command performances and received leading actors in her homes. This appreciation was symbolised by her knighthood for Henry Irving in 1895, the first such honour for an actor; the respect was finally sealed with Edward VII's avid patronage of the theatre and its people.

Whereas the national census of 1881 counted 4565 actors, there were 18,247 in 1911, and during those thirty years twenty-one new theatres were opened in London's West End. Following the precedent set by Irving's knighthood, six more actor-managers received the same honour between 1897 and 1913. At the same time, more actors were coming from the landed gentry and from educated backgrounds. The profession's standing continued to improve in the popular estimation, higher classes of society were depicted onstage, amateur theatricals expanded, and repertory companies multiplied as even the Church took an eager and sustaining interest in the actor's life.

At the Central School there was one emphasis above all others – that of speech training. Former actress Elsie Fogerty (then fifty-eight) had leased rooms for lectures and rehearsal in the upper regions of the

Albert Hall in 1906, and there she began to teach the primacy of 'healthy and natural speech'. All the courses in her haphazardly arranged syllabus supported her emphasis on elocution and proper voice production: physical training and dance classes were aimed at correct breathing, and fencing was taught to develop rhythmic movement as an aid to coherent speech. Even Herbert Norris's costume seminars and Ethel Radmar's recitations on deportment had felicitous speech as their goal. Norris described the effect of wardrobe on breath control, and Radmar stressed the social and professional benefits of fine diction.

Despite her rather one-sided approach to the craft, Fogerty did influence teacher-training programmes in voice: in 1913 the Bishops of London and Birmingham were sending young clerics to her, and the following year she opened a clinic of speech pathology at St Thomas's Hospital, where she and a small staff treated patients. One of the tough, eccentric maiden ladies dedicated to advancing the British theatre, Elsie Fogerty was nothing like the polite clerics of All Saints and St Edward's. John Gielgud, who was already acting in London in 1924, recalled her as a shapeless, dowdy old lady, but imperious. Wearing a large plumed hat and an array of mismatched costume jewellery (and often with a colourful petticoat boldly creeping below her hemline), she directed students in her commanding baritone, often waving a cheese sandwich with one hand and suggesting a breathing exercise with the other.

Her advice was resolutely unorthodox. In 1933, when he was acting in *Richard of Bordeaux*, Gielgud had some minor voice trouble and consulted Fogerty. She at once sat him down and told him to imagine that his head was a pot of marmalade that could communicate a kind of oozy relaxation to every muscle in his body. For reasons Gielgud never fathomed, the advice worked.

Peggy Ashcroft, who enrolled at the Central School in the same term as Olivier, recalled that Fogerty was insistent on what the students derisively called The Voice Beautiful, but that although the fencing instruction, movement and elocution classes were superb, the teaching of acting itself was virtually non-existent. Ashcroft accurately described the era; indeed, the reputation of the Central School's early years gleams brighter in doctored history than is warranted by honest assessment. Occasionally, established actors (Gielgud, Thorndike, Edith Evans) sought Fogerty's assistance for temporary voice problems, but very few of her students graduated to theatre careers. Of the fifty-five students in 1924, fifty were young society ladies content to work harder for a good marriage than for a diploma. Mostly debutantes, they were at the school only to learn deportment and the social graces necessary in polite life.

And so in June 1924, seventeen-year-old Laurence Olivier joined four other young men (George Coulouris among them) auditioning for Elsie Fogerty. He chose to recite the 'Seven Ages of Man' speech from the second act of *As You Like It*, bringing what he thought was a fiery, youthful intensity to the text:

> All the world's a stage,
> And all the men and women merely players . . .
> And one man in his time plays many parts . . .

But it was too fiery, too intense, he was told at once by Fogerty, who called him aside. 'When you say sudden and quick in quarrel, it is not necessary to make fencing passes.' And then Elsie Fogerty did something else. 'You have,' she said, placing her finger on his brow, 'a weakness – there.' Olivier, in repeating this statement, always used it as a justification for his elaborate make-up and false noses. But Fogerty was apparently correcting his evident timidity, his inability to gaze directly at other players onstage, for which he compensated by frenetic actions.

Notwithstanding the overstated recitation, Olivier was admitted to the school on full scholarship and with a fifty-pound bursary to defray his living expenses for the nine months his studies would last. Life on little more than a pound a week at a time of postwar inflation was woefully frugal. 'I lacked for food,' he said later of this time. 'I was hungry and terrified.' Perhaps because of his father's indifference, at this time Olivier did not receive even token financial support from him. Peggy Ashcroft remembered him as energetic and eager, but acutely awkward and downright uncouth, rather shabbily dressed in clothes inherited from his brother and uncles. Several students recalled that Olivier walked across Hyde Park carrying his shoes to preserve the leather, for he had only the one pair, and could not afford to replace them.

By this time, Laurence Olivier had reached his full adult height of five feet ten inches. But he was also very thin, and according to his classmate Evelyn Ascherson he could never afford a winter overcoat. 'But he was full of life – uncontrollable, and that included his hair, his hands and his feet. He was always being told he was waving his hands too dramatically, but he could also produce extraordinary bits of busi-

1. *Right* Agnes and Gerard Olivier at Tower House, Dorking, 1904. *From the collection of Felix Barker*

2. *Below* Laurence Kerr Olivier, aged about two, 1909. *National Film Archive, London*

3. *Below right* Aged seven (1914). *National Film Archive, London*

4. *Bottom* Laurence Olivier (second from left) with All Saints schoolfriends on a summer outing, 1915. *From the collection of Felix Barker*

5. *Top left* Dressed for a fancy-dress party, aged about eleven. *From the collection of Felix Barker*

6. *Above* Aged fourteen, as Katharine in *The Taming of the Shrew*, All Saints production at Stratford-upon-Avon (1922). *From the collection of Felix Barker*

7. *Above left* As a member of the Birmingham Repertory Theatre, 1926. *Photo: H.J. Whitlock and Sons/Felix Barker Collection*

8. *Left* As Mat Simon in *The Well of the Saints* (Birmingham, 1926). *From the collection of Felix Barker*

9. *Above right* As Tennyson's *Harold* (London, 1928). *From the collection of Felix Barker*

10. *Above far right* With Lillian Harvey in the film *The Temporary Widow* (1930). *From the collection of Felix Barker*

11. *Right* At a May Wine Festival in Berlin (1930): Olivier (fourth from right) with cast and crew of *The Temporary Widow*. *From the collection of Constance Cummings*

12. *Left* With Bromley Davenport, in the film *Too Many Crooks* (1930). *National Film Archive, London*

13. *Above* Noël Coward. *Culver Pictures*

14. *Below* In the London production of *Private Lives* (1930), with Adrianne Allen, Noël Coward and Gertrude Lawrence. *Culver Pictures*

ness nobody else thought of.' One of those original bits included a deliberately startling appearance for a scene from *The Tempest* that autumn. When he entered as the deformed Caliban, the female students suddenly wanted to leave the room, one fainted and several required smelling salts, for Olivier had covered himself from head to foot with a green slime and had applied coloured plasters to his face and hands with spirit gum, to resemble suppurating carbuncles. He had taken with utter seriousness the playwright's description of Caliban as 'a freckled whelp, hag-born, not honoured with a human shape'. The gasps from his classmates were as heartening as laughter or applause.

Not long after, he and Ashcroft appeared in the court scene from *The Merchant of Venice* (he as Shylock, she as the clerk), and by this time, as George Coulouris said years later, they were the star girl and boy in Fogerty's mind. Apparently Olivier was learning to modulate and refine his voice and manner, for the actress Athene Seyler (who had already achieved great success in Restoration comedy) remembered his subtlety in the *Merchant* extract, and felt he was leaving something for the audience to discover in Shylock. His hair, she recalled, grew very low over his forehead, and with his big eyebrows and his added makeup, she could hardly see his face.

On 30 November and 1 December, Henry Oscar (an occasional lecturer at the Central School) presented and starred in two performances of a new play at the Century Theatre, Bayswater, under the auspices of the Lyceum Club Stage Society. (The Society offered four performances annually, financed by subscription. There were many such theatre clubs in London at this time, staging new plays in brief runs; they preceded the establishment of Equity rules and the distinction between amateur and professional performances.) In *Byron*, by historian Alice Law, Olivier – his first name misspelled in the programme as 'Lawrence' – played the very small role of a Byzantine officer, for which he was forbidden any distinctive make-up. It was his first professional appearance in London, and it earned him no recognition at all. Nor was there any indication that Oscar would employ him again, for he felt that around Olivier was 'an invisible wall of discomfort'.

There would have been numerous causes of such discomfort, apart from Olivier's awareness that a seventeen-year-old Englishman could not, without the right greasepaint, appear very convincingly as an Oriental. In the first place, it would have been natural for him to feel socially inferior. Overnight, the priest's son had leaped from the rough, conformist, insulated artificiality of the all-male, clerical school into an environment for which he was painfully unprepared. For the first time, he was faced with classmates who were mostly well-bred and well-read young ladies from the wealthier families Elsie Fogerty had privately tutored and courted. They found him amusing at times (and, as Caliban, shocking), but he was poor, invariably untidy and inclined to vulgarity.

More removed than ever from his family, Olivier was without affectionate advice. Since the age of nine, his main role models had been severe clergymen (and a few lay teachers who were just as stern and remote), at schools where uniforms were worn and where there was no preparation for adult heterosexual society. No one had advised him on grooming, dress and manners, and this uneven training had made him a socially unsophisticated young man alienated from the world he tried to embrace. The young Olivier, like many who require attention, often unwittingly alienated others in his muddled attempts to win acceptance, and – feeling rejected and confused – he would quite naturally withdraw behind 'an invisible wall'. The feeling of social inferiority must have been even more poignant in light of his financial situation, for he had barely enough for his own meals; to invite a young lady to tea, a dance or an entertainment was beyond the realm of possibility.

There was, then, an array of conflicts facing Olivier as he approached his eighteenth birthday, in addition to the normal quandaries attending that age. If it is crucial for every young adult to find approval and support, surely that need is trebled for an artistic personality. Forced to a lonely independence on the brink of maturity, he required and longed for peer and professional acceptance – not only because he had virtually no family to turn to, but because he was a richly endowed young man, and his gifts demanded recognition and refinement. But just as his dress and manner were crude, without polish and in need of modification, so his aptitudes – of which he could not yet be certain – were still raw. His genius, in other words, was as yet unharnessed to talent.

To supplement his meagre budget, Olivier scanned the theatrical call boards and sat on agents' doorsteps in Charing Cross Road, hoping for a job. Occasionally his waiting obtained a modest reward. At Christmas 1924, he worked as assistant stage manager and understudy in a children's play, *Through the Crack*, at St Christopher's School, Letchworth; this added only three or four pounds to his income. In February, he was seen briefly at the Regent, London, taking two small (and critically ignored) roles in *Henry IV, Part II* – Snare, who comes to arrest Falstaff, and Thomas, Duke of Clarence. As eager for a good part as for a hot meal that winter, he may well have envied the actor who played Shallow: for his own enjoyment, Olivier memorised much of the role, and years later it became one of his most famous and favourite characterisations.

That same month, he sacrificed several meals for a cheap seat at John Barrymore's *Hamlet* at the Theatre Royal, Haymarket. In retrospect, it provided nourishment for years of inspiration. Barrymore had exquisite diction, consummate charm and two techniques that greatly impressed Olivier. First, he seemed to select from each line a single word for emphasis, and this he uttered with a great ring of passion; the result was a rhythm of alternating stresses and varied volume that kept the audience bound to him. Second, there was Barrymore's roaring athleticism: his Hamlet sprang to life with sudden leaps and unexpected, flashing gestures. At the time Shakespeare was often performed with an almost anaemic languor, but Barrymore made Hamlet's agonies credible.

There were other influences. Most films shown in London were American imports (only thirty-four English films were made in 1925, compared with over 300 American), and for a few pence Olivier could see which actors kept the packed cinemas in rapt attention. Ronald Colman, an Englishman who had recently emigrated to Hollywood, was Lillian Gish's choice as her co-star in *The White Sister*. One of the most popular in the grand exodus of actors to America (Clive Brook, George Arliss and Victor McLaglen were others), Colman seemed the embodiment of gentlemanly elegance. The American matinee idol Rod La Rocque (in *Forbidden Paradise*) appealed to both men and women with his striking, confident sexuality. And the portrayals by Douglas Fairbanks (in *The Thief of Baghdad*) and Lon Chaney (in *The Phantom of the Opera*) tapped and exposed for Olivier a new kind of bold carnality, and rich varieties of costume and make-up.

There was very much of America in the London air that year. 'Tea for Two', 'Indian Love Call' and 'California, Here I Come' were heard all over town, and Americanisms ('the bunk','sugar daddy', 'baloney', 'okay', 'yeah') were peppering the conversation of British youth. In July 1925, the Charleston arrived at a Soho tea dance; Olivier was persuaded to try it by a schoolmate. Her name is unknown, but she was a carefree flapper and he found her laugh and high spirits infectious. They danced for an hour before she left on the arm of an older man.

The cocktail and cabaret age had begun in London, and it was the era of the Bright Young Things. Those who could not afford to see Beatrice Lillie or Sophie Tucker at the Hotel Metropole's 'Midnight Follies' or the bands and variety acts at the Piccadilly Hotel's 'Revels' found their way to one of the endless theme parties. Cliques all over London seemed to be in constant rivalry for the most outrageous requirements for dress and decor: there were Wild West parties, Jungle Savage parties, Greek, Russian, Nearly Nude and Baby parties. Some of them offered cocaine (first called 'snow' in London) as an alternative to the Pink Lady cocktail, and although drugs were not illegal some of their effects were, and soon morally vigilant citizens were marching to suppress vice. Olivier was exposed to it all – through those he met in the daily crush of postwar London life, through the pages of *The Era* and *The Stage* (which he scoured for jobs), through the agents and producers he hounded, and in his frugal lunches with equally penurious but more worldly apprentice actors. He still attended All Saints every Sunday, often serving as acolyte, and Father Mackay, observing how thin Larry was, wrote to Gerard; thereafter an occasional pound note from Father Olivier arrived in the mail at Castellain Road.

As his classes at the Central School concluded in mid-1925, Olivier acted in a brief scene from Pinero's *Trelawny of the 'Wells'*. Peggy Ashcroft remembered suddenly sitting up as if seeing him for the first time and saying to herself, 'My goodness, he can act!' For all his roughness, he was dynamic. Olivier and Ashcroft were (to no one's astonishment) awarded the Dawson Milward Cup, a school prize named for a popular actor of the day. This was given for their achievements in general, but particularly for an absurdly amateurish comic piece called *Mr and Mrs Inkpen*, of which both actors were slightly ashamed.

Late that summer and autumn, Olivier was engaged by manager Julian Frank to appear in *The Unfailing Instinct*, a music-hall curtain raiser with the actress Ruby Miller. (The teenage character's name, Armand St Cyr, was more impressive than his role, as a fan who discovers that his great idol is his mother.) After four weeks on tour with this trifle in Manchester, Liverpool and Brighton, his salary of two pounds was slightly augmented when he was asked to be assistant stage manager and play the silent policeman in a melodrama, *The Ghost Train*, in which Miller had scored a great success in London. No such success was Olivier's: the Brighton drama correspondent alluded to him only to note his unintentionally dramatic entry onstage. Heedless of the stage manager's warning about the set's raised doorsill, Olivier reduced a tense scene to giddy farce as he tripped, sliding precariously toward the footlights.

He fared no better in his next employment, although there was a different reason for both the hilarity and the brevity of his tenure. In October, Olivier secured a position in a modest repertory company managed by Lena Ashwell, another of the stalwart ladies of the British stage. Like Elsie Fogerty, she was both maternal and encouraging to him – and, as it happened, she was eventually less patient.

The relationship with the Ashwell Players began auspiciously. Lena, aged fifty-three, told Olivier that she too had lost her mother very young, and her father had turned to the ministry late. She had first appeared onstage in 1891, and four years later she triumphed as Elaine to Henry Irving's King Arthur. The theatre soon became a mission for Lena Ashwell, and during the war she organised twenty-five acting companies to entertain troops. Thereafter, she established the 'Once-a-Week Players' to provide good cheap entertainment in various town halls at home, and in 1924 she acquired the Bijou Theatre, Bayswater, and renamed it the Century (Olivier's performance in *Byron* with the Lyceum Club Stage Society had taken place here). In addition, she took her casts nightly to play for the poor in various settlement houses, public baths, piers and town halls, in places like Battersea, Ilford, Deptford and Camberwell.

Olivier was impressed by her commitment to the theatre, but not by the excessive frugality of her productions. For a stage, boards were shunted over swimming pools, lights were hastily strung round an ancient, unelectrified school hall, and players were asked to take multiple roles in the same play. Evidently he could no longer take the enterprise seriously when he had to double as Flavius and Antony in *Julius Caesar* before a crowd of schoolboys. Another player's trousers fell to the stage from beneath his costume, and Larry – freely joining the audience in a fit of unsuppressed laughter – simply quit the scene. Next day, the unamused Lena Ashwell summoned him and insisted he also quit the company.

It remains unclear how the renewal of their acquaintance occurred, but in December 1925 Olivier was working with Sybil Thorndike and her husband Lewis Casson, who with manager Bronson Albery were producing plays at the Empire Theatre, Leicester Square. For three pounds a week, he was a servant in Shakespeare's *Henry VIII*, and Carol Reed – later famous as the director of films such as *The Third Man* and *Oliver!* – was his cohort in holding Thorndike's heavy robe as Queen Katherine. Offstage, the two young men were rivals for the attention of the production's Anne Boleyn, Angela Baddeley, who was quite happily married and ignored the infatuated young actors. 'They used to quarrel like mad [over Angela],' according to Thorndike. 'I had to say, "You shut up, you two, and attend to what you're doing."'

Onstage, Olivier generally attended to his responsibilities, despite an occasional fit of amateurish laughter at something like a missed cue or at what he considered an absurd line. Offstage was another matter. As assistant stage manager (of the same plays in which he took his small roles), he once rang down the curtain a full minute before time, and he shocked Bronson Albery (whom he did not recognise) by asking him to keep silent during a rehearsal. The impossible infatuations, the onstage giggling, the sloppiness at duties that bored him – all these were signs of a protracted adolescence, causing some colleagues to doubt the seriousness of his professional goals. Sybil Thorndike, for one, thought he was altogether too casual that season.

But she and her husband Lewis (who were like parents to him) continued their kindly patronage, and in March 1926 Olivier played Orsino's servant – one brief appearance with twenty-seven words – in their revival of Shelley's *The Cenci*. He was glad of the money, but the roles were still unchallenging and life, as he approached his nineteenth birthday, seemed drearily static. Writing to Dickie in India, he claimed to be very near to abandoning the theatre and taking the voyage out.

CHAPTER THREE

⚜

1927–1930

Let schoolmasters puzzle their brain
With grammar and nonsense and learning;
Good liquor, I stoutly maintain,
Gives genius a better discerning.

Tony Lumpkin, in Goldsmith's *She Stoops to Conquer*

Outside London – most notably in Liverpool, Stratford, Manchester and Birmingham – the repertory system flourished in England even before World War I. Repertory companies offered one play on Monday, another on Tuesday, a third on Wednesday, sometimes even a fourth or fifth thereafter, and actors appearing in one were usually rehearsing a second and learning lines for a third. Repertory theatre was a superb training ground, exercising a player's memory and extending his range; appearing with established actors, an apprentice quickly learned both classical roles and parts in new plays.

Barry Jackson, the wealthy heir to the Maypole Dairies, had directed an amateur company called the Pilgrim Players before opening the Birmingham Repertory Theatre in February 1913. Jackson personally supervised the design of the company's building, insisting on an intimate auditorium with no seat more than seventy feet from the stage, and in addition to revivals of standard classics he also subsidised productions of the works of new and controversial playwrights. His stated aim was to enlarge and increase the aesthetic sense of the public . . . to give living authors an opportunity of seeing their works performed, and to learn something from the revival of the classics; in short, to serve an art instead of making that art serve a commercial purpose.

George Bernard Shaw, whose mammoth, five-part *Back to Methuselah* had its premiere (spanning a whole week) at Birmingham, benefited from Jackson's idealism, calling the Repertory Theatre a place where 'all genuine artists have found themselves happily at home', and plays opening there often continued in London and beyond (among them Besier's *The Barretts of Wimpole Street*). Early Birmingham players who went on to substantial careers included Felix Aylmer, Leslie Banks, Gwen Ffrangçon-Davies and Cedric Hardwicke. Noël Coward appeared there briefly in 1919, and among the Birmingham alumni were Peggy Ashcroft, Edith Evans, Ralph Richardson and Laurence Olivier, who was received into the company during their London season at the Kingsway Theatre in the spring of 1926.

Although his first role was a small one, it guaranteed a month's wages (at six pounds ten shillings per week) and the promise of more parts to come. As a minstrel in *The Marvellous History of Saint Bernard*, Henri Ghéon and Barry Jackson's reworking of a religious mystery play, Olivier made his first appearance on 7 April. He was duly impressed by the expense Jackson had obviously incurred for the elaborate set representing a tripartite heaven-earth-hell – the effect was very like a page from a medieval illuminated book of hours.

Gwen Ffrangçon-Davies, who played a bride abandoned by her pious fiancé, remembered that there was nothing sensational about Olivier's presence or performance at all; and actor Denys Blakelock retained a clear memory of an undistinguished-looking young man with bad teeth, eyebrows that grew thickly into a straight line and a thatch of unmanageable hair. Blakelock also recalled that Olivier could be surprisingly candid. Once, as they sat in a restaurant called the Cabin in the Strand, Blakelock had his hands spread out on the table. Olivier looked down at them and said, 'Funny stumpy little hands, aren't they?' Also in the cast was a young actress named Muriel Hewitt, for whom Olivier developed a romantic fixation that was doomed to be unrequited. Like Angela Baddeley, she was also married and immune to his idolatry.

The run of *Saint Bernard* was interrupted in early May by the General Strike, the worst of over three hundred labour disputes afflicting Britain that year. In support of the coalminers' grievances, virtually every union struck on 4 May. London trams, buses and underground and other essential services were manned by volunteers and guarded by police, and Olivier worked as a tube conductor on the Circle Line for the nine days of the strike, which won no concession for the beleaguered miners. Forever after, he remembered this brief work only as a bit of a lark.

34

Saint Bernard closed on 12 June, but by this time Olivier had rehearsed for a small role in D.T. Davies's *The Barber and the Cow*, a pallid Welsh comedy about a local haircutter, a comatose animal and rural elections; it has been justly ignored since shortly after the premiere in Clacton-on-Sea. Ralph Richardson, who was married to Muriel Hewitt, had a leading role; he, too, would fare infinitely better in coming years.

Born in 1902 in Cheltenham, Richardson had been acting with amateur companies since 1921. He and his wife (nicknamed Kit) joined the Birmingham Repertory in 1924, and soon after he went on tour with Eden Phillpotts's popular and lucrative country comedy *The Farmer's Wife*. By summer 1926 he hoped for a major London debut, and his rivalry with Olivier for some of the same roles was aggravated by the latter's open adoration of Kit. Richardson judged his colleague 'a cocky young pup full of fire and energy', and in turn Olivier thought him stuffy and pretentious.

One day during the summer tour of *Barber*, Richardson and his wife offered to bring Olivier with them from Clacton to Bridlington. Driving his new Morris Cowley on a particularly warm day, Richardson noticed the radiator gauge approaching the boil. While Olivier and Kit chatted gaily, he stopped to inspect the car's innards. As steam hissed around him, Richardson saw Olivier approaching. 'I want to ask you something, Ralph,' he said portentously.

'What the devil is it, Larry?'

'Would you mind – would you – if I called Muriel "Kit"?'

Fastidious about using a diminutive, Olivier could however be annoyingly reckless at the wheel, as was soon clear to Richardson – himself no timid soul: in his seventies he was still wildly driving a motorcycle in London traffic. Driving to Brighton several months later, Olivier approached a dangerous crossroad without a traffic signal. Instead of slowing, he increased to fifty miles an hour and without any concern for danger sped across the intersection. 'Laurence,' Richardson said deliberately, 'never – never – as long as I live, will I forgive you for that.' But the driver was jaunty: 'It is a well-known thing, Ralphie, that when you get to a point of danger, get over it as quick as you can.' The tour of *Barber* continued into autumn, when Olivier was cast as Richard Coaker, the lovesick country lad in *The Farmer's Wife* (the role had earlier been Richardson's). After several weeks playing the role in Brighton and elsewhere, Olivier made his Birmingham debut in December. Throughout 1927, his circumstances remained frugal, for like the rest of the company he was paid only six pounds a week and could afford only a modest room in a boarding house.

In the evenings and on some afternoons, Olivier performed on the steeply raked stage of Jackson's Station Street Theatre, where he was seen in more than a dozen roles that year. 'The versatility I wished to dazzle people with was being gradually developed all the time,' he recalled later. 'I didn't want to be recognised from one week to the next.' Often he was not. From a non-speaking cameo to the title role in a classic play, Olivier was employing a diversity of styles, accents, costumes and make-up.

But his irrepressible sense of fun still occasionally endangered his career. In January, for example, he took the role of a wealthy young man with monocle and Oxbridge accent in Eden Phillpotts's *Something To Talk About*, a one-act comedy about a thief who breaks into a manor house early on Christmas morning. As the polished son, Olivier enjoyed himself immensely and could not resist an interpolation. To the intruder's angry 'Who are you?' he was to say, 'We are Conservatives!' But that did not sound funny enough to him, and instead he replied, 'We're Freemasons, Frothblowers and Gugnuncs!' The director, W.G. Fay, was furious and demanded Olivier's dismissal, but Jackson let him off with a gentle lecture on professional decorum. His behaviour improved markedly for the remaining winter roles: a simpleton in Synge's religious fantasy *The Well of the Saints*; a young romantic in R.R. Whittaker's *The Third Finger*; another well-to-do young lover in Murray McClymont's *The Mannoch Family*; and a wordless walk-on in Henri Ghéon's *The Comedian*.

In April 1927, there followed two major roles. As Chekhov's Uncle Vanya, Olivier pasted on such great quantities of make-up and facial hair that colleagues at first did not recognise him backstage. He also appeared as the sneering, cynical and mendacious Parolles in a modern-dress production of *All's Well That Ends Well*, the most complex and challenging role he had so far assumed. Although the man is thoroughly reprehensible, his final unmasking and downfall are accompanied by an awareness of his own deficiency:

> If my heart were great,
> 'Twould burst at this. Captain I'll be no more
> But I will eat and drink, and sleep as soft
> As captain shall: simply the thing I am

Shall make me live . . .
There's place and means for every man alive.

Years later, Birmingham colleagues recalled that Olivier (not yet twenty at the time) captured both the grim humour of the role and the sympathy Parolles must evoke from the audience. For spring and summer, he took small parts in Beatrice Mayor's *The Pleasure Garden* (as a dreamily romantic young man in a public park) and in J.M. Barrie's *Quality Street* (as the bland Ensign Blades, longing for a pretty dancing partner). The *Birmingham Mail* first mentioned him after his performance as the boorish brat Tony Lumpkin (in dark greasepaint and a wild wig) in *She Stoops to Conquer*; he was praised for showing Tony as more than merely a churlish clown. By then, Jackson was ready to cast Olivier in a romantic lead. On 3 September he appeared with his former classmate Peggy Ashcroft in John Drinkwater's *Bird in Hand*, as a squire's son who falls in love with an innkeeper's daughter. One critic gently scolded Olivier for sentimentally kissing the door of his sweetheart's room.

That little touch may have been his way of compensating for his silly role, lead or no. But the kiss also certainly reflected his feelings toward his co-star. Long afterwards, he told Ashcroft that when they visited a fellow player's flat that year, he intended to propose to her when their host excused himself for a moment. Olivier hesitated, the sound of a flushing toilet broke his Byronic mood, and the question was never asked. She also remembered a weekend in Stratford, chaperoned by the author of *Bird in Hand*. After an elegant dinner they all attended a production of *Antony and Cleopatra* staged at a local cinema (the Memorial Theatre had recently been destroyed by fire). She remembered it as a romantic but platonic weekend.

Later in September, he appeared more rambunctiously as Mervyn Jones, the love-smitten admirer of a character named April Mawne in Herbert Farjeon and Horace Horsnell's comedy *Advertising April*. With particular relish he tore into the young man's romantic anguish, wildly declaiming:

I feel as Hamlet must have felt when he chastised his mother. 'Such an act, that blurs the grace and blush of modesty.' And then she said he'd cleft her heart in twain. And he said, 'O throw away the worser part of it, And live the purer with the other half.' That's what I say to you – you – actress! . . . All the world isn't a stage. And all the men and women aren't merely players!

37

'The only player genuinely in character was Mr Laurence Olivier,' said the *Birmingham Post*'s reviewer.

He brought a similar honest energy to his next role, that of a dissolute in John Galsworthy's *The Silver Box*. The curtain rose on Olivier's entrance in full evening dress and his long monologue as a well-bred man who arrives home drunk. He completed the autumn season in Elmer Rice's *The Adding Machine* – his first American play – and in Thomas Holcroft's eighteenth-century *The Road to Ruin*. Between them came his performance as an aspiring inventor, the weak husband in Harris Dean's thin comedy *Aren't Women Wonderful!*

The constant cycle of performances, rehearsals and memorising sessions left players little time for pursuing a private life. At twenty, Olivier was refining his professional skills, but offstage he was still the gauche, overaged choirboy. He was certainly attracted to women (Angela Baddeley, Muriel Hewitt, Peggy Ashcroft and Jane Welsh, who joined the company for six months), but these affections were unreturned. Later he claimed that 1927 was a year of intense sexual desires he felt should be legitimately satisfied only as a husband – a view not widely shared by young men.

Additionally, Olivier seems not to have been entirely sure of himself at this time: in the first draft of his memoirs (written in 1980–81), he admitted that the homosexual experiences of his schooldays had endured well into his late teenage years, and since neither courtship nor overt sexual advances were requisites to dating at that time, he may have approached young adulthood in mild, unexamined conflict about his fundamental sexual identity. The claim of frustrated desire was of course easy to make then and later, and the woman he chose to marry when he was twenty-three was, as it happened, as confused as he seemed to be.

Non-romantic socialising continued very early in 1928, when Olivier's acquaintance with Ralph Richardson was transformed into friendship during the Birmingham Repertory's London season at the Royal Court, Sloane Square. They discovered a joint distaste for the conventions of dated acting styles and a shared preference for long drinking sessions at the local pub; both had astonishing capacities for alcohol. In addition, they were united in their concern about the gradual but unmistakable signs of illness in Kit. (Eventually her condition was diagnosed as encephalitis, which ravaged her for fourteen years until her death in 1942.)

At the Court, Olivier's first assignment in January 1928 was the same role he had played earlier in Rice's *The Adding Machine*, an expressionist indictment of postwar chaos and man's transformation into a machine. Olivier was concerned about the unsuitability of his English accent for an American character, so he rang Denys Blakelock, then appearing in the West End in Sidney Howard's *The Silver Cord* with the American actress Clare Eames (Howard's wife). He asked Blakelock to introduce him backstage, and there he immediately asked Eames to coach him in a tough New York accent. 'Larry looked down at me with the eyes of a conqueror,' she said later to Blakelock. And conquer he did. His efforts and his quick mastery of the diction earned him a line of praise from critic St John Ervine, who wrote in the *Observer* that Olivier's brief appearance on 9 January marked the best performance in the play. This was, it seems, the first time he took special pains to achieve a particular vocal quality he felt a role required; henceforth, this search for the proper timbre and texture would be a constant and crucial part of his preparation for a naturalistic approach to character development. In so doing, he systematically increased the volume, colour, accent and inflection that enabled him to portray the widest variety of characters and emotions with the utmost credibility.

Up to 1920, performers had depended instead on rhetorical skills, expansive gestures and sweeping movements which often seemed almost comically artificial. However brilliant they were, Henry Irving and Herbert Beerbohm Tree, in the nineteenth century, were always obviously 'acting'. But after World War I, there emerged a more realistic and casual style that emphasised the role more than its exponent. Part of the change had to do with the contemporary subjects and settings of many new plays (social upheavals, postwar inflation, poverty, psychological illness and even the decadence of the genteel life), and much had also to do with the freewheeling and boldly creative spirit of the time. But the trend towards more natural acting depended most of all on the breadth of the actors themselves. The man most often credited with this shift away from overt histrionics to an almost invisible realism was Gerald du Maurier, whose art was precisely that he disguised his art.

Olivier himself had once believed that du Maurier was not acting at all, that he was merely reproducing onstage his own drawing-room behaviour in, for example, *The Last of Mrs Cheyney*. 'We thought he was being really natural,' he said many years later, '[but] of course he was a genius of a technician giving that appearance.' As du Maurier's friend Raymond Massey wrote, 'The smooth naturalness of his performances came from laborious preparation.' Massey watched the actor practise expressions for hours in front of a mirror with bits of business involving a drinking glass or a cigarette. 'Little things like that don't come easily to me,' du Maurier said.

Nor did they to Olivier, who by 1928 very much admired Gerald du Maurier's technique. Thus he began to spend many more hours alone in private preparation, and soon he was regularly attending a first rehearsal with every line memorised and most visual details planned. He, like du Maurier, worked from exterior details (voice, gait, costume and make-up) towards the interior truth of a character, and eventually he would far surpass du Maurier in range, depth and fame. And so Olivier, too, abandoned the exaggerated mannerisms of the preceding generation and cultivated a more realistic approach to each part.

Like du Maurier's, Olivier's technique would never be 'natural'. All his performances were comprised of carefully calculated externals, meticulously applied make-up and diligently practised modulations of voice and nuances of gesture, stitched together in private and developed in consort with directors and other players. He was 'natural' only insofar as this triumph of achieved technique was (almost always) entirely believable and recognisably human – characters sprang to life and emotions were deeply felt by audiences. The genius of Laurence Olivier would be to extend perhaps farther than any actor of his time the scope of these emotions and characters – beyond Irving's heroic portraits and du Maurier's salon gentlemen – to include the widest gallery possible.

On 6 February, Jackson presented *Macbeth* at the Royal Court, with Olivier as Malcolm. Jessica Tandy, who had recently made her London debut and joined the Birmingham Repertory, recalled that only Olivier was memorable: the production was unsatisfying, perhaps because of its inept modern dress and setting. The play, after all, does not transcend its era by the simple transformation of the witches into London charwomen and of Scottish thanes into Mayfair gentlemen wearing silk dressing gowns and flannel suits; nor is the banquet scene made more compelling by the addition of champagne, Peach Melba and cigars. On 5 March, Olivier appeared as Martellus in the fifth part of Shaw's epic *Back to Methuselah*, set in the year 31,920. By this time, according to his co-star Gwen Ffrangçon-Davies, he was reading modern verse magnificently and demonstrating more professional and personal confidence.

Then, for his first leading role in London, Jackson gave Olivier the title role in a revival of Tennyson's verse drama *Harold*, which opened on 2 April. Ponderously solemn, the play, about the events of 1066, was doomed from the first rehearsal. Colourful sets, inspired by the Bayeux Tapestry, were the only successful element: even the carefully enunciated speeches by Olivier (wearing a long blond wig) could not compensate for the tediously undramatic text and for his own inability to assume a convincing romantic-heroic posture (he was not yet twenty-one).

On 30 April he took a much smaller role (a lord) in the modern-dress staging of *The Taming of the Shrew*. After his brief opening scene, Olivier was to join a few other actors as an 'audience' in an onstage theatre box – and from the first performance he decided to stir up some fun at the expense of their colleague Ralph Richardson, who was playing the comic servant Tranio. First he affected every kind of inappropriate grimace and gesture to make Richardson 'corpse' – laugh onstage and 'kill' his character. Olivier waved at Richardson, whispered to others, stuck out his tongue, feigned sleep the moment Richardson began to speak – none of which put the actor off his stride, for he refused to look directly at Olivier. Finally, the mischief-maker sat absolutely still with a deadly serious expression, watching Richardson with rapt attention until he was unnerved with anxiety and finally had to look at Olivier, who maintained the same frozen, serious gaze. That did it: Richardson and the audience collapsed with laughter.

As he reached his twenty-first birthday that May, Laurence Olivier was – despite *Harold* – still very much an obscure repertory player who received only an occasional nod from one of the forty or fifty daily drama critics in London. To improve his prospects, he was now working with an agent named Peacock, who scoured producers' offices, telephoned managers and used influential contacts in the hope of solid leading roles. Olivier also withdrew that spring from Jackson's repertory company.

'Of course I wanted to be a West End actor,' he said later, 'of course I wanted money. I wanted violently to get married, I wanted to have all the earmarks of success – they appealed to me as they appealed to everybody else.' He wanted, in other words, 'to reach some heights'. But the heights were not to be immediately scaled, and soon he was literally penniless. One day Evelyn Light met him emerging from his tiny flat in Margaret Street. Finding him pale, thin and depressed, she at once offered him lunch; it was, he said, his first meal in almost a week.

Olivier then learned that Patrick Susands, who was appearing in the London revival of *Bird in Hand*, was departing, and the small Royalty Theatre in Dean Street needed a hasty replacement. By late June he was onstage, this time opposite an actress named Jill Esmond. Then twenty, she was a somewhat aloof brunette, attractive rather than beautiful, with a serious manner, an impressive theatrical pedigree and a professional career so far that greatly outshone his. She had none of the airs of many young women from famous families, and she affected neither a flapper's insouciance nor a flirt's coyness. And her shyness with the opposite sex rather resembled Olivier's.

Jill Esmond Moore (as she sometimes preferred to be known) was the daughter of actress Eva Moore and actor-playwright Henry Vernon Esmond (who early on abandoned his family surname, Jack). Jill had studied at the Royal Academy of Dramatic Art, and after her 1922 debut as Nibs in *Peter Pan* she worked consistently in London or on tour – most memorably in Noël Coward's *Hay Fever* and Sutton Vane's *Outward Bound*. When she met Olivier, she was still living with her widowed mother in the house where she was born, a mock-Tudor maisonette in Whitehead's Grove, Chelsea.

It is impossible to know whether Olivier saw the ironic connection between himself and his role in *Bird in Hand*, but it was soon clear that he intended to bring the play to life offstage, with the roles reversed. Instead of being the well-born squire's son wooing the modest innkeeper's daughter, he fancied himself the needy apprentice ready to wed the child of famous parents. At once he decided that no one better would come along, and since her credentials were acceptable and he was desperate to be married, he chose Jill Esmond. But she remained determinedly cool. When, after several modest suppers, he asked her to become Mrs Olivier, she smiled and politely refused, suggesting only that they become better acquainted before taking such a step. This he chose to interpret simply as feminine wiles, and he intensified his efforts to appear an attractive prospect. Under her friendly tutelage, he undertook important cosmetic changes over the next several months, clipping his thick brows, slickly styling his hair in the movie-star fashion of the day and submitting to major dental work that cleaned and straightened his teeth. At the same time, he presented himself to Jill's mother, who found him amusing and acceptable, for Eva Moore was eager that her daughter should find a good husband – preferably a theatre colleague, as she herself had once chosen.

The run of *Bird in Hand* continued through the autumn, with Olivier also appearing in the single performance of a wordy costume drama called *The Dark Path*, set in nineteenth-century Japan. By December, he was out of work again, but there was considerable speculation in the London theatre world about an elaborate production director Basil Dean was preparing – a stage version of P.C. Wren's novel *Beau Geste*, which had recently been a great success on film with Ronald Colman. It was common knowledge that Dean was scouring London for a dashing leading man after Brian Aherne, who had initially accepted, decided he did not like the script. Olivier was one of a dozen actors hopeful of landing the role, and so he decided to accept the lead in two theatre club performances of a play called *Journey's End*, which, it was widely thought, would vanish quietly – but not before Basil Dean attended the Sunday evening or Monday matinee performance. For his appearance in *Journey's End*, Olivier deliberately modelled his appearance on Ronald Colman in *Beau Geste*, cultivating a trim moustache and carefully parting and greasing his hair, as Jill counselled.

R.C. Sherriff was a salesman who had poured into *Journey's End* his heartache and frustration as a soldier in the trenches of the Great War. His play romanticised nothing; like *All Quiet on the Western Front*, it was a bitter and poignant indictment of war. But in 1928 no producer or actor gave it a chance of commercial success: it was considered too uncompromisingly grim. On 9 December the curtain of the Apollo Theatre, Shaftesbury Avenue, rose to reveal a dugout, and there the action remained. Olivier played Captain Stanhope, a once idealistic soldier now dependent on alcohol to calm his nerves and his fear of death. In the role of a young soldier was Maurice Evans, also hopeful of playing in *Beau Geste*.

In his memoirs and in later broadcast interviews, Olivier maintained that Dean, not wishing to embarrass Evans, asked him to leave their joint dressing room while he offered Olivier the role of Beau Geste immediately after the Monday performance of *Journey's End*. According to Evans and others, however, Dean appeared with two scripts: he wanted Olivier for the lead and Evans for his brother. Evans believed *Journey's End* had a future (and he did not wish to be a supporting player to Olivier so soon again), and so he declined Dean's offer. Olivier, who received only polite applause for his Stanhope (which some critics thought overheated), accepted on the spot for *Beau Geste*.

But he soon had second thoughts, for Basil Dean often resembled a howling sergeant-major. Madeleine Carroll, the leading lady, was often in tears as Dean shrieked condemnations at rehearsals, and Olivier himself came close to weeping at the fiery insults to which actors were singularly susceptible after a ten-hour day of rehearsals and costume fittings. The entire cast was terrified of Dean, and this seems to have been his ploy to maintain their attention and endurance. All the men were forced through a punishing two-hour exercise class each morning, followed by an hour's marching. Then came eight hours of rehearsals and an hour singing soldiers' choruses and marching songs. Absence from any of these activities warranted dismissal.

Everything in *Beau Geste* had to be authentic, demanded Dean. Hobnailed army boots were required at rehearsals as onstage, and Foreign Legion uniforms were imported from France – their desirability not much helped by repeated fumigation. Meanwhile, *Journey's End* (with Colin Clive replacing Olivier) reopened at the Savoy Theatre on 21 January 1929, after the American actor-producer Maurice Browne raised the needed funds for its transfer. There it began a successful run of 600 performances, and soon there were companies playing it in New York and around the world.

On 30 January, the lumberingly overproduced, patchily written *Beau Geste* came to His Majesty's Theatre. Dean, the critics wrote, failed to tell a coherent story about the three brothers Geste and their desert exploits under the French flag. Gravid with sentimentality, the text resembled a children's pageant rather than a believable picture of men in the Legion. The final scene, in which Olivier's character, Beau, was to be cremated by his brothers, capped a disastrous premiere. As the smoke rose from a small, fanned fire nearby, the theatre fire warden – new to his job and unfamiliar with the text – leaped to his feet and lowered the asbestos fire curtain, which crashed heavily to the stage. By the time it was raised and the cast gathered for the applause, His Majesty's Theatre was empty. A month later the play closed, for London critics and audiences were unwilling to accept the play's 'tedious nobilities' (*The Times*), nor were huge sets and technical wizardry proper substitutes for compelling characters in a drama. '[Olivier] is overwhelmed,' wrote critic Charles Morgan, 'by the sickliness of his part and by the weight of the stage trappings.' After nine London productions, Olivier's stage career was stalled – and so it would remain for five years.

But Basil Dean had an option for his services, and on 14 March Olivier appeared in yet another exotic spectacle – *The Circle of Chalk*, James Laver's adaptation (via Klabund) of the Chinese tale of a young prince (Olivier) who rescues a girl wrongfully accused of a crime. Bloated Chinoiserie, ill-fitting costumes and a wretched case of laryngitis on opening night did not aid the hapless Olivier.

At least Jill was not at the New Theatre to see his misfortune. She had departed for New York, there to make her Broadway debut in the durable *Bird in Hand* on 4 April. During her absence (and because they were not officially engaged), Olivier went out with Betty Chester, best known as a song-and-dance comedienne in the annual series of revues called *The Co-Optimists*, which opened that year in July and ran for seventeen weeks. But Chester, twelve years older, was not interested (according to actor Alexander Clark, who knew them both at the time), because Olivier spoke constantly of Jill. Absence apparently made his heart grow fonder.

At the end of April, he played a supporting role opposite Herbert Marshall and Edna Best in Philip Barry's comedy *Paris Bound*, and in June a chorus girl's lover in a dreary piece called *The Stranger Within*. Both plays closed quickly, and thus it was not surprising that Olivier immediately accepted an offer for his American stage debut. Frank Vosper was starring in the London production of his own play *Murder on the Second Floor*, and he decided not to travel with it. New York producer A.H. Woods offered a ten-week guarantee at five hundred dollars a week, and on 10 August Olivier boarded the *Aquitania*.

He had kept his arrival secret from Jill, and his unexpected appearance at her dressing-room door a week later must not have been entirely unwelcome, for within days he had proposed marriage again. This time she accepted, with the mysterious proviso of a year's delay. Had Olivier not been so eager for marriage and yet apparently so shy of its financial and sexual responsibilities, he might have thought that her demand now cast him as the forlorn hero of a lost tale by the Brothers Grimm, a lover constantly put off by his inamorata. There was, however, no tangible reason to complain about Jill, for she made no demands of any kind on him – except the postponement of the banns.

Murder on the Second Floor opened at the Eltinge Theatre on 11 September, with Olivier in the role of a playwright who spins a murder tale to impress his beloved: the story he tells her is then enacted, utilising all their neighbours as characters. New York was unimpressed, and Olivier made little more impression than the play: one critic remarked that he acted 'with an alarming suggestion now and then of Alfred Lunt', while another cited his 'engaging and straightaway manner', which was about as enthusiastic as the notices he had been receiving at home. As it happened, the play closed after five weeks.

The remaining five weeks were therefore a paid holiday, but because Jill was still performing their encounters were limited to daytime excursions. For companionship in his hotel room he took in a stray dog, but the poor animal had to be given up after becoming addicted to bathtub gin: the Algonquin's management had a tradition of welcoming eccentric guests – even those who had a private stash of whiskey in those days of Prohibition – but a dog habitually fainting in the lobby and elevator was too much. Just as the stock market crashed at the end of October, signalling the Great Depression and instantly altering the general ebullience of New York social life, Olivier bade Jill farewell and boarded the unglamorous *Lancastria*, bound for Southampton. In November, he was travelling daily from a small flat in Notting Hill to rehearsals for his role as a shell-shocked pilot on leave during the war in Frank Harvey's soggy spiritual melodrama *The Last Enemy*, which opened on 20 December and closed after ten weeks. By that time he was rehearsing for a one-week run at the Arts theatre in late March as Ralph, a prim young artist in John van Druten's synthetically sentimental family melodrama *After All*.

The failure to land major roles, the ongoing series of appearances in doomed plays and the lack of financial and emotional preparation for an imminent marriage – all these conspired in early 1930 to threaten the ego of the twenty-two-year-old Olivier. He could not be certain of success, and he had no reason to feel that he should not, after all, have followed Dickie to India. Fear and insecurity often conspire to produce an ungenerous and superior manner towards others, and in few worlds is this as understandable as in the theatre – a profession employing only a small number of its members even in the best of times. In 1930, only the fortunate minority were appearing in long runs like *Journey's End*, Coward's *Bitter Sweet*, or Shaw's *The Apple Cart*. In light of this, a kind of viral insecurity is easy to comprehend, and Olivier was not immune to it, as his fellow actor Denys Blakelock remembered. Blakelock was driving his friend to an appointment during rehearsals for *After All* when Olivier said, 'I suggested you for the leading part in it but John [van Druten] said, "Denys is a very good actor, but he hasn't got star quality."'

Then, in that spring of 1930, Olivier was offered a film role, and because he desperately needed money he accepted at once. Despite the general contempt in which film work was held by stage actors, such players as Ivor Novello, Isabel Jeans, Malcolm Keen and Sara Allgood had appeared on screen, and that year Herbert Marshall starred in Alfred Hitchcock's *Murder!* while George Arliss, in the title role of *Disraeli*, greatly dignified the image of the English film actor.

Since the first 'kinetoscope parlour' opened on Oxford Street in 1894, the British film industry had had an uneven history. Two years later, short narrative and 'reality' films were shown (with nonprofessional actors) in every major music hall in the country. The new medium was still a novelty until 1908, when Godfrey Tearle's *Romeo and Juliet* became the first British film to star stage actors like Tearle himself; Herbert Tree was paid the princely sum of one thousand pounds to appear in a film adaptation of *Henry VIII* three years later. Before the World War, there were forty-three major production companies in England, and professional actors often appeared in films: the work was considered easy and lucrative in comparison to the theatre, and they were pleased to have a record (though silent) of their stage perform-ances. By 1916, there were over 4000 cinemas in England, selling many millions of tickets annually.

But the war grievously affected the industry, taking a heavy toll of the talent and limiting material resources; by 1926 less than 5 per cent of films shown in England were British. Hollywood, with more favourable economic, geographical and climatic conditions, was producing movies that dominated the world market, and there was a large drain of English talent to the United States. British producers were often compelled to import American and German actors and crews.

Responding to the crisis in 1927, the Cinematograph Films Act stipu-lated that a percentage of motion pictures released in Britain must be produced by British companies – a quota that was set to increase to 20 per cent by 1935. Still, American films arrived in profusion, and a new, 3000-seat cinema opened somewhere in Britain every week of 1930. Studios, forced to comply with the law and eager to provide products for the new movie palaces, struck collaborative deals, often registering companies in London and actually making the films elsewhere as co-productions, especially with the thriving German film industry based in Berlin, where technical facilities were superior. It was to just such an Anglo-German collaboration that Olivier was invited by producer Erich Pommer.

*

Olivier departed from Croydon airfield on 7 April and arrived in Berlin eight hours later after stopovers in Rotterdam and Hanover. The picture, based on Curt Goetz's play *Hokuspokus* and eventually titled *The Temporary Widow*, featured Olivier as an artist who pretends to have been murdered in order to attract publicity for his work. During the six weeks of filming (for which he received three hundred pounds), Olivier and his colleagues attended the Berlin opera and a May wine festival at a lakeside hotel outside the city centre. He was back in London on 18 May, eager to repeat the lucrative job of movie-acting.

He didn't have to wait long. In mid-June he was at Twickenham Studios near London, as a rich playboy in a mystery-comedy called *Too Many Crooks*. Although he worked only four nights and the product was less than forty minutes long, Olivier received a favourable (if tendentious) trade review from *The Bioscope*: 'If his future work is up to the standard he has set here, his appearance in the leading role of a more ambitious film is assured.' Of far greater importance, however, *Too Many Crooks* brought Olivier a lifelong friend.

Laurence Evans was a young sound recordist and technician at Twickenham when, in June 1930, he met Laurence Olivier. The facilities were in operation day and night, with two shifts of workers so that films could be made round the clock. Evans was assigned to the night shooting of *Too Many Crooks*, and bore the responsibility for recording the dialogue. He remembered Olivier as friendly, unassuming and remarkably patient about re-recording lines of dialogue that, typically in that first year of British sound films, had not been clear during a take. (Both of them apparently dispatched their jobs well, for *The Bioscope* also commented, 'All the voices have been recorded perfectly, not a word being lost throughout the production.') The Olivier–Evans friendship continued over the next sixty years, eventually encompassing both creative and business enterprises, and often they greeted one another with the words, 'What have you been doing since *Too Many Crooks*?'

Although the shooting took place at night, Olivier's days in late June were not for sleeping. On the morning of the eighteenth, he was invited to the home of Noël Coward, who received him while he was breakfasting in bed. Olivier was impressed with Coward's casual elegance, his wit, his ingenuous style and his expensive silk pyjamas. The playwright handed him a cup of coffee and a typed script.

Coward had recently completed *Private Lives*, in which he and his great friend Gertrude Lawrence would soon star as the wittily scrappy

Elyot and Amanda, a divorced couple who accidentally meet on their honeymoons with new spouses and find that their old love, however problematic, is indissoluble. The narrative line was thinner than the paper on which it was typed, but the dialogue flashed with brilliantly acerbic humour, and Elyot and Amanda were recognisable denizens of the champagne-and-dressing-gown world of 1930 high society.

Coward required two attractive players in the roles of Victor and Sybil, the hapless second spouses who are finally abandoned when the others sprint back together. He admitted that the supporting roles were mere foils for the leading couple. But Adrianne Allen (Raymond Massey's wife) had agreed to play Sybil: since Coward believed that only an attractive actor should portray a bore, would Olivier like to play Victor? *Private Lives* would be a triumph, Coward said without arrogance, and would thus assure Olivier a good showcase; it would also pay fifty pounds a week, a very handsome salary. To Coward's surprise, Olivier said he would prefer the leading role, but since he was now scheduled to marry Jill at last – on 25 July – he needed the job. Rehearsals for *Private Lives* began earlier that same month, by which time there was as much emotional confusion offstage as on, for Noël Coward had fallen in love with Laurence Olivier.

CHAPTER FOUR

1930–1933

Victor: You know I feel rather scared of you at close
quarters.
Amanda: That promises to be very embarrassing.

Noël Coward, *Private Lives*

Thirty-year-old Noël Coward – tall, slim and patrician – had been acting since the age of twelve and producing his own plays since his early twenties. When he invited Laurence Olivier for morning coffee at his home in Gerald Road, Belgravia, he was already firmly established as a master of the theatre, author of sober dramas (*The Vortex*, *Easy Virtue*) as well as dazzling comedies (*Fallen Angels*, *Hay Fever*), composer of songs for his plays and lyrics for his songs. He also supervised every aspect of the productions, often as director, and was the superlative exponent of each as leading actor. Still greater successes were to come, beginning with *Private Lives*.

Above all a sophisticated wit, Coward was quick with repartee on paper and with a riposte in person. When the King and Queen once came to a Coward play, the entire audience rose to applaud their entrance to the royal box. 'What an entrance!' whispered Gertrude Lawrence as she and Coward waited in the wings. 'What a part!' he replied.

Aristocratic but candid, Coward loathed pretence, and his plays ruthlessly attacked it. To a letter from a business executive, written on paper headed 'From the desk of . . .' Coward wrote, 'Dear Desk of . . .' When a singularly sarcastic newspaper critic came backstage after a performance in a play by another writer, the critic told Coward, 'I've always said you could act better than you write.' There was no pause before Coward rejoined, 'And I've always said exactly the same about you.' He was also devoutly and exclusively homosexual.

As rehearsals for *Private Lives* progressed that summer, it was clear to everyone in the company that an affectionate and symbiotic bond had formed between the actor and his writer-director. Olivier knew his lines perfectly at first read-through, he presented an extremely handsome appearance, and thanks to the money from his two films, he also dressed fashionably. He took direction easily from Coward, admired his charm and intelligence and asked his advice on matters both professional and personal.

Only eight years older, Coward was a willing mentor. When Olivier admitted he had read little but the plays he performed, Coward gave him a list – the Brontës, Maugham and Arnold Bennett at first, then poetry, more novels, history and the classics. Much later, when Olivier was asked to name the people who had most influenced his life, he replied,

> Noël Coward, in all kinds of ways . . . He was a great mind-opener and very inspiring . . . I think Noël probably was the first man who took hold of me and made me think, he made me use my silly little brain. He taxed me with his sharpness and shrewdness and brilliance and he pointed out when I was talking nonsense, which nobody else had ever done before. He gave me a sense of right and wrong.

For his part, Coward's attentiveness and devotion were the natural result of an attraction to Olivier that quickly flourished into tender love. According to Cole Lesley, one of Coward's closest friends (and his biographer), 'Noël adored Larry, there is no other word for it.' The London theatre world was small and insular, however, and Coward had reasons to suspect (from friends and his own perceptions) that the Olivier–Esmond marriage was ill-advised – even doomed.

Nevertheless, on Friday, 25 July 1930, Laurence Olivier and Jill Esmond exchanged vows in a brief ceremony at All Saints, Margaret Street. (At the register office, Olivier – who had been moving almost monthly from one flat to another – wrote the church's address as his own.) The marriage was newsworthy mostly because of the bride's much greater fame; she had come back from a successful New York tour and joined another West End hit, Aimée and Philip Stuart's *Nine Till Six*, in which she was still performing at the time of her marriage. Her family's theatrical history and her own celebrity had given Jill a keen sense of the value of publicity, and before the wedding she confided in a newspaper reporter with astonishing directness. She did not, she said straight away, 'expect married life to be one long dream –

nobody could endure such a mental condition for long . . . One settles down on an even keel [after] a mutual readjustment . . . I should certainly have secrets and friends unknown to a husband of mine.'

The interview had been published on 22 May, her fiancé's twenty-third birthday, and it must have dismayed Olivier, who was surely not contemplating the untimely dullness of an even keel. But reasons for alarm were only just beginning.

After a reception at Whitehead's Grove, bride and groom left for a honeymoon weekend in the country, at a house owned by a friend of Eva Moore. Years later, Olivier claimed that he and his bride shared 'the same unspoken dread of what was expected of us before going to sleep'. Then, after some embarrassingly awkward fumbling, 'at last we turned away from each other'.

Olivier later claimed that Jill 'could not and did not try to deceive herself into believing that she was in the slightest degree in love with me, and she knew that I was fully aware of it'. But he was so avid for a respectable marriage (as had been enjoyed by his friends the Cassons and the Richardsons, among others) that he went ahead, apparently certain he could overcome both her hesitation and his own shyness.

If the prospect of sex with Olivier was apparently uncongenial to Jill in 1930, the full truth was discovered only gradually by them both over the next few years. Although she evidently believed she might sustain the marriage, she much preferred the company of women, to whom she turned increasingly for comfort, and by the time she was thirty it was well known that she was exclusively lesbian in her sexual preference. As the press had been warned, she had her secrets.

What may have been her own uncertainty and confusion at the time of her marriage had the predictable unhappy effect. The trauma of the wedding night, as she turned away from her husband with a resolute revulsion for sex, must have caused him to feel not only unattractive and ashamed but also inadequate and incompetent. For a young man so needy of professional and personal endorsement as well as womanly comfort, the experience was devastating. And while he hoped *Private Lives* might bring him one kind of fulfilment, he could never have expected marriage to deny him another. For some time afterwards, the marriage remained unconsummated.

'Larry never really enjoyed playing it very much,' Noël Coward said of Olivier's performance as Victor Prynne in *Private Lives*. 'But I think he enjoyed acting with me, we had great fun, and curiously enough, it did him a lot of good.'

While Olivier's marriage was a sham, at least he was working in a more rarefied and glamorous society than he had ever known. One day that summer, Denys Blakelock met him dashing from a long luncheon at the Ivy (a popular theatre restaurant near Covent Garden) to a cocktail party in Belgravia; that same evening, dinner at the Savoy was to follow. To this new world Olivier quickly adjusted, learning how to conduct himself in the most sophisticated settings, to make himself agreeable and amusing, to command attention amid a crowd. The means, after all, were not so very different from the polish he was observing in Coward: ironic and sometimes risqué wit, elegance of dress and manner and the adroit employment of subtle body language. By inviting him to social events, Noël Coward provided Laurence Olivier with an entrée to society's most desirable echelons. Thus, at the same time as he suffered from Jill's aloofness, Coward was always at hand with both social education and affectionate support.

But Coward perhaps discerned early on that, whatever his own inclinations towards Olivier, the actor did not seem an apt candidate for the real-life role of his lover. More to the point, Coward was professionally established, highly respected and genuinely concerned for Olivier's unformed talents. And so he provided a masculine affection and camaraderie hitherto denied the young actor. The relationship in fact seems to have been more enriching for Olivier than for Coward, for whom the situation was quietly poignant. In his memoirs, Olivier referred to a 'nearly passionate involvement with the one male with whom some sexual dalliance' was possible, and the man he left unnamed was Noël Coward. Whether or not Olivier was disingenuous in his insistence that he never wavered, and whether the relationship with Coward was in fact briefly carnal is impossible to ascertain; what is certain is the reality of a deep and constant affection that lasted over forty years.

The tour of *Private Lives* began in Edinburgh and proceeded to other cities before its London run; it was, as Coward noted, 'swathed in luxury', with first-class railway carriages and hotels provided by producer Charles B. Cochran. At dinner one evening, Olivier regressed to schoolboyish conduct, tossing bits of bread across the table at Coward, then advancing to leftovers from his plate. Coward gave as good as he got, and soon the two of them turned the fight into a Mack Sennett custard-pie comedy.

Private Lives opened at the Phoenix in London on 18 September and was an immediate success. It closed three months later while doing sell-out business, only because Coward refused to risk the boredom of a long run and had booked a New York engagement to follow. Of Olivier, Coward later wrote, 'Larry managed, with determination and much personal charm, to invest the wooden Victor with enough reality to make him plausible.' That was the most extensive review Olivier received, the critics dedicating their paragraphs to the play, Coward and Lawrence.

That autumn, Jill made a film of John Galsworthy's play *The Skin Game* (not one of Alfred Hitchcock's finer directorial achievements). At the same time, in addition to his evening performances, Olivier played a leading role in Maurice Elvey's film *Potiphar's Wife*, shot at the same studio, Elstree in Hertfordshire. The Oliviers' shooting schedules were so varied that they usually met only in passing, but since they had (as he wrote) 'precious little to make conversation about', their separate lives were not resented.

Appearing more than ever like a Ronald Colman stand-in, Olivier acted the role of chauffeur to a rich and unhappily married woman who, when he rejects her amorous advances, hauls him into court with allegations of assault (thus the film's biblical title). The irony of the story in contrast to his own forlorn status as a rejected husband may well have occurred to Olivier; in any case, he was simply too suave and too meticulously turned out to be credible as a man for whom the seductive Nora Swinburne would have meant danger rather than allure.

On 27 January 1931, *Private Lives* opened at the Times Square Theatre in New York – with Jill Esmond, at her own suggestion, replacing the pregnant Adrianne Allen in the role of Sybil. America was in the thick of economic crisis, but there were still theatre audiences for several long-running hits (*Strictly Dishonorable*, *The Green Pastures*, *Once in a Lifetime*, *Girl Crazy* and *Grand Hotel*); *Private Lives* was at once an even greater success than it had been in London. Onstage, the Oliviers were seasoned players; off, they were able to maintain a reasonably cordial friendship since their association with Noël Coward assured both welcome publicity and invitations to the best soirées in the city.

Also onstage, Olivier learned an important lesson. His tendency to break character by laughing at the most inappropriate moments had not been conquered, much to Coward's annoyance. 'If I did anything that was at all funny, Larry would be in fits of laughter instead of being cross, so I said, "From now on I'm going to try and make you laugh, and every time you do so, I'll kill you."' Coward's method, planned in advance with Gertrude Lawrence, was simple and effective. If Olivier laughed onstage one more time, Coward warned, he would be severely reprimanded backstage before the entire company. And next night Coward put him to the test: When Lawrence spluttered over her coffee in one scene, Olivier was to slap her hard on the back. Instead of continuing with her lines, however, she choked, turned round to him and said (ad-libbing), 'You great clob!' To which Coward added, 'The man with the clob foot.' Olivier had to restrain himself from giggling, and Coward had cured him at last.

With Coward's departure after three months in New York a new cast was rehearsed for *Private Lives*, and when they opened on 11 May, the playwright and his leading lady were preparing to return to London. The Oliviers, meanwhile, were packing for California.

Every Hollywood studio maintained East Coast offices in order to recruit from Broadway well-trained, articulate performers for the movies, and both their film experience and their attractiveness as a couple made it natural for talent scouts to approach the Oliviers in New York. Representatives of several studios invited them to submit to wardrobe and voice tests, Metro-Goldwyn-Mayer and Paramount among them. Reacting to one such test, a young Paramount executive named David O. Selznick cabled his superior that the verdict on the Oliviers was 'DIVIDED, WITH MAJORITY BELIEVING ESMOND MORE DESIRABLE FOR STOCK [roles] THAN OLIVIER . . . [who still has] EXCELLENT POSSIBILITY.'

RKO Pictures also offered to test them, and in a cramped Manhattan studio, dressed in white tie and tails, Olivier addressed the camera and recited his own speech, meant as a bouquet to the studio:

> Ladies and gentlemen, may a comparatively young English actor utter his very humble congratulations to those who have initiated this enterprise. Hollywood has set a very high standard of production, but I know perfectly well that the British brain and the British capital embodied in this and the other studios will make the British picture Hollywood's most successful rival.

His somewhat ineptly patriotic statement was certainly not a masterpiece of logic (nor even of tact), but the men at RKO noted a smooth, clipped English accent they might be able to use. Jill's screen test (which was eventually lost) was apparently more impressive, for one RKO executive recommended the studio sign her without her husband: 'He has no chance – he tries to look like Ronny Colman.' The resemblance to Colman was indeed striking (and quite intentional, since the time of *Beau Geste*), and in fact it persuaded the complainer's colleagues to take the opposite view. Hoping to market Laurence Olivier as their answer to Goldwyn's Ronald Colman, RKO finally offered contracts to him and to Jill.

Within days of the test, the Oliviers signed – for salaries of $700 per week with a forty-week guarantee, an extremely handsome income for 1931 (but not outrageous by Hollywood standards). 'I went for the money,' Olivier admitted, 'and the chance of fame.' He went with alacrity, as it happened. Leaving Jill to convalesce alone in New York after an emergency appendectomy, he departed for Los Angeles, where he rented a Tudor-style bungalow at 8856 Appian Way. Dramatically perched in the hills above Los Angeles, the house afforded a spectacular southerly view over Laurel Canyon towards the city.

When Olivier accepted the offer to come to Hollywood, he may not have known until arriving that the name actually designated only a small section of a sprawling city. H.H. Wilcox, a Kansas prohibitionist, had laid out a portion of Los Angeles as a real-estate subdivision known as Cahuenga Valley; he settled on a huge ranch there in 1887. The following year, his wife renamed it Hollywood, after a friend's home in Chicago. The name was extended to the entire village, incorporated in 1903. In 1910, needing the city's water supply and sewage system, Hollywood (with a population of about 5000) joined Los Angeles, but the name of the area endured.

From the end of the nineteenth century, most American movie-making was centred in New York and Chicago, but southern California's perpetually hospitable climate and the variety of topography (seashore, desert, rolling hills and snow-capped mountains all nearby) soon attracted film technicians and businessmen. In 1913, director Cecil B. De Mille, musical impresario Jesse L. Lasky and Lasky's brother-in-law, the glove salesman Samuel Goldfish (later Goldwyn) formed Jesse L. Lasky Feature Plays in New York. Three years later they merged with Adolph Zukor's Famous Players, and eventually Zukor headed the studio which derived its name from a small distribution company, Paramount.

Other companies also flourished. By 1931, Metro-Goldwyn-Mayer was in Culver City, south of Hollywood; Universal Studios had its own municipality (Universal City) near North Hollywood; the Fox Film Corporation was located on two corners of Sunset Boulevard and Western Avenue; and Columbia Pictures had facilities at Sunset and Gower Street, as well as a ranch in Burbank, just over the Santa Monica Mountains in the San Fernando Valley. Three brothers named Warner also had their studios in Burbank from 1929.

RKO, the studio to which Olivier reported, was formed after David Sarnoff, president of the Radio Corporation of America (RCA) had patented a sound system and needed a studio for its use. He found one – called the Film Booking Offices of America, owned by Joseph P. Kennedy, a Massachusetts entrepreneur. From the agreement between Sarnoff and Kennedy in 1928 was born RKO (its letters taken from RCA and from the Keith-Orpheum theatres they bought to show the pictures). Located at the corner of Gower Street and Melrose Avenue in Hollywood, the studio's biggest success (indeed, its only major hit) had been *Rio Rita* in 1929, a lavish musical western with Bebe Daniels and John Boles.

Laurence Olivier was joining many English actors who had come to the movie capital. After Ronald Colman and George Arliss, a veritable colony settled in southern California – among them, eventually, Cedric Hardwicke, Claude Rains, Herbert Marshall, Nigel Bruce, Charles Laughton, Ray Milland, Cary Grant, Basil Rathbone, C. Aubrey Smith, William Henry Pratt (soon to be known as Boris Karloff) and *Journey's End* director James Whale (who directed Karloff in *Frankenstein*).

Olivier's closest friend in Hollywood was the American actor Douglas Fairbanks, Jr., son of the silent-screen star and at the time husband to Joan Crawford. He recalled that Olivier was generally considered a good-looking but rather stiff young Englishman with a French name, who was not keen on films and much resented Jill's greater popularity. Fairbanks had the impression that Olivier would have liked to return to London almost immediately. Nevertheless, by June Olivier had been cast with Lily Damita, Adolphe Menjou and Erich von Stroheim in *Friends and Lovers*. Handsome though he was in the film (wearing British colonial military garb and Colmanesque moustache) Olivier was miscast opposite the sensuous Damita and the suave Menjou, and he seems quite insubstantial and immature before the camera. His arms and shoulders look wire-thin, perhaps because of his boyish saunter, and there is something epicene about him, with no indication that he could ever be more than a slick romantic foil. Neither compelling nor subtle (and ill served by a turgid script) Olivier is credible only when reciting Robert Browning: 'Oh, to be in England now that April's there!' *Friends and Lovers*, on release, registered a loss of $260,000 for the studio, with a budget only slightly higher.

During production, Jill arrived from New York, and on loan to Paramount she immediately appeared in a film called *Once a Lady*. Olivier, meanwhile, quickly finished his scenes for *Friends and Lovers*, and at night he and Fairbanks began to tour Hollywood's exotic lounges. One such night spot was the Russian Club, where they frequently joined the balalaika musicians in song, clinked many glasses of iced vodka and boozily swore to help restore Nicholas II as czar. There a vaudeville performer they had once seen at Grauman's Chinese Theatre offered them cocaine, and in a devil-may-care attitude they accepted – once only, according to Fairbanks.

Olivier's next assignment was to have been a melodrama with Pola Negri, but just when principal photography began that July of 1931, Olivier succumbed to a case of hepatitis and was replaced by Basil Rathbone.

Scarcely had Olivier overcome his jaundice and lethargy than RKO rushed him into his next picture, ironically titled *The Yellow Ticket*. The script by Jules Furthman and Guy Bolton derived rather heavily from *Tosca* but lacked that story's passion and colour, while nothing about Olivier was very impressive; director Raoul Walsh merely stressed his handsome profile and gleaming smile and asked the make-up department to apply great dabs of brilliantine. The picture's release that October did little credit to anyone connected with it. Jill, meanwhile, returned to RKO, playing secondary roles in four forgettable pictures while Selznick (hired away from Paramount to reverse RKO's sinking fortunes) continued to search for an appropriate starring vehicle for her.

The Olivier marriage was no more a reality than it had been in London. He was twenty-four years old, attractive and curious, and there was no lack of women who were the same; in fact he confided to friends like Fairbanks and Laurence Evans (who was also working in Hollywood at the time) about long nights with Lily Damita and later with Elissa Landi; there is every reason, in light of his honesty about the few extramarital romances he pursued, to accept his word.

'It was a wild, wild place in those days,' Olivier said of Hollywood at that time, 'and [the actor] Bob Montgomery, Doug Fairbanks and I were the wildest.' Once that summer, Fairbanks told Olivier that a beautiful and very rich woman had fallen in love with him. But the arrangement was a classic set-up, typical of their frequent practical jokes. Fairbanks knew no such woman, and instead he engaged a studio extra to meet Olivier for a drink. When the couple met, a genuinely fervent romance began. Fairbanks, continuing the prank, arranged for them to meet privately at his uncle's Hollywood apartment. When he knew the couple had settled in for the night, he signalled to a burly stuntman he had brought along, who burst in on the couple, shouting, 'What are you doing with my wife?' Olivier, according to Fairbanks, promptly keeled over in a cold faint.

Olivier's genial attitude encouraged such antics. Early in the production of his next film, he accepted an invitation to join Fairbanks and Montgomery, who had chartered a yacht, for a weekend of fishing near Mazatlán, Mexico. But more mischief was planned. When he arrived by single-engine plane, Olivier was greeted by unsmiling soldiers who without asking for his identification papers hustled him off to the local jail; they apparently expected a bribe. After several hours of anxiety, Olivier was released when Fairbanks turned up and explained that he had arranged the caper with the jolly assistance of a cooperative mayor. But Olivier explained the good reason for his panic: he carried no visa or passport.

Back in Hollywood, Olivier joined Ann Harding in Selznick's production of *Westward Passage*, an appealing film that owes much to Harding's warm onscreen personality. She also provided Olivier with a brief lesson in untemperamental, generous film-making collaboration, insisting that his role be expanded and often arguing that close-ups favour him. Her performance was artless, and Olivier's too became natural and unselfconscious. For the first time, something of his personality was evoked by the camera. As they dance to the music of 'Wonderful One', his devotion is entirely credible, and when he recites loving lines from Milton's *Paradise Lost* there is in his film acting an adult confidence for the first time. In *Westward Passage*, a new aspect of Laurence Olivier emerged, a screen actor with a flair for both cruelty and comedy.

But unfortunately Selznick had no plans for Olivier after the film was completed in autumn 1931, and according to Helen Hayes (who was also in Hollywood that year), 'Larry was left to gather dust on the shelf, and he was very unhappy.' He felt, as Douglas Fairbanks, Jr., added, the frustrated eagerness of a talented person waiting impatiently for his time to come.

His restiveness was justified, for not since his two performances in *Journey's End* three years before had he assumed a role bringing either challenge or celebrity. The septet of stage roles which had followed that had been long forgotten by everyone, and although his appearance in *Private Lives* widened his social circle and gave him the valuable association with Coward, it had failed to advance his career. And this year in America, so full of glamorous promise, had availed him nothing but a few fleeting romances with leading ladies, diversions from which he never derived the psychological sustenance acting provided.

Olivier's professional zeal could only have been intensified when he went to the Biltmore Theatre in downtown Los Angeles on 23 December to see *King Lear* performed by the visiting Stratford Festival Company. After the performance, he went backstage to meet the leading player, Randle Ayrton. 'Listening to the compliments flying,' he wrote later, 'I came to a decision . . . I was determined to be the greatest actor of all time.' For the next forty years, every personal and professional decision supported that vow, every element of his life was subordinate to that commitment.

Indeed, he took swift action that winter. Since the Great Depression and a lack of box-office hits had pitched RKO into serious trouble, Selznick had decided to cut the salaries of all players; if they accepted an offer of contract renewal, they would receive little more than for their first year. Olivier had no intention of remaining a minor player, and so he told Jill – who was being considered for the lead in the film *A Bill of Divorcement* – that they must return to London at once: only the theatre, only great roles such as Ayrton had played, could establish him as the greatest actor of all time.

Years later, Olivier insisted that he convinced Jill that her career, too, would never progress at RKO. He had seen a contract in Selznick's office, he said, and according to its terms the New York stage actress Katharine Hepburn had just been contracted to RKO. This, he said, spelled the end of Jill's chance to be the studio's new leading lady, for surely Hepburn and not Jill would star in *A Bill of Divorcement*, regardless of Selznick's stated indecision. But Olivier's account cannot be true, as he could not have seen such a document in Selznick's office at the end of 1931. Katharine Hepburn's contract was not finally negotiated until just before she began filming *A Bill of Divorcement* in July 1932. Olivier's insistence that Jill return with him to London seems to have been based on jealousy – and perhaps also on other factors.

First, he did not want a separation from Jill – that would be disastrous for an already tentative and problematic marriage neither of them was as yet prepared to abandon. The role of husband was an important one for the still insecure Laurence Olivier, and he may have felt compelled to make this marriage work, to feel that he could eventually be an effective and attractive spouse and perhaps even the father of her children. In addition, her success might be of more use to them both in London, where she had a solid reputation in theatrical circles. Finally, he had received an offer from the American actress Gloria Swanson, who had just married an Englishman and wanted Olivier as her leading man in a film to be made in London. And so Jill, whose personal life was no happier than his and who felt no great affinity for Hollywood, agreed to depart with her husband.

By early February they were in London, after a voyage with Douglas Fairbanks, Jr., and his wife Joan Crawford. Fairbanks recalled that Jill kept very much to herself, and it was clear that the Olivier marriage was in difficulty. In London, the tensions were somewhat defused by work, as Olivier was rushed into a busy schedule for the Swanson production, a pallid and somewhat unsavoury domestic comedy called *Perfect Understanding*, which turned out to be a disastrous commercial failure. The role was perhaps too close to his own life, for he played a man whose wife suggests they have a perfect understanding about their freedom to pursue intimacies outside their marriage.

Olivier had brought back from Hollywood an image of sleek glamour. Anthony Quayle, eighteen and making his stage debut, remembered seeing him on a Chelsea street corner, nattily dressed, with two schnauzers on leads. Attractive he certainly was, and elegantly attired; but the talent, because it had had so little opportunity, was still mostly raw, unrecognised and untapped, and the success was entirely in the image. He had no offers for work except another dreary filmscript, scheduled for production later that year. Many of Olivier's colleagues, however, were thriving. The major West End hit that spring was Coward's latest, *Cavalcade*, and still another (*Words and Music*) would soon open – but Coward had no role for him. Russell and Eileen Thorndike (Sybil's brother and sister) greeted Olivier backstage several times after their Shakespeare performances that spring: they appeared as the Macbeths, then in *The Merchant of Venice, The Taming of the Shrew, Romeo and Juliet, Twelfth Night* and *Hamlet* – all in repertory, within a single week. The new Memorial Theatre in Stratford opened in April, and Olivier attended at least two performances there in June, while in London Peggy Ashcroft and Ralph Richardson were in plays by Shaw. The aspiring 'greatest actor' seemed stymied.

Because of his own idleness, such theatre-going could not have brought him unalloyed pleasure, for producers and managers considered twenty-five-year-old Laurence Olivier a pleasant supporting player, one among hundreds of young English actors with nothing exceptional in his credits. From the London stage – where nine of his last ten appearances had been in failures – he had been absent for a year and a half; out of sight, he had drifted out of the public's collective mind.

The savings from their RKO salaries enabled the Oliviers to buy a house in Chelsea, but serious refurbishing and redecorating were required, and for a year (from March 1932) they rented a furnished flat at 13 Roland Gardens, South Kensington. Meanwhile, he and Jill accepted roles in a film comedy called *No Funny Business*, which, alas, was just that. In this mesmerically tedious movie they were cast as professional co-respondents engaged to entrap an adulterous couple; predictably, they fall in love with one another. But however cordially they worked together at the studio, there was still no romance between the Oliviers offscreen. Nevertheless, grounds for divorce were strictly limited in 1932, and because they did not want to submit to the usual indignities of a case for adultery (hired co-respondents, ugly fabrications and the kinds of entrapment detailed in *No Funny Business*), the Oliviers remained together. But there was no happiness at all, recalled Laurence Evans, who had returned to London about the same time. Olivier seems to have quietly resigned himself to their arrangement, while Jill became rather bossy, and was soon known among his friends as 'The Colonel'.

When the offer to appear in a new play came in the spring of 1933, more than two years had passed since Laurence Olivier had acted onstage in London. The actress Gladys Cooper, who had seen him in *Journey's End* and *Private Lives*, suggested Olivier for the young schoolmaster Stevan Beringer in *The Rats of Norway*, Keith Winter's morbidly Gothic melodrama set in a Northumberland school. This venture added nothing to Olivier's reputation, nor to his expectations of a leading role, and during the first half of 1933 he was often quite severely depressed. The day after his twenty-sixth birthday, he was invited to judge a performance at the Central School of Speech and Drama, and there a colleague remembered him as behaving uncharacteristically badly, speaking with brisk contempt about the standard of students' make-up.

Olivier was also not much elated at the prospect of leaving London for New York later that year, but Noël Coward had convinced him and Jill to accept an offer from the American producer-director Jed Harris. Visiting London that season seeking West End plays for transferral to Broadway, Harris had selected Mordaunt Shairp's successful and controversial drama *The Green Bay Tree*. The play was no more cheerful than *The Rats of Norway*, but at least each of the Oliviers would receive over a thousand dollars a week, and for leading roles; with their heavy expenses, and at the height of the worldwide Depression, it was an opportunity they had to accept.

In June, they finally moved into their new home, 74 Cheyne Walk, on the Thames Embankment near Chelsea Old Church. Consisting of eight rooms on three floors, the house featured thirty-foot-high ceilings and a minstrels' gallery in the main reception room. They added white silk curtains, a vast fireplace, a grand piano, overstuffed furniture, tapestries and a ring-tailed lemur in a gilt cage. At once they began to entertain, often opulently. 'He has such illusions of grandeur,' said a bemused Noël Coward about Olivier that year, disappointed that his friend was resorting to affectation as a substitute for achievement.

CHAPTER FIVE

1933–1935

He jests at scars that never felt a wound.

Romeo, in *Romeo and Juliet*

Soon after the premiere of *The Rats of Norway*, Olivier received a telegram from Frank Joyce, his Hollywood agent: Metro-Goldwyn-Mayer were offering ten months of film work at a thousand dollars a week. At first he declined, since he was committed to *Rats* and to *The Green Bay Tree* on Broadway the following autumn. But the overtures from MGM continued, one enticement following another. His initial assignment would be *Queen Christina* with Greta Garbo, who had the right to select her leading man; impressed by his performance in *Westward Passage*, she had requested Olivier. Rouben Mamoulian, who was to direct, had already urged caution: the final choice of Olivier, he told Garbo and MGM, would have to depend on whether or not, once in costume and make-up, he could hold his ground in experience and authority opposite Garbo. As negotiations continued through May and June, the studio agreed to Olivier's salary demand of fifteen hundred dollars a week for a minimum of four weeks on the Garbo film alone; he was also assured that he would be in New York at the appointed time for rehearsals for *The Green Bay Tree* with Jed Harris.

On 7 July 1933, the press announced that an agreement had been signed between MGM and Laurence Olivier. The following week he arranged to leave *The Rats of Norway*, and on 23 July he and Jill arrived in Los Angeles. They rented a bungalow at the fantastic Garden of Allah hotel (a notorious Hollywood rendezvous) and settled in for a three-month stay.

But their plans soon changed. On 1 August Olivier arrived at the MGM studios in Culver City, where he met the shy, withdrawn Garbo.

Attempting pleasant conversation, he found the atmosphere awkward, and she barely replied to anything he said. Mamoulian called for the first shots and Garbo ended Olivier's monologue by muttering, 'Oh, well, life's a pain, anyway' – and with this typically enigmatic proclamation she preceded him onto the set. Her coolness was unwarmed by the scene they played, in which Olivier (as the Spanish ambassador Don Antonio) had to embrace Garbo with such passion that Queen Christina would completely alter her destiny for him. They rehearsed several times, but Garbo never reacted to her co-star, and despite repeated takes, the scene remained lifeless. Greta Garbo, it seems, was as dispassionate and unmoved by Olivier's advances as Jill Esmond. That morning in Culver City did nothing to enhance his self-esteem either as an actor or as a man confident of his sex appeal.

Within days, Olivier was summoned to the producer's office, where he was told that both star and director found him unacceptable. 'Although he had qualities that suited the part,' Mamoulian commented, 'he didn't have enough maturity, skill and acting weight to balance Garbo's. In short, he was too young and inexperienced for Don Antonio.' (The role, at Garbo's insistence, was given to her friend and former co-star, John Gilbert.) Years later, Olivier claimed that he 'wasn't really surprised . . . I simply wasn't up to [Garbo].'

But he was not so phlegmatic that summer of 1933, and two days after his dismissal he and Jill cancelled their lease at the Garden of Allah. Because they were not expected in New York until early October but still had Olivier's guaranteed four-week salary, they booked passage for a holiday in Honolulu. Soon after their arrival, Olivier broke a toe while riding the waves on a surfboard and most of their time was spent in quiet indolence. They did, however, learn their lines for *The Green Bay Tree*, and by the end of September they were in New York awaiting Jed Harris's call for rehearsals. There, the theatre was prospering despite the country's economic tribulations during the worst year of the Great Depression. (Among the many successful productions of the 1933–34 season were Sidney Kingsley's *Men in White*, Eugene O'Neill's *Ah, Wilderness!*, Jerome Kern's *Roberta* and dramatisations of Erskine Caldwell's *Tobacco Road* and Sinclair Lewis's *Dodsworth*.)

Since leaving the Birmingham Repertory in 1928, Laurence Olivier had not achieved his goal of becoming a leading man of the theatre, much less the world's greatest actor. He had earned occasional praise for minor or supporting roles (in *The Adding Machine*, *Private Lives* and

The Rats of Norway), but he had also appeared in over half a dozen failures or limited-run showcases. He had come to depend on a studied resemblance to Ronald Colman for his juvenile appeal, and although there were thousands of talented young actors, only a handful of successful British playwrights were providing material (Coward was the most prolific and popular). This partly explains London's reliance on the classics, in which Olivier obviously lacked solid experience. Denied both a stable career and a happy marriage, he was an impatient young man without any clear professional or personal prospects beyond the next gloomy play. And in social life he depended on his attractive appearance and a casual, blithe charm – qualities which made him an agreeable companion but could be found elsewhere in profusion.

As for Jill, despite her family background and a blare of Hollywood ballyhoo, she was now mired in a series of indifferent secondary roles and was unsure whether she should seek a new career. This quandary was made more poignant by her long struggle to accept her lesbianism, which was at last painfully clear to Olivier by 1933. In California and in New York, she fulfilled her promise to have 'secrets and friends unknown to a husband of mine', and she led a quite independent life among a coterie of lesbian producers, agents, writers and actresses – a discreet but large and influential group that included actress Alla Nazimova, writer Mercedes de Acosta, producer Cheryl Crawford, and impresarios Natasha Rambova and Elisabeth Marbury.

By an odd coincidence, Olivier and Jill had to confront the issue of homosexuality in their new play. In *The Green Bay Tree* he was to play a young man whose yearnings for maturity and freedom are destroyed by his own selfishness and an unhealthy, mutually exploitative attachment to an older male lover. Jill had the part of a woman who temporarily wins his affections, only to lose him when he returns to a sybaritic life.

The play was an unpleasant experience from the first day of rehearsal, for they found that Jed Harris was not the polite and amusing gentleman they had met in London. That had been the convenient and effective negotiating persona for which Harris was notorious: he was in reality a man much disliked for his bombast, sarcasm and generally dyspeptic behaviour.

Overbearing and snide at rehearsals, with a sarcastic smile usually forming as he prepared a vicious attack on an actor's scene-reading, Harris made the three weeks of preparation a nightmare for his cast. He had, it was known, a whipping-boy in every cast, and for *The Green*

Bay Tree his choice fell on Olivier, whom he derided in the middle of a speech, mocked for his hairstyle and ridiculed for his accent. To this treatment the victim responded with admirable patience and calm, refusing to give Harris the satisfaction of seeing him distraught. But Olivier never forgot this cruelty, and later he based his stage and screen portrait of Shakespeare's Richard III on Jed Harris. Jill, too, was subjected to his frequent outbursts, and several times Olivier spoke out in anger against Harris's abuse of her. For several weeks that autumn the couple was united by a mutual antipathy towards their director.

Shrill and divisive though he was, Harris was an effective interpreter of the warped, menacing atmosphere of Shairp's play, and despite his misery with the whole enterprise, Olivier received only favourable notices after the opening on 20 October at the Cort Theatre. Typical were the observations that his acting was 'not acting, but an exhibition of emotional collapse . . . an extraordinarily searching and progressive study of a nimble-minded weakling, [a performance with] design and movement and tragic emotion'. By all accounts, he rose above the conditions of rehearsal and his own distaste for the role; indeed, he seems to have summoned enormous reservoirs of energy, and the result was a performance that displayed a new level of talent. The play ran almost six months and won Olivier considerable fame and a loyal following among New York producers and playgoers.

Jill, too, was praised in *The Green Bay Tree*, but she had increasingly withdrawn from the theatrical social life they were expected, at least occasionally, to participate in. From the time of the transatlantic crossing with Fairbanks, her aloofness had been noted, but by now the genial public manner she had been able to adopt when necessary had all but vanished. Alexander Clark was back in New York that season, and he invited the Oliviers to his parents' home in Pound Ridge, Westchester County. The atmosphere was thick with tension, and Clark noted Jill's coldness, distance and apparent unhappiness; he had the impression she simply wished to be elsewhere.

By coincidence, Noël Coward was in New York at the time. After encouraging the Oliviers' appearance together in *Private Lives*, urging their subsequent journey to Hollywood and their joint performances whenever possible, he added that they might ultimately become a kind of British version of the Lunts: Lynne Fontanne and Alfred Lunt were the premier American acting couple, playing Coward's *Design for Living* that same year. Such advice from his mentor was an incentive for Olivier to stay with Jill. (Coward may have had another parallel in mind, for the Lunts' marriage was also platonic, each of them being homosexual.) Clark, who had recently acted in the eight-month run of S.N. Behrman's play *Biography*, then told Olivier that Coward was going to direct the forthcoming London production. (Olivier, during rehearsals for *The Green Bay Tree*, had seen *Biography*.) Within days of the visit to Pound Ridge, Coward and Olivier were reunited. The prospect of working with Coward and of playing comedy in London was attraction enough, and Olivier accepted his offer of a supporting role.

The Green Bay Tree closed on 10 March 1934, and at once the Oliviers returned to London after an eight-month absence. The house in Cheyne Walk had not been long inhabited when they had departed for Hollywood the previous July, and they enjoyed the privacy afforded them both by separate bedroom suites. Just as Olivier began rehearsals for *Biography*, Jill was cast in the London production of another American play (Kingsley's *Men in White*), and they resumed distant professional and social lives.

In *Biography*, Olivier played a fanatically idealistic magazine editor whose ideals obstruct his ability to conduct ordinary human relationships. His performance could not bring much nuance to so contemptuous a character, and Olivier read the closing notice with some relief: *Biography* put its cast on half-pay at the end of the first week (1 May) and closed soon after. (Jill's play kept her employed for four months, until mid-autumn.)

But there was a new role for him immediately. During rehearsals for Gordon Daviot's *Queen of Scots*, it became clear to everyone that Ralph Richardson was miscast as Bothwell, the brawling, passionately romantic schemer who becomes the queen's third husband after plotting the murder of Lord Darnley. A replacement was suggested by the leading actress and the director: Gwen Ffrangçon-Davies, who had known Olivier since Birmingham Rep days; and John Gielgud, who had seen him onstage several times since *Journey's End*. Gielgud was a celebrated actor and a perceptive director, and like Coward he recognised a talent that promised more than Olivier had as yet delivered. Bothwell was the perfect supporting role for a handsome apprentice, and Gielgud had no difficulty contracting him for it. With only a week of preparation before the 8 June premiere, Olivier memorised the role, rehearsed fourteen hours daily with Gielgud and the cast and assumed the part of 'the greatest brawler in Scotland – red-haired, well-built, [with] vitality radiating from him' (thus the text).

In doublet and high boots and sporting a red goatee, Olivier sprang into the role of the philandering earl who, even while he kisses Mary Stuart, admits that, to him, all women's lips are the same. This was a portrait created *con brio*, impressive to both colleagues and audiences, but it was presented at a time before air-conditioned auditoriums, and the torrid weather forced an early cancellation that August. The costumes were brutally heavy, as Ffrangçon-Davies said years later, and in addition the attendance fell sharply as people avoided the steaming theatres.

Notwithstanding the summer heat, Olivier was vitalised, and backstage he was a genial host, pouring drinks for the cast every night after the performance and taking a late supper and more drinks with one or another player. The actress Constance Cummings (whose husband Benn Levy had co-authored *The Temporary Widow*) remembered that Olivier was very gregarious at that time, that he loved drinking and carousing with his colleagues. With his marriage virtually dead, as Gwen Ffrangçon-Davies added, he really counted more than ever on his friends.

Olivier evoked various effects in his next role. Brian Aherne, who was contracted for a play to be directed by Noël Coward, was detained filming in America. Coward asked Olivier to substitute for Aherne during the pre-London tour only, and although Olivier was reluctant to be a provincial stand-in, he felt he could not disappoint Coward. He accepted the hundred pounds a week salary and assumed the supporting part of Anthony Cavendish in *Theatre Royal*, George S. Kaufman and Edna Ferber's satire on the Barrymores (called *The Royal Family* on Broadway).

Based on John Barrymore, the part gave Olivier the opportunity for a comic exaggeration of everything he knew about that actor and everything he relished in a role: elegance, athleticism, romantic dash, high comedy, satiric braggadocio. After the gloom of *The Rats of Norway* and *The Green Bay Tree*, after the fatuous dialogue of *Biography* and the period drama of *Queen of Scots*, this was a comic part he did not want to abdicate. Accordingly, he brought such panache to it and was so loudly approved by audiences and the rest of the cast that word of his success reached Aherne. Disinclined to follow so splendid a performance and simultaneously offered work in New York, Aherne cabled his withdrawal, thereby promoting Olivier's career a second time. The play opened in London on 23 October 1934 and ran nearly six months.

Swathed in fur coats and cashmere scarves, wearing a snap-brim hat and tweeds, applying greasepaint and powder that emphasised his strong chin and expressive eyes, Olivier seemed taller than his five feet ten inches, more imposing than a man with his slim (thirty-inch) waist and lanky frame. Cavendish is the same man at home as onstage: at any moment he can leap into a swordfight with a tray-bearing servant, vault a staircase to greet a guest, or swoop towards his mother like Hamlet confronting Gertrude.

Olivier's portrayal was certainly based on his own familiarity with John Barrymore's sweeping performances, but he also tempered the character's frantic bohemianism with a glamorous sexual allure. He flirted with the actors onstage, he often played shamelessly to the audience and he used every hoary mannerism of the dandy to create a caricature of a self-absorbed theatrical stylist. No physical challenge was beyond him as he bounded over balconies, dashed round landings and slid down banisters. The role was an incandescent showcase for a showoff, and he despatched it with blazing élan, relishing the chance to surprise and shock his audience. Critics and playgoers again adored his performance.

Constance Cummings recalled Olivier saying that he would gladly break a leg to get a laugh. As it happened, during one performance in December he made a bounding second-act entrance. 'Hello, folks – farewell appearance!' he cried in character, darting onto the set's upper balcony. Then, as usual, he headed for the staircase, but that night his spirits were somewhat too high. Olivier attempted a leap over the balcony towards mid-staircase but misjudged his mark and seconds later was carried offstage, wincing in pain with a fractured ankle – the first in a lifelong series of injuries sustained during work.

Not long before the mishap, Olivier had been contacted by producer Gilbert Miller who offered him, in light of his success as Anthony Cavendish, the highest salary of his stage career (almost two hundred pounds a week). In early 1935, Olivier met with playwright Keith Winter and director Raymond Massey (who had the identical credits on *The Rats of Norway*) and signed to appear in *Ringmaster*. As a further inducement and to help with publicity, the role of the character's wife was offered to Jill. Anticipating great success in a thoroughly different role, Olivier abandoned the antic comedy of *Theatre Royal* (to which he had returned, mended) and took on the bitterness of *Ringmaster*.

The role of Peter Hammond seemed to augur well. A former matinee idol disabled in a traffic accident and thenceforth attended by a long-suffering wife, he operates a guest-house on the Devon coast. Apparently charming but actually manipulative and spiteful, Peter becomes the ringmaster of his guests' lives, prying open their affairs, using their weaknesses to bolster his own and finally causing such strife among those who have trusted him that he is abandoned by everyone.

Olivier's speeches had moments of consummate charm that lightly veiled a complex malevolence – just the kind of emotional network to keep an audience alert and astonished. But like *The Rats of Norway*, the prevalent tone of *Ringmaster* was politely sordid in its oak-beamed, chintz-covered country-house way, and the dialogue was full of foreboding for the implosion of family resentments, of love denied or paid for but never earned. Winter's dramatic writing was, as before, competent; it was also cheerless and formidably static. Olivier lacked the literary sophistication to see that *Ringmaster* was simply a bad play. He needed to work, and the plain truth is that *Ringmaster* was comparable in quality to most new English plays that year. He must have sensed an opportunity for a new sort of bravura – not as a leaping athlete but as a chair-bound antagonist subjugating others, alternately snapping commands and counselling gently until at last, in an emotional outburst, he collapses to the floor in a howl of pain. It was another showcase piece, and he filled the stage with nervous energy, his immobile Peter Hammond as dynamic as his whirling Anthony Cavendish.

But the satisfaction endured only a week, after which the play closed on 18 March 1935 for lack of good reviews and a healthy box-office. This marked his first leading role; because he had left *Theatre Royal* for it, he may have remembered the unwise decision of six years earlier, when he departed *Journey's End* for *Beau Geste*. His disappointment was heightened by the fact that he had paid for the performing rights to *Ringmaster* and was therefore legally a partner with Gilbert Miller. He had, therefore, lost money as well as prestige.

Nevertheless, two more projects occupied Olivier in rapid succession during that busy year of 1935.

First, he accepted an offer from Alexander Korda to appear in a motion picture Korda was producing under the banner of his production company, London Films. In doing so, Olivier took a small role in a minor picture but simultaneously began an important association with one of the major figures in British entertainment. Korda had made films in his native Hungary and in Austria, Germany, Hollywood and France before settling in England, where with his brothers Vincent (an artist and designer) and Zoltàn (a director), he produced enormously successful and stylish pictures.

Conquest of the Air, however, was not among his more memorable products. Planned as a feature about the history of aviation, it was begun, abandoned and resumed over a period of seven years, and the final product (released in 1940) revealed its patchy development. There were sequences about da Vinci and about the Wright brothers, and Olivier appeared briefly as Vincent Lunardi, the first aerial traveller in England, who in 1784 sailed bravely over London in a balloon. For his few scenes, he had only to stand and smile confidently in a studio-prop balloon. But Korda saw Olivier's potential as a screen actor with charm and presence, and he promised him a leading role for later that year.

His work on *Conquest of the Air*, at Korda's Denham studio, required only a few days in early April. Immediately after, Olivier undertook a more ambitious project as he accepted an invitation to co-produce with Maurice Browne a new play called *Golden Arrow*, by Sylvia Thompson and Victor Cunard. (Browne had made a fortune when he assumed production rights for *Journey's End*.)

In *Golden Arrow*, Olivier would have the leading role of a rising young English politician who refuses to take his American mistress on a Continental business trip (aboard the train called the Golden Arrow). She decides instead to travel with a handsome Frenchman, but before virtue is further compromised she is reunited with the Englishman and marries him. The play was little ado about nothing; its shallowness was not apparent to Olivier – or he chose to ignore it, for the offer from Browne was significant. Producing a play in London meant directing it, and the great ambition of his generation, as he said later, was to assume the responsibility of being one's own boss.

Producing-directing was a new and important function in the English theatre since the World War. Earlier, actors were expected to know the traditional moves and gestures of a role, and advice or 'direction' was rarely given – it was in fact considered unnecessary and insulting to a professional. But the great modern actor-managers (Gerald du Maurier, Charles Hawtrey, Nigel Playfair, Ben Greet and Seymour Hicks, among others) had begun to alter that tradition. They presented a play by raising funds, leasing a theatre, gathering fellow actors, assuming general responsibility – and also giving directions to the cast.

By 1935 the influence of the actor-manager had greatly declined, and directors (who were called producers) emerged. They were needed, first of all, because theatrical entrepreneurs were now mostly financiers or businessmen and also because the technical aspects of production (lighting and electronics, for example) had become more complicated. In addition, new kinds of plays in the postwar era demanded new thinking: psychological motivations for action and gesture were less obvious, and dialogue was often oblique and subtle, contrapuntal to action and at times requiring explanation and guidance for the actors. David Belasco was already an established director in New York, and in Europe there were Max Reinhardt, Konstantin Stanislavsky and Jacques Copeau.

Olivier assembled his cast, and after a first reading of *Golden Arrow* he announced a revolutionary way of rehearsing. Instead of building a play slowly over weeks with painstaking attention to the details of inflection and gesture in each scene (a method that had often left him angry and bored), he got his players through the entire text in five days. This, he insisted, gave actors a sense of their parts and of the play as a whole; then they continued to rehearse scene by scene, altering and adding necessary emphases of word and gesture.

But these first rehearsals quickly revealed to Browne that *Golden Arrow* would not be the success they had hoped. He withdrew, and Olivier – either heedless of Browne's warning or convinced he could give the play a quality of wit it sorely lacked – assumed complete responsibility. As well as directing and starring in it, he now saw 'Laurence Olivier Presents' on the marquee and in advertisements. He was the star, the producer and the manager.

Despite the flawed script, Olivier took his multiple responsibilities with utter seriousness, and this brought forth previously hidden abilities. No longer concerned only with his own role but with its coherence within the entire play, his imagination soared. He encouraged variant readings and stresses in a character's line, he learned the dramatic function of silence, he saw the modulation of a spotlight shift the mood, and from a place in the auditorium he observed several pacings for scenes. Avid to attempt anything to enliven the play and encourage the players, Olivier also had a relaxed manner with his cast. He would never be like Jed Harris; his style would be more like Noël Coward's – gentle, ironic, amusing, supportive, provocative, always polite.

For his leading lady Olivier had selected a pert, twenty-six-year-old Irish redhead named Greer Garson. Rather than mimic the action for the cast, as she recalled years later, he encouraged them to stretch their imaginations, 'to try out little things on our own. There were always little exercises he invented, adventures of the imagination, to keep the material fresh.' There was also some adventure offstage, for during *Golden Arrow* the star-director and his leading lady were briefly lovers. But the entanglement ended with the play's run: after a mid-May tryout at the New Theatre, Oxford, the play opened at the Whitehall in London and closed, after two weeks, on 15 June. (Only Garson received favourable notices – for her 'lively impudence . . . vitality and charm' – and very soon film producer Samuel Goldwyn brought her to Hollywood.)

Two nights after the last performance, the playwright and actor Emlyn Williams invited Olivier to a performance of his play *Night Must Fall*. Afterwards at a pub, Olivier downed several whiskies and muttered disconsolately to Williams, 'I'm washed up – I'll never make it! Hollywood just didn't want to know me, Garbo turned me down for *Queen Christina*, *Ringmaster* was a flop . . .' Williams thought Olivier looked 'as lost as an abandoned orphan who has stumbled into a deep puddle . . . We tried to cheer him up, to no avail.' After twenty-one professional (post-Birmingham) stage appearances in London and nine films, Laurence Olivier saw no substantial advancement in his career.

Nor was he comforted by praise offered to him earlier that same evening. In the audience at the Duchess Theatre was a slender, dark-haired beauty with skin like porcelain, sensuous eyes, a bright smile, an infectious laugh and a sharp intelligence. Forthright, literate, impeccably mannered and attired, she had (the same week of Olivier's disaster with *Golden Arrow*) made the proverbial leap to stardom in a comedy called *The Mask of Virtue*. She approached him during the interval of *Night Must Fall* to express her admiration for his work in *Theatre Royal*, which she had seen three times, and *Ringmaster* which, remarkably, she had seen twice. Her name was Vivien Leigh.

Born on 5 November 1913 in Darjeeling, India, Vivian Mary Hartley was the offspring of an unlikely and eventually unhappy marriage between a stern Catholic mother (Gertrude Yackjee) and a philandering, stockbroker father (Ernest Hartley). At the age of six she was deposited by her mother at the Convent of the Sacred Heart in Roehampton, and this sudden withdrawal of parental presence and attention – perceived by the child as a virtual abandonment – affected her deeply and sowed the basis for much of her later character and conduct. Vivian demonstrated a keen desire to please strangers and acquaintances, as if she could compensate for the absence of her parents by earning or buying the affection of both classmates and teachers. She remembered every schoolmate's birthday, worked ceaselessly to endear herself to the nuns and excelled in every class. Not surprisingly, she showed a flair for recitations and dramatic readings: nothing was so gratifying as holding the attention of the teachers and the other students.

In adolescence, Vivian continued her education at several European schools and blossomed into a polished, much admired seventeen-year-old who spoke superb French and German and had taken leading roles in several school plays. In early 1932, at eighteen, she began studying at the Royal Academy of Dramatic Art, but before the end of the year she left school to marry a wealthy lawyer named Leigh Holman, who was twelve years her senior. Serious, respectable and indulgent of her, Holman offered Vivian many of a father's qualities.

In October 1933, their daughter Suzanne was born, but Vivian never showed anything like a strong maternal devotion; denied sustained parental affection herself, she had no idea how to give it. Instead, bored with domesticity and the mundane requirements of motherhood, she signed with a theatrical agent, played in several films, changed her name to the more feminine Vivien and, as if to seal her own childlike identity with the paternal role of her husband in her life, took his name as her professional surname and was henceforth known as Vivien Leigh.

Although she was no longer in love with Holman, she regarded him for the rest of her life as friend and protector. By early 1935, Vivien had begun an affair with a handsome but emotionally unstable young actor named John Buckmaster (son of Gladys Cooper). When she met Olivier, her agent was negotiating with Alexander Korda, who had offered her a long-term film contract.

An important part of the theatrical social scene centred round late supper at the Savoy Grill. The night Vivien opened in *The Mask of Virtue*, Laurence Evans was dining there as she entered with the play's director, Sydney Carroll. Evans recalled that everyone in the room stood and cheered this previously unknown actress who had just made such an impact on first night. But the public's enthusiasm owed more to her appearance than to her talent. 'Though she had taken the critics and public by storm,' according to John Gielgud, 'she knew that her youth and beauty were the chief factors of her immediate success, and she was modest and shrewd enough to face the challenge of developing herself.'

*

75

If her words to Olivier during the interval of *Night Must Fall* did not have the buoyant effect she hoped, at least her presence did. He thought her charming and cheerful, and within a week he had gone to see her in *The Mask of Virtue*. He recalled her as having 'beautiful poise [and] an attraction of the most perturbing nature I had ever encountered'.

In late June, Korda fulfilled his promise and summoned Olivier for three weeks' work as the leading man in the film *Moscow Nights*. His part was that of a Russian captain, wounded during the World War, who is convicted of treason but finally acquitted and wins the hand of a beautiful nurse who had cared for him. Twenty-eight and in his first major film role in over two years, Olivier had visibly matured, and his performance remains a model of comic inventiveness counterpoised with tragic desperation. In the scenes with Penelope Dudley Ward (as the nurse) he exploits a winning smile, tempers his voice for every emotional effect, and – despite a weak script and excessive lip rouge – appears every inch the strong, confident suitor. Later, in the trial sequence, he affects a dry-mouthed anxiety that communicates more than the verbose screenplay. There is nothing mannered about his performance, and Korda felt his initial confidence in Olivier's screen presence was vindicated. But no subsequent film role came available for him. By midsummer 1935, Jill was rehearsing her role in a play called *The Black Eye* when Olivier received a telephone call from John Gielgud.

Then thirty-one, Gielgud (the grand-nephew of Ellen Terry) was London's pre-eminent Shakespearean actor and director, having earned enormous critical and popular acclaim as Romeo, Richard II, Macbeth and Hamlet. Successful in roles requiring both outer strength and interior reflection, he was admired for an aristocratic poise and a mellifluous voice that made any speech poetic, and his range as performer and producer-director extended to the widest variety of plays classical and modern.

That year, Gielgud realised that he would soon be too old to repeat his portrayal of Romeo, and that gave him an idea. Since the nineteenth century, it was not extraordinary for actors to alternate important roles in the same production – Samuel Phelps and William Macready (and later Henry Irving and Edwin Booth) had alternated Othello and Iago – and it was Gielgud's intention to do the same with Romeo and Mercutio that autumn.

> When I suggested to [theatre manager] Bronson Albery that he should do *Romeo and Juliet* for me in 1935, I first approached Robert Donat to alternate with me as Romeo and Mercutio, but he turned

down the offer. I had seen Larry quite often on the stage [and directed
him in *Queen of Scots*]. When I asked him to be in my production
he demurred, as he said he was hoping to mount the play for himself
and Jill Esmond. But finding I was already determined to have Edith
Evans as the Nurse and Peggy Ashcroft as Juliet [who had played
these roles with Gielgud in 1932], he immediately agreed to join us.

It would have been very difficult for Olivier to have staged the play,
with or without Jill. Since his school performances, the insignificant
appearances with Lena Ashwell and the Cassons and the disastrous
modern versions he had acted in in 1928, he had not played Shakespeare
at all. Considered in 1935 an appealing but lightweight exponent of
modern (mostly comic) plays, Olivier would have aroused considerable
surprise (not to say amusement) with an announcement of a forthcoming production of *Romeo and Juliet*. On the other hand, he may
have hoped an enterprising manager would find the idea sufficiently
intriguing to profit from it, at least as a curiosity.

Gielgud's offer was both generous and judicious, although its pertinence would not be immediately evident. *Romeo and Juliet* was to open
in October with Olivier as Romeo and Gielgud as Mercutio; they would
exchange roles six weeks later. Rehearsals began in early September, but
with muted excitement. The settled tradition (of which Gielgud was
prime guardian) was to stress the poetic lyricism of Shakespeare's verse.
But from the first reading, Olivier spoke his lines as if they sprang from
blunt feeling and were not lines of venerable iambic pentameter: he was
clearly preparing to play Romeo as a hot-blooded adolescent seething
with sexual eagerness. Cast and director heard the verse as if it were not
verse at all, but a spontaneous rush of passionate desire, impossible to
suppress. Gielgud tried to restrain Olivier, and the atmosphere at
rehearsals was frequently charged with tension. 'He felt that I was too
verse-conscious and exhibitionist in my acting of Shakespeare,' Gielgud
reflected years later. 'Of course, he was a great exhibitionist himself, but
in quite a different way – daring, flamboyant and iconoclastic.'

Olivier's speech as he prepared Romeo was natural and credible –
not a recitation for the academy, but a ringing cry for the audience.
This approach to Shakespeare sprang not from a reasoned, intellectual
and consciously artistic approach but from the fact that he was 'rebellious [against] John's power and gifts', as he later admitted. Gielgud
was well-bred, literate and familiar with all the classics, as Olivier was
not; Gielgud was only three years his senior, but he was the most
famous and respected actor in England.

Since his schooldays, Olivier had wanted to 'knock their bloody eyes out' with his acting, and in 1935 his attitude was still, as he said, one of defiance: 'I will show them, I will show them, I will show them . . . I'm going to be a simply smashing actor.' In his case, this goal was neither idly ambitious nor blindly vainglorious; the prophecies were based on creative intuition, however dimly the outcome could be perceived. Now, confronted with an actor-director he had to admire and whose achievements he coveted, and cast for the first time as the lead in Shakespeare, Olivier's ambition perfectly matched his genius; he had indeed benefited from the harsh experiences of *The Green Bay Tree* and his multiple responsibilities with *Ringmaster*. As so often with authentic creative growth, both impetus and depth were provided by the accumulations of professional frustration, artistic abrasion and emotional torment. To his performance as Romeo he brought everything that was himself.

The critical reaction might have been predicted, for the opening night on 17 October at the New Theatre (later the Albery) provoked virtually unanimous denunciations: with a single exception the London critics – worshipping the traditions of tremulous verse-speaking and chary of any new style – did not appreciate Olivier's performance. Among others, *The Times* and *Sunday Times*, the *Evening Standard* and the *Star* published scathing comments about his 'inexpertness' and 'gabbling', claiming that he was 'temperamentally ill at ease' and – worst of all – had neither the lyrical voice nor the poetic diction for Romeo. There was rousing praise for Gielgud, Ashcroft and Evans, and this added to Olivier's resentment of the general critical reaction. Within days, Glen Byam Shaw (who had acted with him in *Queen of Scots* and had become an amiable drinking partner) found him 'terribly depressed – almost suicidal – [over] the notices for Romeo'. But the respected critic St John Ervine (in the *Observer*) praised the revolutionary naturalness of his performance: 'I have seen few sights so moving as the spectacle of Mr Olivier's Romeo . . . [an] impetuous boy, struggling to be articulate . . . I think [Shakespeare's] eyes would have shone had he seen this Romeo, young and ardent and full of clumsy grace.'

In later reminiscences, Olivier omitted Ervine's important endorsement, perhaps because it lessened the dramatic poignancy he wished to attach to his chronicle of the moment. He also overlooked the enthusiastic response he had from audiences who, as Alec Guinness recalled, cared not so much for the adherence to an established style as to the dramatic effect, which was immediate and popular: 'He didn't have a bad way of reciting the verse, it was just a new and very different way.' And critic J.C. Trewin, who was in the audience that first week, recalled that Olivier 'almost sprang on the stage, a young gallant from the Renaissance. I can still remember the gasps of admiration in the theatre.' Nor was he cheered by the most important notice from an American correspondent: 'Mr Olivier was a fresh, impetuous Romeo, intoxicated with love.' The consensus of Americans, who had no hallowed expectations about Shakespeare, was that Olivier's Romeo was above all emotionally accessible, and with this achievement, his value to American producers, agents and visitors was vastly increased. But he was long familiar with rejection, and so he almost wallowed in the customary pain. No matter the encouragement offered or the optimism engendered by colleagues, Olivier was, as Gielgud felt, 'inclined to be obstinate'.

Laurence Olivier's first appearance as a Shakespearean lover was in a notoriously difficult role demanding a combination of impetuosity and dignity. Told of Juliet's death, Romeo has only one line to convey a complex reaction: 'Is it e'en so? then I defy you, stars.' He then sets to action: 'get me ink and paper, and hire post-horses', and at once plans to obtain poison from an apothecary – a teenager's spontaneous reaction, perhaps, but a major challenge for an actor to make credible and coherent. Romeo can be played as a helpless victim of fate or a tragic collaborator in his own frenzied destiny. By playing the impulsive adolescent, Olivier attempted to fuse the two aspects, and the immediate reaction of critics was to reject the unfamiliar tone.

'He was deeply hurt,' Gielgud recalled, 'and he went on all his life about the way he resented this [critical rejection].' Olivier was not consoled, either, by Peggy Ashcroft's support, even though he admitted later that she was the most attentive and encouraging co-star. (She thought his Romeo was the best she ever saw, 'because he played him as a passionate boy'.) There was to be a permanent rancour in Olivier's account of this time, a testimony to his lifelong hypersensitivity about negative criticism tendered by anyone other than himself. Forever after, he presented himself as a benighted victim rather more than was really the case – as if the critics had summarily demolished his career, as if presently he did not equal (and eventually even perhaps surpass) Gielgud in fame and achievement.

For Olivier the issue seemed precisely that Gielgud had the superior notices. A pungent, churlish envy – as he had felt in Hollywood about

Jill's success – was aroused in him that October, and he never lost a sense of rivalry with Gielgud. 'John had a preoccupation with the beautiful and the poetic, at the expense of reality . . . He was conscious of his gifts, of music and lyricism.' Variations on this theme ran through Olivier's interviews for the rest of his life. None of his achievements mitigated this attitude, and as late as 1986, three years before his death, he wrote: 'I was the outsider and John was the jewel . . . Everybody was in his favour.'

No such tone characterised his colleague, for Gielgud always came to Olivier's defence: 'Larry had a great advantage over me in his commanding vitality, striking looks, brilliant humour and passionate directness. As Romeo, his love scenes were intensely real and tender, and his tragic grief profoundly touching.' But Gielgud was ever aware of Olivier's resentment, which made them, he felt, 'rivals rather than colleagues, which I was sorry about'. (In his will, Olivier stipulated that each of ten close friends were to select a small memento from among his personal effects; to Gielgud he left an early rehearsal edition of *Hamlet*.)

On 28 November the two actors exchanged roles, and the critics replaced their cold words for Olivier with warm. As Mercutio he was, according to the same critics who had spurned his Romeo, 'brilliant . . . sparkling . . . every word struck fire with a . . . quick and lusty vitality . . . and extraordinary power'. The most notable aspects of Olivier's earlier Shakespearean performances – the vitality of his Puck, the exuberance of his Kate, the volubility of his Parolles – found ideal reincarnation in Mercutio's irrepressible vigour and impish love of repartee, his naturalistic speech now considered appropriate. 'My Mercutio went down very well,' he wrote years later, adding, 'but this could never be a compensation for me' (for the earlier reaction to his Romeo).

Curiously, it was Olivier's Mercutio that was more difficult for his colleagues; Peggy Ashcroft, for one, recalled that he was furious at having to play the role, which affected his performance. Despite the formal courtesies that marked their greetings and normal business, the tension between the two leading men continued. Olivier – taking advantage of Mercutio's quicksilver character – quite regularly spoke on Gielgud's cues, cutting off half a line of his partner's verse. This was especially jarring since Gielgud was on a punishing schedule that autumn, working all day filming the complex and physically demanding lead in Alfred Hitchcock's *Secret Agent*.

At times during his four months as Mercutio, Olivier's zeal (and perhaps his resentment) overcame him. He insisted on absolute realism during the fight scene with Harry Andrews (as Tybalt), who recalled that although they were well-rehearsed with two-handed swords and buckler and dagger,

> we used to knock each other about quite a lot, slashing away as if we really meant it. Not a night passed without one of us causing the other some damage; years afterwards Larry often referred to this fight, saying he still bore the scars.

Thus continued Olivier's penchant for risk and danger, always justified as a passion for authenticity. Henceforth he would insist on performing the most dangerous feats – even in films, for which professional stuntmen are ordinarily employed. In this regard, it is easy to understand that such endurance would have an additional importance for Olivier at this time, as evidence (against the barrenness of his marital life) that he was manly.

By 1935, Laurence Olivier had thus become – almost by default – a major actor, and his participation in Gielgud's *Romeo and Juliet* was a historic moment in London theatre. Very soon what he had attempted was accepted: his new approach to the verse signalled a stylistic turning-point in playing Shakespeare – a true revolution from which even John Gielgud learned, as he admitted. Olivier's career (despite the critics' reactions) was in no way hurt; indeed, the controversy over his Romeo won him new admirers even before he began to play Mercutio. At last he was noticed – he was 'showing them' – and he was being regarded seriously in a strenuous role, as lover, athlete and swordsman. Once he began to play Mercutio, the shift towards success was assured; thenceforth, the New Theatre was every bit as much his territory as that of his co-stars. Olivier had more than vindicated John Gielgud's confidence that here indeed was a kind of genius wanting only opportunity and the unpredictable amalgamation of timing with talent.

Everything came into focus that season. Searching for his professional identity, he was selected by the great John Gielgud, exponent of a different style against which the obstinate showoff in Olivier reacted. Since his schooldays, he had desired to shock others with special effects and to surprise them with athleticism. Now, his lifelong desire for attention was paying dividends as his craving to grip an audience coincided with a preference for natural speech, and his longing for a romantic life perfectly matched the temper of Romeo. He was becoming, at last, his own man – by becoming, onstage, two other men.

And yet there was a thinly disguised ungenerous streak in his envy of and rank ingratitude towards John Gielgud, without whom he would not have had this important breakthrough. *Romeo and Juliet* played until the end of March 1936 – the longest continuous run of the play on record. Olivier always attached great importance to this period, and on his eightieth birthday he recalled that he had indeed, in 1935, been driven by 'ambition – without it, I couldn't have made it'.

In late november the Oliviers were dining at the Savoy Grill after a performance, and among the diners were Vivien Leigh and her husband Leigh Holman. They chatted briefly while waiting for their taxis home, and the Oliviers invited the Holmans for a weekend at a modest country cottage they had just rented near Maidenhead – 'and so we went and we played football,' according to Vivien, 'and I remember Larry roaring around one minute and then unaccountably falling fast asleep under the piano the next.' The weekend was otherwise unmemorable.

Vivien, in a stagnant period after *The Mask of Virtue*, attended several matinees of *Romeo and Juliet*. Before one performance she breezed into Olivier's dressing room to invite him and Jill for dinner at her home in Little Stanhope Street. There was only a moment of superficial conversation, and then she kissed him quickly and swept out. What Olivier did not know until much later was that Vivien, in addition to her affair with John Buckmaster, had by this time briefly become the mistress of Alexander Korda, who was (according to Vivien's biographer Hugo Vickers) exploited to advance her career and steer her towards working with Olivier. Since both actors were under contract to Korda, Vivien badgered him to cast them together in a film. The reason for her insistence was simple, as Vivien had confided to her friend Beryl Samson in May of that year: 'Some day I am going to marry Laurence Olivier.'

By Christmas 1935 – to the astonishment of all who knew the Oliviers – Jill was expecting a child. Given the nature of their relationship, it is probable that the pregnancy was deliberate: her homosexuality would not have precluded a strong maternal instinct. As for Olivier, he neither commented nor confided on the matter.

During the first week of 1936, Vivien Leigh invited Laurence Olivier to join her for lunch – alone – before his matinee. Within a week, they met again, for a late supper after his evening performance. Like him, Vivien Leigh was, as her friend Fabia Drake wrote, 'intensely ambitious'.

CHAPTER SIX

⚜

1936–1938

O! how full of briers is this working-day world.

Rosalind, in *As You Like It*

'I was trying to sell realism in Shakespeare,' Laurence Olivier said of his controversial Romeo. 'I believed in it with my whole soul.' Among those convinced during the late autumn of 1935 was the German refugee actress Elisabeth Bergner. After agreeing to play Rosalind in a movie version of *As You Like It*, she saw Olivier onstage and immediately asked for him as Orlando. Despite his doubts about how well Shakespeare could be presented on film, he could not refuse a salary of six hundred pounds a week, for over two months.

However lucrative, the experience of filming *As You Like It* that winter was uncongenial. Olivier was exhausted from rushing each day from the studio to the New Theatre for evening performances, often still in make-up and the padding he wore beneath his tights for his roles as Orlando and Mercutio. (Throughout his life he considered his legs spindly and unattractive.) In addition, the film – directed by Bergner's husband, Paul Czinner – was an inconsistent melange of styles and moods, and ultimately it could not bear the weight of its clumsy artiness. Czinner's production was a fussy agglomeration of realism and fantasy, alternately crowded with a menagerie of peacocks, dogs, geese and sheep, and moments later monastic in the frugality of its sets and props. Arden, cheaply constructed indoors, seemed more a thicket than a forest, and too often the camera battled against the cast, swirling dizzily when it should have recorded calmly.

But the direst liability of *As You Like It* was the star. Elisabeth Bergner's fey charm was overplayed too coyly for the resolute Rosalind, and her heavily accented soprano – inappropriate for Rosalind disguised as a boy – elicited politely suppressed smiles from the English cast and crew; rarely has an actress been so miscast. Nor did Bergner ingratiate herself by arriving late, or by refusing to react off-camera to Olivier's lines and to recite her own so that his reaction close-ups would seem natural.

Orlando is an awkward part even under the best circumstances. At the outset he is a brave and articulate nobleman, and then he becomes tongue-tied, ambling about in the forest while the action focuses on Rosalind. Olivier rightly saw that Bergner's close-ups as a girl disguised as a boy would be unbelievable, and to counter that problem he played Orlando with a mild touch of comic lunacy; his forest scenes are just slightly askew, never quite predictable and amusingly idiosyncratic.

Olivier's crowded schedule in early 1936 was matched by that of Vivien Leigh, who could not therefore pursue him as immediately as she hoped. Eager to play Shakespeare, she won a role in John Gielgud's production of *Richard II* at Oxford and later played Anne in a Regent's Park open-air staging of *Henry VIII* – roles for which she was still praised more for her beauty than for her acting.

The marriage to Leigh Holman, meanwhile, was further strained by her absence from home much of the season, by her assignment of her daughter's care to a hired nanny (much as her own mother had dropped her at a boarding school), and by her growing obsession with Laurence Olivier, for whose sake (although Olivier was entirely unaware of this) she had withdrawn from John Buckmaster and ended the brief affair with Alexander Korda. Early that spring, seeking Olivier's advice on verse recitation, she invited him several times to her Mayfair home; a quiet lunch in Shepherd's Market often followed their discussions.

Throughout the first half of 1936, the Olivier–Leigh relationship remained nonsexual. Because of Vivien's evident seriousness about her career and her shrewdness in presenting herself simply as a friendly colleague, Olivier was not entirely certain of her intentions; she was, after all, a wife and mother (and he knew of her attachment to John Buckmaster). His sense of responsibility to his pregnant wife made him additionally cautious with Vivien, just as his history with Jill and the other women in his past made him insecure as a possible lover. But their meetings continued, Vivien always showing herself an engaging companion. She told risqué jokes without losing her elegance; she matched Olivier drink for drink and never slurred a syllable; she was intelligent, a quick winner at card games who could also complete the *Times* crossword with amazing speed. Most important, however, was her fierce attention to every word he uttered. Vivien had a gift for making Olivier feel attractive, virile and important – a talent that rarely fails to secure a man's allegiance.

If such matters were discussed, they would have found much common material in their histories, for both had been grievously hurt: never close to his cool and remote father, Olivier at twelve had lost his mother, and Vivien forever bore the wound of being abandoned in what was essentially a foreign country at the age of six. In his choice of Jill and his remaining with her, Olivier had found someone at first more maternal than romantic, and Leigh Holman was very much the protective father-figure for Vivien. It was clear that the similar emotional histories, frustrations and ambitions of Laurence Olivier and Vivien Leigh provided the arena for mutual consolation, compassion and encouragement. Both were motivated by a love for theatre, by an intense desire to be acknowledged and accepted, by the actor's basic wish to gratify others. For Olivier, this was manifested in the increasing cultivation of a variety of roles – almost as if he were saying: 'If you don't like me this way, then wait just a moment' – while Vivien showered friends and colleagues with tangible tokens of affection.

By April, she was touring in Max Beerbohm's comedy *The Happy Hypocrite* and Olivier was involved in plans to present and direct, with Ralph Richardson, a new play by J.B. Priestley. The playwright's recent triumphs with *Dangerous Corner* and *Eden End* must have convinced them the new play was sure of success, but *Bees on the Boatdeck* was as unfortunate as its title. A political parable, it opened at the Lyric Theatre on 5 May and concerned the steamship *Gloriana* (whose officers were played by Olivier and Richardson), threatened with destruction by a cynical capitalist, a crackpot scientist, a Communist agitator and a scheming fascist (none of whom, it may be added, held much interest for Olivier, who – a patriot at heart – was essentially apolitical). The two caretakers foil the plots, only to have the ship's doom finally ordered by its owners. A frankly didactic and unplayable mixture of allegory and farce, *Bees on the Boatdeck* lasted less than a month; the two actor-directors (who had shared the inexpensive funding with Priestley) lost more confidence than cash. Playgoers found Olivier unsuited to his role, and critics (recalling *Golden Arrow*) questioned his directorial ability.

On all counts the timing was perfect when in June Olivier received a call from Alexander Korda, who had a screenplay ready for production that summer – *Fire Over England*, an elaborate costume romance.

Olivier would receive first billing in the leading role, a stalwart British fighter and passionate suitor in the time of Queen Elizabeth named Michael Ingolby, who undertakes dangerous missions on the crown's behalf, uncovers details of the Armada and wins not only the love of Cynthia, the Queen's beautiful lady-in-waiting, but also a knighthood into the bargain. He was about to enact on screen the kind of absolute Englishman he would eventually represent in life; Cynthia, he learned at the same time, was to be Vivien Leigh, who had much importuned Korda to cast them together. According to Michael Korda, the producer's nephew and biographer, Alexander Korda was like a benevolent uncle or godfather to them over the years – first because he adored Vivien and considered the advancement of her career to be one of his major roles in life, and also because he valued Olivier's talents.

Filming was scheduled to begin in August at the Denham Studios; meanwhile, the American director William K. Howard and cameraman James Wong Howe worked with a large English crew on the lavish designs and intricate production requirements (sea battles, vast palaces, complex miniatures and special effects).

The two leading players lost no time in fixing daily meetings to discuss the script, and in late June or July they became lovers. (Leigh Holman was sailing with friends in Sweden, and Jill – nearing the term of her pregnancy – withdrew from the London summer to her mother's country cottage in Hurley.) Soon Olivier and Vivien were seen together at the Savoy Grill and the Ivy restaurant, popular theatrical salons. Such appearances were not, of themselves, particularly indiscreet or scandalous, although there was a flurry of rumour in the West End when an actress recognised them early one morning coming out of a bedroom suite at the Savoy Hotel. (According to Gwen Ffrangçon-Davies, Olivier and Leigh were surprised by none other than the venerable Marie Tempest, who had acted with Olivier in *Theatre Royal*.) The Olivier–Leigh affair blazed passionately that summer of 1936, and by the time of their first scenes in *Fire Over England*, their lives had forever altered.

Primed for an exclusive, amorous relationship, Olivier greatly needed Vivien, and to her he attached all his hitherto unexpressed feelings and needs; for her part, she needed the devotion of a handsome, vibrant and stable man whose talent she respected. She had inherited her mother's single-minded concentration and refinement and her father's love of glamour and romantic adventure, and like Olivier, Vivien may also have found additionally exciting the inbuilt risk of their relationship; like him, too, she had a respectable life that did not fulfil her needs. Yet as late as mid-autumn, the affair was still unknown to their spouses.

On 21 August, Jill gave birth to a son, baptised Simon Tarquin and always thereafter called by his middle name. His father, in an apparently grandiloquent preference for royalty that year, named the boy for an emperor celebrated in Macaulay's *Lays of Ancient Rome*: 'It came to me in a mad moment,' he admitted. 'It has such dramatic overtones.' Olivier's filming schedule and, more insistently, his new life with Vivien, kept him distant from his family; he did, however, host a lavish christening party at Cheyne Walk, attended by a crowd that included the child's godfather, Noël Coward, and Michael Redgrave, who recalled that '[Olivier] liked the grand scale in everything about him. The party was at his enormous Chelsea studio with enormous windows and enormous fireplaces – a setting that would have dwarfed lesser men, but he was very much in his element.'

Korda's fourteen-week filming schedule brought fire over Denham in several ways. First, the entire company was immediately aware of their affair, for during any break in shooting Olivier and Vivien fled to the bolted privacy of a remote dressing room, whence they could be summoned back to work only after repeated requests and much rapping on the door. They also adopted pet nicknames and openly exchanged the affectionate winks and touches by which lovers proudly proclaim their relationship to observers. It was clear to everyone there, recalled actor Alexander Knox, that they were most desperately in love, and the intensity of their affair is noticeable in their scenes together in *Fire Over England* – although one exchange of dialogue was oddly prophetic:

> Cynthia (Vivien): We've got a right to be happy! Everyone has a right to be happy, Michael.
> Michael (Olivier): Everyone. Yes. That is why we can't be.

For a hazardous scene, Olivier as usual insisted on performing his own stunts as Vivien stood by, admiring. He was to spring aboard the studio galleon and throw a flaming torch along the oil-soaked floor, leaping over the side of the ship into a safety net below as the deck burst into flames. The director, assured the fire brigade was nearby and alert, called for action. Olivier jumped up and tossed the firebrand, but the flaming oil floated on the water and sped towards him. Making a swift but crooked dive overboard, he landed precariously on the net below, merely wrenching his back instead of breaking his neck or sustaining severe burns. To everyone's astonishment and against the producer's wishes, Olivier then insisted on doing numerous retakes. But only the love scenes and action sequences enlivened an otherwise foggy screenplay, gravid with unresolved subplots and odd conglomerations of speech patterns (Question: 'Hath not the Queen forsworn her anger?' Reply: 'You can say that again!').

Prominent though it was, Olivier's affair with Vivien was (away from Denham) remarkably discreet. For him it was certainly not considered a prelude to marriage, and he spent every weekend with his wife – which brought, at a garden party held by her mother late that summer, an unexpected development. Olivier was approached by a guest who had specifically asked Eva Moore for an invitation. He was Tyrone Guthrie, widely respected as supervising director at the Old Vic theatre. Impressed by Olivier's Romeo and Mercutio, Guthrie offered him a place in the company; his first role would be Hamlet, played (as rarely) in its entirety.

Built on reclaimed marshland south of the Thames near Waterloo Bridge, the Old Vic was opened as the Royal Coburg in 1818, and for its first sixty years was a hall for cheap melodrama and farce. Important actors occasionally played there, but despite their visits and a name-change to the Royal Victoria after the theatre-loving princess visited in 1833, the surrounding neighbourhood remained seedy and dangerous. Then, in 1880, a social worker named Emma Cons took over the management and transformed the place into the Royal Victoria Coffee and Music Hall, 'a cheap and decent place of amusement along strict temperance lines', as she announced.

Cons's niece Lilian Baylis succeeded her, and from 1914 the theatre (billed as the Old Vic two years later) became a noted forum for opera, ballet (she engaged Ninette de Valois and formed the first Sadler's Wells company) and, most important, for a famous cycle of Shakespeare's plays. By 1936, every serious English actor had performed there; no one earnest about performing would decline the opportunity to work cheerfully for its absurdly low salary (ten pounds a week was standard pay; players in leading roles sometimes received twenty).

Guthrie had just returned to the Old Vic that summer of 1936 after a two-year absence, and he had already engaged Edith Evans, Michael

Redgrave and Alec Guinness, among others. Introducing the custom of eight-week runs with a different cast for each play, he offered as incentive the promise that Olivier would be free to choose other Shakespearean roles after his Hamlet. Still smarting from the previous year's critical blows, Olivier realised that he was indeed at a crucial moment; at twenty-nine, he required an important association like this to advance his career. Friends encouraged him, Vivien promoted the idea, and within days Olivier telephoned his acceptance to Guthrie. That year, recalled Alec Guinness (who was to play Osric in *Hamlet*), he was certainly eager to be recognised as a serious classical actor.

Olivier knew that the role of Hamlet was even more risky than Romeo, and that once again he might be considered an upstart rival of Gielgud's acclaimed performance as the prince (which had opened on 8 October and would run simultaneously with Olivier's). 'I knew I was putting myself up in a kind of stupid rivalry,' Olivier admitted years later. In 1936, the challenge was too tempting to ignore, and three decades later he told critic Ronald Hayman that he 'would never have gone to the Old Vic if John had not gone there first'.

Despite some favourable notices as Mercutio, as Peggy Ashcroft said years later, 'Larry had got it in the neck as Romeo, but he went to the Old Vic to go on with Shakespeare and to prove them all wrong. It was really quite courageous of him.' He may also have realised that it would be unnecessary to risk further exposing his sometimes poor literary judgment if he worked at the Old Vic: his miscalculations about new plays (by Keith Winter, Sylvia Thompson and J.B. Priestley) would be no impediment to playing Shakespeare. He needed only his genius, not his intellect.

Throughout the final weeks of shooting *Fire Over England* in September, Olivier was memorising Hamlet. The following month, he agreed to accompany Jill on holiday to Capri, where after several days Vivien suddenly turned up, chaperoned by a family friend named Oswald Frewen (who later discovered that he had been invited only so that Vivien could visit Olivier without open offence to Jill). Vivien's arrival was typical: her devotion to Olivier had an obsessive quality, and she had to reassure herself that his absence with Jill was nothing like a second honeymoon.

She need not have worried – and indeed, not long after her arrival she was the gayest of companions, planning activities, buying gifts and trinkets and keeping the others awake into the small hours with card and word games. As the four continued on to Naples and Pompeii,

Olivier had no time alone with Vivien. His resentment and frustration were clear after she departed Italy, for he wrote to her that he found life quite insupportable in her absence and was ready to leave Jill. That was not, however, a settled plan of action.

Returning to London, Olivier rehearsed *Hamlet* for four weeks in December before he was finally taken to meet the legendary Lilian Baylis. Short, dumpy and untidy, with gentle eyes and a bespectacled, grandmotherly mien, Baylis had a slightly crooked mouth, the result of facial nerve damage from a swimming accident. She spoke in a South African accent that was usually taken for Cockney, and she was nothing like an intellectual. Baylis presented Shakespeare not because she was particularly scholarly, as Peggy Ashcroft confirmed, but because she knew what was good box office. She treated people as if they were her Sunday school children, and her stinginess with salaries and production costs was well known – some of her Old Vic productions cost about twenty-eight pounds, excluding salaries – but she was a magnificent impresario.

'She's an absolute scream,' wrote Sybil Thorndike to her brother Russell about that time. 'I'm sure Shakespeare is roaring at her, for she runs the place like parish rooms and looks like a church worker. She has two smelly dogs, Scamp and Snoo, of whom it is said you never know which end you are patting.' Baylis was parsimonious to the point of niggardliness about salaries in those days before government subsidies; 'O God, send me some good actors – and cheap,' was her constant prayer. Yet Lilian Baylis inspired from her company enormous affection – some of it based on her genuine concern for their spiritual and temporal health, some springing from the amusement she unwittingly inspired.

A devout spinster, Baylis was a glorious eccentric in the tradition of Elsie Fogerty and Lena Ashwell. 'Are you pure, dear boy?' she once asked a young acting candidate. 'Mind you, I'm not narrow-minded, but I won't have anything going on in the wings.' Fearing neither man nor beast, she was known to have continued with a performance of *King Lear* while bombs fell during World War I. 'Now, boys and girls,' she said to her adult audience before the curtain rose, 'we're not going to let Kaiser Bill interfere with the Vic. If you people upstairs would feel any safer, you can come down and sit here and I won't charge you extra. And will all those who wish to leave, do so at once – we are carrying on!' Weeks later, catching some actors taking shelter during

15. *Above* Leaving New York for Hollywood, with Jill Esmond, 1931. *National
Film Archive, London*

16. *Below* Jill Esmond, Douglas Fairbanks,
Jr., Joan Crawford and Laurence Olivier
— in Hollywood, 1932. *From the collection
of Felix Barker*

17. *Above* With Ann Harding in *Westward Passage*, 1932. *National Film Archive, London*

18. *Below* Headed for Hollywood, 1933. *Culver Pictures*

19. *Below* With Jill, flying to New York, 1933. *Courtesy of the Academy of Motion Picture Arts and Sciences*

20. *Right* As Julian in *The Green Bay Tree*, New York (1933). *Culver Pictures*

21. *Above* As Romeo, with Edith Evans and John Gielgud (1935). *Victoria and Albert Museum*

22. *Left* With Elisabeth Bergner, in the film of *As You Like It* (1936). *National Film Archive, London*

another air attack, she scolded them, 'If you have to be killed, at least die at your job!'

Her fearlessness extended to the royal family. When Queen Mary arrived late for a centenary performance in 1918, Baylis was there to greet her: 'I'm glad you've turned up at last, dear,' she said airily to Her Majesty while the Board of Governors blanched. 'I know it's not your fault being late, as I hear that your dear husband, going to the Union Jack Club, has held up [traffic in] the road. But we've got a long programme to get through, and so we had to make a start.' Leading the great matriarch into the theatre, Baylis pointed to a painting of George V: 'Here's your husband's portrait. It's not as large as Aunt Emma [Cons], because your dear husband has not done so much for the Old Vic.'

In her messy, cramped office, Baylis greeted Olivier that December: 'Of course, you really oughtn't to come here at all when you can get so much more money elsewhere, but still, that's your business.'

'I adored her,' Olivier said frequently throughout his life, and the reason is easy to understand: aged sixty-two, Lilian Baylis was a surrogate mother (and not only to Olivier). He liked to tell of resting between matinee and evening performances at the theatre, when Baylis herself would come to tuck him into a quilt and wish him a prayerful blessing. Baylis's gentle piety also struck a chord of memory in Olivier – with certain sensory alterations: 'The theatre still had a lot of the atmosphere of the parish hall, with the smell of hard-boiled eggs and stale tea, plus a hint of something I could only describe as dead cats.'

So warm a bond formed between them that when she complained about cash, he felt free to suggest that a bar be opened at the Old Vic. Referring to the earlier ill repute of the Royal Victoria and its environs, she parried: 'Dear boy, if this theatre hadn't been a gin palace with men coming home from it to beat their wives, we'd never have got this place!'

Olivier found the *Hamlet* rehearsals unexpectedly provocative. Guthrie's psychoanalytic reading of the text, based on a famous paper by Freud's biographer Ernest Jones, maintained that Hamlet felt guilty about his subconscious love for his mother and therefore – desiring the very relationship Claudius now had with her – could not kill the man with whom he identified. The play thus becomes a dilemma of unresolved Oedipal conflict. Baylis, who many blithely claimed was prudish, did not object to Guthrie's theories, as she had not when some of her

Measure for Measure cast felt shy of the play's sexual content. 'My dears,' she told them, 'all we can do is go on our knees right now and pray for lust.'

Although something of the Jones reading is certainly justified by the text, Guthrie fell into the unfortunate trap of subjugating the entire play to his obsession with it; and Olivier, impressed by Guthrie's persuasive academicism, developed the character along these lines. Instead of the usual Hamlet – gentle, sad and sonorous – Olivier prepared a vivid, sardonic and resolute portrait of a Renaissance athlete, reminiscent more of Barrymore than Gielgud. Exploiting a make-up kit Vivien had given him, he arrived at the final dress rehearsal having shaved the hair at his temples and plucked his eyebrows. To suggest a kind of distracted exhaustion, he had drawn a faint line under his eyes that started at the tear ducts and ran down over his cheekbones.

But the opening night of *Hamlet* (5 January 1937) was not an unqualified success. 'He moved with catlike agility,' according to Guthrie; 'it was evident that here was no ordinary actor, not everyone's cup of tea . . . not necessarily well cast for Hamlet, but inevitably destined for the very top of the tree.' Critics approved Olivier's vitality and resolve, but some still complained about his recitation of verse and, except for the lascivious kiss he planted on the lips of Gertrude, the Freudian motif was neither clear nor recognised.

Vivien, who frequently attended, once approached him backstage with tear-stained cheeks. She knew how the death of Agnes Olivier had darkened his youth, and she always claimed to have seen through the subtleties of his performance to his grappling with a poignant array of memories: she was convinced that her 'Larry-boy' – her pet name, with its hint of slightly condescending juvenility (he called her 'Puss' or 'Vivling') – was confronting in this role his own feelings about his mother. Persuaded that her life was destined to be linked to his, Vivien now longed to play Ophelia to his Hamlet.

But Olivier may have brought to his Hamlet more of his anguish over Vivien than over his mother. 'Larry was profoundly unhappy at the time,' Tyrone Guthrie said years later.

> It all had to do with the conflict [over] his violent and immature love for Vivien . . . He was literally in a quandary as to what to do. When I first talked to him about *Hamlet*, he said, 'Oh, how I'd love to do it, I already know what it feels like to be a Hamlet in real life.' . . . He believed he had a great deal of personal Hamlet-like anguish and spiritual paralysis to bring to the part.

The entanglement with Vivien was not undilutedly joyful, and Olivier always felt guilty about these two years of furtiveness and lying. He called the affair 'fatefully irresistible, this thing . . . sometimes felt almost like an illness . . . love was like an angel, guilt was a dark fiend . . . [it was] rapturous torment.' However typically florid the Olivier diction, his words reflected a severe ambiguity in his feelings then and his memories later. He always insisted that their trysts occur in all possible secrecy – no more of the studio cavorting as in the days of *Fire Over England* – and at this subterfuge he was so successful that Jill was still oblivious that winter.

The ambiguity of Olivier's intentions became clear when he asked Guthrie (against Vivien's loud opposition) to cast his wife as Olivia in *Twelfth Night*, which was to follow *Hamlet* in February; he still had not resolved to leave his family. The complications of guilt may at least partially explain his ragingly physical and dangerous performance as Hamlet. Week after week, backstage crew were sent to fetch cotton and antiseptic, and next day the press would report that Olivier had been wounded during the duel with Michael Redgrave (who played Laertes). Redgrave was neither careless nor over-acting: Olivier, not surprisingly, had insisted that Laertes lunge violently. This Hamlet seemed intent on self-laceration, for by mid-January bits of flesh had been nicked out of his scalp, arm and chest. As always, Olivier was passionate for realism, with little fear for the extremes to which his insistence frequently led. Lilian Baylis, meanwhile – who chose to ignore the Olivier–Leigh affair – grew bored with the protracted swordplay. Stuart Burge, the Player King in *Hamlet*, recalled that one evening, when the poisoned sword was about to change hands near the play's finale,

> unfortunately, the sword went sailing offstage, into the audience. We didn't know what to do, since you can't finish the play without the poisoned sword. Finally a loud voice came from a box seat: 'Oh, come on, dears – won't someone give him back his sword so we can get on with the play and go home!' It was Lilian.

Olivier's love for Vivien, then – like the continuing critical debate over the merits of his Hamlet – was both affliction and consolation. She adored him, and with her Olivier's self-estimation flourished as never before. By the midpoint of the run, he was perfectly at ease as the cast spokesman, frequently stepping forward at the end of the evening to make announcements or give words of appreciation to the audience. Michael Redgrave remembered this clearly, for on Saturday,

30 January 1937, Olivier at the curtain call made a speech: 'Ladies and gentlemen, tonight a great actress has been born. Laertes has a daughter.' The newborn Redgrave was named Vanessa.

'I was looking,' Olivier later said,

> for a way that I could show off my versatility . . . First Hamlet; then Sir Toby Belch [in *Twelfth Night*], a complete contrast; and finally Henry V. Not bad for a first season, I thought . . . I like to appear as a chameleon . . . I want the joy of dressing up . . . So all my career I've attempted to disguise myself.

And so he did. After the clean youthfulness of his Hamlet, he gave an outrageously amusing performance as Sir Toby, the self-indulgent, blustering sensualist. With a prominent putty nose, plaster pouches under his eyes, drooping moustache and red cheeks bulging with chunks of sponge, he was 'only now and then recognisable' as Olivier (*The Times*). He wanted nothing so much as to surprise his audience by appearing as a comic buffoon after the rigours of Hamlet.

His star was quickly rising, for after the premiere on 23 February of *Twelfth Night*, *Fire Over England* was released, and London journals praised the screen's new romantic pair. At the same time, Vivien performed in two short-lived plays: on 5 February she opened in *Because We Must* and on 11 March in *Bats in the Belfry*; she also completed two films, *Dark Journey* and *Storm in a Teacup*. But none of these appearances furthered her career as much as the film with Olivier. Still considered a pleasant, light-voiced, twenty-three-year-old actress of beauty but no great talent, Vivien begged her lover for exercises to deepen her vocal range and for advice on how to play Ophelia – which, she insisted, she one day would. And Vivien had still another role in mind for the future: on opening night of *Because We Must*, she presented her fellow players with copies of Margaret Mitchell's novel *Gone With the Wind*. It was widely known that producer David Selznick had already begun searching for the perfect actress to play Scarlett O'Hara in his forthcoming production, and Vivien confidently claimed the role would be hers.

Meanwhile, she and Olivier gave what might be called their first joint performance that spring. Appearing casually as friends only, they and their spouses spent Saturday, 11 April at a country inn and next day visited Oswald Frewen's cottage. The weekend was a kind of dual celebration – for Olivier's third Old Vic opening (as Henry V the previous Monday) and for contracts he and Vivien had just signed with Korda, to make a second film together the following month.

As before, when intimacy with Vivien was forbidden him in Italy, her presence (alongside his wife's) fired Olivier's resolve. Within a week he confided to Frewen that he felt Vivien should live with a fellow artist, not with Holman; he added – rather hyperbolically, as Frewen might have suspected – that only the passionate Vivien could keep Olivier from being a promiscuous wanderer.

Before the end of April – exactly when and how may never be known – Jill learned or was told of the affair with Vivien. Calmly and coolly, she told her husband she would not consider a divorce, despite their loveless marriage. Jill had devoted herself fully and responsibly to her child, and because she had sacrificed her private life she expected some display of paternal duty at home. As Noël Coward noted later in his diary, 'Jill, rather surprisingly, has been a wonderful mother to [Tarquin, Coward's godson] and he quite genuinely adores her. Larry, as a father figure, has not come off quite so well.' Just as Vivien had allowed her mother to assume parental duties for Suzanne, so Olivier ceded emotional and practical responsibility for Tarquin to Jill – a surprising desertion in light of his clear and poignant memories of his father's distance. There was never any question of the fierce devotion that united Olivier and Vivien; but as often with such relationships, its exclusivity was not without painful consequences for others.

At first, Olivier had been indifferent to Guthrie's suggestion that he play Henry V, but this was to be the Old Vic's coronation play, honouring the accession of George VI that May. Guthrie had planned a spectacle with over a hundred actors and with sopranos from the Sadler's Wells Opera singing in the betrothal scene; furthermore, he persuaded Olivier that the grandeur of Henry's ringingly patriotic speeches were just the sort of heroics to further extend the actor's range.

At Guthrie's suggestion, Olivier worked on the speeches as if they were arias, until finally he felt 'in complete control of body and mind, the whole machinery meshing perfectly . . . I was heroic – none could have been more so – but I was truthful, I was not showing off.' By extending the range of his remarkable tenor voice to previously untried heights and depths, Olivier built Henry's major speech from steady encouragement ('Once more unto the breach, dear friends . . .') through controlled excitement ('Then lend the eye a terrible aspect . . .') to open confidence ('On, on, you noblest English . . .')

and certainty of victory in a rhetorical climax ('Cry "God for Harry, England and Saint George!"') to which he brought the actor's equivalent of a high C. Complementing this operatic diction were Olivier's fresh timings, which could give the verse a startling piquancy. On the lines

> Good morrow, old Sir Thomas Erpingham:
> A good soft pillow for that good white head
> Were better than a churlish turf of France

Olivier paused after 'turf', adding 'of France' like a derisive afterthought. His entire performance had, according to one witness, 'lucidity, the ability to sustain a train of thought, unstressed feeling and quiet pathos . . . The question as to whether Olivier was truly a Shakespearean actor – still advanced a good deal by the Vic audience at this time – was finally settled' by this role.

Henry's character marked an important moment in Olivier's career. When Charles Laughton asked backstage if Olivier knew why his performance had been so fine, Olivier replied he did not. 'You are England, that's all,' Laughton said. The comment went deeper than the praise of one actor for another's performance. Laughton had located what his biographer Simon Callow called his belief that acting could 'transfigure the raw material of the actor and the character into the embodiment of huge ideas and human realities'. In the playing of Henry, Laughton implied, Olivier had somehow communicated what every Englishman felt – an almost dangerous pride in the achievements of the Empire and a simultaneous feeling that everything could be lost at any moment. Thus Olivier had become a kind of corporate personality, and when asked later how he enacted the role so well on film, he replied, 'I don't know – I'm England, that's all.'

That year Olivier's life was characterised by the upheavals of an ecstatic and confusing romantic life accompanying a demanding range of types – the anguish of Hamlet, the antics of Toby and the heroism of Henry. But in developing these men, Olivier, after all, had only the raw material of his own life experience and his own imagination on which to draw. This is not to suggest that his acting was autobiographical or that he was playing himself; but it is true that he had to find something of the part in himself and of himself in the part. He had, to be sure, the obvious gifts of voice and presence and the mysterious gift of intuition about a role. But at least part of his sense was provided by a deep access to his own inner life. He felt the indecision and conflicting attitudes of Hamlet; he shared Toby's love of fun and roistering; and like Henry he had a burgeoning self-awareness and the sense that in some way he, too, was mustering the troops. Not despite but because of his personal growth and 'rapturous torment', Laurence Olivier began to invest his acting with a new level of realism grounded in emotional truth, beyond mimicry and mere external technique.

Olivier could not be called a 'Method actor', as later described by the American actor and teacher Lee Strasberg. Instead of deliberately seeking personal antecedents on which to base the expression of a specific emotion, he simply observed and felt; later, he pretended. Other than a lifelong regime of physical fitness, he had no dedication to any theory or set of specific 'actors' exercises'; there was for him simply a direct frontal attack on a role – the result of ordinary perception joined to extraordinary genius. Throughout his life, Olivier had no patience with theories; he wanted simply to get on with it, to play and to pretend – to be somehow every man. 'I am England, that's all.'

None of this richness was required (or evident) in the Korda project Olivier and Vivien began in May at Denham. Based on John Galsworthy's *The First and the Last*, the film told of a man (Olivier) who in self-defence kills the husband of his lover (Vivien). An innocent suspect is wrongly accused of the crime and remanded to prison for twenty-one days before trial, but he dies of heart failure, thus conveniently freeing the lovers.

Despite a screenplay by Graham Greene and direction by Basil Dean, *Twenty-One Days* (the release title) somehow contracted a fatal languor never relieved by the participation of real-life lovers. At their first entrance, Vivien rushes into Olivier's arms crying, 'Oh, Larry!' – the character's name – and thenceforward their dialogue is interesting only because of that coincidence. Olivier underplayed the man's hysteria admirably; Vivien, on the other hand, gave an annoyingly grand performance, evidently confusing seriousness with artiness. As a result, *Twenty-One Days* seems to last about that long. Korda wisely shelved it until 1940, when, he thought, the names of the stars could sell the film; he was wrong, and even the two leads walked out of a New York screening after a few minutes.

The couple, of course, needed no amusement other than themselves and their future plans. With Korda's encouragement (since he would benefit financially from a loan-out), Vivien continued to speak to the press about her desire to play Scarlett O'Hara. Otherwise, according to Basil Dean, the two players of *Twenty-One Days* were notable for their joyful awareness of each other, laughing and giggling constantly on the set. By this time, Olivier was apparently considering leaving Jill, for he even asked the advice of Dean, who was neither confidant nor friend.

By the end of May, he had decided. With his salary from *Twenty-One Days* he bought Durham Cottage, a compact seventeenth-century house behind high walls at 4 Christchurch Street, Chelsea. Quaint in a doll's-house kind of way, it could have sprung to life from a fairy-tale engraving: there were low windows, climbing vines and flowers, small rooms and a general cosiness. Because refurbishment was necessary, their move to Durham Cottage had to be delayed several months.

But Laurence Olivier and Vivien Leigh were not to be separated. Earlier that year, the Danish Tourist Board had invited Lilian Baylis and Tyrone Guthrie to bring the Old Vic's *Hamlet* to its setting in the play, Kronborg Castle at Elsinore. Olivier at once approached Guthrie, asking that Vivien replace Cherry Cottrell, the actress who had so touchingly played Ophelia that winter. Guthrie refused to consider such unprofessional conduct, and in this Lilian Baylis supported him.

What followed was most unfortunate. When Olivier told Vivien the news – ironically during her filming of *Storm in a Teacup* with Rex Harrison – she broke down in wild hysteria, anger and anguish. No one knew quite how to react to this off-camera scene, but Olivier returned to Guthrie and implied that if Vivien were not engaged for the role he would withdraw. With great reluctance, Guthrie yielded; in his later interviews and written accounts of the Denmark visit, he never mentioned Vivien Leigh. Cherry Cottrell was emotionally devastated by the news that she had been replaced, for this sort of thing simply was not done.

At the end of May, *Twenty-One Days* was still not complete, but Korda gladly released Olivier and Vivien for the Elsinore *Hamlet*. The play was to be staged on the castle ramparts and terraces. Because tourists had free access, rehearsals were restricted to night-time; a week of chilly rain brought chaos to these preparations and afflicted Vivien with a hacking cough and fever, but she neither complained nor absented herself from a single rehearsal.

As the weather had not improved by the day of the first performance (3 June), it was obviously impossible to stage *Hamlet* outdoors. Baylis, Guthrie and Olivier met hastily that afternoon. The performance could not be cancelled, for the Danish royal family was en route from Copenhagen and the international press had arrived. Baylis stood forlornly gazing up at the torrential rain and, ever on intimate terms with God, demanded, 'This has got to stop!' Olivier sprang to action. Once he and Guthrie had decided to stage the play in the ballroom of the Marienlyst Hotel, he fairly sparkled with *ad hoc* ingenuity. While Guthrie supervised the placement of chairs around a central playing area, Olivier conducted a complete rehearsal, improvising exits and entrances, rearranging cues and action and effectively employing the principles of theatre in the round.

The performance that evening was necessarily untidy; it was also important for Olivier's reputation, for it confirmed that his sense of theatre was (despite his unfortunate history as stage director) acute and instinctive. 'It was the most remarkable example of technique responding to sudden emergency,' recalled critic J.C. Trewin, who was present.

> Here was Hamlet, in the centre of his audience, in and out among them, acting on the smallest of playing spaces and involving us all in it . . . All the company followed him, and it was really the performance of a lifetime – so new, astonishing and exciting.

Vivien's Ophelia, on the other hand, was only politely received; the actors, the company and the audience thought her performance immature and unconvincing.

Perhaps in a misguided attempt to keep the lovers apart by her presence, Jill had insisted on joining the company in Elsinore. Alec Guinness (again playing Osric) was delegated to take her sightseeing during that week; Olivier and Vivien, meanwhile, spent the afternoons together – because (as he wrote later) 'we could not keep from touching each other, making love almost within Jill's vision'. Earlier, Jill had certainly been insolently independent of him with her own affairs, but they were not conducted in such proximity. She was humiliated by Vivien, and Olivier's remorse was fitting – no matter that he thought he might compel her to a divorce.

Back in London by 15 June, Vivien lost no time. On the sixteenth, she announced that she was leaving Leigh Holman, who (surely believing the affair would not endure) replied he would not divorce her for at least three years. At once, Vivien left her husband and daughter and rented a small house at Iver, west of London and very near Denham, where *Twenty-One Days* had to be completed. Olivier soon demonstrated as much daring as he had when improvising *Hamlet*: at a time when the cohabitation of unmarried lovers was not as commonplace as it later became, he at once moved in with her.

The scandal broke immediately after Elsinore, as Laurence Evans recalled. 'For a while they were dropped socially by Lord and Lady So-and-so, but they were never dropped in West End theatre life. They were simply much too attractive – and in any case most theatre people were quite tolerant.' As for Jill, the thought of public humiliation and of single parenthood apparently caused her to panic, and she rushed for comfort to a sympathetic friend, Gwen Ffrangçon-Davies, crying that she wanted a traditional, stable home for her son, at least until he was mature.

Once *Twenty-One Days* was completed, Olivier and Vivien decided to travel to a warmer and even more romantic spot than Elsinore, so they departed quietly for Venice. There, with her quick mind, her language fluency and her richer general education, Vivien began to assume what might be called the polishing of Laurence Olivier. Despite his initial resistance, she taught him the fine points of the cultivated life, explaining the differences between Italian and French wines, between dessert and berry spoons, between knives set for fish and those for fowl. Noël Coward had advanced Olivier's informal education and had introduced him to a glittering social circle in the West End, and Sybil Thorndike, Peggy Ashcroft and John Gielgud represented a professional success to which he had long aspired. Even Jill, early on, had made recommendations about refining his manner and appearance; but Vivien's cultural tutelage completed the process. At the same time, he took pride in training her professionally, being Pygmalion to her Galatea and thus calming her doubts. For an astonishingly long time, this rare symbiosis brought them mutual rewards.

Returning to England in September, Vivien hurried into a supporting role in *A Yank at Oxford* while Korda took up his option and cast Olivier in a film with Merle Oberon (Korda's leading lady since 1932 and soon to be his wife). Filmed in Technicolor, *The Divorce of Lady X* was considered a daring drawing-room comedy of manners *à la* Feydeau, with bedroom doors opening and closing, mistaken identities, and open discussions about 'what happened' and 'what didn't happen that night'. Seen years later, *The Divorce of Lady X* has scarcely a single amusing line, nor enough action or absurdity to be farce. Bloated with dialogue, it was made to unite the dark exoticism of Oberon with the candid charm of Olivier. But only in one stingingly misogynistic speech does Olivier find a mature tone; otherwise the screenplay offered him little and the audience less.

Offscreen life was far more pleasant. Ralph Richardson's company was invariably amusing during breaks in shooting, and often on weekends they tootled round London in Ralph's car, enjoying an easy camaraderie. By the end of October, Olivier and Vivien had settled into Durham Cottage, where with exquisite care she at once set to redecorating the place and to designing a Regency dining room to be added later. Selecting soft shades of blue and cream as the dominant colours throughout the house, she began to pore through antique and auction magazines, and eventually, she selected original works of art by Sickert, Epstein, Degas and Corot. Olivier admired her taste but not her airy unconcern for economy, and one observer thought the house had 'an almost claustrophobic prettiness [in which] Larry was rather like an unfortunate bull in a china shop'. His tastes were simpler – his small study, for example, was never as tidy nor as fancily designed as Vivien wished – and several years would pass before he felt comfortable in such elegance.

When the furniture was in place and the paint had dried, they invited Ralph Richardson and his wife to celebrate the coincidence of Vivien's birthday with Guy Fawkes Night on 5 November. Richardson, arriving at Durham Cottage with a box of fireworks, went to the garden and set off a rocket which unfortunately flew back into the dining room, burning the new curtains and destroying expensive antique crockery. Vivien was incensed, Olivier merely inconvenienced; Richardson summoned his wife and they departed, but not before the front doorknob came off in his grasp.

Olivier had no time to supervise the cleaning up, for he was in the midst of rehearsals at the Old Vic. With the respected French director Michel Saint-Denis, he was preparing to play Macbeth, a role he had coveted since his early days as Lennox and Malcolm. The murderously aspiring general and king was, he felt, at last within reach of his talent: 'I was just thirty, very fit, mentally very much in control and still bursting with ambition.' Judith Anderson, who had been John Gielgud's Gertrude in his New York *Hamlet* in 1936, was engaged as Lady Macbeth.

Saint-Denis and Olivier had long offstage discussions about finding the meaning of the play through the verse – not by ignoring it, as Olivier sometimes did. According to Basil Langton, who taught with

Saint-Denis at the London Theatre Studio (and who played Lennox and was Olivier's understudy), Saint-Denis was committed to theatre as an actor's art:

> He taught Larry the primacy of the text and insisted the stage was the actor's medium, a place for the actor's art – the director was only a temporary mentor . . . For Michel, the text was a primary devotion and technique came from the text: no system or personal method could be imposed on it.

The influence of this collaboration cannot be overstressed, for henceforth Olivier always studied a verse text with almost religious fervour. Ever mindful of the injunctions of those he considered more schooled than himself, he devoted many hours to studying the placement of words within a metrical scheme. In so doing, he discovered those rich, manifold subtexts which give a character depth and complexity.

The rehearsals loped towards the planned premiere on Tuesday, 23 November, but as if to fulfil the hoary superstition that 'the Scottish play' curses its presenters, the production was overcome with trouble. Saint-Denis barely escaped death in a taxi accident; Olivier was nearly brained by a falling stage sandbag; the scenery did not fit the stage; Darius Milhaud was not happy with his musical score and kept tearing up pages of composition; and Lilian Baylis's favourite dog died, pitching her into depression. The company continued gamely, and the final dress rehearsal lasted until well after midnight on Monday, but serious lighting problems could not be corrected and this, along with Olivier's heavy chest cold and incipient laryngitis, forced the postponement of opening night until Friday, 26 November. Then, on Thursday evening, Lilian Baylis died suddenly at her home in Stockwell; the play opened next night, but with a weary and heartsick cast.

Unaccountably, given Saint-Denis's theories, the actors were overwhelmed by a rather hysterically overdecorated production, top-heavy with grotesque props, make-up and costumes. Olivier wore a huge false face, a putty chin and forehead, enormous eyebrows and a yellow pallor – an appearance inspiring Vivien's description on opening night: 'You hear Macbeth's first line, then Larry's make-up comes on, then Banquo comes on, then Larry comes on.' As Olivier himself admitted much later, 'I "made up" to play Macbeth, instead of letting Macbeth play through me. I had everything outwardly and not enough inwardly. I think, in that production, Macbeth was nearer my sleeve than my heart.' But audiences loved it and were entertained rather than offended by the production's many gaffes. Tickets were sold out, and the run was held over and transferred to the New Theatre.

For all its difficulties, Olivier earned the best reviews of his career. Attacking Macbeth with a nervous intensity, he traced a process of moral deterioration with an odd dignity. Terrifying in the short night-scene before Banquo's murder, he was also Machiavellian in briefing the murderers and simultaneously doomed by his own character. Vigilant and crafty, his Macbeth was a weak man but a bold soldier, and the performance was full of dazzling subtleties revealing Olivier's close study of the text. In later years, he dismissed the performance as negligible, but it was certainly not so for him in 1937. Indeed, it was his most intense performance thus far, conveying a profound sense of the usurper's guilt: he seemed, according to one who saw the play, 'closed in by darkness' when performing Macbeth, and early on performance days his mood altered noticeably. Olivier's mind was entirely wrapped in the verse, and those who heard him never forgot the sense of doom as he said: 'Light thickens; and the crow makes wing to the rooky wood: good things of day begin to droop and drowse, whiles night's black agents to their prey do rouse.'

As Basil Langton recalled, Olivier's shrieking on seeing Banquo's ghost became louder and more protracted, an unearthly howl that eventually gave him laryngitis. Equally memorable was Olivier's spectacular onstage fight, acted so lustily that the various Macduffs were all hurt. Once he gashed Ellis Irving so badly that he had to be replaced in mid-performance by Roger Livesey, whom Olivier led forward for a solo bow at the curtain call.

During the run of *Macbeth*, Olivier and Vivien were plagued by the refusals of Holman and Jill to grant divorces, and this introduced a new strain. Additionally, they both felt the pain of separation from their children; their guilt must have been sharpened when a few friends, expressing shock over such abandonment, withdrew from their social circle.

Vivien was often at the Old Vic on her own business that December, for she had been cast as Titania in Guthrie's production of *A Midsummer Night's Dream*. Company members recalled that sometimes she arrived bearing oysters and champagne, and she and Olivier would disappear into the privacy of his small dressing room; by such behaviour she was, it seems, trying to force their spouses to action.

*

At the beginning of 1938, Olivier was still wearing the heavy make-up of Macbeth for the three-week extension at the New Theatre (a transfer necessary to accommodate the Christmas hold-over of *A Midsummer Night's Dream* at the Old Vic). In mid-January, he and Judith Anderson joined a small crew at Alexandra Palace, whence excerpts from *Macbeth* were broadcast to the few cumbersome television sets in London. To no one's surprise, the Old Vic then announced that Laurence Olivier would appear in three major roles during the latter half of the 1937–38 season – the first of these being Iago to Ralph Richardson's Othello, directed by Guthrie.

The evening of 'Ralph's Rocket' (as the two men always called it) had not shattered the friendship along with the crockery. Richardson was a genial soul, serious about his craft but not so driven with ambition as Olivier. Offstage, mischief and a bit of risk were still Richardson hallmarks, and he often pub-hopped with Olivier after work. But onstage he was earnest and prudent, and Olivier often asked his friendly advice before undertaking a role or making a major decision. Richardson's approach to acting was a plain and instinctive attack, without detailed analysis or deliberation; the beauty of a play, he insisted, was in 'the magnificence of its rhetoric – never mind your psychology!'

To such a style no director could have been less sympathetic than Tyrone Guthrie, whose approach to *Othello* repeated his method with *Hamlet*: he would first discuss the play with Ernest Jones. At Guthrie's request, Olivier accompanied him to Jones's office in Regent's Park for two long evenings of textual analysis, during which the Othello–Iago relationship was easily interpreted for them by the Freudian acolyte. Iago was not, they were told, jealous of the Moor; rather he was subconsciously in love with him, and this homosexual attraction led to his destruction of Othello's marriage to Desdemona. Olivier later asked Guthrie his opinion of such an idiosyncratic reading. 'It's inescapable – on an unconscious plane, of course,' Guthrie replied. 'Of course,' Olivier said, 'but I don't think we dare tell Ralphie.' (In his autobiography, Guthrie quickly passed over the *Othello* production, and his reference to Jones coyly avoids any mention of the Freudian reading.)

But the odd idea of Iago's subconscious love became quite overt as rehearsals proceeded: Othello's third-act words, 'Now art thou my lieutenant' evoked an almost amusingly lascivious tone in Iago's reply, 'I am your own forever.' Richardson coped with all this by ignoring it – until the moment Olivier threw his arms round his neck and kissed him full on the mouth. 'There, there now, dear boy,' Richardson said gently. But Olivier went even further in the first matinee. Othello had to collapse in anguish over Iago's goading, and Olivier fell beside him, deliberately simulating an orgasm. 'I'm sure I have no idea what you were up to when you threw yourself on the ground beside Ralph,' said Athene Seyler to Olivier backstage. Thus ended the blatant sexuality of the performance, on which Richardson later simply commented, 'Bold. Laurence was always very bold.' Laurence was also continuously inventive, for he played Iago as a witty rogue, clever and insinuating: instead of shock he now went for comedy. To the actor playing Brabantio he said, 'You are . . . [pause, smile] . . . a Senator.' ('He played for laughs [and] always got them,' according to Audrey Williamson, the Old Vic historian.)

Following her appearance as Titania, Vivien filmed *St Martin's Lane* with Charles Laughton and Rex Harrison (and, in a supporting role, Tyrone Guthrie); otherwise she was professionally idle until September. This enabled her to beg Leigh Holman to grant her a divorce. Since 1857 (when divorce first became possible without a private Act of Parliament), adultery was effectively the sole ground for the legal dissolution of a marriage. In January 1938, progressive liberalisation of the law extended the grounds to include desertion, cruelty and incurable insanity; the reward for the offended party was financial support and child custody. Offering her husband the opportunity now to claim desertion instead of (or in addition to) adultery, Vivien was again rebuffed; Holman still expected her to return, and he permitted her a few awkward visits to Suzanne.

As for Jill (who was occupied with a series of minor West End roles and a more satisfying personal life with a lady companion), she too stood adamant. Olivier had scarcely any contact with her or with Tarquin; in an odd way, he was so involved with his career that he seems to have expected the matter to resolve itself – or to have Vivien resolve it for him.

Iago was Olivier's sixth major Shakespearean role in sixteen months, and despite critical and popular division over his portrayals there could be no doubt of his astonishing range and versatility. As with Gielgud's invitation in 1935, he may not have undertaken these roles had Guthrie not approached him, nor would he, by 1938, have so developed without them as to be considered a serious classical actor.

But Guthrie was not limited to traditional plays any more than he was to traditional interpretations of them. He hoped the Old Vic might be the seed of a national theatre, and because part of that goal was to include new works he offered Olivier the leading role in *The King of Nowhere*, by James Bridie, whom Guthrie had championed throughout the decade. Rehearsing daily and performing Iago at night, Olivier opened in Bridie's anti-fascist diatribe in March. As a half-mad actor who escapes from a lunatic asylum and, at the instigation of a rich spinster, becomes the leader of a new political party, Olivier luxuriated in the tragicomic tone and gave a performance superb out of all proportion to the play's merits. From his first entrance, he played the actor with a haunted vitality and insolent bitterness, and he particularly revelled in the opportunity to recite the madman's sudden leap into lines from *King Lear*:

> Blow, wind, and crack your cheeks! Rage!
> You cataracts and hurricanoes, spout
> Till you have drenched our steeples . . .

Otherwise, the play's message about the rise of dictators was, however timely, drowned in a sea of muddled simplicities.

The role of Miss Rimmer, the rich woman, was taken by Marda Vanne, with whom Gwen Ffrangçon-Davies shared a home in Holly Place, Hampstead. One evening they invited Olivier and Vivien to dinner and included Sybil Thorndike and her husband Lewis Casson. The evening was auspicious, for Casson, who had been invited by Guthrie to stage *Coriolanus* at the Old Vic in April, offered Olivier the unsympathetic and demanding title role; Sybil was to play Volumnia, his furious, steely mother. Far more laborious to prepare than Bridie's unstable actor, the Roman aristocrat is another kind of dictator – the arrogant patrician unable to control both his temper and the people he must court to achieve his coveted position. Prior to 1938, the play was only rarely performed except at Stratford and the Old Vic, for *Coriolanus* was not generally ranked among Shakespeare's great tragedies, and extreme physical stress is placed on the leading actor. Perhaps for precisely these reasons, Olivier at once accepted Casson's offer, and as he prepared the part, deeper affinities became clear.

*

Laurence Olivier at thirty had not come to his success easily, and despite fierce efforts of mind and body, continual learning and constant risk, he felt he had not yet achieved anything like complete mastery of his art nor of himself. The demands on his memory, the physical challenges he assumed for each role, the meticulous textual study, the experiments with make-up, the steady effort to require more of himself in a new role than he had in the preceding one – these had become habits consistent with both duty and ambition.

His was a collaborative craft, and he relished the professional camaraderie and the occasional moments of relaxation with fellow actors. His private life, too, now provided him with great satisfactions. But to neither friends nor to Vivien would he ever give himself with the complete abandonment he reserved for his art.

Olivier's closest associates and lovers always noted something elusive and remote in him. The reservoir from which he drew was fed not only by his own emotional history but also by a sense of emptiness and a consequent neediness. This awareness of inadequacy was suffused by a mysterious gift, enabling him to pass the single beam of his own humanity through the prism of a role – and the emerging, manifold ray reached the countless different lives of his spectators. His wide empathy made the roles astonishingly, often alarmingly effective – and this he accomplished onstage with remarkable frequency. His portraits were credible and the play rang true because from emptiness he was able to convey something of that complete humanity always just beyond anyone's individual grasp.

In his Romeo, Mercutio, Hamlet, Henry, Macbeth and Coriolanus, audiences beheld something recognisably true about human life – not because Olivier communicated himself, but because he submerged himself. Sometimes this was done through the externals of make-up and what appeared to be mere bodily bravado. But there was in this proud and ambitious man a paradoxical humility. He was most himself when he was pretending to be another. Familiar with both frailty and failure, he always suspected that even at their best his intimate relations might abandon him; they had, of course, in the death of his mother, the distance of his father and the disappointment of Jill. This suspicion can be called cynicism; it can also be a sign of a maturity that does not ask of anyone more than he can provide.

Precisely through his own humanity – deeper by far than that of Coriolanus – he acted the role with a combination of icy pride and a thawed tenderness to the character's wife and mother. Creating a

Coriolanus both austere and humorous, he was splendid in wrath and cloaked in a royal fatalism. Sybil Thorndike, as his mother Volumnia, was an ally in this creation, and Casson's direction of the scenes with her elicited much of the complex pathos of Olivier's performance. Those who saw the production long remembered the nightly hush falling over the audience near the play's end, when – in perhaps the character's only moment of inner epiphany – Olivier poignantly and literally stressed Shakespeare's own stage direction: 'He holds [Volumnia] by the hand, silent,' and says with exquisite gentleness to her who had taught him unyielding arrogance: 'O mother, mother! What have you done?'

There was critical praise for the resonance in Olivier's voice, admiration for the daringly majestic death scene in which he toppled down a flight of stairs, rolled over three times and came to a dead stop just short of the footlights. He was, as one usually diffident critic wrote, 'the nearest thing we have today to the heroic tradition'.

In this, his last London stage performance for six years, Olivier revealed a soaring artistic maturity. Arriving at the Old Vic in late 1936 as a virtually untried Shakespearean actor, he departed less than two years later as a first-rate performer capable of giving the rhetoric of Coriolanus a musical poetry and a human depth. In a role that Garrick had ignored and that had confounded Kean and Irving, Olivier had finally established himself as a classical actor of the highest eminence.

In little more than a year at the Old Vic, Laurence Olivier had undertaken a professional schedule for which formidable is too weak a word. Playing the exhausting role of Hamlet each night, he was memorising the lines and rehearsing the gestures of Toby Belch onstage by day. He then at once learned and rehearsed the demanding part of Henry V while performing Toby at night. The rigours of absorbing thousands more lines as Macbeth – in a difficult and stylised production – accompanied his study of Iago, and while in that role he memorised the harsh, staccato dialogue of *The King of Nowhere*. Performing that part each night, he was memorising and rehearsing each day for Coriolanus, one of the most intimidating roles in Shakespeare, physically demanding, emotionally draining and intellectually taxing: the role contains more than three thousand lines of verse.

From winter 1936 to spring 1938, then, he had learned more than twelve thousand lines of Shakespeare in a schedule of performance and rehearsal that remains perhaps unique in the history of acting. Such demands would leave any man with no time for a personal life, but this period was dense with conflict and with the clash of duties and devotions. Leaving Jill and Tarquin was no easy decision whatever his passion for Vivien, and Vivien herself – mercurial, hyperactive, exquisitely sensitive – was never an easy companion. Ambitious, driven, subject to guilt, full of energy, a lover of pranks and drinks, he drew from his work the confidence to pursue his much needed private life with Vivien. And because every element of that private life was delicate and precarious, he pitched himself – with the utmost vengeance – into all the exigencies of an arduous craft and an exhausting schedule that would have daunted any of his great predecessors in the theatre.

The last performance of *Coriolanus* was on the eve of Olivier's thirty-first birthday, and in early June he and Vivien departed for an eight-week holiday, touring through France (in her old Ford), where they sampled the richest offerings of *la route gastronomique*, idled on the Riviera and poked through the ancient towns of his Huguenot ancestors. 'Idyllic,' he later called the journey that provided 'the glowing fulfilment of every desire of the wayward lovers'.

Their itinerary had been left with their London agents, and in early July a cable awaited Olivier at a Provençal hotel. Alexander Korda had arranged for a loan-out of Merle Oberon to producer Samuel Goldwyn, who for her first starring vehicle had chosen to make a film of Emily Brontë's *Wuthering Heights*. Would Larry and Vivien be interested in joining the cast? Olivier replied cautiously; he had, after all, no glowing memories of Hollywood – and if Merle Oberon were to be Cathy to his Heathcliff, Vivien, they reasoned, must have been destined for the subordinate and therefore unacceptable role of Isabella.

In Roanne-sur-Loire two weeks later was a detailed letter for them from Olivier's agent. *Wuthering Heights* was to be a major film and the director, William Wyler – who had seen Olivier onstage in *The Green Bay Tree* and *Ringmaster* – awaited them in London. There was also a copy of the screenplay by Ben Hecht and Charles MacArthur; even a quick perusal revealed its excellence. (Hecht, one of Hollywood's most brilliant and prolific screenwriters, had suggested Olivier to Goldwyn.) During dinner at Durham Cottage, Vivien sweetly but steadfastly insisted to Wyler that she would not play a role supporting

Merle Oberon, despite Wyler's protests that Isabella was as fine a part as she could expect at this point in her career.

This caused a dilemma for Olivier: Wyler had readily convinced him that Heathcliff was a role not to be rejected, but Vivien was almost frantic at the thought of his departure. Encouragement for Olivier's signing was also forthcoming from Ralph Richardson, again his cinematic co-star in an inconsequential spy comedy called *Q Planes*, made quickly in September. (Olivier was required to do little more than pose handsomely in the film.)

That same month, Vivien was onstage in *Serena Blandish*, alienating her director during rehearsals by bringing Olivier for additional coaching. Because she had agreed to repeat her Christmas appearance as Titania at the Old Vic, she would, Olivier reasoned with her, be occupied until mid-January – by which time he would be near to completing *Wuthering Heights*.

And so, on her twenty-fifth birthday – 5 November 1938 – Vivien drove him to Southampton, where he boarded the *Normandie*. Among the other passengers was Noël Coward and the actor Leslie Howard, who was going to Hollywood to appear in Selznick's *Gone With the Wind*. Olivier studied the screenplay of *Wuthering Heights* each morning during the crossing; in the afternoons he wrote to or telephoned Vivien; in the evenings he dined with Coward or producer Herbert Wilcox and his wife, the actress Anna Neagle.

On 10 November he arrived in New York and three days later was in Los Angeles, where he went to the Goldwyn Studios for make-up and wardrobe tests and meetings with the producer and director. To his surprise, he received a cable from Vivien within a week. Sprung free from her Old Vic commitment and unable to bear the separation, she had purchased a steamship ticket, and on the twenty-seventh she embarked for America.

But loneliness was not the primary inducement for her departure. Although her agent's long-distance arguments had failed to convince Selznick, Vivien herself was still determined to play Scarlett O'Hara in *Gone With the Wind*. While the *Majestic* and its passengers pitched and rolled amid wild seas and a severe storm, Vivien was calmly undiverted. She read for the fifth time Margaret Mitchell's novel and she studied three volumes of American Civil War history. As her Larry-boy had often claimed, even the elements could not withstand the strength of Vivien's will.

CHAPTER SEVEN

1938–1940

I have night's cloak to hide me from their sight.

Romeo, in *Romeo and Juliet*

Like almost every English actor of the 1930s, Laurence Olivier was frankly contemptuous of movie acting: it was something serious players did only for the fame and the money, returning as quickly as possible to the theatre, the only true forum (they maintained) for the craft. Nothing in his Hollywood experience from 1938 to 1940 encouraged him to alter that view, for the movie roles he undertook were essentially supporting characters in the shadow of women, parts unlikely to advance his goal of a major stage career. Nevertheless, in November 1938 he applied himself diligently to preparing for Heathcliff. During the ten days of wardrobe fittings and camera tests he memorised the entire role, attempting to build a coherent character according to the logic of theatrical preparations although, as he knew, the scenes would be shot out of continuity, according to the schedule of all those variables affecting filming, among them set construction, actor availability and weather.

The rigours of the theatre had not only toughened Olivier: they had also won him rich psychological satisfaction in the praise of critics, the applause of audiences and the approval of colleagues he respected. The call sheet for the first day of rehearsals on *Wuthering Heights* (Monday, 28 November 1938), listed no other actors with his theatre background, and neither producer Samuel Goldwyn nor director William Wyler had ever worked in the theatre. This, Olivier reasoned, made him different from his colleagues, and perhaps also a better judge of fine acting. Thus Olivier brought to this task (as he later freely admitted) a smug, superior attitude, perhaps exacerbated by his edgy impatience over Vivien's impending arrival. *Wuthering Heights* was merely a job to endure before returning home richer. Trouble could have been predicted, and the entire picture (which began filming on 5 December) was painful for just about everyone involved.

First, Olivier much resented Merle Oberon, whom he had liked well enough during *The Divorce of Lady X* but who was now cast in what he felt should be Vivien's role. During production, he seemed to assume aspects of Heathcliff's character, treating Oberon as if she were (in his own words) 'a little pickup by Korda, which she was' – an especially brutal description of one about to marry a friend. This aggravated Oberon's unhappiness, for she was already enduring grief from their director: Wyler reduced her to tears in his efforts to evoke the desired reactions, and submitted her to such an ordeal in the studio-generated storm scene that she had to be admitted to hospital. When she later complained that Olivier's saliva bespattered her during an intense scene, he flew into a rage and drove her from the set: 'Why, you amateur little bitch! What's spit, for Christ's sake, between actors, you bloody little idiot?' To the director's credit, it was remarkable that none of this persistent animosity shows in the finished film.

Olivier's first scenes were grossly overacted, and both producer and director were duly alarmed. Goldwyn, uneducated but successful as an independent producer, was then as always involved in every aspect of his productions, and Wyler was a meticulous craftsman and an exacting perfectionist. The former was not remarkable for tact, nor was the latter notably articulate or specific in directing actors, who were simply asked to repeat a scene until he got what he wanted. (Nevertheless, the Goldwyn–Wyler partnership resulted in, among other classic films, *The Little Foxes*, *Mrs Miniver* and *The Best Years of Our Lives*.)

'How do you want it?' Olivier demanded of Wyler after more than a dozen takes of a single line of dialogue. 'I've done it calm, I've shouted, I've done it angry, I've done it sad, standing up, sitting down, fast, slow – how do you want me to do it?' Wyler's reply was typical: 'Better.' Olivier found this attitude galling and wasteful of time and talent: 'He would just go on to take sixty-three, saying, "That was lousy, do it again."' Accustomed to the more polite and politic ways of Coward and Gielgud, the rarefied intellectual deliberations of Guthrie and the calmly articulated directions of Saint-Denis, Olivier resented what seemed to him crude Hollywood practices.

His mood was not brightened when, after exterior filming north of Los Angeles (in Chatsworth, which stood in for the Yorkshire moors), he contracted severe athlete's foot. Bandaged and leaning on a cane, he expected Goldwyn's sympathy, but instead heard him say to Wyler: 'Willy, if this actor goes on playing the way he is, I close up the picture. Look at him – he's dirty, he's ugly, his performance is rotten, it's stagey, it's hammy!' Olivier, humiliated in front of the entire company, said in quiet defence, 'Heathcliff's a stable boy, you know.'

But Olivier still required chastening, and Wyler – thinking only of the final product – saw to it. 'What do you think you're doing?' he shouted at Olivier during a scene. 'You think you're at the Opera House in Manchester? Get off your ass and come down from that cloud, will you? I want it so I know you mean it!'

Finally, one day during production Olivier at last turned to his director: 'I suppose this anaemic little medium cannot recognise great acting.' Everyone on the set burst into laughter, and on that December day began the refinement of Laurence Olivier as a screen actor.

> He knew I couldn't be told anything. He knew I'd come to my senses in time, to some true feeling . . . [but] at the time I merely thought him a cruel bastard . . . 'I want you to be patient about this,' he said. 'You're quite wrong to take up this despising attitude . . . Don't sneer at it.'

'What Wyler was really trying to teach me was humility,' Olivier later admitted, and according to Wyler's wife Talli, by the time *Wuthering Heights* was completed the two men were great friends. But Merle Oberon resented Olivier to the end of her life, never missing an opportunity to say how uncooperative he had been and how difficult a time he had made it for everyone.

Olivier received an Academy Award nomination for his Heathcliff, but still thought film acting beneath the dignity of a serious actor. The reason was simple – his own lack of control over the finished performance. 'I haven't yet the authority to boss the director,' he said,

> [and] he is the chap who has all the fun . . . The sum total of the actor's work in a picture depends entirely upon the arbitrary manner in which the director puts together his mosaic . . . I play in films for one thing only – money.

(Gregg Toland won the Oscar for black-and-white cinematography, and Wyler, Geraldine Fitzgerald and Goldwyn were among eight others nominated; it was the year of *Gone With the Wind*.)

Olivier's Heathcliff remains one of his truest and the cinema's most deeply felt characters, with an unsentimental vulnerability and a quiet, tragic grandeur. First seen in long shot standing before a fireplace, with a threatening mastiff growling at an intruding stranger, Olivier seems the prototypical Gothic antagonist – enigmatic, handsome and miserably withdrawn from any human communion. But as the history of his character unfolds, he is shown as the victim of others' emotional caprice and deliberate cruelty. His face registers astonishment at both, until the look of innocence finally bears the traces of wariness.

When Cathy rejects Heathcliff in favour of Edgar Linton, Olivier has some of his finest moments onscreen, his pain mingled with a compelling gaze of moral outrage. 'Cathy,' he says in a voice dry with anguish and the fear of loss, 'why did you stay so long in that [Linton] house?' In that single, simple line, the actor conveyed the lucidity of a love both whole and uncritical, thinking only of being with the beloved no matter the cost to himself, no matter how painful. Then, as she berates him for his rude background and his dirty, workman's hands, he glances down at them piteously, almost choking with humiliation: 'That's all I am to you, a pair of dirty hands.'

But as he tells the housekeeper Ellen soon after, 'I want to crawl to her feet, whimper to be forgiven for loving her, for needing her more than my own life – for belonging to her more than my own soul.' Wyler's direction and Olivier's access to his own feelings fused sublimely, for there was in Heathcliff a longing for a deep attachment and the gradual awareness that in that consuming love he was losing something of himself. For the naked emotion in his delivery of these lines he may have drawn, however unconsciously, on his own passion for Vivien, to whom he always felt culturally and intellectually inferior, and whom he sometimes resented for precisely the grip she had on his life. Wearing little make-up, Olivier achieved a portrait beyond dissimulation; an unusual clarity of expression gave his Heathcliff a raw power and tenderness that remain a standard for classic film acting.

Before the first week's shooting was complete, Vivien was sharing Olivier's suite at the Beverly Hills Hotel – but not for long, for his agent Myron Selznick introduced her to his brother David in circumstances straight from the pages of a romantic novel.*

* To further identify her career with Olivier's and to advance her own, Vivien was taking steps to leave her London agent, John Gliddon, and sign as a client of Myron Selznick, whose offices were powerful in both London and Los Angeles and who represented (among many other major stars) Olivier, Helen Hayes, Katharine Hepburn, Carole Lombard, Merle Oberon, Ginger Rogers, Fred Astaire, Gary Cooper, Henry Fonda and Fredric March.

To make room at the Selznick studios in Culver City for the construction of *Gone With the Wind*'s Tara and for the Atlanta railway station, long unused standing sets (for *King Kong*, among others) had to be removed. The plan was to dress these sets with appropriate false fronts and set them afire, thus enabling Selznick to film the burning of Atlanta sequence. Thirty-four pieces of Los Angeles firefighting equipment stood nearby on that Saturday evening, 10 December. Myron brought Olivier and Vivien to the conflagration as seven Technicolor cameras rolled. As the flames leaped up against the night sky, Myron approached David. 'I want you to meet Scarlett O'Hara,' he said.

'I took one look,' the producer wrote later, 'and knew that she was right [for the part].' Next day, Vivien read lines for director George Cukor (she at once undertook diction lessons for a Southern accent) and the following week she stood for camera tests. At a Christmas Day party at Cukor's home, Vivien learned she had won the role against dozens of other candidates (among those who had been considered since 1936 were Tallulah Bankhead, Bette Davis, Paulette Goddard, Lana Turner, Jean Arthur, Joan Bennett and Anne Baxter). She was ecstatic, but Olivier was not, and no one quite understood his subdued congratulations. He seemed, in fact, to fear (as he had with Jill) that she might win the major stardom that still eluded him.

According to the mores of 1939, the lovers could not continue to cohabit at the Beverly Hills Hotel. Selznick at once rented a house for Vivien at 520 North Crescent Drive, Beverly Hills, and there he installed her and a companion-secretary named Sunny Alexander (later Sunny Lash), an employee of the Myron Selznick agency. Olivier moved in as well. But Selznick wanted to ensure, Lash recalled many years later, that the world thought of Vivien Leigh as a perfect little lady who would never think of sleeping with a man not her husband. Thus Olivier maintained his address at the Beverly Hills Hotel, but was rarely found there. He spent almost every night at the house on Crescent, arriving and departing at odd hours, and sometimes in disguise – because after it was announced that Vivien would play Scarlett, reporters kept a vigil around the place.

Not much time passed before Selznick's lieutenants informed him that Olivier was to all intents in residence, and one quiet Sunday afternoon in January he arrived unannounced and ordered Olivier out of the house, reminding them both that Vivien could be dismissed from *Gone With the Wind* on the basis of the clause forbidding 'moral turpitude'. Such was the standard of public decency required of Hollywood actors in 1939 – and such the power of the studio chief – that the lovers had, after that day, to redouble their efforts at discretion. Olivier, for several weeks, shared a house with Leslie Howard while Selznick posted round-the-clock guards at Crescent Drive. These men were rather more understanding of the situation, and mostly they chose to believe that the disguised visitor – exploiting a talent for changing his appearance – could certainly not be Miss Leigh's lover.

While the romantic intrigue continued, Selznick completed negotiations with Alexander Korda for Vivien's services. But before her participation in *Gone With the Wind* was formally announced in mid-January 1939, Olivier's fear and jealousy became clear. The day after he completed *Wuthering Heights*, he approached Selznick, at first protesting about Vivien's fee of $20,000 for *Gone With the Wind*. Nonsense, Selznick replied: her lack of fame and American film experience warranted nothing higher. But he intended to marry Vivien one day, Olivier said, and they could not endure the separations inevitably imposed on them by a seven-year contract. Besides, they intended to work together onstage in England; neither he nor Vivien was about to give that up for film acting, no matter how financially rewarding. Selznick cooperated, including in Vivien's contract a clause allowing her time off for stage work. She signed on Friday, 13 January 1939.

Olivier's interference suggests a subtle exchange of tensions between them: Vivien brought the force of a bonding passion to the affair, but he was not so stunned by it that he failed to keep a clear eye on his professional life. 'For Larry, career was his priority,' as Sunny Lash said, 'but for Vivien, the priority was Larry.'

He thought her a clever, engaging actress, but only many years later did he begin to defend her as one whose gifts were underestimated. At the time, he seems to have had a quite modest view of her talent. But he needed her presence as a kind of consort to his increasingly grand life, her extravagant homage to his ego and her conviction of his greatness. He loved her, to be sure; but his ultimate commitment was to the theatre. This was not cold escapism or an avoidance of the responsibilities of love. It was rather the natural behaviour of an artist who had a clear image of himself and his destiny. Nevertheless, for the time being, he preferred that his work and her presence correspond.

Vivien had perhaps a simpler reason for wanting to guarantee their union. She needed his blessing on her efforts to be a serious actress and his effective advancement to her stage career. Of her adoration there can be no doubt; but she was unable, at the age of twenty-six, to carve out her own identity apart from him. And much of this, it must be said plainly, had to do with their intense sexual life at this time. They were obsessed with each other, according to their friend Douglas Fairbanks, Jr.

> They seemed to be constantly impatient to get the trivialities of everyday life over with so they could just rush madly back to bed. Or anywhere else handy and preferably private . . . Vivien was extremely libidinous.

A disruption in this hothouse atmosphere was perhaps inevitable, and it came in late February – as an invitation from the actress Katharine Cornell. She was to produce and star in a new Broadway play by S.N. Behrman, who had written *Biography* and now recommended Olivier as her leading man. Olivier read the script and accepted – not because it was the role of a lifetime, but because he preferred not to wait idly while Vivien filmed *Gone With the Wind*: she had begun work on 26 January, and would be employed for six months. In addition, Vivien was upset when Selznick replaced George Cukor as director with Victor Fleming, and she had got into the habit of asking Olivier to coach her each night for the following day's scenes. The function of director *manqué* did not appeal to Olivier, and so, in the absence of any other offers of movie work after the completion of *Wuthering Heights*, he accepted the offer from Cornell and Behrman as an escape from an awkward situation.

No Time for Comedy was not so fine an addition to his career. Olivier was cast as a writer of plays for his actress wife (Cornell). He totters on the brink of an affair with a woman who persuades him that his gifts should serve more serious purposes than mere theatre comedies, and the play's three long and verbose acts present and predictably resolve the triangle the meddling woman creates. Olivier's role could hardly be described as a fitting sequel to Macbeth and Coriolanus. Vain, petulant, easily led astray and just as readily taught a tidy moral lesson, the part of Gaylord Esterbrook was from the tradition of comedies about ingenious women controlling duller men (a genre popular from *Lysistrata* to *I Love Lucy*). Written for Cornell, the play gave her its little humorous aphorisms, while Olivier (only an acolyte for the star) had to resemble the bland ideologue of *Biography*, managing to enliven the character only by comic overplaying and improvised burlesque, as when he occasionally juggled a drinking glass onstage.

Prior to its Broadway premiere, *No Time for Comedy* was presented in Indianapolis, where Olivier learned of his father's death from a stroke on 30 March. Gerard, sixty-nine and retired to country life in West Sussex, was attended by his second wife; his son's only regret was that he had never told him that his attitudes were often ignorant and full of prejudice.

At the same time, there was disturbing news from California. Vivien, scheduled for almost every one of the picture's seven hundred scenes, was dangerously exhausted from a schedule that kept her working over ninety hours a week. Up at five in the morning no matter how late the night shooting had lasted, she never complained. Apart from a Sunday brunch she offered the Hollywood English crowd almost every week (the Colmans, George Sanders, David Niven and others), she had no social life, and she was constantly miserable without Olivier, as Sunny Lash recalled.

Unaccustomed to southern California heat, Vivien submitted to the arduous demands of a complicated epic film and to Selznick's endless orders and changes, even while she found it difficult to respond to the directions of the blunt Victor Fleming after the dismissal of her gentle friend George Cukor. During the first week of April, after rehearsing the complicated sequence of the mass flight from Atlanta, dodging animals, props, caissons and four hundred extras, she ran crying from the set and demanded Olivier. Selznick, concerned, at once summoned him; released from the Indianapolis tryout, he flew to her side.

Afraid of being alone and abandoned as she was in childhood, Vivien required Olivier's protective presence – just as she had when she followed him to Hollywood in 1938, with the additional incentive of this role. By the time he arrived she was cheerful and energetic, and two quietly romantic days ended tearfully only because Selznick, requiring her on the set, denied Vivien permission to see Olivier off at the airport. After No Time for Comedy opened in New York on 17 April, he visited again for a weekend (and returned late, missing the Monday performance), and for a third visit she hounded Selznick to allow her two days with Olivier at a geographic mid-point – the Meulbach Hotel, Kansas City, which the lovers never left for two days and nights. Vivien could be cunning and conniving to get her way, according to friends like Sunny Lash and Douglas Fairbanks, Jr., but this she did with such charm no one could resist her – Olivier least of all. The visits during No Time for Comedy were the only times in his life that he compromised his professional duties for romance, and for it he bore both resentment and guilt.

He sometimes found Vivien's love, and the prodigious energies she devoted to it, overwhelming; he had such reserves only for his work, and for everything else his strength and interest were strictly rationed. But he admired her dedication to her career. Obsessed with the quality of her performance, Vivien impressed every colleague on *Gone With the Wind*, giving on camera no indication of the enormous physical demands of her role, nor of the loneliness of her separation from Larry. When, among the film's twelve nominations and eight Academy Awards, Vivien was cited as best actress of 1939, whatever feelings of jealousy Olivier may have borne – that his own performance as Heathcliff was passed over – were submerged in his clear happiness for her, and his pride in her achievement. 'I could never love anybody who wasn't talented,' Olivier said to Rachel Kempson about this time. Vivien had struggled to live up to his expectations of her, and when he saw *Gone With the Wind* he admitted that she exceeded anyone's hopes. Spoiled, haughty, amusing, romantic, strong-willed, capricious, generous, determined – her Scarlett O'Hara was shaded with every nuance of a real woman, not a Hollywood stereotype.

Olivier's life that spring of 1939 was a constant whirl of activity. Back in New York for performances of *No Time for Comedy*, he was (notwithstanding his pallid role in that play) an instant matinee idol, for the release of *Wuthering Heights* on 13 April had brought about a radical shift in his public image, if not in his movie marketability. Crowds gathered outside the Ethel Barrymore Theatre for a glimpse of the wildly tender Heathcliff offstage; autograph-seekers milled in the lobby of his hotel; stacks of fan letters were delivered daily, often containing offers of marriage.

His favourable press and instant celebrity immediately aroused the interest of Selznick, who was rushing from the set of *Gone With the Wind* to nightly story conferences with Alfred Hitchcock. Selznick had imported the English director for a seven-year contract, and their first project was to be a film of Daphne du Maurier's 1938 bestseller *Rebecca*. Before the end of June, Olivier was signed for the leading role of the coolly autocratic Maxim de Winter – an important but nonetheless supporting role to the nameless heroine. Ronald Colman was Selznick's first choice, but he sensed that the picture was centred round the leading lady, and William Powell's price was too high. (Myron Selznick, who had negotiated $20,000 for Olivier on *Wuthering Heights*, eventually got him $30,000 for *Rebecca*.)

Vivien, whose last scene in *Gone With the Wind* was completed on 27 June, at once swung into action to land the role of the nameless heroine who in marrying the widowed Maxim replaces Rebecca as mistress of Manderley. Selznick tested her (and as many hopeful actresses as he had for Scarlett), but he and Hitchcock found her too eager, too aggressive for the passive, virginal and beleaguered young wife. But they agreed to keep her under consideration as the script was finalised that summer. Confident that she would again overcome Selznick's hesitation, Vivien left Los Angeles in high spirits on 1 July. Joining Olivier in New York, she accompanied him for a weekend at the home of Katharine Cornell and her husband Guthrie McClintic in Sneden's Landing, on the Hudson River. Typically, Vivien was recreation director, arranging card games and rounds of charades. When Olivier retired early, she kept her hosts awake until the small hours with spirited theatre talk and her lively hopes that she and Larry would act together in *Rebecca*.

Since filming would not begin until September, they boarded the *Ile de France* on 11 July, and in London they again discussed divorce with their spouses and had brief, awkward reunions with their children. Durham Cottage seemed cramped and forlorn after their American accommodations, and everywhere there were preparations for war. Not as cavalier as Scarlett about impending conflict, Vivien was tense and ill at the summer news: Nazi troops moved into Danzig and into North Africa, and France began mobilising.

On 17 August, Olivier and Vivien returned to New York; with them was Vivien's mother, Gertrude Hartley, treated to an American holiday. During the crossing, a cable from Selznick informed Vivien that she was simply wrong for the part in *Rebecca* and that her career, about to be greatly enhanced by the release of *Gone With the Wind*, would be damaged if she undertook an inappropriate role. At the same time, Selznick cabled Olivier, reminding him that Vivien had been entirely uninterested in *Rebecca* before Olivier was signed, and since they would both in any case be working in Hollywood she need have no fear of further separations. At the end of August, Olivier rented a house at 606 North Camden Drive and Vivien officially returned to Crescent – although (to the dismay of her mother) she spent most nights with Olivier.

On Sunday, 3 September, Douglas Fairbanks, Jr., and his wife together with David Niven, Olivier, Vivien and her mother were aboard a boat anchored off Catalina Island. They gathered round a radio to hear Neville Chamberlain's declaration of war against Germany, and then poured drinks. Olivier became quite vociferously drunk, lowered himself into a rowing boat, and went out into the harbour, shouting to those in the other boats, 'This is the end – you're all finished – drink up and enjoy yourselves – it's all over!' At last his friends hauled him back onboard. Within an hour, the harbour was lively not only with war news, but with the scandalous report of a drunk and disorderly Ronald Colman (whose yacht had also dropped anchor there). When an apology was demanded of Colman by the harbourmaster, he had no idea what the man was talking about, and it was some time before he found out the identity of his double.

London issued no immediate call for potential soldiers from among residents abroad; indeed, if every eligible young Englishman returned, there would have been an enormous drain on an unstable economy. Soon the British ambassador to Washington, on orders from his government, issued a directive: British actors in Hollywood were representing the best of their country,

> partly because they are continually championing the British cause in a very volatile community which would otherwise be left to the mercies of German propagandists, and because the continuing production of films with a strong British tone is one of the best and subtlest forms of British propaganda.

The British in Hollywood, in other words, were to be effective means of galvanising American sympathy for England and, it was to be hoped, for eventual active collaboration.

Among 'films with a strong British tone' none is more exemplary than the Selznick–Hitchcock *Rebecca*, which began production on Friday, 8 September. Set in Cornwall, directed by an Englishman and produced by an anglophile, the picture had an authentically English atmosphere, and the cast was virtually a roll-call of the British community abroad – among them Gladys Cooper, Nigel Bruce, Leo G. Carroll, C. Aubrey Smith, Melville Cooper and Joan Fontaine, whose American mother had married an Englishman.

Selznick demanded of Hitchcock and his writers as much fidelity to the popular novel as the film form would allow, and with some concessions to censorship *Rebecca* closely follows du Maurier and the genre of modern Gothic romance. Selznick's lavish production values and Hitchcock's unerring use of camera, light and shadow resulted in a film of quirky humour and ominous, desperate romanticism, and some of the story's neurotic gloom was reflected in the circumstances of production. Olivier, resentful of Joan Fontaine as he was of Merle Oberon during the filming of *Wuthering Heights*, is entirely convincing when his character treats her brusquely and condescendingly; indeed, he barked obscenities freely during rehearsals. Hitchcock urged him to mind his language, adding that Fontaine had just been married. On hearing that the groom was the actor Brian Aherne, who had given up two roles which Olivier had assumed with great success, he strode off, saying to Fontaine over his shoulder, 'Couldn't you do better than that?'

Olivier's dour mood was certainly due partly to Vivien's absence from *Rebecca*, and partly to Hitchcock's method, which was diametrically opposite Wyler's: Hitchcock placed his camera where he wished and fitted his actors into a scheme of which they were only one function. Olivier found him genial enough, but he did not offer him much direction – which was often Hitchcock's way with his leading men. Likewise, the role of Maxim de Winter (in which Olivier was deliberately presented to resemble Ronald Colman) required only competence, and any actor might have felt frustrated. Even his friendly colleague Gladys Cooper, who had admired him since *The Rats of Norway*, thought him quite wrongly cast, as she wrote home to her family, 'but he is a big draw here now since they saw him in *Wuthering Heights* so what does it matter!' To Olivier, apparently, it mattered; the role was unsympathetic and certainly secondary to Fontaine's. Sophisticated and handsome but smug and condescending, de Winter is a two-dimensional character who rescues a simple girl from a boorish employer only to pitch her, ill-equipped, into the demands of her new station as a great lady.

His performance is frequently one of mere perfunctory elegance. Uncomfortable with his co-star, his role and his director's apparent diffidence, Olivier as de Winter grasps the bridge of his nose, rubs his temples, shuts his eyes and sighs, rather as if he confused spiritual anguish with a sinus headache. His pacing, too, was unnaturally tardy, as Selznick remarked to Hitchcock: 'his pauses . . . are the most ungodly slow and deliberate reactions I have ever seen. [He acts] as though he were deciding whether or not to run for President instead of whether or not to give a ball.' Except for a few final retakes, Olivier completed work on *Rebecca* in December.

23. *Above* At Denham Studios with Vivien
Leigh, 1936. *Culver Pictures*

24. *Above right* With Vivien in the film *Fire
Over England* (1936). *Culver Pictures*

25. *Right* With Vivien in *Twenty–One Days*
(1936). *National Film Archive, London*

26. As Hamlet, with Vivien as Ophelia: at Kronberg Castle, Elsinore, Denmark (1937). *Culver Pictures*

27. Unrecognisable for the first time onstage: as Toby Belch in *Twelfth Night* at the Old Vic (1937). *Theatre Museum, London*

28. In the film *Q Planes*, with Ralph Richardson (1938). *Culver Pictures*

29. Arriving in America for the film of
Wuthering Heights (1938). *Culver Pictures*

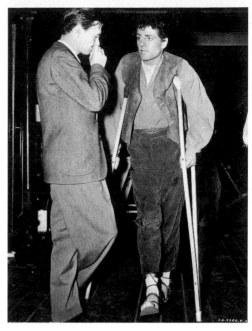

30. Suffering athlete's foot during the
filming of *Wuthering Heights*. *Culver
Pictures*

31. As Heathcliff, with Merle Oberon as Cathy. *National Film Archive, London*

32. *Above* At Selznick Studios during the filming of *Rebecca*, with Reginald Denny and Nigel Bruce (1939). *National Film Archive, London*

33. *Left* Preparing his production of *Romeo and Juliet*, while filming *Pride and Prejudice* (1940). *Culver Pictures*

34. *Below* The Rev. Gerard Kerr Olivier. *From the collection of Felix Barker*

That same month, he and Vivien rented a Spanish colonial house at 1107 San Ysidro Drive, Beverly Hills; her mother had returned to England in October to care for Suzanne. Also in December, the premiere of *Gone With the Wind* brought the cast to Atlanta. The Governor of Georgia had been persuaded by MGM (the distributors and co-financiers of Selznick's production) to declare a three-day holiday prior to the 15 December screening. More than 300,000 people jammed the city streets to hail the film stars, and for two days the *Atlanta Constitution's* front pages carried no war news – only details of the film and of the visiting stars. In an experiment, executives of the National Broadcasting Company sent four television cameras and a small crew to the premiere and beamed a live image of the celebrities' arrival to about five hundred sets then in American homes. Olivier escorted Vivien, and the story was put out by Selznick's office that he was present only to promote *Rebecca*. No journalist was that gullible, for Olivier was never seen anywhere but at Vivien's side. On Christmas Day, *Time* magazine's cover bore a colour photograph of Vivien in emerald green, as Scarlett.

The new year 1940 began with a rush of dashed expectations. In November, Olivier had signed to play Darcy after reading Aldous Huxley's literate screenplay of Jane Austen's *Pride and Prejudice*. George Cukor was to direct the film for MGM, and together they hoped that chief executive Louis B. Mayer would borrow Vivien from Selznick for the leading role of Elizabeth Bennet. But Cukor was transferred to direct the picture *Susan and God*, and Selznick loaned Vivien to Mayer not for *Pride and Prejudice* but to co-star again (after the success of *A Yank at Oxford*) with MGM's Robert Taylor in *Waterloo Bridge*. Vivien begged Mayer to replace her with Joan Crawford and put her in *Pride and Prejudice*, but Mayer assigned the role of Elizabeth to none other than Greer Garson. That winter, while Olivier was filming on one stage in Culver City, Vivien worked on another. He needed to earn money, he explained to Garson during the first week of production in January; indeed, there were two major expenses requiring immediate funds: his forthcoming marriage to Vivien and their intention to stage *Romeo and Juliet*. Both events were most energetically advanced by Vivien.

The long-coveted wedding seemed closer by 5 January when Herbert Leigh Holman filed a petition in the Probate, Divorce and Admiralty Division of the High Court of Justice, London, naming Laurence Olivier as co-respondent in an undefended suit charging adultery and seeking a divorce which would become absolute the following August. Three weeks later, Jill Esmond Olivier also sued. 'Evidence was given on affidavit,' stated the court record, 'in support of a charge that Mr Olivier and Mrs Holman had committed adultery at Christchurch Street, Chelsea.' Both injured spouses were granted child custody.

The news broke during the filming of *Pride and Prejudice*, and Olivier had to confront studio publicists and enquiring journalists while coping with the flat and humourless supporting role of Darcy. Subordinate to Elizabeth in the script, Darcy became even more so in the actual filming, for producer Hunt Stromberg – under orders from Mayer – ensured that, in close-ups, director Robert Z. Leonard and his cameraman favoured Greer Garson over Olivier by a ratio of about twenty to one: *Pride and Prejudice* remains in every sequence a celebration of her sturdy charm. Somewhat churlishly, Olivier always claimed that 'darling Greer seemed to me all wrong as Elizabeth . . . [playing her] as the most silly and affected' of the Bennet sisters. Quite the contrary: both the script and Garson's confident performance established, over every other character in the story, the quick-witted, appealing maturity of Elizabeth – exactly the qualities for which Garson rightly won the role and which she communicated directly. But Olivier was jealous of his 'discovery', as her name preceded him onscreen and in billings.

Just as with *Wuthering Heights* and *Rebecca*, Olivier's disappointment over Vivien's absence from the film was aggravated when he saw that his basic function was again to serve a leading lady. 'Acting for film,' he said at the time,

> is about as satisfying as looking at a Michelangelo fresco with a microscope. I just don't like the motion pictures: it is a director's medium, and actors just fit into a puzzle as it is being made up by the director.

But with his impeccable comic timing, Olivier infused the role with an epicene languor without effeminacy and an arrogance without cruelty.

The idea for *Romeo and Juliet* had been spearheaded by Vivien and her friend George Cukor, with whom she maintained contact during and after *Gone With the Wind*. The great tragic romance starring famous real-life lovers could not fail, Vivien and Cukor reasoned; it would also enable her and Olivier to act together, onstage and away from Hollywood, for the plan was to open in San Francisco and Chicago before proceeding to New York. Before the end of January, Cukor had matched their own investment of $48,000 with funds from Warner Bros. The expected profit would enable them to maintain their expensive lifestyle, to pay alimony and child support and to provide money for Vivien when Olivier entered military service, an eventuality of which he and his peers felt certain.

Preparations were under way while he was filming early that year. As Greer Garson recalled, he was quite preoccupied with his own plans for *Romeo and Juliet* during the shooting of *Pride and Prejudice*. And plan he did – every detail – in order to triumph abroad in the role in which he had been criticised five years earlier at home. There was also something in his self-assessment that made *Romeo and Juliet* oddly apposite, for Olivier sometimes considered himself a benighted lover, an outcast in his passionate fidelity, scorned by polite society, an exile underappreciated and underutilised by Hollywood. In support of this feeling, he saw that Vivien was regarded as more desirable by the film industry in 1940; so much was clear to Olivier from the roles they were offered and the publicity they received.

For her part, Vivien longed to establish herself as his theatrical equal, to vindicate his guidance and training of her, to be the consort of her prince and to prove that she was a serious, gifted actress and not just a Hollywood star. This unacknowledged rivalry strained their relationship, as did time itself. By 1940, the initial intensity of their great passion had predictably cooled, and their different and constantly shifting professional fortunes did little to bring them closer together. *Romeo and Juliet*, they may have felt, would enable them to recover, by a kind of sympathetic magic, the original intensity.

That they were not fairy-tale lovers was now clear to their friends. At a Cukor party, writer and director Garson Kanin overheard and later reconstructed a revealing conversation demonstrating the tarnish that had marred the golden couple. Seeing Olivier chatting with Greta Garbo, Vivien was furious with jealousy and at once demanded that Kanin drive her and Olivier home.

This would be, Kanin recalled that Vivien insisted, 'the last time I *ever* go to lunch with you! Do you hear? The last. I'd rather starve.'

'Now be reasonable, Puss –'

'Why should I be? Are you?'

'Of course.'

'Hah!'

'Oh, my God, will you give it a rest?'

'Floating around the garden like a moonstruck ninny.'

'She asked me if I would like to walk a few steps. What was I to say?'

'Did you try "No"?'

'Of course not.'

'Why not?'

'I was being polite. It's as simple as that.'

'What was so enthralling?'

'Enthralling?'

'That conversation. What was it about?'

'All right! If you insist, I'm about to tell you what it was about.'

'Thank you – and do not dissemble, if you please. You know what a rotten liar you are and how I always know when you're lying.'

'I have no intention of lying this time – there's no need.'

'Ah! Then you admit that sometimes you *do* lie?'

'Jesus, Puss! How many battles do you expect me to fight at once?'

Olivier then told Vivien that his conversation with Garbo was simply about gardens – English as compared to Swedish gardens, vegetable contrasted with fruit gardens.

'I don't believe one bloody word of all that,' Vivien said when he finished.

'No, I didn't think you would.'

It appeared that a love affair once so intense, liberating and full of promise had become – with time, geographic dislocation and shifting professional fortunes – tinged with resentments. At the core was an unforeseeable dilemma, for Vivien often performed better in pictures than Olivier, and thus far she had certainly had better roles. She seemed not quite so overwhelmed as he by the camera's proximity – like many actresses, she seemed to reveal herself willingly on film. This Olivier did better onstage; in movies he sometimes withdrew, as if the camera were a threat to his privacy. A consummate stage actor, he brought audiences to himself. Vivien went to meet them.

Additionally, in 1940 there were stronger and more complex roles for women than there were for men (and in this regard, it is perhaps important to remember how much a woman's medium film was; women provided beauty and emotion, men mere action). The best-loved, most enduring and most admired male actors tended to portray quite ordinary men, even if in extraordinary circumstances: Henry Fonda, James Stewart, John Wayne, even Errol Flynn and the glamorous types like Cary Grant and William Powell were very much of this world. The faces of women were more malleable to the transforming effects of lighting and make-up, and the great male directors exploited their beauty to express fantasies that were to some extent universal: the innocence of Lillian Gish, the erotic danger of Marlene Dietrich, the quiet anguish of Greta Garbo, the fresh, elegantly sensual allure of Vivien Leigh.

Her American film debut had made her enormously popular not only in America but around the world, but for Olivier – restless to continue the serious career he had advanced in so short a time at the Old Vic, when he was the star and she the student – there was little endorsement other than fan mail, weekly cheques and a comfortable life at a time when his country was enduring the war. Ambition, guilt, the natural fear of failure and the inevitable insecurities of any public life of performance – all these clashed with his expectations.

Their appearance together in *Romeo and Juliet* would meet their professional desires and restore his, and in a way might effect through art the idealisation of love they had not achieved in life. This is not to say that the love between Laurence Olivier and Vivien Leigh was not true and deep on its own terms; but their ambitions and their fantasies for themselves and one another were certainly nourished by the deliberate pretence (one might say the totem) that is the business of acting. And in 1940, no actors had to pretend more studiously for the press and the public than this couple. They wanted to be Romeo and Juliet.

While they filmed *Pride and Prejudice* and *Waterloo Bridge* daily during the first months of 1940, Olivier and Vivien rehearsed Shakespeare at night, at the Warner radio studio on Sunset Boulevard. He personally cast every speaking role and each extra, devoting whatever private time was necessary to evoke the character, as he had learned, through the verse. With seasoned professionals like Dame May Whitty, Ben Webster and Alexander Knox he was deferential but ready with brief, pointed suggestions, while younger actors (Cornel Wilde, Edmond O'Brien and Wesley Addy) he drilled long past midnight. Vivien, ever the perfectionist whom rehearsals invariably left dissatisfied and exhausted, regarded her own performance with an almost savage intensity, but Olivier's direction was wisely gentle and encouraging. Thoda Cocroft, engaged as publicist for *Romeo*, recalled that during every break on *Waterloo Bridge* at MGM, Vivien ran to her dressing room and worked with Dame May Whitty on their dialogue.

At home, Olivier shut himself up in his room to prepare his Romeo, working with a large mirror and reciting into a wire recorder. Everything had to be just right – the walk, the tone of voice, the historically accurate costume. But Olivier did more. He supervised the selection and adaptation of music by Palestrina, and on costume and set designs he worked closely with the trio of gifted women who called themselves collectively 'Motley' – Elizabeth Montgomery and the Harris sisters, Sophie and Percy – and he selected the red hue of Capulet Hall, the ostrich-egg blue of Juliet's room, the style and weight of each costume fabric and drapery. Olivier also insisted that the tragedy's twenty-one scenes must unfold swiftly: Romeo and Juliet meet on Sunday, marry on Monday, are separated on Tuesday and die on Thursday morning, thus giving the production an intense kinetic energy. Additionally, he supervised the construction of a massive revolving set. The exterior of the Capulet house turned to reveal public rooms and a staircase leading, after a further revolution, to Juliet's room and a balcony – which turned further to the exterior of the balcony and the garden below, with the wall for Romeo to scale with an ardent leap. Expensive, complicated and meticulously engineered, the scenes were designed like storyboards for a film.

For his second Romeo, Olivier was preparing a young, humourless and totally uninteresting boy who gradually takes on colour and character after his meeting with Juliet. At first he would be simply a bumbling colt moving with the sprawl and bounce of adolescent awkwardness – until the Mantua scene finds him almost adult, and the final act in the tomb marks his complete development as a full-grown man. This Romeo, very different from that of 1935, was a reflection of Olivier himself in the early stages of his affair with Vivien – culturally unsophisticated and requiring the transforming effects of a delicately aggressive lover. Addressing his cast one evening, he could have been speaking of Laurence Olivier and Vivien Leigh. Juliet, he said, provided the polish, the humour, the incentive for Romeo's courage; she effected the maturing of a man by the simple radiance of her fragile beauty; it was her destiny 'to pop on the cap and bells, like so many women in everyday life' whose emotional energy and humour refine their men.

Further crowding his schedule, Olivier added to daily filming and nightly rehearsals another task. Each morning before dawn he raced to Clover Field in Santa Monica, where he climbed into a small plane for flight training under Cecil Smallwood (who had also taught James

Stewart, Katharine Hepburn and Olivia de Havilland, among others). This was no mere hobby: Olivier had his hours of instruction duly logged and credited.

Olivier was in fact terrified of flying, but he saw this fear as something he had to conquer. His efforts, however serious, resulted in little skill but several close escapes from death. Olivia de Havilland saw him narrowly miss several planes in midair, and before he had completed his two hundred hours of instruction that year he had smashed into three landed aircraft and caused damage ten times at landing fields from Monterey to San Diego. Vivien was sick with worry, for he was certainly among the worst fliers in history, just as he was an absolutely reckless driver, always taking chances just as he did onstage. Back in England, friends like Ralph Richardson were training for the Fleet Air Arm; Olivier would not, he told Vivien, be known as unpatriotic or cowardly.

Romeo and Juliet opened in late March with completely sold-out performances at the Geary Theatre, San Francisco. But the opening night brought trouble. After many weeks of flying, filming, directing, supervising thousands of details, encouraging the entire company, meeting with executives from Warners, Olivier was exhausted to the point of collapse. When the moment came for him to climb Juliet's wall and bound into her garden, he leaped up and clung to the edge of the wall, too tired to lift himself over and too mortified simply to lower himself. The stage manager had to ring down the curtain. Most Bay Area critics were lenient about this and the unfortunate effects of the heavy props and sets that deadened many actors' speeches and the predominantly upstage action that left some sightlines obscured – problems which might have been avoided had Olivier not assumed virtually every responsibility for the production, losing perspective in the process.

Chicago newspapers had blared the arrival of Heathcliff and Scarlett, and a thousand screaming fans greeted them at Union Station. Olivier, tired and irritable, pushed his way through, ignoring reporters who hurled questions about their divorces. From the train, he had wired instructions for a public address system at the Chicago Auditorium, whose four thousand seats were appropriate for opera but not for Shakespeare. For himself he had no speech concerns, but he was afraid that Vivien's thin voice would not be heard beyond the footlights. That gap in style created another problem at the first Chicago performance:

Vivien, relaxed and in command of her role, could be heard clearly throughout the house – until Olivier bounded onstage. His projection was so intense he required no amplification, and his voice reverberated, drowning hers. The sound system was disconnected, Vivien was thenceforth inaudible, and hundreds of customers demanded refunds at the interval.

Frantic alterations to the production continued in Chicago. Three shipments of lumber arrived for the continual redesign of the scenery; lighting cues were reset; Olivier trained Vivien so exhaustively she nearly lost her voice, and there was considerable alarm that she might not go on to Broadway. By this time she worried that she was humiliating Olivier and ruining the entire production, but the sound was improved and the overwhelming impression was that hers was 'a personal triumph to make Scarlett O'Hara seem meagre'. He, in turn, regarded her favourable notices as unjustified by a merely adequate performance; worse, he was again receiving bad reviews for his Romeo. The entire company found him remote, unwilling to socialise or to receive guests backstage. Vivien, meanwhile – eager to please as always – wrapped gifts for each member of the troupe in anticipation of the New York premiere, but only on the way to New York did Olivier brighten, boozily singing sections of Handel's *Messiah* with Alexander Knox long into the night.

The pleasure was all too brief. On 9 May, *Romeo and Juliet* opened at New York's cavernous Fifty-First Street Theatre. A block away at Radio City Music Hall, *Rebecca* had queues stretching round two corners. *Wuthering Heights* had just been revived at suburban cinemas, and *Gone With the Wind* was still showing at the Rivoli on Broadway. None of these rescued them, for their stage production was judged a failure, smothered under the weight of its own excess and not helped by Olivier's diminished energies.

Quite apart from the unsatisfying production, there was a hidden agenda in New York society. Olivier and Leigh were generally regarded as *arrivistes*, mere movie stars with ideas above their station. With no evidence of his stage ability over the previous seven years and only two recent American movies, Olivier was unfavourably compared to Maurice Evans, the preferred exponent of Shakespeare in America who had been Katharine Cornell's Romeo in 1935 and had then played Richard II, Hamlet and Falstaff. As for Vivien, she was simply an English actress who had won an Oscar but had no consequent claim to theatrical greatness. The New York press meted out a kind of retribution to these two upstarts, and the word of mouth about the tedious three-hour production sealed their fate.

Two days after opening, as ticket-holders clamoured for refunds, Olivier and Vivien left their New York hotel, accepted Katharine Cornell's invitation to save money by residing at her home in Sneden's Landing (an hour's drive north of the city) and posted a notice that *Romeo and Juliet* would shorten its nine-week run to four. By the time the production closed on 8 June, the stars had lost their entire $48,000 investment on a show budgeted at almost $100,000 – an enormous sum for Broadway in 1940.

Olivier's performances were badly affected by this turn of events. He had not achieved his goal of proving himself anew on Broadway as he had at the Old Vic, and now Vivien's ambitions seemed beyond reasonable expectation; he may have felt that this, too, was his fault. All the players sensed some kind of trouble between them after the reviews, according to cast member Joan Shepard.

> Vivien hid in her dressing room when she was not onstage, inaccessible and unapproachable, while Olivier said she was ill. He continued to behave as if everything were fine, inspecting everyone's make-up and costumes each night and treating everyone with utmost courtesy.

Not so Vivien, whose reaction to the crowds at the stage door had changed: she routinely dismissed autograph-seekers with brusque cries of 'Fuck off – now fuck off!' ('She and Larry did not suffer fools gladly,' as Alexander Knox recalled.) They were also forced to cancel plans for a New York company that would offer Shakespeare in the repertory tradition of the Old Vic. Olivier intended to negotiate for some English players as guest performers and to train New York actors as well. This project died with *Romeo and Juliet*.

During the brief run of the play, Olivier continued his flying lessons, making solo excursions in light aircraft over the Hudson Valley each morning; by mid-June he had 250 hours credited. The Third Reich occupied Belgium and Holland, Scandinavia was invaded, France was on the verge of total capitulation and even England seemed in danger of Nazi conquest. Olivier may well have considered war service (like flying over the Hudson) not only a duty but a refuge from his personal disappointments, for he offered himself to his government. Duff Cooper, the Minister of Information, replied that the British conscription law did not apply to overseas residents over the age of thirty-one (he was just thirty-three) and that, in addition, Olivier 'may well be more use where you are'. Just as Olivier was about to intervene directly in the matter by cabling senior officers in London, a call came from Alexander Korda, who had stopped off in New York to see *Romeo and Juliet*. He was on the way to Hollywood with an outline for a film, and he offered them the leading roles.

The picture was to be outright propaganda for the British war effort, filmed safely in America where such support was most needed. Based on the story of Lord Nelson and his affair with Lady Emma Hamilton during the Napoleonic wars, the film would offer Olivier an opportunity to portray an appealing and historic patriot. And Lady Hamilton, Korda added, would be played by Vivien. With their bank accounts bare, they accepted at once, planning, with the monies earned from filming that autumn, to return to England. By mid-July they were back in Los Angeles, renting a house at 9560 Cedarbrook Drive, Beverly Hills, and devoting themselves to research on their roles and meetings with Korda, who was to produce and direct.

To his genuine dismay, Korda found Olivier and Vivien less than the blissful couple he had last seen in England. She seemed to cling obsessively to Olivier, frantically eager to please him, and he in turn appeared to find her slightly hysterical and overwhelming in her devotion; predictably, he began to withdraw and she became more fixated on his presence.

In August, their divorces became final and they planned a wedding at the San Ysidro Ranch, a cluster of bungalows in Montecito, near Santa Barbara. Shortly after midnight on 31 August 1940 – with their acquaintances Garson Kanin and Katharine Hepburn hastily corralled as witnesses – they drove north. Throughout the trip, as Kanin recalled, Olivier and Vivien argued bitterly about the correct route. Finally, in a forty-second ceremony before police judge Fred T. Harsh, Laurence Kerr Olivier and Vivian Mary Holman were wed at last. The groom, thirty-three, gave his address as 4 Christchurch Street, London; in a sly nod to propriety, his twenty-six-year-old bride listed hers as Durham Cottage, Chelsea. Without stopping to accept a kiss from the sleepy spectators, the Oliviers sped south to San Pedro Harbor, where Ronald Colman had offered his yacht for a brief honeymoon. Three days later, they were back at Cedarbrook Drive, and before the week was out they were fitted for costumes as two of the most notorious lovers in British history.

CHAPTER EIGHT

1940–1945

Jesu! Jesu! the mad days that I have spent.

Shallow, in *Henry IV, Part Two*.

Alexander Korda's film *That Hamilton Woman* (released in Britain as *Lady Hamilton*), made quickly and cheaply in early autumn 1940, tells of Horatio Nelson's heroics in the Napoleonic wars at the turn of the nineteenth century, his honour tarnished by a long affair with Emma, Lady Hamilton. Korda, fulfilling a promise to his friend Prime Minister Winston Churchill, deliberately produced a picture alluding to the contemporary crisis: Napoleon as Hitler, Nelson as Churchill ('Look out, Bonaparte,' Olivier/Nelson cries while gazing from a ship, 'by Gad we shall lick you now!'). The casting of offscreen lovers onscreen was a brilliant idea inspired by Korda's affection and admiration for the Oliviers.

With Nelson, Olivier may have thought he was becoming typecast as a player of period roles. Heathcliff and Darcy had been such, and despite modern dress, Maxim de Winter lived in a pre-modern, madly Gothic Cornwall; all of them were moodily unpredictable, scowling autocrats. In *That Hamilton Woman*, his first frankly heroic film part, Olivier epitomised historic valour; unfortunately, the character as written lacked both depth and passion.

His entrance into the action is accompanied by the triumphal music of 'Rule, Britannia!' and he becomes progressively more scarred in battle, more noble with achievement. He ages, whereas Emma matures into a rapturous beauty whose experiences mark her only with depth, and despite the centrality of Nelson, the film narrative was hers; the camera favoured her, and with good reason, for Emma was the more richly written, more sympathetic role. ('I have quite a good part as Lady Nelson,' Gladys Cooper wrote to her family during production, 'but they are making me play her very disagreeable so as not to take the sympathy away from Vivien as Lady Hamilton!')

In addition, the dialogue was invariably double-edged, and even Nelson's crew have the opportunity to read a message hung on flags from the mast, each reciting a word of 'England expects that every man will do his duty.' No amount of disfiguring make-up and no degree of Olivier's understated technique could make the character anything but a wooden mouthpiece for Churchill:

> I would not for the sake of any peace, however fortunate, consent to sacrifice one jot of England's honour. Hitherto there has been nothing greater known on the continent than the faith, the untainted honour, the generous public sympathies, the high diplomatic influence, the commerce, the grandeur, the irresistible power, the unconquerable valour of the British nation.

No wonder the finished film was a favourite of the Prime Minister, who frequently screened it for dignitaries and friends.

But *That Hamilton Woman* was a triumph for Vivien, and this Olivier knew during shooting even before Korda placed her name before Olivier's in the titles and in advertising: she was still the more valuable and bankable star, and she gave a magnificent performance. Her husband may well have recalled Jill's primacy in Hollywood eight years earlier; in any case, the increasing and unavoidable contrast between his situation in film studios and his theatrical career strengthened his resolution to return to England. Vivien readily agreed. *That Hamilton Woman* was the last film they appeared in together.

The Oliviers were not intimately attached to the clubby British contingent in Hollywood, a group that met for cricket at the home of C. Aubrey Smith and for tea at Cedric Hardwicke's. These and others of the clique (among them Basil Rathbone, Claude Rains, Aldous Huxley, Ray Milland, Ronald Colman and Herbert Marshall) Olivier regarded somewhat disdainfully, considering them professional Englishmen who privately hated Hollywood while luxuriating in fat salaries and comfortable southern California living.

His ambitions were greater than his achievements, however, and by late 1940 he looked forward to the risky excitement and challenges of the English stage – or at least, temporarily, the honourable risk of military service. His decision that they would depart as soon as possible after *That Hamilton Woman* was perhaps confirmed by the additional strain put on their marriage by Vivien's popularity – and by the marriage itself, rather an anticlimax after four years of dramatically flouting convention. England, they both may have reasoned, would restore them to their true professional and personal destinies.

Before the Oliviers departed, they met briefly with their children. Vivien visited her daughter Suzanne, who had been shipped out to Canada and lived there with Vivien's mother, and Olivier saw Tarquin, then (with Jill) visiting Robert Montgomery's farm in upstate New York. Later, Jill took Tarquin and moved to the fashionable section of westside Los Angeles known as Brentwood; there she lived happily with Ella Voysey, who was separated from her husband Robert Donat, and there young Tarquin spent the war. Later Jill Esmond settled in a modest semi-detached house in Wimbledon, south London, and there she lived quietly for many years with her friend Joy Pearce. After several years of wretched health, Jill died at eighty-two in July 1990.

Olivier and his son did not form an instant bond; for three-year-old Tarquin, this was a meeting with a stranger, and so his father would remain, for their meetings were infrequent. Indeed, denied warm paternity himself, Olivier was unaware of its ingredients, and he had no idea how to handle contact with his son and a reunion with Jill.

By Christmas the Oliviers had given up the house on Cedarbrook Drive, and after a few days in New York they boarded the *Excambion* on 27 December (with only two dozen other passengers) bound for Lisbon, whence they would find other means to London. At the pier, a reporter asked Olivier why he was returning at such a perilous time, and Vivien was quick to reply for him: 'It is still our home and that's where we want to be.' Fifty years later, the journalist still thought it remarkable that she answered almost every question he put to Olivier.

The circuitous route homeward was the only way civilians could travel to England, since few ships were taking passengers across the North Atlantic. There was another good reason to be returning via Lisbon, for Olivier made several personal appearances for the Portuguese premiere of *Rebecca*. The Oliviers marked the new year onboard with some trepidation, for the ship's passengers were mostly Germans who sang rousing choruses of Nazi marching songs at the midnight celebration. They finally arrived in London to find Durham Cottage cold and dusty but untouched by the devastation that afflicted the city. (During the four months prior to the Oliviers' arrival in January 1941, more than 13,000 Londoners were killed and 18,000 severely wounded by German bombs. Before the end of the war, more than 60,000 civilians had been killed in air raids.)

The early months of 1941 were a restless period for Olivier. After a medical examination disclosed minor nerve damage in one ear, he was rejected by the Royal Air Force but accepted into the Fleet Air Arm – thanks to helpful recommendations from Ralph Richardson, who was already serving in that same branch of the Royal Navy which, since 1937, had charge of shipborne aircraft. Olivier was told to report in May.

Professionally, there were two brief engagements. On the soundtrack of a morale-boosting documentary called *Words for Battle*, Olivier's voice was heard reciting selections from poems by Milton, Browning and Kipling; the accompanying images were of uniformed soldiers, sailors, airmen and servicewomen among civilian crowds. This eight-minute call to arms concluded with the last words of Lincoln's second Gettysburg Address, which he read with tranquil dignity.

His second project took him in February to the Denham Studios for a role in Michael Powell's propaganda film *49th Parallel*; the title refers to the Canadian-American border. (In America, the picture was called *The Invaders*.) Partially financed by the Ministry of Information, the anti-Nazi story concerned a crew of Germans who, stranded in Canada after their U-boat is destroyed off the coast of Newfoundland, cut a bloody path in their effort to infiltrate America. As the amiable, rustic trapper Johnnie Barras, Olivier played a man innocent of war's cruelties, appalled at German inhumanity when he learns of the invasion of Poland and the killing of refugees; he is finally their first victim in North America.

Freed from the demands of the doomed romantic (Heathcliff), the enigmatic sophisticate (Maxim de Winter), the Regency snob (Darcy) and the national hero (Nelson), Olivier performed with earthy charm and a crusty, benevolent humour. From his first appearance in a hip bath (singing 'Alouette'), this was his most amusing and effective screen acting up to that time, a delicate counterpoise between comedy and moral outrage which remains one of his finest performances ever. After studying with a French-Canadian language coach, Olivier perfected a flawless accent, but beyond mere technique he brought to the role of Johnnie an integrity that gave the character simplicity without stupidity and common decency without sticky sentiment. Told that a famous missionary in Canada was really a German spy in disguise, he replies incredulously, 'A good priest like that?' And to the enemy's rejoinder – 'And a good Nazi' – Olivier casts a side glance of surprise, a moment later turning astonishment to quiet contempt for German racism. Johnnie is brutally shot, and there is a lengthy close-up as he dies, whispering, 'When we win the war – we will send you some – missionaries.' This was no simple, virtuosic movie death scene, for Olivier communicated the man's painful end as he had his early hopeful humour – with an alert innocence that made the character immediately lovable.

Vivien, at this time, was welcome everywhere as an international film star, and she was eager to exploit that fame in her quest for stage work. At the same time, she cavalierly ignored the contractual obligations she had to David Selznick who, for the present, chose not to prosecute on behalf of his rights to her acting services. Accordingly, the Oliviers went to see Tyrone Guthrie about a place for her at the Old Vic, but Guthrie turned her aside as too glamorous for a repertory company that avoided casting stars and conferring star billing. This she would willingly forgo, Vivien said, but Guthrie was adamant: 'Not a good enough actress – not on stage,' he said to Olivier, who relayed the decision and at once suggested a substitute – a play by Shaw.

His contract for *Wuthering Heights* had prevented them, in 1938, from performing together in a radio production of Shaw's *The Doctor's Dilemma*. Now, in March 1941, Olivier learned that Katharine Cornell and Raymond Massey were opening in a New York revival of the play (the Lunts had performed it earlier). The Shavian satire, Olivier told Vivien, would be ideal for her. At once he approached Hugh ('Binkie') Beaumont, managing director of H.M. Tennent Productions, and recommended his wife for the leading female character, Jennifer Dubedat, in a new staging. Tennent, rightly expecting audience interest in a movie star, obtained permission from Shaw (who had approval of all castings and productions), and contracts were quickly signed. Rehearsals and a tour were scheduled for the following autumn, with a London opening in March 1942.

The interval allowed Vivien time with her husband, who was first assigned to Lee-on-the-Solent, just opposite the Isle of Wight. Refusing to be separated from Olivier, she stayed at a nearby guest house during his three-week training course, telephoning him during the day and visiting every evening. This attention was not at all comforting or flattering; it was on the contrary rather suffocating, for Olivier wanted very much to establish some distance and independence from the increasingly possessive Vivien.

By the end of May he was posted to the Royal Navy Air Station at Worthy Down, a few miles north of Winchester, but Sub-Lieutenant Olivier of the Fleet Air Arm was not exactly a member of an elite corps. Squadron 757 was a motley group of men eager to serve but lacking the best flying credentials: his companions included a few ex-convicts and jockeys, some tired singers and vaudevillians and a handful of actors, Ralph Richardson among them. For Olivier, the reunion with Richardson was a pleasant buffer against his discovery that the squadron was less than important. At the same time, Vivien leased a small house at nearby King's Worthy, and when she learned that Olivier was permitted to commute and live there she insisted on it. Within days she had toted furniture and pictures down from Durham Cottage, intent on making their temporary quarters snugly familiar. Encouraged by Richardson, Olivier bought a second-hand BMW motorcycle, not only for the short commute but to enable the two friends to zoom to local pubs on free days.

Olivier's life with the squadron became literally another crash course in disappointment. The airfield at Worthy Down was a bleak backwater for air-gunner fledglings, and his main job was to take trainees on trial runs in ancient training biplanes. Attempting on his first day to demonstrate that his American aeronautic experience had made him an expert, he leaped into an open cockpit, started his engine and prepared for take-off. But he had not waited until the chocks were removed from his front wheels, and at once the Blackburn Shark spun round in a shaky half-circle and crashed into the adjacent plane. Olivier was unhurt but the complete destruction of two planes was an inauspicious beginning. After that first day, nothing could remove the aura of ineffectual celebrity that enveloped him like fog from the Channel.

But this was only the preamble to a series of Air Arm disasters – some life-threatening, some hilarious – and Olivier's later claim to aerial expertise ('I think I may describe myself as a decent pilot') was an outrageous hyperbole. Like the equally accident-prone Richardson, who smashed up old planes as if on assignment from the enemy, Olivier destroyed no fewer than five aircraft in his first seven weeks. As one of his comrades recalled, 'Olivier couldn't fly his way out of a paper bag.' The mishaps were caused not only by the antiquity of the aircraft and the bumpy field of Worthy Down: Olivier was taking the same risks airborne as he did onstage, still eager to prove himself.

Fearing disaster, the commanding officer finally grounded him and Richardson. Disconsolate and bored, they got roaring drunk and went to Winchester, where their inebriate attempt to join the cast of *Night Must Fall* onstage precipitated their ejection from the theatre. Later, a tipsy Olivier approached Richardson and announced, 'The trouble with you, Ralph, is that you can't hold your liquor.' And with that, as Richardson recalled, Olivier fell flat on his face.

By mid-summer it was clear to Olivier that in the Air Arm he could promote neither England's cause nor his own honour. Vivien, rehearsing *The Doctor's Dilemma* in London, spent August weekends at their Victorian cottage near the airfield, bringing plays she thought they might one day perform together and urging him to apply for a release from service. He read them, desiring to take on a major classical role more than to appear with Vivien. That, to put the matter plainly, was his hierarchy of values.

Olivier and Richardson were eventually given a new task, repacking parachutes after trainees had drifted onto the Hampshire downs. This was hardly a promotion, and the persistence of occupational frustrations after Broadway and Hollywood took a toll. Lunching with Olivier that summer of 1941, Noël Coward found him unhappy, and by autumn Olivier had become openly miserable.

The reasons were obvious. His incompetence as an aviator, the very means he had chosen to serve his country and associate with ordinary men, must have been a severe blow to his ego. Not only had he patently failed in the 'real world' (often considered by artists as desirable, elusive and distant), but he was simultaneously being denied access to the place where his own reality flourished – the theatre, where illusions touched deeper than visible truths. To compound his frustration, Vivien – protégée, mistress, wife – was now enjoying the success he had imagined for himself. Her brilliant opening in *The Doctor's Dilemma* at the Haymarket on 4 March 1942 was another triumph while his career stagnated.

Years later, he recalled this time as one of discovering that

> ordinary people [were] so terribly ordinary, so lacking in imagination, I'd hate them for it. They didn't understand each other's feelings at all. I thought when I joined [the Air Arm], 'How marvellous, now I shall know real people, instead of this froth that I've been living amongst all my life.' My God, give me the froth every time . . . Real people are artists. Ordinary people aren't. They just exist in a kind of vacuum. Without any pity, feeling, imagination about each other's troubles or woes or sensitivities or sensibilities. Almost inhuman, I found the real people.

Once demobilised, he never again sought temporary release from his art, nor did he regard it as less than his sole reality. From 1942, the life of the stage would be for Laurence Olivier neither an escape from reality nor the place where he avoided ordinary people, but rather the arena where the deepest feelings of which anyone is capable could be felt by him and presented to others. He learned what every creative person learns who accepts the unavoidable difference caused by his vocation – that what he is tempted to consider unreal because isolating and interior may be the deepest reality of all.

The release of *Words for Battle* and *49th Parallel* (nominated for an Academy Award as best picture of the year) brought Olivier to London more often that spring of 1942. Invited to give dramatic readings and war-related speeches before schools and civic and church groups, he was readily granted leave by his superiors. Indeed, he had crashed so many planes that the government decided something had to be done to save the remaining ones. Propaganda work was the perfect solution.

From the summer of 1942, things happened quickly. In May, a producer for British Broadcasting named Dallas Bower, who had been an associate producer on the Czinner-Bergner-Olivier *As You Like It*, arranged for him to read the St Crispin's Day oration from *Henry V* in Manchester as part of a patriotic radio programme, and this gave Bower the idea to produce a film of that play. After he failed to convince the Ministry of Information to finance the film, Bower contacted Filippo Del Giudice, an Italian immigrant who had just produced the Noël Coward–David Lean film *In Which We Serve* (based on the naval heroism of Lord Mountbatten). Del Giudice in turn obtained financing from mogul J. Arthur Rank, the most powerful distributor and exhibitor in England. Rank agreed with Del Giudice and Bower that Olivier, whom they had all seen onstage as Henry at the Old Vic in 1937, had the perfect combination of youth, classical experience and movie-star sex appeal.

Olivier's extended release from military service was arranged so that he might play the title role. Bower, his colleagues and the star planned to stress Shakespeare's celebration of brave soldiers who muddle through to victory by improvised solutions – a perfect vehicle, they reasoned, for rousing the British spirit in wartime. (The project was later dedicated to the men of the Royal Air Force who fought in the Battle of Britain.)

While the film of *Henry V* was being developed, Olivier appeared in a picture called *The Demi-Paradise*, intended as a celebration of the contemporary Anglo–Russian alliance. Adding a somewhat awkward Russian accent to his gallery of dialects, he found humour as well as pathos in the indifferent narrative about a proud but confused Soviet inventor in London.

Earlier, overtly propagandistic films financed by the Ministry of Information had been narrowly conceived: documentaries on salvage and rations and on the danger of careless talk supplemented short films like *Words for Battle*, which were simply morale-boosters. The first picture to win wide popular appeal was *Men of the Lightship* in 1940 (perhaps because the sailors shouted 'You bloody bastards!' at enemy planes). The following year, *Target for Tonight* was an important advance, for its story of a raid on Germany cast actors who were really fighters. This and other films (*Coastal Command*, *Desert Victory*) made possible the successful production of *49th Parallel*, *In Which We Serve*, *The Foreman Went to France* and *One of Our Aircraft Is Missing*; now, a production of *Henry V* would present the hallowed prototype of English heroism. And for Olivier, there would be a double advantage: the opportunity to return to acting and to do so in a role in which he would achieve by artistic proxy – in staged battle – the victories he had never known in military service.

The picture would be filmed at Denham, and so the Oliviers rented a house at Fulmer, less than five miles away; Vivien took a room at Claridge's for the remainder of the run of *The Doctor's Dilemma*, travelling to Buckinghamshire at the weekends to be with her husband. When the play closed in early March, she at first moved to Fulmer, but soon she became so restless (with Olivier occupied almost round the clock) that she went on tour to entertain the troops for three months. From May to August she travelled to Tripoli, Cairo, Algiers and Gibraltar in a revue called *Spring Party* with (among others) Beatrice Lillie.

While he worked on *The Demi-Paradise* at Denham in January, Olivier met with Del Giudice and Bower on the pre-production of *Henry V*. Olivier's first choice for director was William Wyler, who had made *Mrs Miniver* (a tribute to British courage during the Blitz) and was with the United States Air Force in England. But Wyler could not be released from service and in any case claimed to be the wrong man to direct Shakespeare. He suggested John Ford, who in addition to his Oscars for *The Grapes of Wrath* and *How Green Was My Valley* was filming documentaries for the United States Navy. Olivier met with Ford, who laughed at the very idea of participating and claimed he had no sense of the classics.

But Ford had a suggestion. He knew a talented writer named Terence Young, who had collaborated in 1942 on the script of a propaganda film called *Dangerous Moonlight* and was about to co-direct an important documentary. Then twenty-six, Young had a gift for overall film design as well as for screenwriting, and since he had not yet directed a feature he could be hired cheaply. Perhaps because he also thought Young would leave him control of his own character, Olivier at once agreed with Ford that he would be the perfect director for *Henry V.*

Divisional Films Officer for the British Army, Young received an invitation to dine with Olivier and Del Giudice at Claridge's in February. While the producers tried to secure Young's release from service, he met at Denham with Olivier, costume designer Roger Furse and critic Alan Dent (who edited the text for the screen). According to Young, Furse was the *éminence grise* of *Henry V*, designing the costumes and sets for Technicolor film in the style of the great medieval illuminated manuscripts – especially the *Très Riches Heures* of Jean, Duc de Berry. In his memoirs, Olivier claimed credit for the idea of the medieval hour books as inspiration for the film's style, but correspondence in 1943 between Olivier and Young confirms that credit for this (and indeed much of the film's overall design) was due to Roger Furse. For his part, Olivier may well have recalled the elaborate medieval designs Barry Jackson had used in *The Marvellous History of St Bernard* in Birmingham seventeen years earlier, and the designs for *Harold* in London thereafter. In any case, only the Battle of Agincourt would be filmed realistically – a brilliant conceit suggested by Olivier – for after the deliberate theatricality of the opening and the storybook sets for the balance of the action, the filmed battle would be at once accepted as the true model for the war then raging.

When it was time to secure Young's release from service, the British Army Council was emphatic that no one under thirty could be discharged for a commercial film. Undaunted, Olivier and Del Giudice invited the War Minister, Sir James Grigg, to dinner. 'They got him drunk as a skunk,' Young recalled, 'and wheedled from him the promise that I could have just ten weeks' leave to direct *Henry V.*' That seemed feasible, and in February Young formally came on the picture as director.

At once there were problems. For the sake of safety from air raids and because it was cheaper to employ non-union labour for the massive

battle scenes on horseback, they decided on Ireland for location shooting. Dallas Bower suggested the vast estate of Lord Powerscourt at
Enniskerry, where there was a campsite used by the Irish Boy Scouts.
Here the film company could bring local horsemen and extras, enjoy
a secured location and have free use of caravan facilities. But by the
end of February, despite twenty-hour workdays by Olivier, Furse,
Young and the pre-production staff, it was clear that the director's
ten-week leave would expire before they could even begin actual filming. With great reluctance, Young returned to military service. (He
eventually directed, among many other pictures, the James Bond
movies *Dr No* and *From Russia With Love*; *Wait Until Dark*; and
two late Olivier films, *Inchon* and *The Jigsaw Man*.)

Desperate for a congenial replacement, Olivier had the odd idea of
contacting his American acquaintance Garson Kanin. Kanin found the
invitation hard to take seriously – he was primarily a director of distinc-
tively Hollywood comedies – and so he suggested his friend, the English
director Carol Reed, but for reasons unknown Reed (Olivier's spear-
carrying partner in the Casson–Thorndike production of *Henry VIII* in
1925) was entirely unacceptable to Olivier.

Exasperated, Del Giudice, Bower and Rank protested that they could
delay production no longer, and that if Olivier was so pernickety about
a choice of director, he ought to assume that responsibility himself.
He took that as an offer, and by 1 March it was announced that Laurence Olivier would star in and direct a film of *Henry V*. This was his
opportunity to mould not only a character but also – with the collaboration of his enormously gifted colleagues on the film – the style and
atmosphere of a classic motion picture. He knew from *As You Like It*
how easy it was to sabotage Shakespeare on film. This was a great risk
in every conceivable professional and personal way, but success would
confirm his status as a pre-eminent creative interpreter of the classics.
In fact, Olivier had hoped from the beginning to direct the picture, as
he admitted years later to William Walton, composer of the music for
Henry V: 'I was ambitious, and I wanted the lot.'

A primary decision was his choice of a cast. Vivien had hoped to
play Katharine, the princess who weds Henry; she could handle the
character's French perfectly, and although Katharine appears in only
two scenes it would be an amusing and romantic part with Olivier. But
when Vivien asked permission of Selznick, who still held her film
contract, he refused, claiming the small part would diminish her career.
In her place Olivier cast a young actress named Renée Asherson, who

ironically had just appeared in a revival of *The Mask of Virtue*, the play that had launched Vivien's stage career. Others among the assembled cast included Felix Aylmer, Robert Newton, Russell Thorndike and Leo Genn. From the crew of *The Demi-Paradise* Olivier knew art directors Paul Sheriff and Carmen Dillon, and from the same picture he also engaged Reginald Beck, who would edit the finished film and direct the scenes in which Olivier himself acted. He also brought in composer William Walton, who had written the score for *As You Like It*. Other talents contributed indirectly to the film: from the crowd scenes in Tyrone Guthrie's *Henry V* in 1937, Olivier took the idea for colourful banners swirling in constant movement.

Despite an able entourage, and no matter how shared the daily tasks, his responsibilities were sometimes overwhelming. In a letter that March to Terence Young, he wrote of the political difficulties in dealing with government ministers of Supply, War, Manpower, Labour and Information, from whom various special permissions and materials had to be obtained; he added that he was greatly relieved to be directing the film himself, since Young could not. Throughout April, Roger Furse and his staff were working on costumes; the miniature set of Elizabethan London for the opening and concluding shots was built at Denham; and Technicolor tests were made of players and wardrobe. On 28 May the company departed for Ireland to film the battle scenes, and on 9 June the first shots were photographed. Roger Furse recalled that although Olivier was nervous and uncertain,

> he exuded tremendous vigour and confidence to all around him. There were hundreds of people to be fed and housed, as well as costumes, makeup, props, horses, dressing rooms and first aid to be seen to. Olivier himself commanded all.

He also involved himself in every aspect of production and asked no physical stunts from his cast that he was unwilling to perform himself. He thought he knew what he wanted, according to William Walton's wife Susanna. 'A famous instance was Larry saying, "Now this is a beautiful tune I've thought of – dum de dum de dum." "Yes," William retorted, "it is a lovely tune; it's out of [Wagner's] *Meistersinger*."' Then, while showing his Irish extras how to drop twenty feet from a tree to attack passing horsemen, he sprained his ankle. And days later, as he was directing the swift approach of horses, Olivier demanded that a rider charge forward, assuming the steed would swerve at the last moment. But the animal knocked over the huge Technicolor camera, and although the operator and crew jumped aside, Olivier – his eye firmly fixed on the viewfinder – received the full weight of the toppling machine. His shoulder was dislocated and the machine tore open his right upper lip. A surgeon was summoned, stitches were inserted, and for the rest of his life Olivier bore a two-inch scar (often hidden by a moustache).

What Olivier could not do on the bumpy fields of Hampshire, he did with panache on the greenswards of Enniskerry, directing 180 horsemen and five hundred footmen from the Irish Home Guard. He was indeed setting an example of how an officer trains his platoon; mustering the troops, acting bravely, leading fighting men and taking the blows of battle. The making of *Henry V* was as close to a kind of totemic representation of Henry as he could achieve.

After thirty-nine shooting days in Ireland, the company returned to Denham on 24 July with sixteen minutes and forty-six seconds of battle scenes – an impressive achievement in light of the attendant complexities. Studio filming began on 9 August and was completed 124 working days later – on 3 January 1944; the producers certainly had no complaint with an average of almost one and a half minutes of film daily. After editing, the addition of music and sound effects, dubbing of voices not recorded earlier and final colour correction, *Henry V* (at two and a quarter hours) was completed on 12 July 1944 – four weeks after the Allied invasion of France. With final expenditures totalling £475,708, it was the most expensive British film ever made.

'Shakespeare in a way wrote for the films,' Olivier reflected later. 'His splitting up of the action into a multitude of small scenes is almost an anticipation of film technique, and more than one of his plays seems to chafe against the cramping restrictions of the stage.' Fully exploiting cinematic technique with swift cuts, dissolves and long, dramatic crane and tracking shots, Olivier demanded approval of every camera movement, and any detailed viewing of *Henry V* reveals the remarkable harmony between the settings and their presentation. He demonstrated once and for all that Shakespeare could be properly and effectively brought to the screen; he also showed how a great play can transcend its form. And he was arguably the first to achieve these goals.

Henceforth, Olivier was warm to the medium he once coolly dismissed as unworthy of him. Now in control, he could indeed exploit the advantages of directorial supervision to convey his own viewpoint. He was also free from the routine aggravations of Hollywood studios, and he was reprising his heroic Henry from the 1937 Old Vic season.

Most important, Shakespeare conferred a benediction not offered by routine scripts. And now Laurence Olivier had played Shakespeare onscreen before Gielgud, Richardson and other noted contemporaries.

The film begins without credits in a languorous shot, over an amazingly realistic miniature of Shakespeare's London south of the Thames and toward the Globe Theatre. There the play of *Henry V* begins as a staged performance, and we see the audience in the year 1600 taking their seats. Backstage life is shown, too, with boys dressing for the women's roles, and actors accidentally dropping props onstage and fussing with sheets of script. This audacious beginning not only makes tolerable the conversational exposition of *Henry V*; it also establishes the frankly theatrical nature of what we are about to see. During the next two hours, the film uses every kind of setting: real country fields, painted backcloths, abstract designs and obviously interior studio sets. For the scenes of battle, Olivier and his associates planned exterior action; for the King's soliloquy he recorded the speech and inserted it as a voice-over, the camera simply panning his own features in a haze of confusion, hope and finally confidence. The film within the production of the Shakespearean play we are seeing does precisely what film should do: it brings the action so close that we become participants in the drama, not mere observers; the abstract and artificial settings allow a retreat from literal reality in order to permit that quiet rumination which the verse encourages.

As we watch *Henry V*, the Globe Theatre is itself transpierced after the first scenes, and we are beyond it, into the play. The grammar of film itself harmonises with the language: as he musters his troops for battle, Henry is seen first in close-up, and as his voice rises the banners pass across our view and the camera pulls back farther and farther until we see the effect of the speech – the gathering of hundreds of men in response to his call:

> In peace there's nothing so becomes a man
> As modest stillness and humility:
> But when the blast of war blows in our ears,
> Then imitate the action of the tiger;
> Stiffen the sinews, summon up the blood . . .
> For there is none of you so mean and base
> That hath not noble lustre in your eyes . . .
> Follow your spirit; and upon this charge
> Cry 'God for Harry, England and Saint George!'

He was also aware of those moments in the text demanding special delicacy – thus his very different inflection (from the 1937 Old Vic performance) of the lines beginning 'Good morrow, old Sir Thomas Erpingham.' Because France was an ally of England in 1943, there was now no light sarcasm, no pause after 'turf' and before 'of France'. With only the minimal make-up required for Technicolor, without a false nose or brow, Laurence Olivier had the consummate appearance of a young king on the verge of greatness. Disguised in cloak and hood for his night-time visit among his men (in the 'little touch of Harry in the night' sequence), Olivier had never looked so beautiful, his face illuminated gently and indirectly, his gaze one of almost mystic calm.

Henry V was rigorously hard work, but it was also fun for him to manipulate an audience not only with his own performance but by controlling every other player and every viewpoint. Olivier had a rare ability to satisfy the guardians of High Art even as he offered audiences exciting entertainment. This picture made him at last a heroic character, star and director, and established by his manifold contributions to the project that he was the quintessential popular exponent of the classics. As a corporate personality greater than Lord Nelson, he incarnated in Henry V the grandeur denied him in the Fleet Air Arm, and with this film he would at last achieve a new level of international stardom. By an odd twist of destiny, the accident during *Henry V* which left him permanently scarred became a kind of symbol, for the subsequent fame and honour marked him for life.

Nevertheless, the authority and control required to be an effective film director have revealed a tyrannical streak in many men. D.W. Griffith was a cinematic visionary and an unbearable martinet; Erich von Stroheim paid meticulous attention to every detail and callously ignored his actors' feelings; and citing his association with Alfred Hitchcock, producer Ivor Montagu made a provocative generalisation:

> It had long been my conviction that a good director must have something of the sadist in him. I do not necessarily mean to a pathological degree, but that his looking at things and telling [actors] to do this, undergo that, is necessarily akin to dominating them, ordering them about.

To this tendency Olivier was no exception, as even admirers recalled. Laurence Evans, his friend since the days of *Too Many Crooks* in 1930, was brought onto *Henry V* as production manager after two incompetents were dismissed; he recalled that Olivier could be terrifyingly demanding in those days. 'Larry was the king and he wasn't going to have any argument.' In fact, that autumn Evans saw a new side to Olivier. Charged with supervising the special requirements for every scene, he met with his director each morning to confer on details of the day's shooting. One day, Evans asked how many horses Olivier would require for a brief medium shot (the meeting between Henry and Sir Thomas Erpingham). The reply was swift: 'I don't know how many fucking horses I want!' To press him for an answer would be to risk an enormous explosion that would have repercussions for days to come. In the evening, out of the role, Olivier was friendly and cordial, pouring drinks and entertaining everyone. But with his make-up and costume back on, as the company knew, an air of menace resumed.

An autocratic side to Olivier's personality was indeed emerging that year. This was perhaps inevitable in a man who would ultimately exploit every aspect of film and stagecraft, an actor able to inspire his crew and draw from his colleagues their own best contributions to a production. On the other hand, playing the monarch evoked a largely dormant aspect of his own character: the posture of aristocracy. From his father and his schoolmasters he had learned not only a grave dignity but also the effect on others of an aristocratic, very proper British mien. This was not mere affectation; it was style deriving from self-awareness.

Complementing his informal geniality, therefore, was a certain imperial pose, and henceforth both styles co-existed equally. While living at Fulmer and shooting *Henry V*, Olivier often invited visitors to accompany him across to the studio stables, where he saddled the horses and conducted a kind of Sunday procession – rather as if he were a royal, trotting serenely with noble friends at Sandringham, Balmoral or Windsor. Olivier himself mounted the horse he had ridden in *Henry V*, trained to break into a gallop at a specific moment in the St Crispin's Day oration.

Olivier's occasional imperial style was sometimes manifest at public ceremonies, too. Invited to address the 'Arts at War' pageant at the Albert Hall that autumn of 1943, he stood onstage in his Air Arm uniform and shouted with almost manic fury:

> We will go forward – heart, nerve and spirit. We will smite our foes, we will conquer! And in all our deeds, in this and in other lands, from this hour on, our watchwords will be urgency, speed, courage. Urgency in all our decisions, speed in the execution of all our plans, courage in face of all our enemies. And may God bless our cause!

The tone and style of the speech were worthy of Henry V himself, rousing the troops at Harfleur. (The filmed speech has been preserved in a documentary tribute to ENSA – the wartime Entertainments National Service Association – produced in Britain by ITV and first broadcast on 29 June 1980.)

Vivien was of course the perfect consort; she not only directed their two servants with impeccable poise, she also rode elegantly and saw to the comfort of their guests with easy grace. Since her return in late summer, she had little to do but set herself to the task of finding a somewhat grander country house. In due course, Vivien would find the right property – appropriately, a king's residence. For the autumn of 1943, she rested; after losing fifteen pounds on her Middle East tour, she could neither overcome a hacking cough nor give up her heavy smoking. For a while Olivier was too busy to notice. He had already spent his last day in naval uniform, and as he was completing *Henry V* there were developments in London theatrical life which would soon critically alter his career.

Since the serious bomb damage in 1941 to the theatre in Waterloo Road, the Old Vic troupe had performed only sporadically elsewhere in London; for the rest of the war, the greatly reduced repertory company had been playing in the provinces. After six years as administrator of all three Old Vic–Sadler's Wells companies offering drama, opera and ballet, director Tyrone Guthrie was exhausted from his multiple responsibilities for its English and foreign tours and wanted a team of stage directors to work with him. First he employed John Burrell as a director. Then in his early thirties, Burrell had been a designer with Michel Saint-Denis at the London Theatre Studio. Painfully dependent on crutches and canes because of polio, he had staged Shaw's *Heartbreak House* at the Cambridge Theatre and was also a successful drama producer for BBC radio. There, Burrell and Guthrie had collaborated on a 1943 broadcast of Ibsen's play *Peer Gynt*, brilliantly read by Burrell's old friend Ralph Richardson.

Immediately, Guthrie and Burrell decided that Richardson should join as a co-director of the Old Vic Theatre Company while negotiations were concluded for its return to London at the New Theatre (later renamed the Albery, in honour of its owner-manager Bronson Albery); the Waterloo theatre required major reconstruction. Richardson realised that a popular and crowd-pleasing actor-director would be necessary to entice audiences back for a London season of the Old Vic

– someone with more glamorous appeal than himself. He and Burrell approached John Gielgud to join them as second co-director under Guthrie's administration, but Gielgud had agreed to play a repertory season at the Haymarket Theatre that autumn. Olivier, although he had not appeared onstage in London for six years (since *Coriolanus*), was the logical alternative.

And so in March 1944, Richardson and Burrell drove to Denham, where Olivier was still working on *Henry V*. Uncertain of success with the film and anticipating only a return to the navy, Olivier was keenly interested. The Old Vic would offer him the great classic roles again, and he accepted their invitation at once. Within days ('with an alacrity that was positively hurting to both Ralph and myself') the First Lord of the Admiralty granted the Old Vic's request that both actors be permanently released from service for artistic work of national import-ance. Olivier's three-year term of virtually non-active war service was mercifully behind him.

With a guarantee against loss from CEMA (the Council for the Encouragement of Music and the Arts, the forerunner of the Arts Council) and with additional subsidies from theatrical managers Howard Wyndham and Bronson Albery, the Old Vic's board an-nounced in May that the triumvirate of Burrell-Richardson-Olivier would that summer begin a three-play repertory season at the New Theatre, St Martin's Lane. Each man signed a contract guaranteeing him a salary of forty pounds a week for five years; their office would be a tiny, windowless attic in St Martin's Court, a few yards away. Once *Henry V* was completed in June and ready for distribution later that year, Olivier and his colleagues assembled actors for their company – among them Sybil Thorndike, Joyce Redman, Harcourt Williams and a young Birmingham Rep player named Margaret Leighton. Intending to draw strength from the imperishable, the Old Vic would emphasise classic plays: for the first two seasons they agreed on Shakespeare, Ibsen, Chekhov, Sheridan and Sophocles (and added Shaw to the reper-tory as well). Astutely, Olivier engaged his friend and *Henry V* pro-duction supervisor Laurence Evans to join them as general manager, responsible for daily business affairs.

By this time, the Richardson–Olivier friendship lacked the easy camaraderie of earlier times. Olivier took himself with utter serious-ness, while Richardson was much the merrier and more sanguine of the two – especially since (after the slow death of his first wife) he had married a lovely young actress named Meriel Forbes.

Olivier, on the other hand, was completely absorbed in his career plans. He was also somewhat anxious for Vivien. Unemployed for a year (since the Middle East tour), she had felt estranged from him during his filming and was bored with her tenancy of the house at Fulmer. Still thin and frail from a chronic respiratory infection, she was nevertheless (as John Gielgud said) 'relentlessly energetic – there was just no stopping her'. In June she announced to her husband that she was pregnant, and that same month, against her doctor's advice, she began working at Denham on a film of Shaw's *Caesar and Cleopatra* (Selznick earning almost a hundred thousand dollars on the loan-out fee). Apparently a surprise to Olivier, the news of her pregnancy was not an unalloyed blessing, for he foresaw the coming year as even more demanding than the last and the duties of parenthood as a potential burden. He urged her to withdraw from the film, but she was obsessed with work, as friends like Rachel Kempson recalled.

Intending to vary the programme, the triumvirate agreed to stage a comedy, a tragedy and a poetic fantasy. To capitalise on the success of the earlier radio production, they would begin with Richardson in *Peer Gynt*, Olivier taking the small role of the Button Moulder. The second production was to be Shaw's *Arms and the Man* (with Olivier and Richardson co-starring). Olivier would then play Richard III.

The three leaders were not a particularly congenial group, however, as Evans and others recalled years later, for the truth is that they did not have much in common apart from their commitment to the theatre. Their personal styles and manners were very distinct, and as time went on they were always just on the edge of strife with one another. Diana Boddington, stage manager at the Old Vic for three decades from 1941, felt that John Burrell was really the third man, somewhat dominated by the other two.

Because the New Theatre was still being used for opera, the company rehearsed all three plays for ten weeks in a large hall at the nearby National Gallery. Throughout June and July, following the Allied invasion of Europe, almost 3000 Londoners were killed, many more wounded and hundreds of buildings destroyed by 8000 pilotless V1 bombs. The cast sometimes read their lines under a table, and because there was a glass ceiling in the gallery, they were threatened with danger every moment of an air raid.

The season opened at the New on 31 August with Guthrie's production of a mercifully edited *Peer Gynt*. A fantasy of cavernous gloom describing the title character's odyssey and his surrender to the life of the senses, the play offers in its final moments a pointed moral lesson: men, like buttons, are designed with a definite shape and function, to hold things together with order and harmony. But Peer, the Button Moulder says, has set his life's design in chaos, and has thus lost himself by acting without principle. Olivier brought to the brief five-minute role both chilling intimidation and stern benignity.

This was followed by Shaw's satire on romantic notions of war. As the pompous, cowardly and egomaniacal Major Sergius Saranoff in *Arms and the Man*, Olivier had to strike absurdly heroic postures. (Shaw describes Saranoff as 'a tall, romantically handsome man, with the physical hardihood, the high spirit and the susceptible imagination of an untamed mountaineer chieftain'.) In his elegant white uniform, rakish pill-box hat and movie-villain moustache, he clicked his heels flamboyantly and played for comedy, but during the preview perform-ances in Manchester before the London premiere, Olivier found the role inordinately unsympathetic and unappealing. He mentioned this to Guthrie, who commented, 'Well, if you can't love him, you'll never be any good.' As Olivier wrote years later, 'I began to love Sergius, and my whole performance seemed to get better and better. For the rest of my life, I would apply this.'

The remark has been misunderstood even by Olivier's admirers as an almost psychic identification with the character's basic humanity, or as a noble (and slightly condescending) Tolstoyan forgiveness of his sins. But as the following weeks would amply reveal, this 'love' of a character meant neither empathy nor moral superiority, but rather an understanding of the rationale for a man's conduct – an exercise in seeing the character as another, with his own inner logic and integrity. For this Guthrie preferred to use the term 'love', and so Olivier will-ingly redefined his portrait for the London premiere on 5 September. Now extravagantly amusing and subtly inventive, Olivier's portrait of confident braggadocio had an edge of disarming warmth that saved Sergius from simple burlesque caricature.

During the second week of performances, he received an emergency telephone call. Feeling ill while filming *Caesar and Cleopatra* at Den-ham, Vivien had had a terrible fall and within hours had suffered a miscarriage. But although the producer shut down the picture to allow her several weeks of recovery, she was out of bed two days later. Her husband was bound by a tense and demanding schedule of eight performances a week and daily rehearsals for a forthcoming premiere, and she intended to use her own enforced interval to assist him. Each morning and late each night she cued his lines.

The miscarriage was evidently not as traumatic for Vivien as some have assumed. She thought she wanted a child, and she certainly hoped to give Olivier an heir to reinforce their union. But Vivien did not relish the responsibilities of parenthood now any more than a decade earlier, and she refused to take the care required by her fragile constitution during pregnancy. Work was her child as it was Olivier's, and to it they gave the obsessive attention that became devoted commitment. Months later, she returned to complete *Caesar and Cleopatra*.

The Vic's third offering that season, *Richard III*, turned a merely successful beginning for the company into a thundering personal triumph for Olivier. He had shaped his portrait of Shakespeare's royal arch-villain from carefully selected externals, some of them based on memories of Jed Harris's sneering sarcasm and steely vocal sophistication. His hunchback Richard was also wily and irresistible, perhaps because his victims were so weak and unimaginative. Every detail of make-up, costume, glance and gesture had been calculated and rehearsed to create a portrait of honey-coated malignity. From this careful assemblage there had emerged a fully-drawn historical character sprung alarmingly to modern life. Diana Boddington never forgot the hush that prevailed backstage at rehearsals as Olivier's colleagues observed his terrifying display of artifice.

But the night before his first performance, Vivien and their friend Garson Kanin kept vigil with an insomniac Olivier in a suite at Claridge's, since Durham Cottage was undergoing repairs after fire-bombing. Unable to hold the lines in his memory, he shook with panic, convinced that Burrell and Richardson had suggested the role of Shakespeare's royal arch-villain (recently played to great acclaim by Donald Wolfit) in order to destroy him. Finally, at four in the morning, he fell asleep from exhaustion. Awake at eight, Olivier still had trouble with several scenes. Fearing the derision of critics and colleagues, he telephoned several friends, among them the actors John and Mary Mills (frequent visitors to Fulmer and Durham Cottage) and asked them to meet him in his dressing room an hour before the performance. They arrived to find him in costume but pacing nervously.

'Sit down, darlings, and listen to me,' he said. 'I just want you to know that you are going to see a bloody awful performance. The dress rehearsal was chaotic. I dried up at least a dozen times. It's a dreadful production, and I was an idiot to let them persuade me to play the bloody part. You are in for four hours of boredom.' He then asked the Millses to warn anyone they knew – before the curtain went up – that he was going to be appalling.

Olivier was not only exhausted, he must have been terrified of the role: how does one love Richard, in the way Guthrie had said he must love a character to play him well? In this case, the actor had been forced to go deeper than 'love', for this was the first undilutedly wicked role he had created, and he found it daunting. So monstrous a character could only alienate his audience, after all. But to his surprise he found that Shakespeare had forestalled this hesitation, for Richard is the most compelling character in the play, the only one who forces the audience to a complex set of moral reflections. And Olivier found that as a character Richard was – in the perverse way of such parts – unavoidably fascinating, and not at all alienating. It was the definitive portrait of ambition, and ambition was a brother to his own imagination.

From the moment the curtain went up and he limped down towards the audience and addressed to them the opening soliloquy ('Now is the winter of our discontent made glorious summer by this sun of York . . .'), Olivier dominated the stage as never before. First, there was an astonishing self-transformation even beyond the padded humpback and the grotesque limp: he had designed a wig of patent-leather black, his lips shone with dark grease, the eyelids were tinted and the putty nose was long and pointed as if to impale with mere enquiry.

But his Richard was no fancy-dress-party guest. Fascinating in his poisonous self-absorption, Olivier drew the audience to himself, creating a sense of quiet collusion in a deadly course towards the throne and presenting evil as familiar, alarmingly tempting, recognisably human and therefore impossible to dismiss as foreign or other-worldly. Addressing the audience, winking at them, whispering asides, he said in essence, 'Watch me!' – but it was to a purpose grander than scene-stealing. Devoted brother, seductive lover, uncle, courtier: this schemer offered a series of playlets on the twilight of the Plantagenets. Venomous, lethally acidulous, Olivier's Richard was like a hideous accident: too ghastly to see as something possible for oneself, too fascinatingly grisly to ignore. His death seemed like the writhing of a pinned spider, each spasm a clawing response to the deadly sword-thrusts until he was literally torn away from life. When the final curtain fell, there

35. *Above* As Darcy, with Greer Garson as Elizabeth in *Pride and Prejudice* (1940). *Globe Photos*

36. *Below* The New York production of *Romeo and Juliet*, with Vivien Leigh (1940). *Culver Pictures*

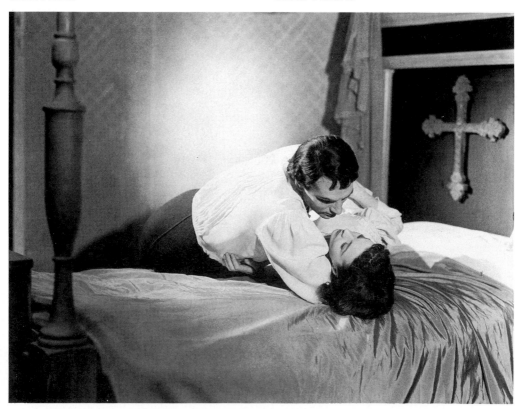

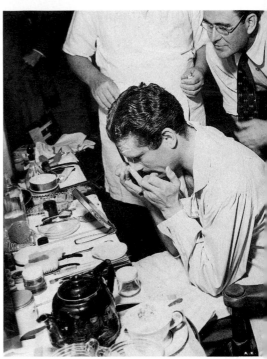

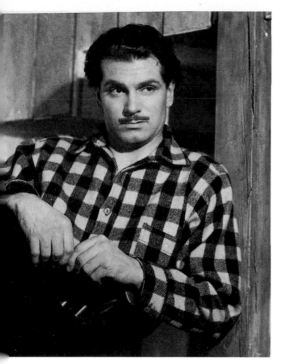

37. *Above far left* The Oliviers, soon after their marriage in 1940. *Culver Pictures*

38. *Above left* Preparing his false nose as Nelson in *That Hamilton Woman* (1940). *Culver Pictures*

39. *Left* With Vivien as Emma in *That Hamilton Woman* (1940). *National Film Archive, London*

40. *Above* As Johnnie in *49th Parallel* (1941). *Culver Pictures*

41. *Above right* Holiday snapshot by Vivien: Olivier falls through a deckchair at Warsash (1941). *From the collection of Felix Barker*

42. *Right* Training Air Scouts at Worthy Down (1942). *From the collection of Felix Barker*

43. *Above* In his film of *Henry V* (1943). *National Film Archive, London*

44. *Below* As Henry (1943). *National Film Archive, London*

was often a moment of silence, as if the horrors they had seen had made the audience incapable of an immediate reaction. Then, as John Mills said, 'People seemed to go raving mad. Everyone knew we were all watching something very, very unusual and very great. We had just seen a man in a weird, strange, frightening, intense mood – and there he was, taking a curtain call, apparently as normal as anyone. But not really.'

Typically, Olivier frightened his colleagues, too – among them George Rose, making his professional debut in a small role. Lunging at him with a sword, Olivier tore through his pikestaff and opened a gash on Rose's head. Nor did Olivier spare Richardson, duelling with him in the role of Richmond: 'Do you really need to go so quickly, old chap?' Richardson often asked Olivier offstage after his eyes, ears and hands had been threatened by all too realistic swordplay.

Laurence Olivier had as usual prepared his part from small external details. Working gradually inward from the outside, as he always insisted, he built from a basis of observed characteristics and found 'a creature swimming about somewhere in the midst of them'. Henceforth he was often to be asked about this method, which he claimed enabled him to find the part in himself; but an actor who began from the inside, he maintained – seeking a personal history on which to build a role – found only himself in the part. The difference was crucial, for Olivier discovered something of Richard's ambition and envy within the larger truth of Laurence Olivier, but he did not submit to the larger truth of the part and discover Laurence Olivier therein. Role-playing was not a technique of self-disclosure; it was a disclosure of another character, in whom Olivier and his audience found something recognisably human. His acting enabled him and others to associate with a parcel of truth (not to identify with it), and in the case of Richard he may have understood the pretender's ambition as well. In preparing a part, he said years later,

> things begin to emerge that help you reinforce the character. And since it is really you, you begin to love this new side of your own character as you have loved the old side. Possibly you love it more since it is all so new and different, yet still you. This is still working from the outside in, but in a much more substantive way than most actors do it, which is simply to impose their own beings on the characters.

Otherwise, Olivier was not given to grandiose theories about the art of acting. He liked to cite a remark of Margot Fonteyn who, when asked to explain what she had communicated in a ballet just completed, replied: 'I explained it while I was doing it.'

He had made his first entrance as Richard 'frightened, heart beating, because I think everybody was rather in despair about the whole production, and nobody believed in my performance'. But the following morning the critics were unanimous in ransacking their vocabularies for superlatives, and within three days every Old Vic play that autumn season was sold out.

His second performance as Richard was the following afternoon. 'There was something in the atmosphere,' Olivier recalled years later.

> There is a phrase – the sweet smell of success*. . . and as I went on to the stage I felt that for the first time the critics had approved, that the public had approved . . . It was overwhelming, and it went straight to my head, this complete confidence. I felt a little power of hypnotism. I felt I had them.

Later that week, a patron came to the box office and asked for tickets to 'a Laurence Olivier play'. The seller asked which play the man wanted to see. 'It doesn't matter – whatever Laurence Olivier is in.'

With a redeeming irony, Olivier's triumph was at the New Theatre, where in 1935 his performances with John Gielgud had led him to question his future as a serious actor. Several days after the first *Richard*, a long, slender package was delivered, addressed to Olivier from John Gielgud. Beneath a dozen roses was history's most famous theatrical memento: the sword worn by Edmund Kean as Richard in 1814, which had passed down through two generations of actors to Henry Irving in 1877. Irving had bequeathed it to William Terriss (a member of his company), who was murdered in 1897. His daughter (the actress Ellaline Terriss) later passed it on to her husband, the actor-manager Seymour Hicks, and eventually it reached the Terry family. On its blade that September evening was a new inscription: 'This sword given him by his mother Kate Terry Gielgud, 1938, is given to Laurence Olivier by his friend John Gielgud in appreciation of his performance of *Richard III* at the New Theatre, 1944.' When asked in 1979 to whom he would bequeath it, Olivier replied, 'No one.

---

* The phrase was coined by the writer Ernest Lehman, who used it as the title of one of his short stories and his later screen version of it.

It's mine.' And so it remained. He made no provision in his will for disposition of the sword.

In November 1944, *Henry V* was released in London, where it became the most successful British film in history, running uninterrupted for eleven months. Capturing perfectly the anxiety of the war, its end and aftermath, the American premiere in April 1946 was merely the second stage in a process of increasing worldwide fame for the film – and more, for its director and star. In 1947, Olivier received a special Academy Award 'for his outstanding achievement as actor, producer and director in bringing *Henry V* to the screen'. The project for which he had been paid only fifteen thousand pounds (and for which he agreed not to appear in any subsequent film for eighteen months) produced revenues of millions of pounds.

Olivier was regarded from that autumn as England's most popular actor on both stage and screen, and a part of his self-image altered dramatically. Against Vivien's preference and the advice of friends, he purchased the grand thirteenth-century abbot's lodge she had found, which took its name from the Augustinian friary called Notley Abbey, near Long Crendon, Buckinghamshire, fifty miles north-west of London. Drenched with atmosphere, the main twenty-two-room house had three large living rooms and seven bedchambers, a library, a baronial dining room and a staff wing. There were also tennis courts, orchards, rich farmland and a three-bedroom caretaker's cottage – all set on more than seventy acres. Built of grey stone, with leaded windows, ancient traceries, carved capitals, trefoil arches and detailed spandrels, it could have sprung from the pages of a Daphne du Maurier novel or designs for a Franco-Russian ballet. Founded during the reign of Henry II and built by the Earl of Buckingham near the River Thame, it survived Henry VIII's dissolution of the monasteries; since then, greenhouses, a barn, tangled gardens and poultry houses had been added.

Although it required months of refurbishment, Olivier considered this his predestined residence: it had, after all, been endowed by King Henry V himself, for whom Notley Abbey was a favoured stopping-place. 'It was absolutely enchanting and enchanted me,' he said. 'At Notley I had an affair with the past. For me it had mesmeric power; I could easily drown in its atmosphere. I could not let it alone; I was a child lost in its history. Perhaps I loved it too much, if that is possible.'

CHAPTER NINE

1945–1947

A person's real vocation is known only to God.

Astrov, in Chekhov's *Uncle Vanya*

On 16 January 1945, the Old Vic Theatre Company presented Chekhov's *Uncle Vanya*. Laurence Olivier was Astrov, the doctor who speaks for the doctor-playwright himself, and a role created in 1899 by the great actor and theorist Konstantin Stanislavsky.

A play about people thwarted and broken by failure, there is very little action in *Uncle Vanya*. But much occurs in the cloaked and hooded souls of the principal characters as their confrontations weave a mood of disenchantment with the present and wistful nostalgia for the future. Astrov is a noble and attractive figure, but he immerses himself in work and alcohol – escape mechanisms he can overcome no more effectively than the ecological problems he so clearly diagnoses. Often played as a Byronic hero in lonely isolation against social and material odds, Astrov is a detached but sympathetic moralist, and Olivier aptly played him neither as the stereotype of a tippling genius nor (when he expresses passionate love for Yelena) as an ageing romantic fool. In *Richard III* he had learned to present a misshapen scoundrel as weirdly attractive; no reprobate, Astrov is simply human and frail – but also the prophetic voice of the play. Like him, Olivier had known the bitterness of failure and the refuge of work; like Astrov, too, he was vulnerable, self-indulgent and ambitious. It was not surprising, therefore, that this became a favourite role to which he would return – and which was filmed much later, when he chose it to represent him and his fledgling company at the Chichester Theatre Festival.

Olivier's performance was lightly tinted with subtleties of anger, wistful longing, and unsentimental regret – especially in the long speeches decrying the abuse of creation:

The forests . . . are being felled, the birds and animals are being turned out of their homes, the rivers are becoming swamps, glorious scenery is being destroyed forever . . . Man has been endowed with intelligence and creative power, [but] he has only destroyed . . . Wildlife is becoming extinct, the climate is ruined, and each and every day the earth is more impoverished and ugly.

He managed, through an almost casual charm (as Astrov speaks to the indifferent, cynical Vanya and the innocent Sonya) to prevent his speeches from tipping over the border into mere moral injunction – just as he avoided self-pity in Astrov's lament:

Life, in general, I love. But . . . as to my own personal life: well, by God, there simply isn't one good thing about it . . . I work like no one else in the district. I'm up against every kind of difficulty. Sometimes I'm so miserable I don't know how to bear it. But there's no light ahead of me. I don't look forward to anything. I haven't loved anybody for years . . . But by one thing I can still be touched – beauty.*

With unflamboyant dignity, Olivier rendered Astrov as one who sees clearly the tragic nature of life, a man longing for what he knows he cannot have – a better world, a great love – and sensing the sadness of living even as he retains his capacity to appreciate nature and affection. He never loses his zest for life, and this – not his escapism – is the ultimate key to his character.

That winter, life with Vivien was undergoing a slow but inexorable change. In January, she had completed her role in the film of *Caesar and Cleopatra*. Although she did not relish the work needed to make Notley Abbey habitable for themselves and guests, Vivien undertook the tasks of furnishing and decorating with brisk compulsiveness in order to please her husband. Playwright Frederick Lonsdale's house at Birchington, near Margate in Kent, had been a centre of entertaining for theatre people, and there were similar glittering social salons at Ivor Novello's Redroofs near Maidenhead, Noël Coward's Goldenhurst and Lady Sybil Colefax's Argyll House. The Oliviers' Notley Abbey, with its royal lineage, was to be their *petit château*.

But Vivien was soon thin as an anorexic, afflicted with a constant

* The play was performed in the standard English version by Constance Garnett; these excerpts are quoted from the Tyrone Guthrie/Leonid Kipnis translation (University of Minnesota Press, 1959).

cough, given to chain-smoking and occasionally to excessive drinking
– although as usual she could not rest and insisted on finding another
stage role at once. And so in January – determined to keep up with
Olivier's pace and (as she believed) his professional expectations of her
– Vivien rang Binkie Beaumont, producer of *The Doctor's Dilemma*.
He had recently read the script of Thornton Wilder's comic moral
fantasy *The Skin of Our Teeth* and recommended to her the role of
Sabina, the burlesque maid and Lilith figure. In 1942 and 1943, the
play had been a great success in New York with Tallulah Bankhead;
now Vivien, eager to advance her stage career as his flourished, wanted
Olivier to direct her as Sabina – thus her performance would be as
perfect as he could make it. David Selznick, refusing permission, took
his contractual rights over her career as far as the London courts, but
Vivien's lawyers cagily argued that if she did not work as an actress
she might be drafted into military service, and in any case Selznick had
no British film studio and would suffer no loss if she appeared there
onstage.

Selznick lost his case, and by February Olivier was coaching Vivien
in *The Skin of Our Teeth*. This he readily undertook not only because
he felt an obligation to her career after such absorption in his own,
but also because it would provide the opportunity to direct a play
for the first time since *Bees on the Boatdeck* in 1936. *The Skin of
Our Teeth* is a bizarre, surrealistic mix of symbolism and fantasy,
following the same members of a New Jersey family as they pass
from the Stone Age to modern times. Inspired by Joyce's *Finnegans
Wake*, the play blithely mixes dinosaurs and bathing beauties, Greek
poets and singing telegrams, the Ice Age and radios. After *Henry V*,
nothing could demonstrate Olivier's directorial versatility more
than this.

Although provincial audiences were divided over the play's merits,
they were unanimous in praising Vivien's performance, and when the
play opened in London on 16 May the reviews were favourable enough
to sell out every performance. Olivier, confident of his success, did not
suffer critics any more gladly than he did fools, and when James Agate,
the dean of London's drama critics, returned to his aisle seat after the
second act had begun, Olivier swept down on him, punched him on
the shoulder and snarled, 'You're late, damn you!'

Notwithstanding the dust-up, Agate's subsequent review of Vivien
was highly laudatory. For her, this somewhat softened the news that
within days she was again to be separated from her husband, for after

the German surrender on 7 May, the Old Vic had arranged for an eight-week European tour.

Before the month's end, Olivier and sixty-five colleagues crowded onto a troop ship at Tilbury. Wearing British Army uniforms with the honorary rank of lieutenant, Richardson and Olivier led the company – the former wearing a standard peaked cap, the latter sporting a French beret. They played *Arms and the Man* and *Peer Gynt* in Antwerp, where the British Consul General hosted a lavish party for the company; in Bruges and Ghent there were similar receptions after performances of *Richard III* in ornate Belgian theatres.

The Old Vic moved on, giving a special performance for five hundred British and French soldiers charged with supervising the liberated concentration camp at Belsen. There, 40,000 barely surviving inmates lingered near a field of 10,000 corpses. Sybil Thorndike and a few company members toured the camp's makeshift clinic with a doctor, but Olivier declined to visit the inmates and children: 'Don't forget the matinee, mind,' he bade his colleagues as they departed.

That night, they were at the German State Theatre in Hamburg, performing *Richard III*. Olivier stumbled on a staircase during one exit, gunner-soldier R.B. Appleton recalled years later, and so on his second exit he took the stairs with great care, then looked round and smiled to show he had done it right. He was, according to Richardson, very good-humoured on the tour – and bored to death.

The boredom quickly turned to anxiety when he received a letter from a London friend named Anthony Bartley: after months of self-neglect, Vivien had finally submitted to tests which revealed tuberculosis. Unable to return to London until late July, Olivier followed news of her as he travelled in Germany and France, where he was informed that *The Skin of Our Teeth* had closed after seventy-eight performances and that Vivien was in isolation at University College Hospital. Meanwhile, the Old Vic arrived in Paris, where they performed *Arms and the Man* for two weeks at the Théâtre Marigny. And there Olivier insisted that since Richardson had opened the Vic season in London and Paris, he himself would now rearrange the schedule. He would play Richard when the company transferred to the Théâtre français.

Olivier's Richard was the great triumph of the tour, but it very nearly ended his friendship with Richardson – not to say his life. 'Ralph never forgave Larry for the change of schedule,' according to Laurence Evans, and after the post-performance celebration, an inebriated Richardson stormed into Olivier's fourth-floor room, lunged towards him and dragged him over to the balcony. In a matter of seconds, Richardson lifted him over the edge. Then, slowly and after some quiet pleading by Olivier, Richardson pulled him back to safety.

This event has been understood by many who knew them as merely the result of Richardson's intoxication; the two men were, it has been maintained, the closest friends despite this anomalous evening in Paris. But the event synthesised a lifelong jealousy. Richardson envied Olivier's glamour and his enormous box-office appeal at the Old Vic, while Olivier always feared that any rival actor's good fortune threatened his own. David Fairweather, publicist for the company, remembered the considerable friction between the two stars during the Paris sojourn. After dinner at a restaurant one evening, there was an embarrassing scene between them about their performances – who was getting more favourable notices, which one the public loved more.

Such fears are, of course, common to actors, who must always face the possibility that a particular role may be their last, that memory or voice may suddenly fail, that they will be denied work or awards crucial to their careers. Even Laurence Olivier, with his prodigious gifts, was no egomaniac and his energies often seemed inspired by insecurity. In time, Gielgud and Richardson, sensing Olivier's keenly competitive spirit, sometimes deliberately avoided performing with him. 'I hate him,' Richardson once said, 'until I see him. Then he has more magnetism than anyone I've ever met.' The antagonism always co-existed with contradictory feelings of mutual admiration.

One immediate result of the Paris contretemps was Olivier's astute suggestion, soon after, that in the coming Old Vic season Richardson should open as Falstaff in sequential productions of *Henry IV, Part One* and *Part Two*; in both, Olivier would assume lesser roles (but would make a mighty impression). Falstaff was eventually one of Richardson's greatest triumphs, and he always credited Olivier with the inspiration and encouragement to undertake it.

Returning to London in August, Olivier found Vivien cheerful and about to be released from hospital, and after a brief holiday in Scotland he installed her at Notley Abbey with two nurses. There she rested contentedly for four months, falsely confident her tuberculosis had been permanently arrested. She read Dickens, Oriental philosophy and French classics, occasionally tended one of the neglected gardens and planned the splendid weekends and banquets she would host. She also supervised the importation of antiques, tapestries, wall coverings and silver, converting the house into a virtual treasury. Olivier, meanwhile, gave himself to a lacerating cycle of work, learning four widely different roles and thousands of lines of poetry and prose in three weeks; at no season for the rest of his life did he demand more of himself than he did that autumn of 1945. His craft was now his only consuming passion.

On 26 September, *Henry IV, Part One* opened the new season, with Olivier as Hotspur and Richardson as Falstaff. An actor who was right for Puck and Mercutio was perfect for the voluble, virile and arrogant young rebel, for whom Olivier found a sympathetic touch in the text's reference to his 'speaking thick, which nature made his blemish'. He affected a stutter before every word beginning with 'w', and his death scene was harrowing. After Prince Hal had delivered the fatal blow to Hotspur's neck, Olivier stood, staunching the wound as blood oozed between his fingers and gasping his final line, '. . . thou art dust and food for w-w-[worms]' – and then plunged forward on his face, dying in the attempt to complete the word. Moments later, Richardson bore him, slung over his shoulders, from the stage, and the thumping of Olivier's head on the floor and steps was so painfully realistic that some spectators thought he had fainted in the fall.

'He had a streak of ruthlessness,' recalled Harry Andrews, who had duelled with him in the 1935 *Romeo and Juliet* (and who was playing Scroop in *Henry IV, Part One*).

> This manifested itself in the way he could be professionally jealous of people, even of his old chum Ralph Richardson . . . As Hotspur and Falstaff, usually the applause at the end when they were taking their solo bows rose to a peak when Larry came on and died a bit when Ralph took his. One night, however, I was holding the curtain for him to go on and receive his applause and Ralphy came on just after him and it rose well above his and he said, 'Hell, the bastard, why the hell has he done that to me?' And he meant it.

On 3 October, *Henry IV, Part Two* followed, with Olivier transformed into the old country justice, Shallow. In a further display of virtuosity, he played the small role with sunny senility, speaking in a high, thin tremolo and piling on make-up. ('Make-up is a strange thing, and for me that's where a lot of the magic lies.') Critics and theatregoers duly noted his ability to turn these two parts into unforgettably rich figures. But Richardson, for one, was not so pleased: Olivier, with masterly invention, had decided that Shallow was a beekeeper, and this led to some audaciously comic scene-stealing. In his dialogues with Richardson as Falstaff, Olivier removed his hat, whacked at the air as if swatting a bee, then kept up his running patter, again snatching at the air and flicking another bee. 'You're very, very funny,' Richardson said offstage, asking him to tone down the antics, 'but I have too much important plot to get through!'

Other fellow players found him, as Margaret Leighton said, 'painstaking and perfectionist, [with] moments when he [was] cutting and critical'. Cast as Lady Hotspur, she was seated behind Olivier and Sybil Thorndike during the final dress rehearsal. When the older actress mentioned Leighton's fine performance, Olivier – perhaps unaware of her presence behind them – said, 'Oh, my God, the girl's a fucking parrot!' Later, just before the performance began, Olivier summoned Leighton to his dressing room. Applying his make-up, he asked how quick a memory she had. ('I hadn't the wit or the nerve to say, "Like a fucking parrot's, darling!"' Leighton said later.) Then Olivier told her about important changes he wished to include only a few moments hence, different positions onstage and altered readings of lines.

'I tried to prove how versatile I was,' Olivier admitted years later. 'But it's also infinitely more fun to vary the parts!

> I like to think my face has always been like a blank canvas, ready to be shaped as I wished. It has always been my great joy to surprise an audience. 'My God, is that him?' . . . Nothing has given me more pleasure than knowing I have tricked my audience and been onstage for more than five minutes without being recognised.

Not since the Old Vic seasons of 1937 and 1938 – when he had played Hamlet, Toby Belch, Henry V, Macbeth, Iago and Coriolanus – had Olivier attempted such a variety of roles. But his achievements in 1944 and 1945 were more carefully prepared, more mature and less dependent on the tutelage of Guthrie or Saint-Denis. As Henry onscreen, as the Button Moulder, Sergius, Richard, Astrov, Hotspur, Shallow – and presently, Oedipus and Puff – he rendered portraits enriched by the intervening years with their admixture of professional and personal responsibilities, joys and sorrows. They were performances by a man familiar with disappointment, with success and with early rhapsodic love for a woman from whom he now felt increasing distance. He could not leave himself and these life experiences outside the door of the New Theatre; indeed, they infused his craft with a new richness and humanity. But as he had since the days with the Birmingham Rep, he wanted to look, to sound, to be another because he was always trying to learn about himself. Which role, which voice was Laurence Olivier? Which style was closest to the real man? He never lost a sense of incompleteness, and this is at the heart of his 'guilt' (as he repeatedly accuses himself in his *Confessions*) – not for something he had done, but for what he missed, what he felt was lacking in himself.

Despite this, there was noticeable that season in the thirty-eight-year-old Laurence Olivier a fresh confidence, the fruit of his maturity and an attempt to give to life through his art the structure, reason and control his privacy needed. His art was thus a means of withstanding disorder and anguish; the perfection of a role was a compensation for the insufficiency of reality.

This self-confidence and his sense of both the comedy of success and the tragedy of failure were directly responsible for his insistence that season on playing a riotously funny role in a double bill with one of the most grisly. Olivier accepted Tyrone Guthrie's proposal to direct him in Sophocles' *Oedipus Rex*, in the Yeats prose translation. But Olivier protested that this long one-act play was not a full evening in the theatre, and he intended to counterpoise the forbidding tale of the patricidal, incestuous king with a vivid, glittering burlesque of theatre itself – *The Critic*, Sheridan's eighteenth-century satire on actors, producers, aesthetes and audiences. As a guilt-ridden man who finally blinds himself and then as a comic dandy in charge of recalcitrant actors in a play-within-a-play, he would pour into one evening the extremes of theatre and of his own responses to his life. Guthrie, however, would not hear of this disparate double bill, and when overridden he departed for New York. Michel Saint-Denis assumed the direction of *Oedipus* and Miles Malleson (an Old Vic actor excelling in eccentric comic characters) of *The Critic*.

While alternating as Hotspur and Shallow, Olivier memorised Oedipus' six hundred lines (half the complete play) and the equivalent lines of Puff in *The Critic*. The two premieres occurred on 18 October, and from that evening every Olivier performance at the New was fully booked and great crowds of fans awaited him at the stage door.

That first night was, by all eyewitness accounts, one of the most brilliant in English theatrical history, proving beyond doubt that Laurence Olivier was an artist equally magnificent in tragedy and comedy. Black-curled and thick-nosed, his Oedipus was a nobleman consumed by a quest he only half-understood, and as he opened the play Olivier spoke with a quickened realism and almost dreadful urgency: 'The city smokes with incense and murmurs with prayers and lamentations. Do you know of anything I can do and have not done? How can I, being the man I am, do other than all I know?'

From there Olivier drew a dark path straight to the final tragedy, when he shocked audiences with two chilling cries – one offstage and one on, as he entered with stage blood streaming from his eyes and splattered on his hands and garments. His screams were unearthly, inhuman; indeed, Olivier was inspired by an account he had heard about ermine-trappers, who spread salt on ice. The animals licked the salt, their tongues froze to the ice and they wailed in agony even before the trappers approached to club them to death. Each night Olivier uttered the cries of a creature torn asunder by horror at what he has been forced to confront and almost half-whispered the lament as he gazed emptily: 'Woe, woe is me! Miserable, miserable that I am! Where am I? Where am I going? Where am I cast away?'

This performance alone would have demolished most actors, but fifteen minutes after the curtain fell Olivier was back, bewigged and sporting yet another false nose. Some critics complained that the devastating effect of *Oedipus Rex* was diluted by the subsequent comedy, but Olivier rightly insisted that the emotional strain on his audience must be balanced by a comedy – and in this he had good classical sense, for the ancient Greeks offered a comic satyr-play after the tragedies, although not on the same day.

The Old Vic offered the Sheridan play exactly 166 years after its premiere, and none of its pertinence and humour had dated. Entering in the second scene of the first act, Puff is the major character, and Olivier commanded the stage every second, tossing snuff into the air and catching it in his nostrils, delivering the wittiest epigrams with breathless clarity and (in the play-within-a-play) directing the dress rehearsal of *The Spanish Armada* with a cast of hearty incompetents.

'The number of those who undergo the fatigue of judging for themselves is very small indeed,' Olivier recited with a sly half-grin towards his audience, some of whom, that first night, turned round and smiled at the critics. He played the ingenious, harassed Puff as a dapper elf, a cork bobbing in uncertain waters, expert at planting publicity disguised as journalism. Booksellers and enterprising poets, Puff claims, can learn readily from the 'puff collusive'. They have only to publish a controversial item:

'An indignant correspondent observes that the new poem called *Beelzebub's Cottilion*, or *Proserpine's Fête Champêtre*, is one of the most unjustifiable performances he ever read. The severity with which certain characters are handled is quite shocking . . . too warmly coloured for female delicacy, [and] the shameful avidity with which this piece is bought by all people of fashion is a reproach on the taste of the times.' Here you see the two strongest inducements are held forth; first, that nobody ought to read it; and secondly, that everybody buys it: on the strength of which the publisher boldly prints the tenth edition, before he had sold ten of the first.

For the final scene at Puff's play rehearsal, Olivier perched himself on a plywood cloud above the stage, whence he was swept up and out of sight. The designers implored him to abandon the idea, but he insisted – again with almost tragic results. One night that autumn a wire supporting him snapped, and he escaped disaster only because a stagehand drew him to one side on a hastily tossed rope and he was able to slither down a side curtain.

By early 1946, Vivien was busy entertaining at Notley most weekends. Often, Olivier would have preferred quiet times alone, for only from Saturday night to Tuesday was there respite from the burden of the week's performances. (The Old Vic Theatre Company at the New played eight times a week: evening performances Tuesday to Saturday and matinees on Wednesday, Thursday and Saturday.) Above all, he coveted time to potter in his flower garden, which he supervised and loved as much as the house itself, but Vivien's weekends were a dither of activity. Friends were expected to arrive at Durham Cottage for drinks after the Saturday evening performance; around midnight they all piled into their cars, the Oliviers leading a convoy to Buckinghamshire.

There, Vivien had foreseen every detail and everything was arranged to please the ten or twelve guests (often among them were John and Mary Mills, Douglas and Mary Lee Fairbanks, Michael and Rachel Redgrave, John Gielgud, Noël Coward). A fire had been laid by the servants in each bedroom, where guests found their favourite novels, bottled Malvern water and a single perfect rose on a bedside table. It was close to two in the morning when dinner was announced. They were served cocktails in Notley's panelled library, and around three o'clock a four-course dinner was served, with appropriate wines. No expense was spared, and most of Olivier's salary from *Henry V* supported their grand lifestyle. Notley itself they had purchased out-right with his film salary, her savings from Hollywood, and the additional £15,000 he was paid by Del Giudice not to act in, produce or direct any film for eighteen months after the release of *Henry V*, an agreement that protected publicity and exploitation of that picture.

Visitors, of course, felt very tired after being merrily forced by their hostess to remain awake until dawn. Let Larry go to bed, she would say when her husband's head nodded at five o'clock in the morning and he begged to be excused. Charades or card games then began and no one was let off, although occasionally a mutineer like Rex Harrison would put his feet up, slouch in a chair and snore.

'Larry simply looked in from time to time, wearing tweeds and a country cap,' John Gielgud recalled of several weekends that year. 'He took only a sporadic part in the festivities before disappearing into the garden or secreting himself with models and plans in his private room, to which I was never asked to accompany him. But he had enormous personal charm, and he loved jokes and absurdities of all kinds.' The models and plans were for forthcoming productions, each aspect of which – from design to lighting cues – was always subject to his approval and modification; never was the designation actor-manager more appropriate. Most of all, Olivier loved to tend the gardens at Notley, to discuss fertilisers with salesmen, seedlings with neighbours, compost with local farmers.

Around eight in the morning, Vivien offered breakfast, by which time most of the guests had crawled to their rooms or were fortified to stupefaction with tankards of strong Turkish coffee; she required only a nap in the afternoon before beginning the new day's activities. There were tennis matches and tours of the estate, with stops to visit the cows named for Vivien's characters (Ophelia, Titania and Cleopatra, but no Scarlett) and to admire the arcades of trees and the five hundred rose bushes Olivier loved to tend himself. He loved to play the local squire in this ancient and baronial home, pruning the hedges and pre-paring the ground for sowing, according to Harry Andrews.

Olivier had little other rest that season. The American producer Richard Aldrich (husband of Gertrude Lawrence) had negotiated to bring the Old Vic Theatre Company to New York for six weeks in the spring of 1946. After the last performance of the season, on 28 April, more than 2500 people thronged outside the New and along St Martin's Lane, shouting for Olivier and Richardson. Olivier's coat was ripped and buttons were torn off as adoring fans grabbed at him, and the police had to assist the actors into taxis. The public adoration was unprecedented – and it heralded the new postwar obsession with stardom. Next day, the entire company boarded a Pan Am Constellation Clipper for the seventeen-hour flight to New York. There, Garson Kanin and his wife Ruth Gordon met the Oliviers and escorted them to the St Regis Hotel on Fifth Avenue.

For those denied the pleasures of Notley, New York was almost unnatural in its opulence. Diana Boddington recalled their delight at having everyday items like bananas, chocolate and coffee, which had been rare pleasures indeed for the English during wartime. 'I remember looking at Larry on the plane to New York and seeing the cuffs on his best shirt, frayed to threads. This was typical of us all – we had no clothing coupons.'

The two parts of *Henry IV* opened on 6 and 7 May, *Uncle Vanya* on 13 May and the Sophocles–Sheridan plays (referred to by the company as 'Oedipuff') on 20 May; Olivier was onstage for every performance, most often in the exhausting double bill. At the Century Theatre box office, all 87,000 tickets for the engagement were quickly sold, half that number of eager theatregoers were turned away, and at a time when the top price of a Broadway seat was $3.90, scalpers (sellers on the black market) were easily taking in fifty dollars.

While Olivier had no time for theatregoing in New York that spring, Vivien often went with the Kanins, who noted the edginess caused by her professional inactivity. 'A crazy quarrel last night with Vivien,' wrote Kanin after one evening in May, referring to her insistence on the pronunciation of a word. 'It must be maddening for her, a young actress at the peak of her powers and popularity, to find herself in the position of a hanger-on who has come along for the ride.' They saw *State of the Union*, *Dream Girl*, *Annie Get Your Gun* and Kanin's own hit comedy *Born Yesterday*, which Vivien enjoyed so much that she urged Olivier to bring it to London the following season. He read the text, easily negotiated the rights with Kanin, cabled London to arrange for a lease at the Garrick Theatre, and suddenly found himself with an additional responsibility, for he would produce and direct *Born Yesterday* that winter. At the same time, Vivien – chafing to return to work – prevailed on Binkie Beaumont to re-open Olivier's production of *The Skin of Our Teeth* in London that September.

The rationale for Olivier's decision to present *Born Yesterday* was clear. He wanted to prove that his new status as an eminent classical actor and a co-manager at the venerable Old Vic did not completely define his abilities. His grasp also included modern works (and American plays, as *Skin* had demonstrated); now *Born Yesterday*, with its deftly modern humour and language, would further establish his position as the most versatile Englishman in the performing arts – stage actor, director and manager as well as film actor, director and producer. Such ambition derived not from hubris but rather from a demonstrably reasonable belief in his own talents; at the same time, this secure self-estimation was not inconsistent with ordinary explosions of fear and jealousy.

Although he had little opportunity for New York socialising, Olivier was at a small gathering one night where he was reunited briefly with his old acquaintance Alexander Clark. Frances Tannehill, Clark's wife, was one of several that season who had an impression that Olivier was happy only when he was acting, or talking about acting. Socially he seemed rather shy and introverted, and he often drifted off into his own silence, but it was clear there were wheels turning in that silence.

By early June, Olivier was also exhausted to the point of nervous collapse, and several actors backstage at the Century were not at all certain he could endure the punishing schedule he had set for himself. Anxious, haggard and short-tempered, he was sometimes summoned from a brief nap backstage, startled out of frightening dreams he described to colleagues: that he was falling from a great height or that he was in an aeroplane about to crash. He had also agreed to interrupt his rare free days by reading play excerpts on Sunday afternoon radio broadcasts – a taxing addendum necessitated by the Oliviers' need for cash. His weekly Old Vic salary was one hundred pounds, which did not cover the St Regis bill or Vivien's new mink coat.

Neither audiences nor critics suspected his fatigue. A goodwill visit from those representing America's closest wartime ally – as well as a major New York cultural event – the Old Vic tour was an artistic and commercial triumph, and although the company played as a repertory without star billings, there was no doubt that Laurence Olivier won the greatest attention. His last performance in New York had been in the unfortunate 1940 *Romeo and Juliet*, but that was now forgotten in a swirl of critical and public adulation. 'The Old Vic is repertory showing what it can do,' read a typical press commentary, 'and it is also Laurence Olivier showing himself as an exceptionally fine actor.' Richardson and others received praise for their performances, but always fewer column inches than Olivier, and the six or seven curtain calls the ensemble took each night revealed the heart of the matter: the theatre rang with cries of 'Bravo, Larry!' and 'We want Larry!' Autograph-seekers besieged the stage door and reporters were despatched to obtain interviews and anecdotes. 'The spring seems to be given over to Laurence Olivier,' proclaimed the *New York Times*. The most importunate fans he sometimes resented; the adoration he relished.

Academics joined the critics and the public in honouring him. First among English or American colleges was Tufts University in Medford, Massachusetts, on Sunday, 16 June (the day after the last New York performance). He and Vivien arrived late, and Olivier made the trip hobbling on a cane and with a taped ankle, for on Saturday evening at his curtain call after his final Puff, he turned a double somersault, landed awkwardly and heard a popping sound: his Achilles tendon had been torn. Despite doctors' injunctions, he insisted on proceeding to Tufts, where he received a Master of Arts *honoris causa* for being 'the real interpreter of Shakespeare for our age'. But his pain and the hot, humid weather increased his general exhaustion. When he and Vivien missed their return flight to New York and were forced to wait two hours, Olivier collapsed onto the tarmac, watching the departing plane and sobbing like a lost child.

The following day, he slept fourteen hours and did not attend *Henry V* (screened since April only in Boston), which opened with a traffic-stopping gala at New York's City Center Theatre – a vast auditorium usually given over to dance and opera. There, with almost no advertising, it was screened three times a day for eleven months and earned revenues of more than a million dollars. Because of the highly creative tradition of film accountancy, the worldwide success of *Henry V*, which cost about two million dollars and eventually returned something in excess of five million dollars before 1948, never returned a profit to Del Giudice or Olivier.

The hectic activity resumed on Tuesday, 18 June, when the Oliviers and forty-two other passengers boarded a plane for London; their Old Vic colleagues had already departed. But an hour later, as if his night-mares had been prophetic, the outer starboard engine burst into flames and fell from the wing, and the plane began to swoop. The hydraulic system was burned out, the landing gear could not be lowered, and the pilot circled skilfully for fifteen minutes, finally bringing the craft down in a forced landing at Windham Field, near Willimantic, Connecticut. 'It is very awkward flying around with a motor missing,' Olivier told newsmen an hour later with feigned composure. 'We were in an arm's length of hell, but then we reached the ground safely. We cheered for two minutes.' Next day, the Oliviers departed again from New York and arrived without incident in London on 20 June.

During July and August of 1946, friends were as usual invited to Notley for tennis weekends and summer dinner parties. 'Notley was like Sandringham or Windsor Castle, for it was considered a great coup to be invited in those postwar years,' recalled Laurence Evans, who had left the Old Vic and was now a respected London theatrical agent.

'I thought he played a variety of roles there at Notley,' said John Gielgud of Olivier. 'One day he was the landowner, another the squire, one day the gardener, another the great host, and often the actor-manager in working seclusion. He played roles on and off the stage.'

That summer, Olivier annotated *Born Yesterday* and plans for the upcoming Old Vic season were finalised. While in New York, he had fancied he might like to revive *Cyrano de Bergerac* at the Old Vic and eventually co-star with Vivien in a Hollywood film of it. But this hope was altered when John Burrell called a board meeting and the old rivalries resumed. Richardson (who had first choice of leading roles) at once selected Cyrano for himself. Olivier, aware that Richardson had set his heart on King Lear for a future season and confident that he would immediately agree to exchange roles, countered by choosing Lear. But he had miscalculated, for Richardson let their selections stand, and this left Olivier to undertake one of the most complex and demanding tragic characters in all dramatic literature. And although Olivier and Richardson had acted together in more than a dozen plays and would always remain on polite terms, henceforth they never appeared onstage together again. That season, Olivier performed and directed *King Lear*; Richardson acted in J.B. Priestley's new play *An Inspector Calls* and then *Cyrano*. (Basil Dean directed the first, Tyrone Guthrie the second.) Vivien, for one, considered this professional disengagement a good thing for Olivier. That summer, Richardson had reasserted his innocently destructive tendency on a visit to Notley where, during a tour of the ancient attics, he ignored Olivier's warning and stepped through an unreinforced floorboard – and right through the ceiling of Vivien's bedroom.

Olivier's first task was the revival for Vivien of *The Skin of Our Teeth*. Terence Morgan, who was repeating his role as the son, found Olivier as cordial as before but somewhat overwhelming to the cast. They sat in a semi-circle round him, his back to the empty theatre, and he acted all the parts at the first reading; he knew exactly what he wanted from each player. Georgina Jumel (also in the cast and soon to be Mrs Terence Morgan) recalled that Vivien was like a taut wire, unable to relax, and that her relentless energy was very tiring for Olivier.

After a week of previews in Manchester, the Old Vic season opened on 24 September with Olivier's *Lear* – entirely sold out, as all his performances were that autumn. He had exercised his voice all summer long in preparation, shouting to the cows at Notley, extending his range and breath control, and by performance time he knew where every pause should be and how to shade his tone of voice. As director, this was his first stage Shakespeare since the New York *Romeo and Juliet*, and he offered each actor painstaking counsel. Margaret Leighton (as Regan) recalled that he had a plan for the entire play – how, when and where each character would be placed onstage: every move was in accordance with the text and helped to explain it.

Olivier portrayed Lear not as a blustery old monarch but as an unexpectedly amusing grandfather – witty, choleric and always surprised by malevolence but fully accepting the horrors of lunacy and death. The performance also had an enveloping warmth: to the Fool's pining over Cordelia's departure for France, Olivier delivered an almost unbearably gentle remonstrance: 'No more of that, I have noted it well.' His Lear had a long-repressed sentiment as well, a thirst for affection that was acknowledged almost too late, and in the storm scene his rage was balanced by an equally severe grief.

Some spectators thought him too young for Lear, too calculating in technique, too remote in the role. But Noël Coward (whose friendship never sweetened a severe critical assessment) wrote in his diary, 'Larry's performance as Lear ranks with his Richard III as being unequivocally great. He is a superb actor and I suspect the greatest I shall ever see.' The majority of critics, too, noted a new control and calm in Olivier's art; the power that could invoke a storm could still it with the raising of a hand. After he had seen his first Lear (Randle Ayrton, fifteen years earlier in Los Angeles) he became determined to be 'the greatest actor of all time'. Now very many critics and theatregoers claimed he was just that at the age of thirty-nine; and at seventy-five he would reprise the role to even more wondrous effect.

*

World War II had brought danger and deprivations to the ordinary British citizen, and life in its aftermath was a slow process of material recovery. As the government oversaw the hard and cheerless routine of reintegrating a depressed society, it was perhaps not surprising that England experienced the same desire for association with celebrities that had flourished in the United States.

American movie publicists since the 1930s had developed mechanisms by which the public was satisfied and careers were promoted – 'exploited' was the industry word, and it was just that. Publicists offered to fan magazines mostly fictional, sanitised accounts of a star's private life – 'puff pieces' that glamorised their subjects, routinely omitting mention of anything more controversial than a peculiar taste in wallpaper. Agents invited journalists for carefully controlled interviews at film studios, and producers engaged photographers to wait outside Hollywood restaurants. Columnists nourished the public's appetite for carefully manipulated glimpses of celebrities' private lives, but the gossip was (especially by later standards) remarkably discreet. Some of this was at first a natural distraction from the grimness of life during the 1930s and 1940s, the time of the Great Depression and the Second World War.

The public's desire to be in some way attached to the beautiful people not only derived from a desire to see a better life; it was also a corollary of democracy. If all are equal under God, there must be parity and access because stars, after all, are only human, and everyone could aspire to their station. The inherent contradictions, fostered by the conflicting desire to see both ordinariness and glamour, led to remarkably undemocratic designations: thus Clark Gable was called 'The King', John Wayne 'The Duke', any photogenic leading lady a movie 'queen', and a studio boss was an exotic Oriental emperor, a 'mogul'. Hollywood, in other words, simultaneously fostered democratic ideals and canonised the images of those who transcended ordinary folk.

The same longing – for association with the famous and for their benediction as members of a new, extended kind of royal family – came to postwar England, and no one experienced the effects of this more than Laurence Olivier. The splendid host at Notley was at other times a man of simple tastes, preferring plain talk and plain society, whisky with friends, a ploughman's lunch with actors who proffered no theatre programme or autograph album for him to sign. One part of his life was *comme il faut*, responsive to his increasingly quasi-royal status, while another part was without aristocratic pretence.

An extremely attractive man whose work required an audience, Olivier's eyes could be clear and curious or remote and provocative, and his voice could be appealing and expressive or quiet, metallic and diffident. Moreover, he had a keen theatrical intelligence graced with an immediate and intuitive sense of stage possibilities, and this was complemented by a capacious memory, a fertile imagination for inventive attacks on familiar roles and an ability to inspire and teach his colleagues. His charm and achievement, therefore, brought Laurence Olivier a greater degree of public exposure than he had ever expected – crowds at the stage door each night and constant requests for interviews.

One of the effects of fame became dramatically apparent offstage that November. A twenty-eight-year-old man named Herbert Wanbon applied as an apprentice to the Old Vic, and when he was not immediately engaged in a major role took strong measures. He awaited the Oliviers' return to Durham Cottage on Saturday evening, 23 November, and when they got out of their car he leaped forward and threw himself at Vivien, trying to kiss and embrace her. Olivier struck the first punch and the men went down in a scuffle while Vivien screamed for help. When the police arrived, Wanbon was quite calm and Olivier had a broken finger. 'I thought the Old Vic might change their minds through this publicity,' Wanbon said on 3 December in court; they did not, and he spent six months in prison for assault.

With his hand bandaged, Olivier departed on 25 November for Paris, where *King Lear* was presented for a week at the Théâtre des Champs-Elysées as the Old Vic's offering at an international UNESCO Festival. He was exhausted to the point that he virtually lost his voice one night, according to Terence Young, who saw him perform there, but despite that he gave a stunning performance. By 5 December Olivier was back in London, where his final month as Lear coincided with casting for *Born Yesterday* (scheduled to open in January) and with preparations for *Hamlet*, which he had hoped to film since 1943. Fully immersed in the multiple responsibilities of three plays, he nevertheless could, as the New Theatre publicist John Goodwin recalled, 'turn a light on for a particular task. He could sit and chat with you and suddenly go onstage for an enormously dramatic scene as Lear, and his trumpet voice rang out as if he'd been preparing a mood for hours.'

The voice could be heard less grandly, too, as it was on New Year's Day, 1947. 'I should have been the fucking knight!' he said angrily backstage when he heard that his colleague would henceforth be known as Sir Ralph Richardson. 'I've done every bit as much as he has, look how I've carried the flag abroad . . . and [had] an even fuller record in the classics – and there was a little film called *Henry V.*' The knighthood went to Richardson, it was said, because he was senior and personally liked by the Royal Family. But the dominant reason for ignoring Olivier was his status as a divorced and remarried man, then a significant consideration in selecting candidates for the Honours Lists.

There was little opportunity for brooding. On 5 January 1947 – the day after his last performance as Lear – Olivier began blocking the first scenes of *Born Yesterday*, which opened to superb notices at the Garrick on 23 January and had a healthy run of forty-two weeks. By that time, he was dashing from one meeting to another, planning for an Old Vic tour of Australia and New Zealand, scheduled to commence a year later and to include Vivien. This meant that he would have to complete his film of *Hamlet* (for which Filippo Del Giudice had once again made a financing and distribution deal with J. Arthur Rank) before the end of the year; his schedule with the Old Vic permitted him time off to make an occasional film. And so, to enable him and his colleagues to work expeditiously and without other professional distractions, Del Giudice convinced backers to finance a working winter holiday for the filmmakers on the Italian Riviera. In February, the Oliviers departed London with associate producers Reginald Beck and Anthony Bushell, designer Roger Furse, text editor Alan Dent, cinematographer Desmond Dickinson and art director Carmen Dillon.

In Paris – where they stopped to see Jean-Louis Barrault's staging of *Hamlet* – and in Santa Margherita Ligure, Olivier began planning for his *Hamlet* with unrestrained good humour. For Cecil Beaton and a few friends he offered one evening a lively exposition of his ideas for swirling camera movements and dramatic sound effects, providing satirically outdated gestures and rude, burlesque noises to entertain his listeners. 'Larry's imitations have about them something of the original clown,' Beaton noted in his diary,

> or at least the essential entertainer who can be found in some remote music hall or performing in the street outside a pub. This was the real Larry – the mummer, the ale-drinking Thespian – not the rather overwhelmed and shy cipher with wrinkled forehead that goes out into society.

176

John Mills agreed: 'Larry always had a marvellously bawdy sense of humour, and we were often left crying with laughter. He was a gifted mimic and raconteur.'

But the production of *Hamlet* was no party. After three months of preparation, filming began in late April at Denham and continued until November; personal and professional tensions abounded all that year. When the project had first been announced, Vivien had assumed she would play Ophelia as she had a decade earlier at Elsinore. But Olivier offered the impolitic excuse that at thirty-three she was too old, to which she countered that he was almost forty. He was intransigent, and after interviewing dozens of actresses employed eighteen-year-old Jean Simmons, who had already appeared in a dozen films (most recently as Estella in David Lean's *Great Expectations*). Simmons had the impression that Olivier wanted someone fresh, someone new to the role or even to Shakespeare – someone without preconceived ideas, since the play was to be filmed entirely according to his conception. It was also noted that Simmons had Vivien's delicate features and youthful beauty. But Vivien was soon frenzied, and at once she suspected that Olivier and Simmons were having an affair – a groundless fixation of which she could not be disabused. Her obsession brought her to Denham, where she anxiously watched the filming of Ophelia's mad scene, causing considerable tension for a cast and crew already severely strained by a complicated schedule.

'For days on end,' art director Carmen Dillon recalled, 'we [shot] scenes of unrelieved tragedy, and the gloom and intensity, combined with the almost superhuman drive and endurance of Laurence Olivier, had a chastening effect on [us all]. There were rarely moments when we could relax.' Cinematographer Desmond Dickinson agreed, adding that there was none of the spontaneous fun that enlivens the passage of humbler films through the studios. In fact, he said, he went quite grey on *Hamlet*.

In preparing his script and setting up each shot with his crew, Olivier had the audience in mind at every moment: he cut almost half the text, omitting characters (among them Fortinbras, Rosencrantz and Guildenstern) and subplots (the political crisis between Denmark and Norway), rearranging and simplifying scenes, condensing episodes, changing words and modernising phrases so that this *Hamlet* would be sprung free from its reverential moorings and become comprehensible for the moviegoing public. And because he wanted the sense of every word clear for that audience, he directed the cast – as his Laertes,

Terence Morgan, recalled – not to be afraid of playing a role as broadly as possible; it could be brought down to the right level later.

At the same time, Olivier insisted on realism – especially (as often before) with the duels and fights. Six swords were especially made by Wilkinson for the final duel, and each was broken in rehearsal or during takes. Insisting that Morgan lunge at him realistically, Olivier said, 'Don't worry, I'll parry, I'll parry.' Morgan obeyed the direction and went straight at him, but Olivier did not move on time. The sword point went through his shirt and he looked down, surprised to see a spreading stain of blood; there was a terrifying silence until it was clear he had suffered only a scratch. Even more dangerous was Hamlet's killing of Claudius, for Olivier hurled himself from a fifteen-foot height. When Basil Sidney (as Claudius) demurred, the burly stuntman who replaced him took Olivier's full weight, was knocked unconscious and lost two teeth.

Olivier had devised not a mere digest version of Shakespeare but what he called 'an essay', a single treatment examining a nearly great man damned by lack of resolution. The finished film has alternately the imprecision of a dream and the hazy horror of a nightmare, with images of half-seen faces and heartbeats accompanying ghostly voices. He always said he made *Hamlet* in black and white to achieve the effect of an engraving; in fact, he could not obtain from Technicolor the film stock he required, so he made a virtue of necessity and worked with technicians to perfect deep-focus photography. Everything was arranged to create a sense of enclosure and entrapment – the clarity of distant images, the vertiginous shots, the hallucinogenic dissolves, and the expressionistic castle of Elsinore with its tall columns and arched colonnades.

Hamlet was entirely Olivier's film, from casting to final cut, and every choice revealed something of the man. More than the halls and vast spaces of Elsinore, the film in a way explores the corridors of Olivier's own mind – the inner world of a man who had lost his mother, had been estranged from his father and had endured an unhappy marriage. His *Hamlet* remains, in the final analysis, not so much about a man racked by indecision as about a man tortured by his relationships with women.

There is, first of all, the attitude towards Hamlet's mother. Continuing the Freud–Jones hypothesis of the 1937 production – the Oedipal love of Hamlet for Gertrude – Olivier at forty cast as his mother the twenty-seven-year-old Eileen Herlie, emphasising in both costume and lighting her voluptuousness, stressing the avidity of their kisses and locating their critical confrontation on her bed. In the final moments, as Hamlet's corpse is carried aloft to the battlements, the cortège passes Gertrude's room and the royal marriage bed fills the screen, a talisman of his birth and her betrayal.

As to the Hamlet–Ophelia relationship, Olivier highlighted an important element in the text. After learning of his mother's and uncle's perfidy, Hamlet approaches Ophelia in her chamber. He stares at her silently, moves towards her as if to say something, then puts his hand to his brow and backs out of the room: his desire to speak with her about his responsibility is aborted when he realises she has no life-experience, no basis to understand and therefore cannot help him. So, in an effort to insulate her from the terrible knowledge about his parents and uncle, he says nothing – and thus Ophelia wrongly believes he has rejected her. One of the terrible ironies Olivier stresses is, then, that by Hamlet's attempt to protect Ophelia he destroys her. Her real madness serves as a tragic counterpoint to his own 'antic disposition', his feigned lunacy. Olivier's performance here and throughout the picture remains a textbook of film acting technique, for it is essentially a series of long gazes and subtly nuanced expressions – infinite sadness, mischievous playfulness, ever-deepening confusion, moral outrage. (Among the many awards for *Hamlet* were four Oscars, including best actor and best picture – the first foreign film to be so honoured; the British Film Academy and the Venice Film Festival awards for best picture; and a high civilian honour from Denmark, the Royal Order of Dannebrog.)

There were pleasant intervals amid the gruelling work. Following the London premier of *Oklahoma!*, the Oliviers invited the cast for a typically lavish weekend at Notley. The American visitors were surprised and amused at Vivien's earthy language, for her use of four-letter words was quite casual on any occasion. (Jean Simmons had once been at the theatre with the Oliviers when Vivien held up her white-gloved hands and said calmly, 'Oh, Larry, fuck it! I've dirtied my gloves!')

In May, still upset about the loss of Ophelia to a younger actress and about the aborted plans for her and Olivier to film *Cyrano de Bergerac*, Vivien's mood darkened. That month, she began work on a film of *Anna Karenina*, but this brought her perilously close to the edge of despondency, for she apparently saw all too clearly the similarities between herself and Anna, who leaves her husband and child for a lover, and eventually commits suicide. During the filming, recalled Sally Ann Howes (who played Kitty Scherbatsky), Olivier telephoned Vivien on the set every morning at eleven and every afternoon at four, anxiously asking about her mood. Directed by Julien Duvivier (who believed she was being coached by Olivier) and outfitted in Cecil Beaton's lavish period costumes, Vivien was a darkly haunting figure, an incarnation of guilt and grief. To the last day of production she prophesied (accurately, as it turned out) that the film would be a resounding failure.

This chain of disappointments did not suit her to be a cheerful recipient of the news of her husband's knighthood on 12 June, and when Cecil Beaton congratulated her, Vivien turned 'a face of furious scorn [and said], "Really, it's too stupid!"' Sir Robert Knox, secretary of the Political Honours Scrutiny Commission, confirmed that the award was 'an example of an increasing tendency towards a more liberal outlook' about divorce as a hindrance to the status of Knight Bachelor of the Empire.

On the morning of 8 July, borrowing Ralph Richardson's waistcoat and sporting his dyed blond hair as Hamlet, Laurence Olivier (at forty the youngest actor to be accorded the honour) knelt before King George VI and was tapped on the shoulders. 'I was nervous,' he cheerfully told the press outside Buckingham Palace. 'I like to have a dummy run before I do anything, but there wasn't any rehearsal!' Vivien – wearing a black dress, black shoes and a black hat, her funereal wardrobe unrelieved by jewellery or make-up – smiled tensely but said nothing.

CHAPTER TEN

✠

1948–1952

Sir Peter: I was a madman to marry you.
Lady Teazle: And I am sure I was a fool to
marry you.

Sheridan, *The School for Scandal*

In February 1948, the American comic actor Danny Kaye was just thirty-five years old and entering his peak years of international stardom on stage and screen. Since his show-stopping rendition of 'Tchaikovsky' in the 1941 Broadway hit *Lady in the Dark* – in which he rattled off the names of fifty-four Russian composers in thirty-eight seconds – Kaye had become a master of physical gymnastics and verbal tongue-twisters. Energetic, clownish and unpredictable, the red-haired, volatile comedian was also a gifted orchestra conductor, a gourmet cook and a devoted entertainer of children, whose cause he eventually took up as a volunteer with UNICEF. Although married (to the writer Sylvia Fine), Kaye was a dynamically aggressive homosexual.

Since he first met the Oliviers at a Hollywood party in 1940, Kaye had attached himself to them and visited whenever he could, lavishing attention mostly on 'Lally' or 'Lala', as he called his new friend. Olivier admired Kaye's inventive disguises, his manic humour, his risqué double-talk and his multiple skills as performer. On the evening of 13 February 1948, seventy guests crowded into Durham Cottage, and after a buffet supper Kaye offered a farewell salute to the hosts. Next day, the Oliviers joined sixty cast, crew and staff members of the Old Vic Theatre Company at Euston Station, where they boarded the boat train for Liverpool; from there they embarked on the S.S. *Corinthic*.

The British Council had arranged for the Old Vic to perform in Australia and New Zealand. There were several reasons for this tour: as a

181

gesture of Commonwealth unity after the war, to earn a profit for the Old Vic and to scout for new talent for the eventual expansion of the company into a national theatre. Among the leading players were Vivien (in her debut with the company), Terence Morgan and his wife Georgina Jumel, George Relph and his wife Mercia Swinburne and Peter Cushing and his wife Helen Beck. Aboard ship, actors were paid fifteen pounds a week for rehearsal time; for theatre performances, only twice that. Eager to please the company and sensitive to the fact of their low pay, the Oliviers compiled lists of every birthday and wedding anniversary, duly observing each with a cycle of parties and an array of gifts for their 'dear boys and girls', as Olivier (in the spirit of Lilian Baylis) called them at rehearsals. Unavoidably part of this geniality was a slight air of unintentional condescension.

On this tour, Laurence Olivier became the surrogate monarch which he was in some ways eminently suited to be. Idolised for his achievements and admired for his looks, he accepted the mantle of nobility and wore it everywhere. Notley and knighthood had further fixed him in a kind of popular mythology – and to a great extent also in his own self-estimation – as destined for noble status. Throughout the journey, and indeed for the rest of his life, Olivier saw himself as in some way the embodiment of British history; he was, as playwright John Osborne later said, ever conscious of his place in the English hierarchy. Vivien, with her beauty, intelligence and talent, quickly adapted to the demands of their august status.

Performing many of the functions of royalty, they were everywhere besieged by the press and public for interviews, ship christenings, broadcasts, tours of neighbourhoods and public works, inspections of lines of troops. 'We want to see the country,' Olivier told the waiting press when they docked at Fremantle on 14 March. 'We want to see every kind of animal or bird there is – black swans, for instance.' The crowds, appropriately responsive, treated the Oliviers with unrestrained deference.

On 21 March, the opening night (during a hundred-degree late-summer heatwave), the Old Vic company filled the vast 2280-seat Capitol Theatre in Perth with Sheridan's *The School for Scandal*. Despite the dreadful acoustics, audiences loved the eighteenth-century comedy, laughed at the antics of the scandal-mongers, warmed to the wistful melancholy of Sir Peter (Olivier) and applauded the unmasking of his wife Lady Teazle (Vivien). Notwithstanding the cast's spartan accommodations in guest houses and cheap hotels, the unfortunate acting venues, the weather, the heavily brocaded Beaton costumes and uncomfortable period wigs, company morale for the fully booked two-week run was kept high by their leader's authoritative calmness.

For two weeks, the Oliviers were constantly hounded outside the theatre by crowds of autograph-seekers, and at their cramped, mosquito-infested hotel they received more than 1500 fan letters. Strangers bowed, raised their hats, jostled to touch them as they made their way in open cars through mobs estimated at 8000 strong. But Olivier was soon exhausted from his multiple duties as actor, director and manager, from the constant round of public speaking and social engagements and, during afternoons, rehearsals with his cast for *Richard III*, which alternated with *The Skin of Our Teeth* for two weeks in Adelaide. Suffering a painful case of gout, he often required a cane, but ignored his discomfort, blithely climbing ladders to alter stage lighting and remaining late to inspect each costume for wear. And each night after performances, he and Vivien invited two members of the company to dinner or drinks. On such occasions, Olivier frequently continued to be the star entertainer, imitating birds, animals, rival actors (notably John Gielgud, whose ability to weep convincingly onstage he both admired and resented) and even King George VI, whose stuttering he perfectly duplicated. But he was sometimes moody and introspective during these evenings of *noblesse oblige*, while Vivien fluttered about and kept up a stream of amusing anecdotes about their hosts' accents and customs.

By mid-April, when they were performing all three plays during an eight-week stay in Melbourne, the Oliviers could have announced a political coup and taken over the continent. His speeches, laced with purple prose and shameless jingoism, drew thunderous applause.

> When a man is British [he told a Melbourne gathering], he is constantly finding himself proud of being so. More than once it has been put to me in question form since I have been in your country, that it might be assumed in some quarters that Britain might very well consider herself to be finished. My friends, I say to you that if one of your most loving relations, my countrymen, thought for a moment that your very great kindness was provoked by that feeling of pity which is akin to contempt, I say to you that there is not a Briton alive who would not rather that you never send them another parcel and that you never spare them another thought, wish or sigh. Britain is not finished.

As for Vivien, she rarely made speeches, impromptu or otherwise, but at press conferences she was invariably patient and articulate as columnists gushed over her beauty and fashionable wardrobe.

In mid-June, they reached Tasmania. Vivien, fearing that public adulation would take Olivier away from her (rather as if fame were a mistress), took no pleasure in the public's adoration of herself, and began to spend a good deal of time with a young actor in the company named Dan Cunningham. Although she had always revelled coquettishly in an admiring coterie of friendly peers, she was now for the first time flirting openly. She seemed pleased when Olivier, embarrassed, scolded her for this flirtation: most of all, she wanted to regain her husband's attention.

On 29 June the company began a two-month run in Sydney, where they presented twenty-five performances of *The School for Scandal*, seventeen of *Richard III* and eighteen of *The Skin of Our Teeth* before more than 120,000 spectators; by this time, it was clear that even after expenses the British Council and the Old Vic were realising healthy profits. This gave the underpaid actors a sense of purpose and pride; indeed, among them there was an extraordinary camaraderie, without cliques or rivalries.

But problems arose, as the strain of performances, public appearances and mustering the theatrical troops taxed the Oliviers. He was Sir Laurence, representing king and country; she was merely an attractive consort – so she thought, or so she felt herself treated – and soon the Oliviers became uncomfortably aware that they had little to share in private. Company members with rooms near theirs heard prolonged and loud altercations. Hitherto, their marriage had endured their varying professional fortunes because of frequent separations and 'the glitter of our position' (as Olivier called their public image). Now, with the kind of proximity denied them in recent years – and which they had believed they longed for – the Oliviers found one another's constant companionship awkward and demanding. 'I lost you in Australia,' he told Vivien later; more accurately, he discovered in Australia that they were losing one another.

The growing distance between them took an oddly unexpected toll during the second performance of *Richard III* in Sydney, on 3 July. Lunging too violently at the actor playing Richmond – who happened to be Dan Cunningham – Olivier slipped and fell on his right knee, badly tearing the cartilage. For the remaining performances as Richard he used a crutch, which many thought was a dramatic prop.

A worse kind of pain soon followed. On 15 July, Olivier received a letter from Lord Esher, Chairman of the Old Vic Governors, informing him that the tripartite directorship of Burrell, Richardson and Olivier was to be ended when their contract expired next June; a new administration would be appointed to replace the men who had earned worldwide fame for the Old Vic and knighthoods for themselves. Burrell (in London) and Richardson (working in Hollywood on William Wyler's film *The Heiress*) received the same letter.

As might have been predicted, an ugly political situation had developed, at the centre of which was none other than Tyrone Guthrie, the man who had suggested this joint leadership in the first place. He complained to the Old Vic board: first, that the company's international repertory status was being injured by its identification as 'Olivier's Old Vic', and second, that it was inappropriate to have the company managed by two actor-knights. His complaints may have been caused by envy of Olivier and Richardson's knighthoods.

But the compelling reason for the dismissal (and the one pointedly mentioned by Esher) was that the Old Vic was now associated with the embryonic National Theatre's founding body. Such an institution was exactly the goal to which Richardson and Olivier were committed, and towards which they had, with the board's approval, drafted a twelve-year plan. But Esher and his board intended to appoint a non-actor as full-time administrator, someone outside the profession, free from prejudice, and someone without the kind of popular approval that might diminish their own power. They were also, as it turned out, ignorant of how to proceed, for although a National Theatre Act was passed by Parliament in 1949, no such organisation emerged until 1963, and no building for it until thirteen years after that. With supreme irony, both developments would directly involve Laurence Olivier.

Olivier replied to Esher that he felt like a pioneer abandoned by the mother country in the midst of a crucial battle, which was more a literal description than a simile. He also asked if this sad development meant the abandonment of the plans laid by himself and Richardson for the coming season, which was to begin with a production of Jean Anouilh's *Antigone*. In a series of carefully worded letters from London, the Board of Governors' view was made maddeningly plain. They considered the team – after the 1944 to 1946 seasons – financially extravagant and concerned mostly for their own careers. Richardson and Burrell, like Olivier, made their outrage clear in letters and cables, but the matter was beyond negotiation. Owing to his very eminence, the rule of Olivier could not continue with the star actor so often absent. After a battery of correspondence, Olivier finally persuaded the Old Vic Governors to commit to his final season (*Richard III, The School for Scandal* and *Antigone*), but he was requested to keep the administrative news to himself, which he did, confiding only in Vivien.

The behaviour of the triumvirate was, then and later, impeccable, but Olivier did not merely suffer in silence. If he was being resented as a de facto actor-manager, he would behave like one. At once he revived his ambition to lead a theatrical production company – his own Old Vic. The previous year (with *Born Yesterday*), he had legally established Laurence Olivier Productions with no clear idea of its future; it remained mostly a paper entity with a token board (Roger Furse and Anthony Bushell, with the Oliviers' agent Cecil Tennant as managing director), subsidised by Alexander Korda, who owned a controlling interest. Now Olivier, free from any moral obligation to recruit only for the institution that had treated him so shabbily, eagerly sought actors for LOP, as it was soon familiarly called.

Before the end of August, after seeing a performance of Molière's comedy *The Imaginary Invalid*, Olivier approached a tall, dark-haired actor named Peter Finch. Thirty-two, with rugged features and alert blue eyes, Finch already had considerable experience in Australian theatre and films. The Oliviers considered him one of the best young performers they had seen anywhere, and they invited him and his wife to dinner; within two days, Finch had accepted an offer to come to London to act with LOP. He would arrive early in 1949.

The final five weeks of the tour were spent in New Zealand, where the company gave forty-nine performances in four cities (Auckland, Christchurch, Dunedin and Wellington). Geographically and culturally isolated, New Zealanders after the war did not quite know how to welcome the famous English actors; to most of them, an evening's entertainment usually meant sports or a movie. Restaurants closed at nine, there was little social life, and visitors were politely ignored.

To everyone's surprise, the Vic's seventeen performances of *School* in Auckland brought in crowds totalling 33,000 people, but the players were so exhausted and homesick they took little pleasure in seeing full houses each night. By this time, the Oliviers' tempers were as frayed as the costume linings, and just before the first performance in Christchurch there was a rare public display of marital discord. When Vivien could not find the red shoes she needed as Lady Teazle, she was furious.

45. *Right* In the Old Vic production of *Arms and the Man*: as Sergius, with Margaret Leighton (1944). *John Vickers Archives*

46. *Middle right* As Astrov, with Ralph Richardson as Uncle Vanya, Old Vic (1945). *Culver Pictures*

47. *Below* As Hotspur in *Henry IV, Part I*, Old Vic (1945). *Culver Pictures*

48. *Bottom right* As Shallow in *Henry IV, Part II*, Old Vic (1945). *John Vickers Archives*

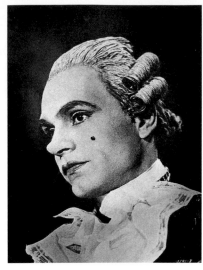

49. *Above left* As Oedipus Rex, with Sybil Thorndike as Jocasta, Old Vic (1945). *John Vickers Archives*

50. *Above* As Puff in *The Critic*, Old Vic (1945). *Culver Pictures*

51. *Left* As Lear, with Alec Guinness as the Fool, Old Vic (1946). *John Vickers Archives*

52. *Below left* Durham Cottage, Christchurch Street, Chelsea. *National Film Archive, London*

53. *Below* Directing *Hamlet* (1947). *National Film Archive, London*

54. *Right* Hal Wallis and Ray
Milland present Olivier with his
Special Oscar for *Henry V* during
filming of *Hamlet* (1947). At far
left, Diana Boddington. *Culver
Pictures*

55. *Below* The daring final leap
during the filming of Hamlet.
National Film Archive, London

56. *Top* Notley Abbey.

57. *Above left* Docking at Tilbury aboard the *Corinthic* after the Australian tour (1948). *National Film Archive, London*

58. *Above* Backstage with Tarquin, opening night of *Venus Observed* (1950). *From the collection of Felix Barker*

59. *Left* During production of *Carrie*, with director William Wyler and Vivien, at Paramount Studios (1950). *National Film Archive, London*

Olivier told her to put on any shoes available and go on, but Vivien was adamant: the red shoes or no performance. 'Get up on that stage, you little bitch!' he ordered, slapping her face. She returned the blow, countering, 'Don't you dare hit me, you bastard!' Moments later, wearing modern black pumps beneath her floor-length brocaded gown, Vivien dried her tears and was soon smiling brightly onstage.

Olivier, too, was putting a brave face on pain. Since the injury to his knee, he had endured increasing discomfort and lack of mobility, and after several consultations with doctors it was agreed that surgery was the only option. On 10 October, after the last performance of the tour, an operation was performed in Wellington by Dr Kennedy Elliott, who removed the ruptured cartilage. A week later, an ambulance drove him to the docks, where he was the last to board the *Corinthic* for London. Unable to bend his plaster-encased leg, he asked to be trussed up in a canvas tarp and swung, like baggage, onto the ship's deck while photographers snapped away to record the moment. It was, according to the company members welcoming him onboard, a brilliant final touch, and pure Olivier: efficient, dangerous and designed for publicity.

After a final dreary month at sea, the company docked at Tilbury on 16 November, nine months and two days after departure. They had performed 179 times before more than 300,000 people and returned with more than £42,000 net profit to the British Council. The Oliviers, who had negotiated a percentage in addition to their hundred-pound weekly salary, also realised £5,000; and each member of the company was given a bonus. Most received sixty pounds – which hardly covered even their personal expenses.

The new year was frantic with activity as Olivier played three roles with the Old Vic and swung into action with LOP, planning to present in March James Bridie's new play *Daphne Laureola*, starring Edith Evans and Peter Finch. Refusing press requests for interviews about his plans for theatre management, he also kept a stoic silence after meetings with Esher that were paradigms of bureaucratic offensiveness. At the same time, he and Vivien spent less time together: she planned minor redecorations for Notley and Durham Cottage and dined quietly with friends like dancer-actor Robert Helpmann while Olivier, after a working day with Roger Furse, often caroused late. Vivien was also carefully studying Tennessee Williams's play *A Streetcar Named Desire*, with an eye to playing the tragic Blanche DuBois in an English production later that year. Olivier, she insisted, would direct her.

On 20 January 1949, *The School for Scandal* opened at the New Theatre, the first time Laurence Olivier and Vivien Leigh appeared together on the London stage. To honour that, he presented her with a portrait of a woman from Sheridan's time and a bottle of her favourite cologne, while (with typically greater extravagance) she offered him a pair of eighteenth-century cufflinks fashioned from garnets, rubies and emeralds.

The first night was an almost riotous triumph. Hundreds of admirers had slept outside the theatre all night in a wintry drizzle for the remaining few seats after more than 5000 postal applicants had been disappointed. Inside, a capacity audience of 2000 brought the cast back for eight curtain calls. Hoping for a glimpse of the Oliviers, more than 3000 fans crowded St Martin's Lane before and after the performance, halting traffic north to Oxford Street and south to the Thames. By this time, journalists had trumpeted the news of the Old Vic firing, and editors of every paper were overwhelmed by letters of protest. This was Olivier's first London appearance with the Old Vic in more than two years, and his legion of admirers intended to celebrate that even though it also began his final season with the company.

The School for Scandal was performed by the Oliviers with a curious lack of bite, and with more sentiment than severity. Exhausted from the tour and depressed by the board's actions, Olivier played Sir Peter with such bittersweet refinement that some critics felt a lack of Sheridan's finely honed satiric edge; at the same time, Vivien was praised for her coquetry but corrected for her reliance on a Gainsborough-like elegance. (Olivier's mood was directly conveyed to the audience one night when he interrupted a performance to scold them for excessive coughing.) His somewhat muted performances continued on 26 January, when his Richard III seemed strangely lacking in the cruel drive and savage irony that had alarmed and excited previous audiences.

But he gave an acutely chiselled and chillingly effective performance as the Chorus in his production of Jean Anouilh's *Antigone*, added to the repertory on 10 February (and preceded by Chekhov's comic curtain-raiser *The Proposal*, which Olivier also directed). Sharply contrasting with Vivien's performance as the fanatically determined and calmly devoted Antigone, Olivier coolly synthesised the Greek sense of fate in one single, piercing speech:

> The spring is wound up tight. It will uncoil of itself. That is what is so convenient in tragedy . . . You don't need to lift a finger. The

machine is in perfect order; it has been oiled ever since time began
. . . Death, treason and sorrow are on the march, and they move in
the wake of storm, of tears, of stillness . . . Tragedy is clean, it is
restful, it is flawless. In tragedy nothing is in doubt and everyone's
destiny is known.

Nightly performances continued throughout February and March,
while Olivier spent days with Edith Evans and Peter Finch at rehearsals
for *Daphne Laureola* which (although he would not direct) he supervised in every detail. In this regard, his position as manager added a
new twist to an old and honoured function: a famous actor was now
appearing in one place and presenting someone other than himself in
a new play elsewhere. This was revolutionary for an actor-manager;
Henry Irving, for example, had presented Henry Irving, and Gerald du
Maurier had always produced plays starring himself.

But in a way Olivier was indeed presenting himself over the next
several years as he guided with unprecedented attention the career of
Peter Finch. From the time of their few meetings in Sydney through
to the opening of the Bridie play on 23 March, Olivier had become
fascinated by Finch's background and committed to his talent, and their
relationship became ever more complex over the next six years.

To begin with, Olivier arranged for Finch to be represented by Cecil
Tennant, his own agent. He then contracted him to LOP for a term of
five years and after *Daphne Laureola* (which ran from March 1949 to
February 1950) put him in *Damascus Blade*, *Captain Carvallo* and *The
Happy Time*. Just as he had demanded of the Old Vic for himself,
Olivier also gave Finch time off for films, reserving prior script
approval. And in perhaps the clearest intimations that he was monitor-
ing a career patterned on his own, he assigned Finch two of his own
most important earlier roles – Iago in 1951 and Mercutio the following
year.

The reasons for this tutelage and benevolent manipulation are not
difficult to understand. On the one hand, Olivier was as touched by
the details of the younger actor's childhood as he was impressed by his
talent. Abandoned by parents who left him in Australia while they set
out for England, Finch had quickly developed an independent, somewhat wild and bohemian character. An amorous, sexually hyperactive
reveller, Finch's brusque and confident manner belied a craving for the
emotional security lacking in his early life, and he harboured a lifelong
yearning to know his parents. Naturally poised, gifted with a quick

memory and perceptive about the seriocomic role of the young Polish romantic in *Daphne Laureola*, he was in a way Olivier's alter ego. Finch also evoked in Olivier a kind of suppressed, compensatory paternity, receiving from him the guidance and recognition Tarquin had been denied. And to many there was at the time no doubt that Peter Finch also aroused a strong (if unexpressed) erotic attraction in Olivier.

Vivien, too, had her reasons – in some ways even more pointed – for feeling attracted to Finch, for his peripatetic childhood was very like her own; more obviously, his glowing virility and sexual allure appealed to her. On his side Finch, though coveting independence, had serious career ambitions and was gratified to become important to the great Sir Laurence Olivier and accepted into the social circle that centred round Vivien. To him, they must have seemed like sophisticated parents, emblems of future possibilities and guarantors of his value.

A clear token of the Oliviers' endorsement was his inclusion in several weekends at Notley, where Vivien immediately disarmed Finch's initial discomfort, enquiring about his ambitions and introducing him to an all-star cast: Orson Welles, planning his *Othello*; Tennessee Williams and his lover Frank Merlo; and Irene Selznick, who had presented *A Streetcar Named Desire* on Broadway, in heated discussions with Olivier about textual cuts in his forthcoming production of that play. Finch was pleased to be Vivien's preferred dinner partner that spring, although he was not alone in judging her hospitality sometimes too calculated to be comfortable.

With the end of the 1948–49 Old Vic season in June, Olivier's contract expired. He and Vivien departed for a holiday on the Riviera, where they discussed the staging of *Streetcar* and the role of Blanche. In the course of this journey (and apparently not, as Olivier wrote more picturesquely in his autobiography, in the winter garden at 4 Christchurch Street), Vivien casually announced that she was no longer in love with him. She did, however, still need him as friend, protector and mentor. This must have been less a surprise than he later claimed, for there was scarcely much physical intimacy in their marriage by this time.

As before with Jill, the new twist to the relationship presented a dilemma. Neither wished to divorce, for their careers were intertwined and in an important way subject to their status as Sir Laurence and Lady Olivier: his knighthood, he admitted, was 'sacred' to him, and another dissolved marriage would gravely tarnish his public image. He also felt responsible for Vivien's career, since her partnership was such a crucial ingredient in that image.

From childhood, Vivien's estimation of her worth had depended on pleasing acquaintances and strangers; for over a decade now, her endless attempt to win the approval and affection (once centred round Leigh Holman) had been transferred to Olivier, her trusted guide. He responded to her deepest needs for a supportive father-image, while she – admiring advocate and charming manipulator – provided many maternal qualities he could not risk losing again. But from summer 1949, despite occasional attempts to revive the once ardent commitment, the marriage was frankly and firmly imperilled; their relationship, very much influenced by the legacy of their past, had concentrated to an extreme and poignant degree the ordinary elements in every romance. And perhaps most cutting to Olivier was Vivien's increasing complaint that he was an unsatisfying lover. At the same time she began to suspect Olivier's sexual ambivalence – in his treatment of Finch and especially in the increasingly frequent visits and almost obsessive attention of Danny Kaye, with whom Olivier spent a good deal of time when Kaye was in London. Her accusations of her husband's sexual languor – a complaint made partly out of need, partly out of fear – had the predictable effect of driving him further from her.

Precisely at this point, Vivien undertook Williams's tragic Blanche DuBois in *A Streetcar Named Desire*. A sad, thirty-year-old Southern belle who has suffered the loss of her ancestral home, Blanche arrives in New Orleans to visit her sister, married to a crudely forceful archetype of machismo (on Broadway, the role brought instant fame to Marlon Brando as Stanley Kowalski). Blanche's airs, affectations and lies are ruthlessly exposed by her brother-in-law, and it is revealed that she – no respectable schoolteacher, as she claims – had been briefly married to a young homosexual whose suicide was precipitated by her cruel taunting. Since then, she has taken to a life of guilt-ridden promiscuity, and when her brother-in-law rapes her Blanche's doom is sealed: she suffers a complete mental breakdown and is removed to an asylum.

By the end of August, they were rehearsing in London, and Vivien confided, in letters to her friend Sunny Lash, that she was 'very, very nervous' about her role; indeed, she placed something like absolute value on the execution of it. During the final days of rehearsal in early October, Olivier pushed her to the limits of her endurance, demanding just one more rehearsal of this scene or another private conference about that moment; and she continually implored him for guidance about every small gesture, all the nuances of a line reading, each pause and turn. Responsive to his slightest suggestion, Vivien was terrified her voice would not carry, anxious she might miss a cue and most of all frightened of embarrassing Olivier by her inadequacy or of interiorising Blanche's desperate state to such a point that she herself would collapse. She also may have feared the emerging parallel in her own marriage, as she goaded Olivier over their marital difficulties. Cast members Bonnar Colleano and Renée Asherson recalled Vivien's pale, shaking anxiety after every performance: they and friends visiting backstage were afraid she might indeed fall very ill. But she did not, and played the role for more than eight months.

With *Streetcar* settled in for a long run, Olivier turned his attention to management decisions. After the failed, two-week run of Donagh MacDonagh's *Fading Mansions* (an adaptation of a French play by Jean Anouilh, directed by Anthony Bushell), Olivier was determined that LOP would have its own theatre. The great actor-managers (Irving, Tree, Wyndham, Waller, du Maurier) had produced, directed and starred in plays under their own roofs, and when the St James's Theatre became available that autumn of 1949, Olivier took a four-year lease from its American owner Gilbert Miller. A small (950-seat) theatre in King Street near Piccadilly, the St James's had a history dating back to 1835. For twenty-eight years (until 1917), Sir George Alexander had been its actor-manager, offering plays by Wilde and Pinero; later, in its plush red-and-gold interior, Olivier had first seen Sybil Thorndike and Lewis Casson, Noël Coward and Gladys Cooper.

'I think audiences are prepared to see good acting even in a bad play,' Olivier said defensively in 1950, after presenting several plays that were financial failures at the St James's. But this was a thesis he did not prove, and under his management there was never a profit. To pay the bills for lavish and expensive productions, he was frequently forced to lease out the St James's to other managers (the Jean-Louis Barrault troupe, for example, and Orson Welles). The ultimate collapse of the venture was partially due to factors beyond Olivier's control: high postwar entertainment taxes, sharply rising costs and, ultimately, the changing style in theatre itself. Meanwhile, he would bring the force of his personality and fame to the enterprise, and when necessary would appear in films to subsidise it. His twenty London productions from 1947 to 1960 (nine of them at the St James's, which was demolished in 1957) provided him, despite his varying involvement and the uniformly poor financial returns, with invaluable experience for the even more important period to follow.

The first offering under LOP management at the St James's was a verse play commissioned by Olivier for himself to direct and perform, a fey romantic comedy called *Venus Observed* by Christopher Fry (recently the author of *A Phoenix Too Frequent* and *The Lady's Not for Burning*). Just before starting rehearsals in mid-December, Olivier flew to New York, where he had been invited to read the Declaration of Human Rights at an anniversary ceremony for the United Nations on 10 December. Two days later (after hurried visits to the Kanins, Thornton Wilder and *South Pacific*) he was back in London, rehearsing with his assembled cast. Among them were Denholm Elliott and Rachel Kempson, who found Olivier in high spirits and good humour. 'One day,' Elliott recalled years later, 'I told him I'd just had a terrific row with a friend, whom I told to go fuck himself.'

'You should never say that to anyone, Denholm,' Olivier said quietly. 'It's very rude.'

'I know. I'm so sorry I did it.'

There was a pause while Olivier thought. He then turned to Elliott: 'What you *should* have said was, "How would you like to go and fuck yourself?"'

As the Duke of Altair, a middle-aged astronomer-amorist in *Venus Observed*, Olivier played a modern, debonair roué who prepares to select at last from among his mistresses – only to learn that his son is a rival for the lady of his choice. The play opened on 18 January 1950 and ran until 5 August; critics and audiences liked the elegant set and Olivier's polished performance, but Fry's play seemed a self-consciously high-flown conundrum. In the popular idiom of rather florid free verse, the play required Olivier to intone orotund speeches reminiscent of ersatz T.S. Eliot.

> Duke: If the earth is ever wise
> To magic, this is the night when wisdom
> Comes rolling in across our sedate equation.
> All the closed hours unlock; rigorous ground
> Grows as soft as the sea, exhaling
> The bloom of the dead everywhere.

Noël Coward had been quiet since *Present Laughter* in 1942, and the plays of Sean O'Casey, Terence Rattigan and James Bridie were respectable but not overwhelmingly successful. Olivier wrongly presumed that Fry would brightly rekindle London's dim postwar theatrical seasons.

During the run of *Venus Observed*, Olivier directed Peter Finch in two plays: *The Damascus Blade* by Bridget Boland and Denis Cannan's *Captain Carvallo*. Rehearsals for the former were slightly worrying for the cast, who found Olivier's meticulous preparation somewhat constraining. John Mills remembered that Olivier's prompt book – with every move and gesture marked with red and blue arrows for each line of dialogue – looked like a blueprint for an army manoeuvre and left little room for the actors' contributions. The venture was, as it happened, overprepared by everyone, since after a few weeks in the provinces the play closed before its London premiere.

Nevertheless, Finch and his career were being monitored by Olivier – and so was his friendship with Vivien. She was delighted when Finch was a weekend guest at Notley, and Olivier, eager to deflect her suspicions about himself and Finch, encouraged the visits. He may not have recognised (or chose not to admit) that the relationship between Vivien and Peter was becoming very tender indeed, although in 1950 it was still platonic.

In any case, there would soon be a long separation. LOP desperately required funds to keep the lease on the St James's, and as if on cue Hollywood came to their rescue. Vivien was invited by Elia Kazan (who had directed *Streetcar* on Broadway) to recreate Blanche in the film version, and William Wyler offered Olivier the co-starring role in *Carrie*, based on Theodore Dreiser's first novel *Sister Carrie*. On 31 July, Vivien flew from London to America for pre-production meetings with Kazan and producer Charles K. Feldman. Two weeks later (after Finch's opening in *Captain Carvallo*), Olivier followed. Stopping briefly in New York, he admitted to Garson Kanin that his emotional exhaustion was caused more by anxiety over his marriage than by overwork: 'We never converse,' he told Kanin of his relationship with Vivien, 'we only confer.'

For the term of their filmmaking, Feldman turned over his Coldwater Canyon home to the Oliviers, whose return to Hollywood after a ten-year absence was cause for considerable press coverage and general industry rejoicing. Sunny Lash was again engaged as Vivien's secretary and assistant, while the adoring Danny Kaye prepared to host a lavish formal ball in their honour at the Beverly Hills Hotel. Among the two hundred guests at this most desirable social event of the year were

Humphrey Bogart and Lauren Bacall, Ronald Colman, Lana Turner, Groucho Marx, Ginger Rogers, Louis B. Mayer and a young contract player from Twentieth Century-Fox named Marilyn Monroe, who was so awestruck by Olivier's poise and charm that she vowed one day to appear with him in a movie. Her agent and sometime lover Johnnie Hyde told her that was a very long shot indeed. After this gala evening, shooting schedules required both of the Oliviers at work six days a week, she at Warner, he at Paramount.

Throughout that autumn, Vivien filmed *A Streetcar Named Desire*, acting with such affecting pathos and controlled hysteria that she earned her second Academy Award. ('She'd have crawled over broken glass if she thought it would help her performance,' according to Kazan.) Nothing in the completed film gave any indication of the stress she felt without Olivier's guidance on the set, nor of the situation Kazan had to manage as Vivien frequently declared, 'When Larry and I did the play in London . . .'

That season, her visiting friend Robert Helpmann took her along on night-time forays, as each sought fleeting sexual intimacies with strangers. These adventures astonished those who knew about them, for Vivien's few brief liaisons (probably her first unfaithfulness since her marriage to Olivier) were completely inconsistent with her own character but very much in accordance with Blanche's. Her conduct later led her friends and biographers to project her emotional instability in the 1960s, exacerbated by recurrent tuberculosis and excessive alcohol consumption, back to the 1950s, and the woman who never failed in her professional obligations (nor, when it suited her convenience, social opportunities) was described as mentally ill during this period of her life. She had become, so the tradition claimed, Blanche herself – a madwoman possessed by her role much as the actress Renée Maria Falconetti, after playing Joan of Arc in a film by Carl Dreyer in 1927, had believed herself to be the martyr, suffered a breakdown and was committed to an asylum.

Love and loyalty for Vivien Leigh, in other words – from friends as well as biographers – prevented an objective understanding of what was really at first simple sensual indulgence. Nothing in her conduct derived from malevolence or hypocrisy, but her behaviour did make her miserable and aggravate the strain in her marriage. There is simply no medical data from that time verifying Vivien Leigh's mental illness (three years later her tactics became more dramatic), nor was there in 1950 any of the uncontrollable paralysis of mind or will warranting

195

the diagnosis of a desperately sick woman who 'became' Blanche DuBois. No such thing occurred, despite the claims of some romantic chroniclers eager to create a character out of Emily Brontë. Vivien simply found certain correspondences with Blanche, her most successful role to date, apt and attractive, and she decided to live them out. If she was indeed certifiably demented, it was remarkable that so delicate a woman could act in more than three hundred performances of *Streetcar* and then undertake a film of it, a production during which neither Elia Kazan nor her co-stars ever noted any irrational conduct. It would also have been unconscionably unprofessional for Cecil Tennant, who knew Vivien as well as anyone, to promote her to Hollywood as Blanche had he (and Olivier) had any doubt that she could despatch the role superbly and without endangering herself. A conviction of Vivien's dementia also implies that Olivier, forcing a sick woman beyond her limits, was imperceptive to the point of cruelty.

In fact her actions had a less mysterious and quite concrete rationale, for by this time Olivier was deeply involved in a sexual affair with Danny Kaye. At first Vivien had merely thought Kaye rude, since he arrived at their house unannounced at odd hours, without invitation or permission. But Olivier was also spending long, late hours with him, and the affair – at first rampant gossip and then a widespread belief in Hollywood, New York and in the Caribbean (where the relationship continued irregularly for several years) – was no secret to Vivien, nor did he deny it.

For Olivier, the affair with Kaye revealed what the earlier relationship with Coward had – more, that is, about his need for affection from those he admired than for sex itself, about which he was for most of his life remarkably diffident, as Vivien was the first to make public (and as he confirmed in his *Confessions of an Actor*). She had always been the aggressor, demanding sex, facilitating it, taking control; yet for him it remained something perfunctory, and to it he never brought his fullest passion. Kaye was not simply amusing, but vibrantly intelligent; not merely encouraging and admiring of Olivier, but also quick-witted, original and capable of discussing the fine points of art, literature and music history – much like Vivien. He was irresistible when Olivier could not resist overt displays of tenderness, no matter to what physical expression they might sometimes lead.

Much of his emotional life, after all, had long been blunted and subjected to the self-imposed demands of a rarefied art. The death of his mother and the emotional distance from his father had been a profound loss of early nurturing and of the only source of youthful endorsement. Later Jill Esmond, who seemed the perfect passport to social and professional respectability, also surprised him and 'died' to him, at first withholding affection and then bestowing infrequent sexual favours that were as unaffirming as his brief Hollywood affairs of the early 1930s were impersonal. This had thrown him into a paroxysm of doubt about his abilities with women that was further complicated by his attachment to Noël Coward. And so, like many who are deprived of early love, Laurence Olivier sought fulfilment elsewhere – not in promiscuity, not in an endless and loveless quest for tangible surrogate affection, but onstage. Only with a woman of Vivien's prodigious erotic manipulation (born of her own poignant history of childhood abandonment) did he feel safe and gratified by a woman. But as he always confided to friends, her sexual demands became repugnant and burdensome. With Danny Kaye, Olivier – accepting affirmation where it seemed genuine, from one he respected – simply yielded to the adoring blandishments of a powerfully seductive man. Olivier above all wished to please, to make himself attractive, to make himself loved – for such is the goal to some extent of every actor (if not every human being).

And so in 1950 Danny Kaye effectively insinuated himself into Olivier's intimate life. He spent many weekends with them both in Los Angeles and London; he arranged his own work to coincide with Olivier's commitments; he turned up in foreign cities when they were travelling; he hosted an inordinate number of parties and dinners in their honour; four times, he corralled the Oliviers into performing vaudeville numbers with him at charity benefits; and he acquired invitations to an astonishing number of events on their schedule. All this and the fact of the affair would perhaps remain unremarkable had not Olivier written a letter to Vivien in 1961, weakly describing as merely transitory and unimportant the sexual intimacy between himself and Kaye. The letter, written to Vivien when she was living with an actor named John Merivale, survived her death and remained with Merivale until his. Additionally, the first draft of Olivier's autobiography (written in 1981) frankly admitted the numerous homosexual escapades of his adult life – events his third wife prevailed on him to remove from the book. As for the relationship with Kaye, it was certainly everything Vivien suspected and far more than Olivier admitted. She was singularly unamused when she saw photographs taken at one riotous all-male gathering at the Caribbean home of Noël Coward. Kaye and

Olivier had performed impromptu song-and-dance duets, dressed alternately as bride and groom. This was pure British music hall, but to Vivien it betokened something true about the relationship, and something with which she could not compete.

Amid the anxiety of these months, Olivier created one of his greatest film portraits, the doomed George Hurstwood in *Carrie*, a performance that decades later remains almost unbearable in its exquisite delineation of a man being destroyed by love. Olivier and Wyler worked in much greater harmony than on *Wuthering Heights*, for Olivier's intervening directorial experience had taught him both the subtleties of film acting and the necessity of patience in working for exactly the right emotion for the screen. With a neat moustache and a flawless midwestern dialect (perfected after practice with Spencer Tracy), Olivier developed Hurstwood's passage from ardent lover to desperate, thieving bigamist without losing any of the character's essentially tragic nobility. His performance is remarkably understated, all sad, longing glances and whispers; in some subconscious way, he may well have drawn on his own experiences with Jill and then Vivien to create the portrait of a man who takes refuge from a loveless marriage in a grand passion that deteriorates before his eyes. Spare in his gestures and with a voice full of dark, quiet intensity, Olivier gave a portrait of one almost fatally destined to be deprived of love. Longing to be trusted and yet fearing that he may not deserve trust, Olivier's Hurstwood depends on the fragile truth of his own desperate passion. 'I want you more than I've ever wanted anything in my life,' he says flatly, his tone suggesting that he is knowingly losing himself in a hopeless love. Spoken aridly, almost without emotion, the line has a fresh pathos, as if the character had suddenly found himself not, after all, without feelings.

To his final scenes Olivier brought a dreadful intensity that corresponds to the greatest portraits in his career. Evicted from a flophouse, the once rich Hurstwood – now destitute, tubercular and starving – shuffles unsteadily, seeking in vain for food and lodging. He finds Carrie, who has left him and is now a successful actress, and approaches her from the shadows of a theatre alley:

> Excuse me, Carrie. I tried very hard not to do this. I need help – just tonight – I need a little help. I'm – hungry. Could you spare me a little something? Anything? I don't want to bother you. I won't again – but just tonight.

He backs away from her in shame, then tentatively extends his hand, begging. She offers to share her wealth with him, but he murmurs heartbreakingly, in a voice thick with illness and shame, 'I've come for a handout – please don't make me go through too much to get it.' Olivier closes his eyes in exhaustion, as if imagining a tide of memories, the recollections of a once sacrificial love fading at last into oblivion. Perhaps no actor has ever relied less on externals for the ultimate impact of a scene than Olivier here, as he fashioned an image of devastating misery without shifting tones of voice or reliance on tears, without gesture or even a clear gaze. His fertile imagination had perhaps never been so keenly parallel to the contours of his own life as it was that year, nor so directly nourished by his own apprehensions. After a reckless romance that had now declined into a wary, half-remembered passion for Vivien, Olivier had the perfect vantage point from which to recreate George Hurstwood's fatal devotion.

It is in the context of autumn 1950 – of the time in their lives that made Vivien's Blanche and Olivier's Hurstwood possible – that there lies perhaps the most affecting difference between them, a disparity of nature they may have only dimly perceived. Laurence Olivier had an innate self-control and discipline based on a fundamental professional self-assurance that prevented him from yielding the core of his personality to any character. Mastering whatever he found in a role that corresponded to something within, he neither allowed himself to be overcome by it nor blurred the distinction between art and life: his profession was always the craft of calculated pretence. Unnoticed by Olivier, Kazan saw him rehearsing alone one Sunday morning that October, practising the gesture of Hurstwood offering a chair to a restaurant patron: he tried the action first one way, then another; he looked at the imaginary guest, then repeated the movement with a flourish – each action a different angle on Hurstwood as Olivier sought the unerring, telling bit of business for a scene.

But Vivien lacked both Olivier's attention to detail and his artistic self-confidence. Preparing Blanche in London, she had asked him to transform her completely – to create from her own raw material a new and ferociously pathetic woman. The sadness of the Oliviers' progressively troubled union thus unfolded perhaps inevitably but without resentment as, like many creative people, they continually sought in the pursuit of professional excellence a kind of aesthetic release from their private anguish.

*

After both films were completed, the Oliviers and only five other pass-engers boarded the freighter *Wyoming* at Long Beach on 25 November, the slow homeward journey intended as a rest while they read prospec-tive plays for the new St James's season. The death of George Bernard Shaw on 2 November had already inspired them to stage *Caesar and Cleopatra* – not only as a tribute to the playwright, but also to capital-ise on Vivien's fame from her movie version (still in circulation) and on the obvious box-office appeal of themselves as the title characters. They marked the text while reading through it together. 'It is unfortu-nate,' Olivier said not long after, 'that Vivien's and my conversations, which should be normal conversations, are all too frequently confer-ences about some business problem, or some theatrical problem.'

Otherwise the sea voyage was, as he later admitted, 'a dismal failure [that] plunged us both into deep depression'. More clearly than ever during the previous several months, he confronted the vacuity of a marriage sustained for and by publicity, and this led him to identify with Hurstwood: like the man he had just played, Olivier found the idea of suicide attractive (as he later wrote in his memoirs), and he stood for long periods at the ship's rail, staring into the deep.

Olivier's sudden and uncharacteristic depression may have derived from his awareness that in marrying so ardent a woman as Vivien he may have briefly stepped out of character, assuming the real-life role of a lover when his true dedication was to his art. Vivien herself knew that the theatre was indeed his great passion. But the deepest cause of his suicidal temptation must have included guilt over the Danny Kaye affair, for which Vivien constantly upbraided him; it was, after all, a manifestation of a hidden aspect of his character – and it may, at least in part, explain his lifelong public self-denunciation. From this point forward, for reasons which he understandably never elaborated, his life became suffused with the kind of guilt that derives from self-denial. 'It's necessary for the public,' he told an interviewer in 1951, 'to have a sense of happiness about the people they admire. And they are not going to have that if you are not constantly aware of yourself in relation to the public, wherever you are.'

On 18 December they docked at Tilbury and that evening hastened to see their old friend John Mills in one of the last performances of *Top of the Ladder*, an LOP production that had opened on 11 October. Though it was written by Tyrone Guthrie, with whom his relations had been so murky, Olivier was attracted to the story of how a mother emotionally suffocates and a father intimidates their sensitive son. By year's end, it had failed, although *Captain Carvallo* continued into the new year; also disappointing was his importing of Gian Carlo Menotti's opera *The Consul* from New York. This he presented early in 1951 and lost £10,000 on the venture, continuing the losses to LOP and the St James's theatre in the first half of 1951 despite the contributions of his and Vivien's recent combined film salaries of over $100,000. (Like dozens of other major English actors, Olivier worked for a day in early March without compensation for his two-minute cameo – as a nameless police constable who sees one of the first silent 'flickers' – in *The Magic Box*, John Boulting's all-star British Film Industry picture about the life and career of William Friese-Greene, one of the cinema's pioneers.)

There was soon a daring addition to their programme for the St James's. While the board members of LOP sought another play for that spring, Roger Furse half-jestingly suggested that the Oliviers could use the same sets and costumes with only minor variations and present Shaw's *Caesar and Cleopatra* alternately with Shakespeare's *Antony and Cleopatra*. The idea suddenly took hold, and in early 1951 their press representative David Fairweather released the news. The two plays were announced as a sensational *tour de force* for Vivien Leigh and Laurence Olivier. She would portray a wilful and kittenish sixteen-year-old as Shaw's Cleopatra, trained for the throne of Egypt by the fifty-year-old, world-weary Caesar; and as Shakespeare's version she would be the smouldering and sensual *femme fatale*, the Egyptian queen in her late thirties, wily and audacious, cool and grave, skittishly and nervously flirtatious but longing to dominate, whose passionate relationship with Antony helps to destroy them both. This would be the great triumph of their joint career.

The dynamics of the Oliviers' individual personalities and of their marriage again provided them with a background of singular emotional associations with these characters. Written in the year of his marriage, Shaw's comedy presents Caesar as a major exponent of the playwright's turn from socialism to the quest for the superman. But *Caesar and Cleopatra* also bore fascinating parallels to both Olivier and Vivien; he would portray onstage what he had been for her in life: teacher and guide, a man who dallies in love but places it second to his profession. For her part, Vivien would play a child-woman very like herself with Olivier: an adroit, naughty and decorative partner, a novice to flatter and enliven his fancy. There is a straight line from these characters to Henry Higgins and Eliza Doolittle in *Pygmalion*, for a major theme in

Shaw's work is the wryly sceptical and realistic teacher who motivates a younger disciple towards achievement.

The affinities were even more pointed in Shakespeare, whose characters focus the destiny of a whole civilisation in one couple, their unchecked passion clashing with the call to restraint, their spontaneity against prudent common sense. Olivier understood the play's central conflict of public image and duty against the tangle of private pleasure, and he must have dreaded playing a heroic figure turned hesitant sybarite, a man ultimately enchained by indulgence. Just as Richard III had released in him a stern confrontation with the worst ambition can do to a man, so Antony – worn, impulsive, angry, fated to the same self-destruction as Cleopatra – evoked Olivier's perilous relationship to Vivien and the impulses towards death that occasionally (and recently) seized them both. As for her, Vivien shared the Egyptian queen's yearning to dominate through an appearance of equality, and though denied the soliloquies that would provide knowledge of her thoughts, she was (as Cleopatra) the consummate and constant performer for the other characters, a woman tenaciously fixed on the alliance of love with status.

Vivien began to prepare the Shakespeare under Olivier's closest tutelage ('I reminded her of the complete personality change and the formidable technical adjustment that she had made for Blanche DuBois'), and throughout that winter and spring she worked to lower the register of her voice, listening obediently to criticism from Olivier and from Michael Benthall, their director in the two *Cleopatras*.

That season, publicist David Fairweather, with an eye to major coverage of the London premieres in May, invited journalist and critic Felix Barker to interview the couple for a few articles. Barker first met them in Liverpool after a preview performance and found them rather grand, very much the Royal Family, courteous and gracious but with an attitude that said 'We Are Very Special.' Over the course of additional interviews in Liverpool, Manchester and London, Barker found that they had keen memories and spoke articulately, if selectively, about their earlier lives. These conversations comprised the first extensive articles on the couple, appearing daily for several weeks in the *Evening News* later that spring and eventually forming the basis for Barker's book *The Oliviers*, suggested by Olivier himself.

On 10 and 11 May, the plays came to the St James's and logged a total of 155 performances over the next four months. As they had hoped but dared not expect, the Oliviers had a brilliant success; with one exception the critics were as rhapsodic as the public. The dissenting and soon fashionable minority opinion was set forth by Kenneth Tynan in the *Spectator*.

Tynan, then twenty-four, felt it was time for a sober assessment of Vivien's talent, the general praise of which he considered ill-founded. In the Shaw play he rated her sweet but unimaginative, and in the Shakespeare, her 'piercing, candid blankness is superbly pretty . . . but it has nothing to do with greatness'. Worse still, Tynan added, Olivier himself had lowered his range in performing opposite her:

> How obsequiously Sir Laurence seems to play along with her . . .
> With curious chivalry, [he] gives me the impression that he subdues
> his ebullience to match her. Blunting his iron precision, levelling
> away his towering authority, he meets her halfway . . . A cat, in
> fact, can do more than look at a king; she can hypnotise him.

Tynan's estimation of Olivier's attenuated performances opposite Vivien became contagious, and was much touted as courageously visionary long after the fact. But what he failed to note at the time was the freshness Olivier and Vivien brought to familiar roles. Olivier played Caesar as a man weary in his own ambition, lonely in his greatness, sad over the futility of passion and bored with the vacancy of his own achievements. He entered stooping slightly, his hair thinning, his make-up sallow and suggesting pain. And as Antony he rightly tempered the mercurial lover with moments of utter psychic paralysis, giving tenderness to the lust and pathos to the downfall; here was a conqueror conquered by love, victimised (as Olivier said of himself that season) by a nagging 'dissatisfaction with self'. Caesar and Antony were extreme images of Laurence Olivier that year – not diminished examples of his talents (as Tynan held) but dual representations of the actor and boldly fresh readings of the roles. He did not scale down his performances to make Vivien's seem brighter: he played the roles for what they contained and brought to them new perspectives.

With this controversial critique, Tynan began virtually a lifelong assault on Vivien Leigh's professional reputation, which he always considered overrated and threatening to Olivier's greatness. Elaine Dundy, Tynan's first wife, felt that he was utterly unable to see Vivien's talent because he idolised Larry; he was transparently in love with the theatre, and Olivier was theatre to him. Nevertheless, in a brilliant move to charm the critic, Vivien insisted that Olivier invite the Tynans for several weekends at Notley, where she was so friendly towards them that some thought she had misread Tynan's review. But she had not; she intended to defuse its power by ignoring it. She also reduced the chronically stuttering Tynan to nervous incompetence when she stripped and asked him to assist her with a costume. Cleopatra herself could not have bettered Vivien's disarmament tactics.

Tynan's review did not affect the box office at the St James's which, even at capacity throughout the summer, could not make a profit of more than forty pounds a week for the expensive shows with their dozens of players. Eventually, the Oliviers were forced to end the run of the plays only because they had already leased the theatre for other productions. But Cecil Tennant had reached agreement with impresario Billy Rose, owner of the Ziegfeld Theatre in New York: the two *Cleopatras* would transfer there later in the year.

The interval, from late September, allowed some relaxation. After holding a Thames barge party for the cast, the Oliviers accepted an invitation from Alexander Korda – a much-needed holiday, for even her adoring press reported that Vivien looked tired and pale. For a month they joined Korda, Margot Fonteyn, Graham Greene and others on his yacht *Elsewhere*, stopping at Piraeus, the Greek Isles, Istanbul, Calvi and Nice before returning to London on 26 October.

In early December, they sailed for New York on the *Mauretania*, and at the Ziegfeld Theatre there were 133 presentations (from 19 December 1951 to 12 April 1952) of what was popularly known as 'two on the Nile'. Neither of the Oliviers missed a performance, and Vivien continued to impress the large cast by presenting gifts on their birthdays and wedding anniversaries. According to Alec McCowen, who was in the company, Vivien knew her colleagues much better than Olivier did, and often she had to coach him, at photo calls or parties, on who played which role.

Because she was generally so cordial with colleagues, it was surprising to the cast when Vivien began to complain loudly about Katharine Blake, who acted Charmian in both plays: she read a line badly, Vivien said, or she ruined a scene with an inappropriate gesture. One night after Blake had placed the crown on Vivien's head and the final curtain of *Antony* fell, Vivien shrieked at her in a torrent of obscene abuse, accusing her of deliberately making Cleopatra look an utter fool by putting the crown on crookedly. Behind his wife, Olivier stood winking at the astonished cast and raising his hands, as if to calm them and say, 'Just ignore her, let it go . . .' Her mood was only briefly lightened by the announcement (on 20 March 1952), that she had won the Oscar as best actress for *Streetcar*; she chose instead to focus on the coincidence that the statuette was accepted in Hollywood by Greer Garson, her immediate predecessor in Olivier's romantic life.

Since he had become an actor-manager, Olivier's manner with most of his players was characterised by formal courtesy rather than outright friendliness, but in New York he was less than ever a company man. He was also on a vicious schedule, arranging for *Venus Observed* to open in New York with Rex Harrison and Lilli Palmer, rehearsing with them throughout January and early February and then travelling daily to the previews in Philadelphia, returning just in time to apply his make-up as Caesar or Antony. (Fry's play opened to puzzled audiences on 13 February and closed quietly on 26 April.) As if all this were not enough, Olivier agreed to appear later that year in a musical film, and throughout the winter he took singing lessons from Helen Cahoon, Mary Martin's vocal coach for *South Pacific*. There were also public ceremonies at which he presided, among them the New York memorial following the death of King George VI; for that event on 17 February, more than 2000 people stood in wintry rain outside a Fifth Avenue church, awaiting a glimpse of Olivier.

The casts of all three plays recalled Olivier as unusually reserved and uninvolved, and although they liked and admired him there was a feeling of restraint in his presence. One huge elevator took the cast from back-stage to the dressing rooms after each performance, and if Olivier was present conversation stopped until he alighted at his floor, then resumed after his departure. The players' feeling of distance was not alleviated by his good intentions, for several times he came to the large upper dressing room reserved for bit players. 'I want to see if my babies are comfortable,' he began with unwitting condescension, and the actors had to leaven the awkwardness by chiming in with small talk.

Onstage, Olivier was ever the alert manager as well as the convincing actor. They could see his eyes wander up to check the lights, McCowen recalled, and he glanced into the wings to see if anyone was talking, then over the house to check the attendance – and he lost nothing by this, no concentration or involvement in the play. 'But when he was in one of Antony's rages, one hoped he was not looking at us. He was terrifying onstage. We were literally frightened of him.'

As the run progressed, there were frequently rows of empty seats in the vast Ziegfeld, despite the excellent reviews. Some theatregoers may have been discouraged because the tickets cost more than any show in Broadway history – $7.20 for the best seats – while others remained at home as television that year drew huge numbers away from theatre. Americans were watching Arthur Godfrey's *Talent Scouts* and *I Love Lucy* on Mondays; Milton Berle, the *Fireside Theater* and *Armstrong Circle Theater* on Tuesdays; the *Kraft Television Theatre* on Wednesdays; George Burns and Gracie Allen and Groucho Marx's quiz show *You Bet Your Life* on Thursdays. One night, when the applause from the decimated audience sounded rather sparse, Olivier whispered to Vivien, 'Smile at them, baby – smile if it's the last thing you do!' She did, and her smile itself brought a sudden wave of clapping.*

The day after the plays closed (Sunday, 13 April), the Oliviers left New York for a ten-day rest with Noël Coward at his island retreat on Jamaica. They admitted to their host that maintaining two English homes during their recent American tour had pitched them into deep financial trouble, and that they were considering selling Notley Abbey to reduce their expenditure.

After returning to London, they spent another week with Korda on his yacht, returning home at the end of June. Vivien went to Notley while Olivier – who had also assumed the duties of co-producer with Herbert Wilcox – began filming the Technicolor musical *The Beggar's Opera* at Shepperton Studios with Peter Brook, who was directing his first picture. The project was undertaken primarily because the Oliviers needed money and, as often in such cases, some angles were ill-considered. Training with his singing coach during lunchtime, rehearsing intricate swordplay, riding his own horse (with cameras following him atop cars being driven at forty miles an hour), Olivier was eager to demonstrate that at forty-five he had all the vigour necessary for the picture's tough physical demands; as usual, he rejected every offer of a double for the most taxing scenes. But despite four months of laborious doctoring in post-production, the film was a terrific failure and lost its entire investment of £250,000. All his efforts notwithstanding, Olivier's performance as the highwayman Macheath seems disjointed, for he unwisely insisted on recording his songs, and in contrast to the other dubbed voices his baritone came out wilted and thin.

---

* Olivier had his London actors in both plays, and after their departure Actors' Equity changed its rules about non-American casts. Beginning in summer 1952, only 40 per cent of a cast could be foreigners, and to assure they would be stars it was further stipulated that none could appear unless at a minimum wage of $500; hitherto, the minimum had been $80.

Perhaps to compensate, he played the character as puckishly athletic, and while performing a risky stunt lost three weeks' filming when he tore a calf muscle leaping onto a gaming table.

But there was good reason for Olivier's apparent high spirits during the filming of *The Beggar's Opera*. In the role of Polly Peachum was a pretty twenty-two-year-old actress named Dorothy Tutin, who the previous year had appeared in the film of *The Importance of Being Earnest*. At precisely the time of his life when he needed companionship and intimacy, Tutin responded fully to him, and that year a romance flourished. Like Vivien (and before her Greer Garson), she was a willing and admiring apprentice – this was always the most important quality in women to whom he was attracted – but Tutin was also calm and undemanding. Years later, she described him as a most vulnerable man at that time, and in some ways hostage to his own good fortune. Talented, considerate and discerning, she was an ideal companion at this delicate stage of Olivier's life. Their relationship was conducted with the utmost discretion until, quite without Tutin's knowledge or approval, her mother assumed the role of marriage agent. In December, Mrs Tutin rang Vivien, who was astonished to hear the question, 'When are you going to divorce Sir Laurence so that my daughter can marry him?'

Vivien's reaction was not as hysterical as might have been expected. Although she referred sarcastically to 'that Dot Tut' several times during editorial meetings with Felix Barker (who was preparing the final draft of *The Oliviers*), she had an oddly stoical attitude. Perhaps she felt that the twenty-three-year age gap between Olivier and Tutin would soon mitigate their romantic fervour. But her surprising poise at the end of 1952 had another explanation. She was ready to undertake an exotic film called *Elephant Walk*, to be made in Ceylon and Hollywood. After all, she protested when Olivier asked her to reconsider such a demanding project, they very much needed her salary of $150,000. Although producer Irving Asher had hoped Olivier would play opposite her, his duties in postproduction on *The Beggar's Opera* intervened. Not to worry, Vivien told them: she had already chosen her leading man – and Olivier, who had the young actor under contract, was compelled to a decision he instantly regretted. By the time Vivien and Peter Finch departed for Ceylon in early 1953, she was – and Olivier knew it – set on the unfortunate course of romantic retribution, with Finch the instrument of her revenge. This would also, she reasoned, effectively put an end to any danger of an Olivier–Finch liaison.

CHAPTER ELEVEN

1953–1955

Lady Macbeth: Nought's had, all's spent,
Where our desire is got without content:
'Tis safer to be that which we destroy
Than by destruction dwell in doubtful joy.

Macbeth

During the years 1950 to 1957, Laurence Olivier was seen only three times on a London stage, twice with Vivien; by contrast, from 1943 to 1950 he had appeared in thirteen plays, directed eight and produced nine. The year 1953 was the most violent and transforming, but there was no indication of trouble at the outset. Early in January, Olivier contacted Terence Rattigan, whose successful play *The Deep Blue Sea* was still running after almost a year. To his enquiry about a possible vehicle for himself and Vivien, Rattigan replied that he had written a Ruritanian trifle of a comedy called *The Sleeping Prince*, which would showcase the Oliviers prettily enough but was certainly beneath their talents. The script, once read, persuaded Olivier it would be right for Vivien after the rigours of filming in Ceylon and Hollywood were behind her. Rehearsals and a tour of *The Sleeping Prince* were scheduled for late April, with the London premiere at the time of the coronation of Elizabeth II in June. Alfred Lunt was signed to direct.

Meanwhile, as Olivier attended to his producer's duties on post-production with *The Beggar's Opera*, Vivien and Peter Finch flew to Ceylon, where Irving Asher had assembled a crew for location photography on *Elephant Walk*. Within days of their arrival, Vivien and Finch were drinking heavily; before the end of January, they were lovers. But to her dismay, Vivien discovered that although Finch's marriage was disintegrating, she was but one of many liaisons in his life. This blow to her fragile ego precipitated a panic attack: Olivier was all but lost to her emotionally, and now Finch too was a disappointment. Because she was consuming considerable amounts of alcohol it was difficult for her colleagues in Ceylon to determine whether her tantrums were caused by drink, a nervous breakdown, expert play-acting – or a combination of these. Asher did not wait for a professional diagnosis, and when he and Finch were unable to reason with Vivien or to improve her temper, Olivier was summoned, and arrived in Ceylon on 17 February. And then an odd thing happened.

Olivier's response to the situation was remarkably casual. Learning the full extent of the passion between Vivien and Finch, he felt no great rage ('Was he not doing what I had done to her first husband seventeen years ago?') and, unwilling to be humiliated by the situation, he calmly wished everyone luck and summarily departed. The visit was simply *pro forma*: he did nothing. For the record, Olivier later stated only that he liked Finch and that the tangle of his professional and personal relationship with him encouraged him to moderate any hostility about the affair with Vivien. He may also have felt relieved, for a Vivien–Finch affair justified his conduct with Dorothy Tutin.

That in this case (as earlier in Hollywood) Vivien was nothing like a certifiable madwoman is clearly demonstrated by her equanimity on Olivier's arrival, and the fact that when he departed she completed the two sequences assigned for location work and with the company of *Elephant Walk* she continued to California for studio shooting. Her husband's presence, it seems, had an astonishingly sedative effect on her. How was it possible for Vivien to have willed her 'illness' to subside? How could she have so easily returned to her professional obligations?

Vivien was always terrified of being forsaken, of reliving the abandonment of her childhood. When Olivier left Hollywood in 1939 to act on Broadway with Katharine Cornell in *No Time for Comedy*, Vivien became so upset by his absence that she heckled Selznick until he rescheduled her scenes on *Gone With the Wind* to permit a romantic reunion. During the war, she was so agitated at their separation that she insisted they rent a cottage near the Fleet Air Arm, lest she be more than half an hour away from her husband. After her miscarriage and subsequent confinement with tuberculosis, Vivien had refused to be left behind when the Old Vic went to New York in 1946, and in 1947 she formally joined the Vic for the Australian tour. There was, then, a clear pattern in her life. Threatened with being left alone, she knew that Olivier – who had his own secrets and his own guilt, as she reminded him – would rush to her side if she demanded. With malevolent or unloving people, this would be simple emotional blackmail; in the case of the Oliviers it was the logical result of their own deepest and finally mismatched emotional needs. Dreading solitude, she always sought Olivier's company; denied it, she panicked.

But when filming resumed in Hollywood, Vivien's conduct became so impossible that it seemed she had virtually driven herself to madness. She threw fierce and obscene tantrums on the set, screamed speeches from *Streetcar*, and asked friends (Sunny Lash, for one) to procure male strangers for her – a task for which none of them felt quite suited. Asher and Paramount's chief executive Y. Frank Freeman ordered director William Dieterle to close down the picture for several days while they decided its fate. Finch, meanwhile, told Vivien they must end their affair, and this precipitated real hysteria.

By 12 March, Vivien certainly seemed like a character from the early works of Tennessee Williams. Forsaken by Finch, she welcomed none other than John Buckmaster (her lover from the days just before Olivier), who had just been released from his latest confinement in a mental hospital. Buckmaster outfitted them both in towels and was conducting something like a lunatic Roman bath party, pouring potent drinks and suggesting that they invite neighbours for a sexual orgy. Vivien was not so indiscreet that she agreed either to this or to Buckmaster's suggestion that they leap from the rooftop and fly around the Hollywood Hills.

Sunny Lash, who by this time had not seen Vivien for several days, arrived at the rented house on Ambassador Avenue just in time to witness the comic-dreadful scene of Buckmaster's attempted flight in his Turkish towel. Remembering that David Niven was a longtime friend of Vivien, she telephoned him in desperation. Niven at once drove to the house, where he found Vivien who, because of the effects of drink and pills, recognised him only intermittently and sat staring at a television set. When she refused to take sedation and seemed about to act violently, Niven rang their mutual friend, actor Stewart Granger. Neither man succeeded in getting tranquillisers into her and finally they summoned Dr Martin Grotjahn, who often treated Hollywood figures. He prescribed heavy sedation and demanded that Olivier be summoned forthwith. This required almost a day, for Olivier was on a short holiday with William and Susanna Walton at their home on the Mediterranean island of Ischia. On 13 March he left Italy for Los Angeles via New York's Idlewild Airport.

There, he was stopped by a customs officer who inspected his passport and tickets, enquired in a nearly incomprehensible accent about his recent travels and promptly informed him that a body search would be required. Hastily shuffled into a nearby cubicle, Olivier was ordered under threat of police action to strip for a detailed physical examination. He demurred, but the customs officer was, he said, merely doing his job – one permitted by the United States Code; he was searching for unspecified contraband. After submitting to the indignities of an inspection of every inch and crevice of his body, Olivier was astonished to see the customs officer step back and slowly remove a complex disguise (dark wig and a heavily powdered latex mask), and there before the naked Olivier stood Danny Kaye. They spent the night at the St Regis Hotel before continuing to California next morning.

Approaching the house in Los Angeles next day, Olivier and the doctors who met him there saw Vivien standing on an upper gallery in a long white gown. She waved, he returned the greeting, and for a moment it seemed rather like the balcony scene in *Romeo and Juliet*. 'I am in love with Peter Finch,' Vivien calmly proclaimed to her husband. What would he do about it?

Because her conduct was now the news of the day in Hollywood, Vivien was released from her contract without penalty (Elizabeth Taylor was hastily engaged for the role), and on 18 March the Oliviers (without Kaye) left Los Angeles. Two nurses accompanied them on the flight to New York, for which Vivien was provided with prodigious amounts of sedation. On arrival, they were surrounded by reporters and popping flashbulbs, and Vivien turned to the rank of eager photographers. 'I'm so sorry to have made such trouble,' she said hoarsely, choking back tears. 'Please forgive me – so sorry.'

The first-class cabin was given over to the Oliviers, Cecil Tennant, two nurses and a doctor provided by the airline. Stewardess Daphne Webster remembered that for the first four hours of the flight Vivien was pale, whimpering and shaking with anxiety before two courses of medication finally sedated her and she slept for seven hours. Awakening as everyone breakfasted before landing, she became the polite and concerned hostess, asking pardon of Tennant and the nurses and enquiring if they had found the flight pleasant. Otherwise she sat quietly with Olivier, reaching for his hand and resting her head on his shoulder. At nine o'clock on the morning of 21 March they arrived in

London, where Vivien insisted on walking unaided from the plane, wearing her mink coat and carrying a dozen red roses. She was taken directly to Netherne Hospital, near Coulsdon, Surrey, where massive doses of insulin were prescribed to induce a three-week coma (sleep therapy, as it was called). She had achieved her goal: Olivier's undivided attention.

But not for long. Dr Rudolf Freudenberg had as much concern for the emotional health of Olivier himself, who was suffering from 'utter physical strain and spiritual depression verging on a nervous break-down', as it was succinctly reported. Because Freudenberg told him there was little he could do for Vivien, Olivier resumed his holiday with the Waltons on Ischia. In Naples the ubiquitous press (alerted by London) were waiting with their cameras at dawn on 23 March. Appearing to one reporter 'horrible, ashen, drawn, with a quiver about the mouth' and unable to confront the crowds or to be, as he had said, 'aware of [himself] in relation to the public', Olivier asked the Waltons to accompany him on a journey through Italy. Forever after, Olivier wrote much later, he blamed himself 'for not being more alive to my duties [at this time], no matter how painful or how mortally sick of them I was'.

The tragedy of the Oliviers was not the Gothic romance some writers would have it, nor was it a saga of capricious and uncontrollable mad-ness blighting a golden couple. It was more poignant, precisely because more commonplace and in fact avoidable. The histories and the needs of Laurence Olivier and Vivien Leigh had once united them but now drove them apart. His experience of intimacy had been a chronicle of loss and disappointment – from the intervention of death, withdrawal and the withholding of love – with the result that he had become an emotionally inaccessible man, channelling his passion and hope into his career and giving unalloyed devotion only to his audiences. Just as his sense of fatherhood had been affected by a denial of warm paternity, so it was in his wider emotional life. Needs were short-circuited not by coldness of will but by a limit of experience he sought to overcome with brilliant imagination and imitation in art. Vivien, on the other hand, wanted greatness only insofar as it could win her Olivier, or at least achievements equal to his. And as she saw that he was gradually becoming lost to her she could only become, in her own eyes first, a madwoman. Unreality was the only realistic alternative.

On 12 April he was back in London with Vivien, who had been transferred to University College Hospital; there she received her first course of electroconvulsive shock therapy, a procedure she would frequently endure for the rest of her life. Under general anaesthetic, usually of sodium pentothal and with scoline as a muscle relaxant, up to half a dozen convulsions were triggered in the brain. Doctors anxious to avoid possible memory loss preferred at that time to use a Shotter-Rich electronarcosis machine; Vivien was not always so fortunate. That she passively submitted to these treatments was not surprising, for by this time she was indeed a hysterical personality, and although her psychological condition did not warrant such drastic therapy, no alternatives were offered to her. Longing for the comfort of attention, bowed with confusion over her relationships with Olivier and Finch and weakened by drugs, she was fair game for the capricious and unwarranted treatments routinely administered at that time.

Olivier took her to Notley Abbey, where they spent a quiet but tense spring. Inevitably, there was a gulf between them, not at all bridged by the friends Vivien spontaneously invited for weekends, who were shown the usual grand time. With his brother Dickie (who, needing work, had been engaged the previous year as manager of the farm), Olivier and Vivien took their guests on tours of the coops bursting with four hundred chickens, the quarter of an acre of pigsties, and the herd of Jersey cows. Peter Ustinov, who visited at that time, found Vivien curled quietly like a cat on a sofa, seeming to dominate her husband by her simple presence, by not saying anything. Every time Olivier looked at her he became buoyant and aggressive.

Two burglaries marred an otherwise quiet period: in April, thieves broke into Durham Cottage and stole Vivien's Oscar statuette for *Streetcar*, and in early July – while the Oliviers entertained the Richardsons and the Waltons at Notley – burglars climbed a ladder and made off with £7000-worth of Vivien's furs and jewellery (a mink cape, a blue fox, a stole, diamond, sapphire and ruby rings and an antique Spanish brooch). On 11 May, because of his postwar visits and his engagement of French acting companies in London, Olivier was awarded the rank of Officer in the French Legion of Honour by Ambassador René Massigli; Edith Evans and Sybil Thorndike were among an informal group present onstage at the St James's Theatre after a performance by the Comédie française. He then pre-recorded a narration for the documentary *A Queen Is Crowned*, since the rituals for the coronation were known in advance; thus the film was released immediately after the actual footage was shot on 2 June.

*

In late July, Noël Coward found Vivien 'calm and sweet and gay . . . papery and rather frail but [without any sign of] a mental breakdown', and soon doctors, to her delight, judged her fit for work. On 31 August the Oliviers arrived at the Haymarket Theatre for the first rehearsal of *The Sleeping Prince*, postponed from April and now with Olivier as director (replacing Lunt, who had other commitments) as well as co-star. The plot was gossamer-thin: In London on the eve of the coronation of George V in 1911, the conscientious, unattractive and philandering Prince Regent of Carpathia (Olivier) meets an American chorus girl (Vivien). Reluctant to be casually seduced by a man for whom love is so perfunctory, she demands royal treatment. With no time to seek a more compliant conquest, the prince yields to her numerous requests – gypsy violins, quotations from *Antony and Cleopatra*, conversations about the burdens of royalty and the Prince's need for the ennobling love of a pure young woman – but with too much success. The girl takes the endearments and the eventual seduction seriously, and refuses to leave the Prince.

Despite its shallowness, the play received Olivier's usual exacting preparation. Terence Rattigan attended rehearsals, naturally delighted that such a minor work had attracted the couple and amazed at the trouble Olivier took, constructing his own and others' performances from small details of dress and manner, continually experimenting, discarding, adding and modifying particulars. More than once, Vivien laughed aloud at a newly invented piece of business Olivier introduced. 'Is it as funny as that?' Olivier asked.

'Yes, marvellous,' Rattigan replied, laughing just as loudly.

'No, I think it's too much,' Olivier often countered. 'It's out.' He was not simply being perverse, just faithful to the text, which he respected down to the stage directions, despite a moment's entertainment for the playwright.

The only London play in which he appeared between 1951 and 1957 (and his only stage appearance anywhere between 1951 and 1955), *The Sleeping Prince* had a brief tour in Manchester and opened on 5 November (Vivien's fortieth birthday) to politely unenthusiastic notices at the Phoenix, the St James's having been leased for other works. Critics remarked on Vivien's loveliness but questioned her credibility as a Brooklyn showgirl, while Olivier's Prince Uncharming was considered polished but beneath him. It was, as usual, a performance meticulously honed, flawless in timing, superbly designed – a stolid, unwitty little man with too much hair grease and a thick monocle. Without overstraining, he created a richly comic character, a complacently smirking middle European with an aptly exaggerated Oxbridge accent. The play managed a run of thirty-four weeks, despite some critics' complaints that 'so much talent should have gone into so little'. At this time there was a growing feeling among newspaper critics that Tynan may have been right: that Olivier was repressing his range and his reach for the sake of Vivien – a consensus that eventually reached its height when John Barber, in the *Daily Express*, claimed that the couple had 'lived on too little for too long', and that Olivier's reputation was no longer justified.

Rattigan, however, hosted a celebration for his cast and crew. 'On behalf of myself and my wife, as actors, and personally as your director,' Olivier said rather grandly (and unnecessarily) during the party, 'I would like to apologise, dear Terry, for mucking up your play.'

'Darlings,' Rattigan replied, 'on my behalf, as an author, please accept my apologies for having written such a mucky, trivial little play.'

The guests were now becoming uncomfortable, and, as often, Noël Coward rescued the situation. 'Children,' he said, 'may I say – on all your behalves – that as an author, producer and actor I have frequently managed to muck up my own acting, plays and productions – and still survive.'

During the nine-month run (until 3 July 1954), Vivien was absent from only two performances – both in early February, after she broke her left wrist five minutes into a performance she nevertheless completed. Olivier, whose understudy was never summoned, increased his income by producing half-hour radio programmes for the BBC, for which he edited Shakespearean scenes and short stories by Conrad, Stevenson and others; Orson Welles, Robert Donat, Michael Redgrave and Ralph Richardson were among the readers.

Because Vivien withstood the run of *The Sleeping Prince* with cheerful equanimity, Olivier yielded to her pleading to join him when he was invited by Anthony Quayle and Glen Byam Shaw (co-directors of the Shakespeare Memorial Theatre Company) to come to Stratford for the 1955 season; she insisted that her great achievements as a classical actress still lay ahead of her. Perhaps because acquiescence was much the easier path when Vivien had made a decision, Olivier accepted the offer, stipulating Stratford's engagement of Vivien. For his first appearance there since 1922 (and for her debut with the company) an impressive and gruelling triple bill was presently announced: John

Gielgud would direct them as Malvolio and Viola in *Twelfth Night*, and they would appear in *Macbeth* and *Titus Andronicus*. As Olivier had predicted, this at once silenced the critics who wondered if he had abandoned classical roles.

But before undertaking this season – sensational in its range, its theatrical and personal difficulties and its eventual success for Olivier – there was yet another major task. Alexander Korda had struck a deal with Ilya Lopert's American distribution company to finance a film of Olivier's *Richard III*, which was made during late summer and through autumn 1954, first on location in the Spanish countryside north of Madrid and then at Shepperton Studios. Vivien, meanwhile, received friends at Notley, studied the roles she would play at Stratford and (late in 1954 and early in 1955) acted in an undistinguished film for Korda based on Rattigan's play *The Deep Blue Sea*.

For the film of *Richard III*, Olivier reassembled familiar colleagues: Roger Furse for production design, Anthony Bushell as associate director, William Walton as composer and Carmen Dillon as art director. He included in his cast three fellow knights (Gielgud, Richardson and Hardwicke) besides his virtual stock company (Nicholas Hannen, Norman Wooland, Russell Thorndike, John Laurie and others) from the films of *Henry V* and *Hamlet*, and Alan Dent returned to work with him on editing the text. 'If you are going to cut a Shakespeare play,' Olivier said later, 'there is only one thing to do – lift out scenes. If you cut the lines down merely to keep all the characters in, you end up with a mass of short ends . . . [*Richard III*] is a really difficult play to film – it's involved, often obscure. I felt it absolutely necessary to do more simplification than I've ever done before.'

To give the film added appeal, Korda and the American backers arranged for Paramount's wide-screen process, Vista Vision, to be exported for Otto Heller's Technicolor cinematography; the result was as visually striking as it was dramatically compelling.

As usual, the most precarious scenes left literal marks on Olivier. Shooting the final battle sequence in Spain, he reined his horse a moment too soon, and an archer trained to pierce the cork padding on the animal's flank instead struck the rider full through his left calf. The stunned bystanders did nothing, Olivier fell as rehearsed, and only when assured the shot was perfect did he shout in pain for the arrow to be withdrawn from his leg.

Back in England after six weeks in Spain, the production fared more smoothly, and Olivier completed the film's 165 scenes in eleven weeks, directing seventy speaking actors and 540 extras with sure voice and hand. He managed to be actor, producer and director without any sign of pressure, recalled Claire Bloom, who played Lady Anne. Already experienced onstage (at Oxford, Stratford and the Old Vic) and in film (as the lead opposite Charles Chaplin in *Limelight*), the twenty-three-year-old actress was chosen by Olivier for her considerable talent and superb vocal technique. In her delicate beauty she also resembled the young Vivien, and like Dorothy Tutin she was both willing apprentice and devoted admirer – and with a similar result; for a short time that season they were discreet lovers. This was a very brief intimacy, however, and Claire Bloom had the clear impression it was really of little significance to him. Once again (as originally with Vivien), the controlling, tutorial capacity aroused Olivier's interest in a beautiful, apparently fragile devotee. And perhaps because the words were simply too ironic in light of this brief romantic episode, Olivier (cagily protesting that 'they didn't seem real to me') cut Richard's line, 'Since I cannot be a lover, I am determined to prove a villain.'

The finished film of *Richard III* eventually won three British Film Academy awards (best picture worldwide, best English picture, best performance by an actor) and earned Olivier an Oscar nomination. But the laurels did not prevent him from mocking his own attempt at solemnity. When receiving the British Academy trophy (from Vivien's hands), he faced the audience very gravely: 'I should like to take this occasion to thank all my associates, artists, technicians and crew with whom – so many of whom – with whom so many of which –' and then he grinned and shrieked – 'AAAAHHHH!' – turning aside and laughing at his own collapsed dignity.

In a bold and unprecedented experiment, the American film premiere of *Richard III* (on 11 March 1956) coincided with a simultaneous television broadcast on NBC. It was estimated that the forty million viewers (only 25,000 of them with colour receivers) formed a larger audience in one afternoon than had seen the play in its 352-year history. The film became an instant cult; it also put the star's image – half-Olivier, half-Richard, in Salvador Dalí's famous painting – on the cover of *Newsweek* magazine. The television premiere (which instantly recouped for Korda $500,000 of the film's cost) did, however, diminish the cinema income, and the experiment was never repeated.

Richard III is entirely Olivier's film, dominated by the fascinating portrait of Gloucester as wickedly masculine yet seductively feminine, personifying an evil so outrageous that he can mock his own audacity. Often speaking directly to camera, Olivier draws us into a kind of voyeuristic complicity in his betrayals, seductions and murders. Boldly calling attention to himself (as Richard does), he shortens the vowels, stresses the consonants, flattens his speech, rolls and raises his eyes and clicks his tongue. This is a record of a relentlessly energetic performance, constantly surprising us with a sudden lowering of voice when we expect it to rise, and vice versa. Apart from Clarence, neither the text nor the film treatment presents us with particularly noble or even strong characters, and this Olivier exploits with a vengeance worthy of Richard himself: everyone else is pallid by comparison. Coy, flirtatious and determined, Richard is a deformed creature of undiluted, sociopathic ambition, but in no sense is he a cliché. Whereas he played Henry and Hamlet with his own face, Olivier's Richard – with his limp and his padded humpback, a deformed hand, elongated nose and silken black pageboy wig – is a gigantic character, an epitome of history's every scheming courtier, unscrupulous lover, villainous uncle and duplicitous brother. Every moment reveals the preparation of an actor who has studied personalities: he blinks his eyes (when lying), points a line by stressing an odd word or pursing his lips (to intimidate his enemies) and creates an integrated world of evil. His Richard has a wholeness of intent the story's other weaklings lack.

Richard is perhaps the quintessential role-player who creates violent scenarios, describes them for us, then sets them in motion and invites us to behold the limits of stupidity and perversity, staging and starring in a series of playlets that forward his approach to the throne. Olivier's performance, in this regard, becomes a kind of existential role-playing. All the many cinematic close-ups scanning his pliant, pointed features reveal as never before the root of Laurence Olivier's ability to enchant: his own primal enchantment by the act of acting. Much of his beguilement sprung from uniting calculation with complete self-donation. He knew with an intuitive understanding that humanity itself enchants, in all its wide, mysterious range from corruption to nobility. In performing, he had access to the entire spectrum of human possibility within himself – ambition, jealousy, greed, lust – and to confront the possible was for him to commence the eclipse of the actual. That is why, in the final analysis, his art can be called transcendent.

From its founding in 1879 to its burning in 1926, the Shakespeare Memorial at Stratford had been a summer festival theatre, and after reopening in 1932 it was considered distinguished but slightly musty with tradition. The Birmingham Rep's Barry Jackson, who was given charge after World War II, saw the need for radical change, and this was ushered in forthwith by Peter Brook's innovative production of *Love's Labour's Lost* in 1946. Younger actors (Paul Scofield, Richard Burton and Albert Finney among them) joined established seniors (Michael Redgrave, John Gielgud, Peggy Ashcroft), and Jackson's successors Anthony Quayle and Glen Byam Shaw continued to achieve an increasingly respected balance of originality and tradition. By 1955, Stratford had not only a fashionable summer theatre, offering repertory in Shakespeare's birthplace from April to November; the Shakespeare Memorial was also the most exciting company for theatrical innovation after wartime austerity, drawing audiences from all over England and abroad. News of the Oliviers' imminent arrival jammed the box-office telephone lines (240 calls were registered in one hour that February), over a thousand requests for tickets arrived each day, and before the end of March the entire season was sold out.

Olivier's first role – Malvolio in *Twelfth Night* – was the least important and, as it happened, the least well received; from the start of rehearsals under John Gielgud's direction, things went badly. For one thing, Olivier was not eager to submit to Gielgud's supervision. Arriving with an entirely settled conception of the role (complete with another pointed nose, thick and crinkly hair and an epicene manner), Olivier played the self-tormentor as an outrageously camp, lisping hairdresser – a frankly homophobic parody that Olivier might have anticipated could not appeal to the dignified Gielgud but would certainly amuse the gallery. Then, in a severe reversal of mood, he gave Malvolio a tone of outraged dignity in the final scenes when he learns how he has been mistreated.

At this time, Peter Finch re-entered their lives and resumed his affair with Vivien, who blithely left Olivier at their rented Stratford house for nights with Finch at his hotel. 'Great actresses have lovers,' she announced airily. 'Sarah Bernhardt did – why shouldn't I?' And that, it seemed, was that. Olivier, fearful of adverse publicity but unwilling to defy her, simply kept quiet; indeed, then as ever, there was little point in trying to oppose Vivien.

'Larry's performance at rehearsal was, I thought, vulgar,' according to John Gielgud, who was working in the theatre with Olivier for the first time since their *Romeo and Juliet* twenty years earlier. 'He strongly resented my criticisms. I thought Vivien delightful [as Viola], but I suspected she was torn between my attempts at directing her and Larry's views, which of course influenced her strongly.' Olivier's control of Vivien onstage was the only kind he could exert, and with this tangle of insecurities, hesitations and a clash of professional and personal responsibilities, a confrontation was perhaps inevitable. Gielgud was not, by this time, at his best, as Maxine Audley (the play's Olivia) and John Goodwin (director of publicity for the company) remembered: the resistance he felt from the Oliviers left him confused and disheartened, and in a vain effort to improve the pacing he introduced last-minute changes in some gestures and entrances. 'Darling John,' Olivier said, stopping the dress rehearsal and addressing the director as the cast fell silent, 'please go for a walk along the river and let us just get on with it.'

The season opened on a gloriously sunny 23 April, Shakespeare's birthday – thirty-three years to the day after Olivier had played Kate in All Saints' Stratford production of *The Taming of the Shrew*. For most of the evening, he played for comedy and got the laughs he desired. Malvolio stumbled on the word 'slough', pronouncing it haltingly first to rhyme with 'thou' and then with 'tough'. And he managed three laughs from one line: 'My masters, are you mad?' he shrieked in a high, effeminate tone, pausing before continuing – 'Or what?' – another laugh – and finally, pointing an amusing variant for reading the line – 'Are you?' But critics found the performance oddly unfunny. Vivien fared worse: admired as always for being graceful and pretty, she was considered by both English and visiting American critics to speak so quickly she lost the poetry of the role. 'What might have been a great occasion,' wrote W.A. Darlington, 'became merely a big one.'

As if tensions had not already been exacerbated, the Oliviers were rehearsing *Macbeth* while performing *Twelfth Night*, and on weekends they drove to Notley, where Vivien insisted on inviting London friends – and Peter Finch. Olivier was exhausted and anxious, and this was one of the most important seasons of his career, but Vivien frankly complained to members of the company that he thought only of himself, and this, she seemed to reason, gave her *carte blanche* for her affair. 'The best you could say about [Vivien and Finch],' as Elaine Dundy remembered, 'was probably the worst you could say about them: they did nothing behind Olivier's back.' For his part, Olivier (whose sexual relationship with his wife was by this time only a memory) may have been glad that Vivien was distracted by her lover.

'I want to be quit of all this,' Finch told a friend in the company, adding as he pointed to the silhouette of Notley Abbey and its lighted windows, 'but I can't face Larry and the Battle of Agincourt down there.'

On 6 June, *Macbeth* opened – for Olivier, one of the great triumphs of his life. Wearing a short beard and small, sharp-pointed crown, he stressed not the stoic butchery or singularity of intent in Macbeth but the spiritual fatigue of a haunted man. His sense of brooding revealed a character who had a pre-history of dreadful introspection before the action of the play began, a man long besieged by nightmares: 'I have done the deed' (the murder of Duncan) was spoken with a kind of arid and detached disbelief, and 'Sleep no more' became an appalling examination of conscience. Speaking the soliloquies quietly, Olivier made Macbeth (as he had made Hamlet and Richard) recognisably human – reluctant, emotionally sallow and ill – and he brought the audience to a reverential hush when he said with frightening menace, 'Light thickens, and the crow makes wing to the rooky wood . . .'

With subtle insight, Olivier found phrases and half-lines within the verse from which he evoked singular relevance. In the scene with the murderers, for example, there are three words often tossed aside and sometimes even cut – 'well, then, now' – but Olivier made sense of them. He stopped, eyed the two killers mockingly, pointed with both index fingers at them and said 'Well' enquiringly. After a pause he said 'Then' in a tone suggesting he wanted them to approach him. But they remained still and his 'Now,' after another pause, was a terrifying imperative. 'The silence in the audience,' wrote one critic, 'beggars description.' The same hush attended his breaking voice in the last act as he almost, but not quite, seemed to weep for his own lost nobility:

> I have lived long enough: my way of life
> Is fall'n into the sear, the yellow leaf;
> And that which should accompany old age,
> As honour, love, obedience, troops of friends,
> I must not look to have . . .

This was, as Harold Hobson wrote at the time, 'the best Macbeth since Macbeth'. Olivier's portrait was not of a man's inevitable self-destruction but of one living a nightmare of guilt, a man not fundamentally wicked but lured by ambition into an iniquity beyond nature. An aura of remorse and terror surrounded him, yet there was no simple posture of despair. At Banquo's second appearance, for example, Olivier leaped onto the table and flailed at the ghost, illuminating not only the courage of the old soldier but the madness of resistance. 'I do not believe there is an actor in the world who can come near him,' Hobson asserted plainly, and almost every critic agreed with him and with Tynan, who exulted that Olivier 'shook hands with greatness'.

Tynan was not alone in decrying Vivien's Lady Macbeth, although none was so damning (her acting was 'competent in its small way'). Pale and delicate, icy and serpentine, she was again criticised for a lack of passion; but in her mad scene, her small and baleful fragility seemed apposite, and she impressed many with her alternation of lunacy and childishness. 'Both she and Larry were to my mind superb,' John Gielgud said. 'I always regretted the film of it fell through as her performance was not projected enough for the unwieldy Stratford stage and the screen would have afforded it full value.'*

Even after the failure of the New York production of *Romeo and Juliet*, Olivier had trained and directed Vivien with astute attention to her voice and bearing, from *The Skin of Our Teeth* to the Old Vic tour, from *A Streetcar Named Desire* to the two *Cleopatras* and *The Sleeping Prince*. She had, however, neither the stamina nor the natural gifts of voice and range for the great stage roles, and so the Oliviers – to her perpetual dismay – never became a great acting team as the Lunts did in America. Nevertheless, it is a fact that Laurence Olivier found Vivien Leigh an attractive performer and enabled her to become a very good if not a great stage actress. She brought to her Lady Macbeth what she bore in life: 'a sort of viperish determination', Noël Coward wrote in his diary, 'and a physical seductiveness which clearly explained her hold over Macbeth. In the banqueting scene she was brilliant, and her efforts to calm Macbeth and keep her guests at their ease were utterly convincing.' That scene could have come straight from a Notley weekend.

The ambition, the thin veneer of polite respectability, the acrid, sexual hypnosis and above all the air of despondent aristocracy – the Macbeths were a *tableau vivant* of the actors playing them that year at Stratford. '*Macbeth* is a domestic tragedy,' Olivier told Tynan in the year of Vivien's death. 'It's the passage of two people, one going up and one going down. And there comes a moment in the play when

---

* For three years, Olivier tried in vain to raise funds for a film of *Macbeth*. Locations were scouted in Scotland and a script was prepared, but the enterprise was sabotaged first by Alexander Korda's death on 23 January 1956 and then by the failure of the film of *Richard III* to realise an immediate windfall in America, where Olivier sought alternative financing.

he looks at her and he realises that she can't take it any more, and he goes on and she goes down.' He was in fact describing the contours of their marriage in 1955, for they were playing the Macbeths offstage as well as on, as visitors like Gwen Ffrangçon-Davies were quick to recognise.

Acting onstage each evening that summer, the Oliviers were also rehearsing every day for the horrific theatrics of *Titus Andronicus*, the third offering of the season, scheduled for its Stratford premiere in August. More involved than ever with Peter Finch, Vivien had by this time all but dismissed her career as a casualty of the critics' assaults. But she retained her glittering hostess image, and each night after *Macbeth* she invited company members to their rented cottage. Usually she detained the guests until after three o'clock, and a demolished Olivier would be fortunate to sleep two hours, for at five he had to be awake and vigilant for Vivien, wandering distractedly through the neighbourhood like Lady Macbeth herself and often perching danger-ously near the Avon, which ran at the foot of the garden. Since she spent the weekends with Finch, Olivier usually stole away to Notley – often with Maxine Audley, who had acted with him since the two *Cleopatras* and was in all three productions that season. Audley, a bright and witty dark-haired beauty then aged thirty-two, remembered that he was miserable that summer, and that when Vivien went off with Finch, she was quite content for Olivier to be with Audley. As with Dorothy Tutin and Claire Bloom, Olivier pursued with Maxine Audley a brief, somewhat awkward amorous interlude. He was not a particularly demonstrative man, and not at all emotional, she recalled.

'[The Oliviers] are trapped by public acclaim,' Coward noted at the time, 'scrabbling about in the cold ashes of a physical passion that burnt itself out years ago. Their life together is really hideous.' And so it was, as Olivier tried to keep hidden the emptiness of their marriage. Nevertheless, the collaboration continued as Vivien played the innocent Lavinia, Titus's daughter who is raped and mutilated (tongue ripped out, hands cut off) fifteen minutes into *Titus Andronicus*. She had few lines to learn, but she moved gloomily about, gazing forlornly, shriek-ing wordlessly and attempting to name her attackers by scribbling on the ground. This she rehearsed sourly and without consideration for her colleagues, often arriving late and embarrassing director Peter Brook and the cast by publicly berating Olivier for his inattentiveness to her, although everyone knew Peter Finch was not far away.

Brook, with whom Olivier had been only coolly polite during the filming of *The Beggar's Opera*, designed and directed *Titus Andronicus* (and composed its musical sound effects), in a production that minimised grand guignol in favour of an austere, formal entry into a world without ethics or basic human decency, a world like Buchenwald or Auschwitz, to whose standards of behaviour the atrocities of *Titus* bore tragic recent resemblance. The result was a historic production of English postwar theatre and the culmination of Olivier's great Stratford season. Critics praised his Titus, a figure of statuesque pathos, a tired veteran bent by a world mad with carnage. His voice cut each word in flint, and his controlling image for the entire role was the ocean (in his *King Lear*, it had been the wind): 'I am the sea; hark! how her sighs do flow,' he whispered, moving downstage, engulfing the audience in the tide of his grief. When Titus received the news of his sons' death and his own betrayal, he leaned against the proscenium arch, slowly bent his head backwards and, after a perfectly calculated pause said, 'When will this fearful slumber have an end?' For the terrifying moment when Titus cuts off his hand, Olivier paused again, after the bone-crunching sound effect (cabbage chopped over a microphone backstage); thus his wail of pain was all the more chilling.

The season concluded in mid-autumn. Vivien, miserable over her rejection by the critics, found Olivier's mere presence insupportable. This would be, she shouted at him one afternoon, the last time they appeared together – a remark she immediately regretted but which proved to be true. And with that, she planned what seemed a wildly improbable elopement. Although afflicted with pleurisy and the threat of recurrent tuberculosis, Vivien packed eight suitcases and summoned Peter Finch to Notley, whence they left in a cloud of confusion for France. Whatever romantic expectations she harboured were unmet, for early in the new year Peter Finch quietly ended the affair again. All the drama of 'Larry and the Battle of Agincourt' – and Vivien too – he at last put behind him forever.

CHAPTER TWELVE

✠

1956–1959

We're characters out of something that nobody
believes in . . . because we're so remote from the
rest of ordinary, everyday human experience.

Archie Rice, in *The Entertainer*, by John Osborne

As if nothing at all had happened, Vivien returned to Olivier after
her last holiday with Finch. She had read Noël Coward's comedy
South Sea Bubble and, insisting she would be in peak form, had cajoled
the playwright into giving her the lead in a spring 1956 production.
At the same time, Olivier's agent Cecil Tennant had been negotiating
with none other than Marilyn Monroe, who wanted the first film
under her own production banner to be made in England with Laurence
Olivier – and wanted it to be a screen version of *The Sleeping Prince*,
a perfect vehicle for a sultry American actress. (Vivien, annoyed that
her stage role should go to Monroe, put a brave face on the announcement, but in a temperate moment she had to admit that she was indeed
too old for the role of a chorus girl.)

Desperate to be more than a sex symbol, Monroe had been studying
the so-called 'Method' of acting with Lee Strasberg, who (apparently
with utter seriousness) insisted that Lady Macbeth was not beyond her
range. Olivier, Monroe felt, was so wildly improbable a movie partner
for her that the match just might be lucrative as well as professionally
advantageous. He, on the other hand, relished the chance to direct and
co-star with one of the world's most famous movie stars. On 5 February
1956, he left London with Rattigan and Tennant; on the seventh they
met Monroe at her New York apartment; and two days later 180
reporters and photographers crowded into a dining room at the Plaza
Hotel for a press conference.

Wearing a clinging black sheath with a scooping neckline, Monroe fielded condescending questions: Would she like to do more than comedy? Which classics? Dostoevsky? Could she spell 'Grushenka'? Had she ever seen any of Olivier's work? Or even a serious play? Mocking and worshipful, loving and loathing the exponent of sex appeal, the press typically subjected her to trivial questions (What did she wear to bed?) and demanded photos as she leaned forward, then embraced Olivier, smiled and winked. In the tradition of such publicity events, Olivier seemed a somewhat ridiculous appendage to the proceedings. Rattigan was completely ignored.

On 13 February Olivier was back in London, privately coaching Vivien for the Coward comedy, in which she opened in April to clamorously favourable notices and settled in for a long run. Olivier, meanwhile, supervised their relocation: having sold Durham Cottage in 1955 because Vivien claimed it was too small for their London social needs, they took a lease on William Walton's house in Lowndes Place, Belgravia; they would reside in its capacious quarters for the reasonable sum of twenty pounds per week. Throughout the year, Olivier also continued his attempts to put together a deal for his film of *Macbeth*.

Marilyn Monroe was due in London for *The Sleeping Prince* on 14 July. On the twelfth, Vivien (then forty-two) announced that she expected a child at the end of the year and intended to leave *South Sea Bubble* two weeks later. Olivier was frankly surprised, the press swung into action, and Coward – the success of whose play largely depended on Vivien – was angered by her atypical lack of courtesy in not informing him earlier. Still slim, no one could have guessed she was four months pregnant, and no medical records confirming her testimony have been uncovered. In view of Marilyn Monroe's imminent arrival and assumption of Vivien's role, there was widespread speculation that the pregnancy was a deception designed by Vivien to maintain a hold on Olivier's attention.

Monroe arrived as scheduled with her new husband Arthur Miller, who was preparing for a London production of his play *A View from the Bridge*. Next day, Olivier went to greet them and asked which shows they might like to see. Miller selected the current offering at the Royal Court Theatre, where his own work *The Crucible* had just been staged. Olivier at first reacted negatively, having seen and assessed John Osborne's *Look Back in Anger* as a 'travesty on England', a nonsensically bitter play that offended his patriotism. But, ever the good host, he capitulated, and the following evening (16 July) he and

Miller left a travel-weary Monroe and went together to the theatre in Sloane Square. Convinced that the playwright would find the evening as tedious as he had, Olivier was surprised when Miller called the play great and urged him to reconsider his opinion. After the final curtain, they went to meet the author and over drinks Olivier asked Osborne: 'Do you suppose you could write something for me?' Noncommittal but obviously interested, Osborne was also surprised, for Olivier and he seemed as unlikely a collaboration as Olivier and Monroe. But the question and the eventual reply (the play *The Entertainer*) significantly altered Laurence Olivier's life and career.

Look Back in Anger had opened on 8 May 1956 and was the first great success of the fledgling English Stage Company, founded earlier that year by George Devine to present new and experimental plays by young dramatists as well as to import the best new foreign work (like the plays of Arthur Miller). Devine, born in 1910, had taught with Michel Saint-Denis at the London Theatre Studio and later at the Old Vic school; he was also a prodigious director, most recently of John Gielgud's *King Lear* at Stratford (which had followed Olivier's *Titus Andronicus*). The ESC's home was the Royal Court (where Olivier had acted in five plays in 1928), a theatre recently reopened after severe damage from wartime bombing. There Tony Richardson, a twenty-eight- year-old television producer and former Oxford University Dramatic Society president, joined Devine as co-director.

The premiere of Osborne's play, directed by Richardson, marked an important date in twentieth-century British theatre, although at first it was disliked, as Osborne said, by 'the entire West End Mafia, including Olivier, who did a characteristically intuitive U-turn-about later – not exactly about the play but what was afoot'. Osborne and others (Harold Pinter, John Arden, Arnold Wesker and Shelagh Delaney among them) were spearheading an entirely new kind of theatre that appealed to a younger audience less interested in stars and glamour than in the winds of change blowing through postwar England.

Committed to theatre as a barometer of social shifts and even as a catalyst for them, the plays, playwrights and actors of the new theatre were drawn from the working classes – in contrast to the middle- and upper-class writers, actors and audiences identified with West End theatre since the times of Queen Victoria and Edward VII. There was now a new breed of proletarian hero, radically different from Coward's dinner-jacketed sophisticates and the polite protagonists of Priestley,

Maugham and Rattigan. Silk dressing gowns, cork-tipped cigarettes and champagne glasses were absent, and a neglected aspect of English life was at last represented – rude, often crude but recognisably authentic working people confronting the real social and personal problems of the 1950s and not merely pretexts for comic relief. *Look Back in Anger*'s hero, Jimmy Porter, was the prototype, bitter and resentful of a class system that crushes his life in a dreary Midlands town. It is no hyperbole to state that from 8 May 1956, the rarefied blank-verse dramas of Eliot and Fry suddenly sounded antique. At the same time, many of the actors who represented the traditional West End theatre were quietly but firmly considered equally passé by the new young breed of non-heroic actors (the young Colin Blakely, for example, and Albert Finney, Frank Finlay, Joan Plowright, Mary Ure and Kenneth Haigh). Even the lack of interest in Olivier's projected film of *Macbeth* was due at least partly to a decline of enthusiasm for the classics, which represented for many producers a resoundingly uncommercial adherence to the past. Not even Vista Vision and Technicolor, after all, had guaranteed the initial financial success of *Richard III*.

But as usual, shifts in theatre were part of a much wider change. Younger actors, often better-educated than their predecessors, no longer considered a grand social life essential for their careers, as it had been when elegance and 'contacts' were crucial for the drawing-room actor. About the time Coward sold his country estate Goldenhurst, the Oliviers realised they could not much longer afford the expenses of Notley Abbey (much less the hectic life prevalent there). Previously, the London 'season' had created a kind of fairy-tale atmosphere, and from this the sub-royal theatrical world had taken its cue; up to the mid-1950s, there was great escapism in this artifice and, by careful design, great distance from the styles of ordinary people; the distance was often increased when a title was conferred. Even advertising supported the cause. Olivier was not the first theatrical celebrity to have a cigarette named for him: when Benson and Hedges won his approval for the manufacture of 'Oliviers', the packages bearing his signature could be aligned near cartons of 'du Mauriers'.

Within the expectations fostered by celebrity and glamour, and the inevitable clashes of schedule and of ambition, intimate relationships could survive only with great effort, and the Oliviers' marriage was a powerful example of that difficulty. One of the most compelling reasons for the maintenance of their marriage was that they were indeed a kind of royal family, and royals did not divorce.

The Oliviers had marvellously fulfilled their regal status, right down to their choice of plays (the two *Cleopatras*, *The Sleeping Prince*). But things were changing swiftly and drastically, and people were no longer looking for regal icons to admire. Simultaneously with these transformations in private life, television was introducing enormous changes into writing, acting and design. On a small screen in a corner of the living room actors had not the same mystery, glamour and mythic quality that surrounded film stars. In fact, television, economics and the so-called 'kitchen sink' theatre were making stars of the man in the street, and there was soon a direct line from this to contemporary television game shows and news broadcasts which include on-the-spot interviews with those directly or even tangentially related to a 'story'.

The Prince and the Showgirl (as the movie of *The Sleeping Prince* was eventually titled) represented a traditional kind of entertainment that was declining. Undisciplined, habitually late, nervous and unprepared, Marilyn Monroe required numerous takes for the simplest shots. Accustomed to being treated professionally and socially as little more than a dumb blonde, Monroe was insecure in the best of circumstances; now, intimidated by Olivier's stature, she was unable to maintain her composure on the set and quickly became terrified that the film would show her to disadvantage. Like previous directors, Olivier found Monroe 'thoroughly ill-mannered and terribly rude . . . the most extraordinary mixture of two clearly demarked people. One was the most enchanting girl I ever met. Then, very, very quickly it became obvious that when she was working she was an entirely different person.'

Early on, Monroe accurately surmised that Olivier wanted her in the film only for her commercial value, and increasingly she saw him as a menace to her equilibrium and a competitor for the film's best moments. She had brought along Paula Strasberg (Lee's wife), and demanded her daily presence on the set for constant coaching and encouragement, and to provide an intellectual and emotional rationale for each line and movement. Exploiting Monroe's precarious self-esteem, Paula Strasberg overwhelmed her with theories and multiple possibilities for every scene. Olivier finally lost patience with this compromise of his direction, and when Monroe asked what attitude he expected for a certain scene, he completely alienated her: 'Be sexy, Marilyn,' he said flatly. 'That's all.' The atmosphere for four months was tense and unrewarding, according to Lee Strasberg's daughter Susan, who frequently visited. Olivier refused to cater to Monroe, and instead asked her to learn an entire new language of acting. This frustrated him as much as it did her, and he ended by doing just what they both feared – competing with her.

By some happy trick of movie wizardry, however, none of this shows in the final film (which, on release in June 1957, pleased American critics more than British). Although protracted and entirely too verbose, *The Prince and the Showgirl* has moments of inspired silliness: Monroe as Elsie, unable to learn the proper address for Olivier as the Prince Regent and always calling him 'Your Ducal'; Monroe, ignored by the busy chauvinist Olivier, hungrily gulping caviar on toast as if it were a ham sandwich; Olivier, acceding to her demands for a romantic scene, attempting a flamboyant seduction when the Prince is familiar only with the swift conquest. Monroe's anxiety, on the other hand, is apparent in those scenes when she proclaims her love, in which the poignant innocence of the character is united perfectly with the doubtful glances of this thirty-year-old, childlike actress. Her last scene is unexpectedly moving as she bids farewell to him – a sad Cinderella necessarily leaving the reluctantly uncharming man locked in his own selfishness. Monroe also had to cope with the ridiculous convention of being poured into a white 1956 gown at least two sizes too small for her ample proportions; nothing about her appearance or manner suggests that the story is set in 1911.

Olivier never seems to falter, perhaps because when there were doubtful moments he allowed himself a few extra takes. During a long close-up in a carriage on the way to the coronation of George V, he regards the showgirl with cold disdain – and slowly, with about five gradations of feeling, he relaxes into a smile. Something more of Olivier himself shines through in what might be called the travelogue through Westminster Abbey. Relying not on the few shots of stock footage but on a boldly indulgent presentation of the atmosphere of a sacred ceremony, Olivier allows an enormous choir to proclaim the glory of the pageant (which we never see), alternating stained-glass windows and statuary with close-ups of Monroe's awe-stricken features – a moment of pure epiphany as the choir bursts into Handel's 'Zadok the Priest'. Here, one detects the heart of the choirboy Olivier, still moved by ritual, still the patriot.

As filming laboriously progressed, so did Vivien's nervy attitude toward Monroe. Irritable and ungenerous, she came to Pinewood

Studios to watch an occasional day's shooting, and no one was left in doubt about her jealous resentment. She left *South Sea Bubble* on 11 August, and next day there came from Notley Abbey the announcement that she had miscarried. The circumstances surrounding this event are still shrouded in confusion, but it is remarkable that a woman supposedly five months pregnant should, without a doctor's attention or even rudimentary nursing care, lose her baby and at once calmly resume her social life. This does seem to have been a phantom pregnancy or a deliberate ruse, despite Olivier's subsequent silence. Alternatively, some have claimed that the lost child was fathered by Peter Finch. Every interpretation of this unhappy time is equally poignant.

The Prince and the Showgirl was completed in late November, and while he began the daily tasks of postproduction Olivier – fascinated by the Royal Court and hopeful that John Osborne might respond to his request – attended the first night of George Devine's production of Wycherley's comedy *The Country Wife* on 12 December. Afterwards, he went backstage to congratulate the cast – among them Laurence Harvey, Alan Bates and a twenty-seven-year-old actress named Joan Plowright. 'He was a top Establishment figure to us,' Plowright said later. 'At the time, we were supposed to be rebels against the Establishment. He came to the theatre in a Rolls – we were on motorbikes. He represented everything we were socially and politically opposed to at the time.'

Soon after, the Oliviers (fighting constantly, he later admitted) joined their friends Paul-Emile Seidmann and his wife Ginette Spanier for a holiday in Spain. They returned to London in mid-January 1957, and although they had negotiated the purchase of an elegant house at 54 Eaton Square, more than a year's refurbishment was required, and so they returned to the Waltons' home in Lowndes Place. Waiting for them was a package from George Devine: the first seven scenes of John Osborne's play *The Entertainer*, and a summary of the remaining six. The story of Archie Rice (a fifth-rate music-hall performer in a coastal town) linked the passing of the British music halls with a fierce commentary on the decline of Imperial Britain at the time of the Suez crisis. 'The music hall is dying,' Osborne commented, 'and with it a significant part of England.'

Olivier's life was at a turning point, too; as was clear even to him.

> I had reached a stage in my life that I was getting profoundly sick of
> – not just tired – sick. Consequently the public were, likely enough,

beginning to agree with me. My rhythm of work had become a bit deadly: a classical or semi-classical film; a play or two at Stratford, or a nine-month run in the West End . . . I was going mad, desperately searching for something suddenly fresh and thrillingly exciting. What I felt to be my image was boring me to death. I really felt that death might be quite exciting, compared with the amorphous, purgatorial *Nothing* that was my existence.

Encouraged by Arthur Miller to reassess the new wave of writers, Olivier had found the answer to his fear of being an outdated performer. Immediately, the freshness and rudeness of *The Entertainer* appealed to his theatrical instincts, even as the tone of resentment exactly mirrored his own. Yes, he told Devine, he certainly saw himself in the role of the elderly father, Billy Rice, the sad prophetic voice of yesteryear who dies offstage. But Osborne and Devine had a different idea: he was to play Archie, the singing, tap-dancing, boozing antagonist. Without waiting for a complete text, Olivier agreed. His entire career had been characterised by a desire to keep people alert, shocked, to turn the business of showing off into the widest variety of role-playing – and to find in characters a kind of redemption within suffering that greatly touched audiences. But the spiritually dead Archie Rice aroused nothing but contempt and perhaps pity; this would be the ultimate disturbance for Olivier's spectators. Apart from his role in the hermetically sealed world of *Venus Observed*, Archie was to be his first contemporary part in almost twenty years.

Olivier prepared for it by learning a mock-shuffle sort of dancing pattern and by attending two of London's last variety theatres, the Collins and the Chelsea. At first, there had been some half-hearted talk of Vivien playing his wife: he put an end to this by stating that at forty-three she was simply too young and lovely to play a frumpy matron of sixty. Her proposal that she could wear a disfiguring rubber mask was not taken very seriously, and the role went to Brenda de Banzie, who had been in *Venus Observed*.

Rehearsals began in mid-March – with Dorothy Tutin contracted, at Olivier's suggestion, to play Archie's daughter Jean. As he wrote in his *Confessions* (without identifying her), their romance resumed and he told Vivien that he was indeed in love with Tutin – to whom he also gave a part in his offstage interests by sending her to make a political statement on his behalf at the House of Commons, protesting against higher entertainment taxes. The affair was ironically pointed during rehearsals and the run of the play, as Archie asks Jean, 'What

would you say to a man of my age marrying a girl of about your age?'
Vivien did not introduce the subject of divorce, but when the actors
began to block scenes onstage at the Royal Court, she made such a
nuisance of herself that she finally had to be escorted to the door.

The Entertainer opened on 10 April for a limited four-week run: not
only were other plays scheduled for the ESC, but Olivier had agreed
to take Titus Andronicus to Europe as part of the International Theatre
Festival. London critics generally estimated Olivier's performance as
superior to the play: he was thought to be at the beginning of a
brilliant new phase in his career. Turning fifty that May, he portrayed a
character unlike anything he had ever attempted: the 'clown, the essential music-hall entertainer' Cecil Beaton had long believed him to be
in real life. His Archie, selfish and seedy, became at once both type
and antitype, his broken, coarse voice aptly stressing the wrong words,
investing a desperate man with a majestic ignorance and a pathetically
unconsidered smallness of spirit. With his bowler hat and thickly augmented eyebrows, his checked suit and bow tie, Olivier created a man
shorn of caricature, somehow superb even in his self-pity. And he
found, as he had in Antony, Macbeth and Titus, an elusive spark of
decency in Archie's lingering memories – a residual longing for
goodness beneath the cynicism as he softly spoke the final words of
the first act:

> Did I ever tell you the greatest compliment I ever had paid to me –
> the greatest compliment I always treasure? I was walking along the
> front somewhere – one day, it must be twenty-five years ago . . .
> And two nuns came towards me – two nuns –

– and then his voice trailed off. He turned slowly, as if hankering for
a lost innocence, and said to Tutin as his daughter, 'Talk to me.' And
with that the light on his features gradually dimmed.

He had, of course, seen dozens of Archie Rices in actors' rooming
houses from Birmingham to Brighton. But the source of his characterisation came from a deeper point than mere observation. 'It's really me,
isn't it?' he asked rhetorically of Osborne and director Tony Richardson
that year, and two decades later he still insisted Archie was the performance he was proudest of because 'It's what I really am . . . I know that
creature. I know him better than he knows himself.' Certainly Olivier
never thought he was a shabby performer in grubby backwaters. But
there are few experiences which cause so sharp a sense of guilt as that
of failed intimacy, few which produce so acute a conviction of emptiness

as a lost love and a severed commitment. And this is precisely what afflicted him in 1957, notwithstanding his professional achievements and despite all his familiarity with acting the full range of human emotion. If it is true that all actors have moments of doubt about their real identity, one as aware as Olivier must have found especially sharp the experience of playing a man who realises he is an outdated fraud. He could say 'That's me' of the character who reflected 'I'm dead behind these eyes – I don't feel a thing' precisely because he so often felt empty.

Olivier had come from the world of the minor Anglican gentry, had lived the staid choirboy and public-school traditions and was a solid example of the old Protestant society of Georgian England. He had passed through the academic pantomime of his Katharine in *The Taming of the Shrew* to the position of a West End apprentice, and then he had assumed the great Shakespearean roles. Later, Olivier was in a sense very like Maxim de Winter: with Jill and Vivien, he lived in a world of French windows opening onto English gardens, and with chums like Ralphie he toodled down Piccadilly in sleek cars. He had been an unquestioning patriot whose 'finest hour' was an invasion of France by proxy when he assumed the role of *Henry V*. During those years, he had refined his theatrical intelligence so that, with a craftsman's skill, he had developed an extremely shrewd, perfectly pitched sense of what worked onstage. And so he took on Archie Rice, which was the logical next step.

In 1956, then, as the Suez crisis forced the nation to rethink its role on the world's stage, English theatrical life was radically shifting, no longer inextricably linked only to Shaftesbury Avenue. Important innovations were occurring in Sloane Square, and Olivier was the first of the 'Establishment' to be there, both his fame and his genius enabling him to be not merely a follower of fashion but a catalyst of change. Because Sir Laurence Olivier was there, the Court Theatre was now indeed Royal.

In the world of the representational, Olivier was the equivalent of Churchill in the world of politics: he came to epitomise England. His marriage to Vivien Leigh and their enthronement as the Royal Family of the theatre coincided with the increasing influence of the press and of film, which made their anointing possible and in the 1950s publicised the decline of that marriage. Henry V, Nelson and now Archie: aspects of Britain itself were synthesised in Olivier and somehow, in a strange and almost accidental way (and surely without calculation) he became the embodiment of the country in a way no other actor could be. Linked to this was a constant shrewd alertness to his own possibilities, so that when he saw the wave of the future he knew he must ride it or perhaps be overwhelmed by it to the point of oblivion. 'I am England, that's all.'

But life provides few clean breaks, and Olivier had to change course again, and radically, relearning the role of Titus Andronicus for the triumphant European tour which began on 15 May in Paris. There Vivien's friends arranged for her to receive the Knight's Cross of the Legion of Honour 'for services rendered to the cultural relations and friendship between France and Great Britain'. This did not cheer a woman who was both dependent on and jealous of her husband as well as terrified of acknowledging that their life together was effectively over. As the company continued to Venice and Belgrade, Vivien was drinking more heavily than ever. Moody and demanding, she flew into a rage if any whim was left unsatisfied, and no one dared cross her, as Maxine Audley recalled, for then she became even more hysterical. As for Olivier, he simply withdrew, unable to cope with her; at the same time, however, the company noted how he liked to show off what they sometimes called 'his royal consort'. The consort, however, screamed obscenities at Austrian and Polish crowds who came to cheer for 'Scarlett! Scarlett!' and although she often seemed quite distracted, she composed herself for the nightly performances.

That spring was unseasonably torrid in Europe, the trains were crowded and uncomfortable, and the most even tempers were tested. During the eight-hour journey from Zagreb to Vienna, and the twenty-two hours from there to Warsaw, the company's mettle was severely tried by Vivien, who gave no one any peace. At one point, she fixed her wrath on Maxine Audley, whom she pursued along the train corridors, chattering wildly and tossing bits of bread at her until Peter Brook finally insisted on summoning a doctor.

Perhaps because by this time he was emotionally already divorced from Vivien, only one event that season seemed to arouse Olivier's anger. On tour, the news of actor Donald Wolfit's knighthood reached them, an announcement Olivier found intolerable – and not only because he disliked Wolfit's acting style. 'He already has the CBE,' Olivier said to Anthony Quayle with almost breathless resentment, 'and that means he takes precedence over me!' Such petty, envious outbursts were fairly common: he had, for example, been unduly enraged for days over what he considered the exaggeratedly good review of a minor player's performance in *Twelfth Night*. An actor to the core of his being, Olivier at fifty feared more keenly than ever the possibility of displacement by colleagues young or old; alliance with a new generation at the Royal Court was a way of keeping ahead of the competition, of defusing the threat.

On 22 June, the weary company returned to London, and four days later Olivier received an honorary Doctor of Letters from Oxford University. ('Whether in tragedy or comedy, he seems to identify himself with the part he plays,' read a translation of the Latin citation. 'It is due largely to him that even those who frequent only the cinema have become Shakespeare fans.') *Titus* began a five-week London run at the Stoll Theatre, Kingsway, on 1 July, and after the eighth curtain call on opening night, Olivier thanked the audience in French, Italian, Serbo-Croatian, German and Polish. For this he had been carefully rehearsed by Vivien, about whom he was now regularly confiding 'ghastly stories' to Noël Coward: '[She] can be so charming and gay,' Coward noted, '[and] also a terrible little bitch. They are undoubtedly a curious couple.'

Coward was not merely still smarting from Vivien's sudden withdrawal from *South Sea Bubble*. That entire month of July, she continued to make Olivier's life ever more intolerable, refusing to let him out of her sight, demanding he escort her to late-night suppers after *Titus* (aptly, to the Caprice restaurant) and inviting friends and strangers alike to Lowndes Place for brandy until dawn. 'I just can't keep up with Viv's schedule when I'm trying to do my job in the theatre,' he complained frankly to a reporter.

Aggravating the situation was the unfortunate fate of several theatres in London scheduled for demolition, the St James's and the Stoll among them. Neither offered performers or patrons comfortable space, both required major repairs to conform to fire regulations, corporations were offering handsome sums to replace them with office blocks, and no one could raise the funds necessary to preserve the theatres. Although the St James's lease had expired (after, as Olivier said, he had made 'mistake after mistake'), he joined a protest walk against the imminent death of the St James's, leading supporters in the rain from King Street down Haymarket, past the National Gallery and into St Martin's Courtyard. There Vivien read an impassioned speech begging the London County Council to save the theatre whose closing was another sign of the end of an era; another shared element in their life was about to collapse.

She did not stop there. Late in the afternoon of 11 July, the Oliviers sat in the Visitors' Gallery of the House of Lords while Viscount Esher described Britain as an artistic desert and demanded an immediate grant of five million pounds for the nation's arts. When Lord Blackford replied opposing public funds for culture, Vivien suddenly rose in her place and, defying all rules of decorum in the Great Chamber, shouted, 'My lords, I wish to protest against the St James's Theatre being demolished!' The robed peers shot icy stares towards her as she was gently but firmly escorted to the door by Sir Brian Horrocks, Gentleman Usher of the Black Rod. An hour later, in her dressing room at the Stoll, Vivien treated the entire incident as a lark and calmly went on as Lavinia. (Winston Churchill offered a contribution of five hundred pounds to a hypothetical fund to save the theatre; he also wrote to scold Vivien for her disorderly conduct.)

For the weekend of 19 July, she invited the entire *Titus* company to Notley. Olivier, who was counting ever more on the company of Dorothy Tutin, arrived late for the festivities, as he did the following Friday. Vivien then insisted that Olivier must cease this romance.

Finally, on the night of 25 or 26 July at Lowndes Place, Olivier could tolerate Vivien no longer. 'In a sky-high phase of scaring proportions', as he later termed it, she determined to keep him awake all night, and when he finally drifted off to sleep she struck his face with a wet towel. Olivier left the bedroom and locked himself in Walton's study, but Vivien pursued him, hammering on the door. Finally he threw it open, grabbed Vivien, dragged her back to the bedroom and hurled her across the room. Her head struck the bedside table, opening a wound precariously near the temple and left eye. 'I realised,' he wrote later, 'that each of us was quite capable of murdering or causing death to the other.'

The results of this violent evening were fourfold. First, since Vivien continued her protest activities, her photograph appeared several times in the press (in the 1 August edition of the *Daily Telegraph*, for example): she was badly bruised and wearing an eyepatch, but told reporters (none too convincingly) that she had been bitten by an insect. Second, the Oliviers henceforth lived mostly separate lives – he at a rented flat or with friends; she ultimately at Eaton Square. Third, when he described the incident to Dorothy Tutin, she and her parents understandably reconsidered her relationship with Olivier (any possibility of marriage would mean an ugly and protracted divorce), and with that the affair ended. Fourth, Vivien fled to Leigh Holman for comfort. Compassionate as always, he invited her and their daughter Suzanne (then aged twenty-three) for a three-week European holiday beginning on 7 August, while Olivier took his son Tarquin (twenty) with him to Scotland for a fishing trip (when he was not scouting locations for the still anticipated film of *Macbeth*). The holidays lifted no one's spirits, and father and son were no closer afterwards than before. At the end of August, Vivien was met on her return by Olivier, and they exchanged kisses and smiles for the benefit of the press. Both insisted that the separate holidays (roundly condemned by no less than a Member of Parliament) were innocent, that talk of divorce was mere rumour, and that Sir Laurence and Lady Olivier were very much in love – still the first couple of the English stage. But London's theatrical circles saw through the pretence: it was commonly known that the Olivier marriage was now an empty legality.

From September to November, *The Entertainer* was revived at the Palace Theatre prior to a provincial tour (minus Dorothy Tutin, who had withdrawn). Tony Richardson asked ESC repertory player Joan Plowright (whom Olivier had so much admired in *The Country Wife*) to step into the daughter's role; this she eagerly did on very short notice, beginning work with Olivier at a stage rehearsal on 24 August.

Plowright was a quick study, an actress of impressive range and fierce ambition. She had played numerous roles both classical and modern in Croydon, Birmingham and South Africa (latterly on an Old Vic tour), but critical notice came only after Orson Welles cast her as the cabin boy in his June 1955 production of *Moby Dick* at the Duke of York's Theatre. There followed a wide variety of parts with the Nottingham Players and, from spring 1956, with the English Stage Company at the Royal Court, where she received one enthusiastic review after another in plays ranging from Arthur Miller's *The Crucible* to Brecht's *The Good Woman of Setzuan*. After her success with *The Country Wife*, Plowright was considered one of England's brightest young talents, whether as appealing comedienne or brooding upstart. There was nothing glamorous about Plowright, and she affected no airs: a plain, dark-haired, brown-eyed young woman, she had a somewhat gauzy, flat voice. But she inflected subtle gradations into that voice, and a remarkable calmness in her stage presence allowed nuances of character to shine through; thus she seemed taller than her five feet four inches.

One rehearsal with Olivier confirmed his high regard for her talents, while she was glad to be in Osborne's play and was calmly 'rebellious against the Establishment', as she had said. 'He got down on the floor with us,' she said later of that early run-through. 'Larry won us over with sheer talent, and when you have that it pulls everyone up on their toes. There was no other side to him – no nonsense at all. His sleeves were rolled up and his braces were showing. He was one of us.' Very soon a friendship flourished between the fifty-year-old star and the twenty-eight-year-old playing his daughter. Joan represented something new and fresh, as Tony Richardson commented years later. 'She was part of an entirely new world he wanted to move into.'

In November, *The Entertainer* went on tour – a week's run each in Glasgow, Edinburgh, Oxford and Brighton – before returning to London for a final seven-week booking. On her forty-fourth birthday, Vivien travelled to Glasgow, where she at once became suspicious of Olivier's friendship with Joan. He denied any feelings other than simple companionship, and so he continued to maintain even after Brighton, where Laurence Olivier and Joan Plowright became lovers. He well may have felt that denial was not only easier (in light of Vivien's recent conduct over Dorothy Tutin) but also ultimately wiser, for there was nothing in this new affair that made marriage inevitable. Emotionally needy he may have been, but after the successive romances of the last decade Olivier was far from certain of himself and his future. Additionally, Joan had been married since 1953 to an actor named Roger Gage, then touring in India.

It is easy to understand Olivier's attraction to a lively, gifted young actress who had none of the neuroses, instabilities or pretensions of Vivien Leigh. Born on 28 October 1929 at her parents' home in Brigg, Lincolnshire, Joan was raised in a solidly middle-class family. Her father, William Ernest Plowright, was editor of the local newspaper; her mother, the former Daisy Margaret Burton, had appeared in amateur productions. 'It was rather an ordered upbringing,' recalled her younger brother David (later a television executive), 'but we were allowed the freedom to develop our self-confidence.' There were few luxuries during wartime, as Joan recalled,

> but we learned music and bridge and sports. Mother produced plays for the local youth club and painted scenery in the garden. In many ways she'd have loved to act herself, but she said she couldn't have taken the rejection and that she didn't have the endurance.

Her parents did not expect Joan to stay with acting, her first career choice, but she did not share her mother's anxieties. 'Joan was naturally competitive,' according to David. 'She couldn't accept that just because she was a girl she couldn't be captain of the football team. Her independence and competition were obvious from an early age.'

From the start, she influenced Olivier's thinking on matters social and political, arenas he had rarely entered: after discussing the matter with Joan, he resigned his honorary post with the International Arts League of Durban, South Africa. 'I do not think any organisation can be truly international unless it is interracial,' he told the press on 26 November. A week later, she encouraged him to speak out on the dilatory progress of a national theatre: 'I am surprised,' he said in a tone more Osborne than Olivier, 'that the English are not ashamed of themselves for being the only nation in Europe without a national theatre.' On 2 December he returned to London from touring for a final month's run of *The Entertainer*. Joan, however, was replaced as Archie's daughter, for she was scheduled to perform in New York in two plays by Ionesco. By this time, Devine and Richardson had negotiated for an American run of the play beginning in February, with the happy result that Joan would remain in New York, there to await Olivier, and together they would have several months away from their spouses and the British press.

The new year 1958 began with a flurry of arrivals and departures. First, the house in Eaton Square was at last ready. In her characteristically obsessive desire for decorative perfection, Vivien had ordered pale colours to make the rooms look larger, Aubusson carpets in the salons, curtains of Thai silk in the dining room, rose chintz in her bedroom and a deep purple motif in his. But she moved in alone. On 21 January, Olivier went to New York and to the Algonquin Hotel, where Joan awaited. Later he telephoned John Gielgud, who was also staying there. 'Larry had just fallen in love with Joan,' Gielgud recalled years later, 'but he talked most touchingly of his years with Vivien, how she had given him the finest moments of his life but also the most painful.' That Olivier should confide in Gielgud of all people, with whom he was certainly never on intimate terms, seems at first curious. But Gielgud was a loyal friend to Vivien, and there may have been an element of self-justification in Olivier's confession.

On 27 January, Olivier and Tony Richardson watched Lee Strasberg conduct several scene studies at the Actors' Studio. Marilyn Monroe, whose tutelage under Paula had already instilled in Olivier a resentment of the Method, was at the Actors' Studio that day; she hid in a lavatory rather than risk a reunion with him. Olivier had accepted new trends in theatre, but the craft of acting was still for him a question of carefully prepared technique and the accumulation of external details from which a character emerges. Reflection on one's personal history (a basis of Strasberg's approach) seemed to him inconsistent with the actor's goal of reproducing not his own but the playwright's vision.

That evening, Olivier met his former Old Vic colleague Basil Langton at the Algonquin bar. 'All this talk about the Method, the Method!' Olivier grumbled. 'What method? I thought each of us had our own method!' Soon after, he spoke more extensively about his impatience with American intellectualism.

> What they call 'the Method' is not generally advantageous to the actor at all. Instead of doing a scene over again that's giving them trouble, they want to discuss, discuss, discuss. I'd rather run through a scene eight times than waste time chattering away about abstractions. An actor gets a thing right by doing it over and over. Arguing about motivations and so forth is a lot of rot. American directors encourage that sort of thing too much. Personally, I loathe all abstract discussions about the theatre. They bore me.

The next day, 28 January, *The Entertainer* opened in Boston, and on 12 February it came to the Royale Theatre; American critics, like their London counterparts, found Olivier's performance as Archie more impressive than the play itself ('a versatile performance [in] a hollow allegory', wrote Brooks Atkinson of the *New York Times* in a typical review).

Although their affair continued, Olivier and Joan were realists. She had acting commitments in London for a year after the limited American run of *The Entertainer*, and for a time he seemed closer than ever (thanks to the keen interest of American movie producer Mike Todd) to realising his hopes for a film of *Macbeth*. (Todd's death in a plane crash on 23 March effectively ended the project, but Olivier continued to beg funds from businessmen and entrepreneurs until that summer, when he finally – and with great anguish – abandoned the project forever. Prospective financiers also observed the failure of *Carrie*, *The Beggar's Opera* and *The Prince and the Showgirl*.) He and Joan may have hoped for a future together, but for the present there was stability only in their work.

Vivien, meanwhile, was to appear in Christopher Fry's *Duel of Angels* (an adaptation of Jean Giraudoux's *Pour Lucrèce*), and when she asked Olivier to help her prepare the role he cancelled four New York performances and returned to England. The visit was not merely a generous gesture, for he intended to raise the topic of divorce. According to Claire Bloom (Vivien's co-star) there was considerable tension during those few days; not only did Olivier depart significantly from director Jean-Louis Barrault's conception of Vivien's role, refashioning it as she wished; in addition, her desperate entreaties to him, her promises of fidelity and a fresh commitment to their life, all went unheeded. Back in New York before the last of ninety-seven performances of *The Entertainer* in May, he told Noël Coward that his life with Vivien was over.

Olivier seemed in no way relieved by this, and Coward sensed that in some way the bond with Vivien remained strong: 'I personally don't think either of them is willing to face the contumely and publicity of a divorce.' As usual, Olivier gave no public indication of this private disharmony. He rented a launch on 9 May and (in a reprise of the Thames party during *Antony and Cleopatra*) invited theatre folk for a midnight cruise on the Hudson River. John Osborne, Richard Burton, Peter Ustinov, Douglas Fairbanks, Jr., Beatrice Lillie, Helen Hayes, Susan Strasberg and almost three hundred other guests were served a supper of stout, fish and chips, jellied eels and (for those with more conventional tastes) oysters and champagne. Two weeks later, Olivier was back in London where Vivien was determined (as she told Robert Helpmann, John Gielgud and Maxine Audley) that Larry would be her husband forever; to that end, she planned the revival of life at Notley and the glamour of their former existence. But Olivier took little part in this, and there were few lavish weekends in Buckinghamshire. Instead, he met Joan regularly at a flat in Walpole Street loaned to them by George Devine.

That summer, Olivier had to honour a commitment to appear in a film of Shaw's *The Devil's Disciple* for its producing stars Burt Lancaster and Kirk Douglas, a project to which he had agreed when he thought they might finance his *Macbeth*. This he undertook in a sour mood – first because the shooting at Elstree interrupted his schedule of meetings with Joan; second, because *Macbeth* was now definitely off; third, because unlike him, the American Lancaster had no trouble raising money for an English film production; and fourth, because Lancaster insistently called him 'Mr Olivier', a gaffe which in any other circumstances would not at all have bothered him (he would normally have asked everyone to call him Larry). Playing the role of John Burgoyne, leader of the British forces against the rebels in New England (a part expanded by the screenwriters beyond Shaw's text), Olivier had to summon little effort to portray the cynical general with a kind of civilised irony: 'It is making too much of these people, to hang them,' he said drily. 'That is the one way to achieve fame without ability.'

The boredom of production was not alleviated by Vivien's attempts to be a charming hostess. Although still performing in *Duel of Angels*, she sped to Elstree or Notley on weekends, eager to demonstrate that she was Lady Olivier, and that any rumours of trouble in paradise were false. Her tactics were often not wisely considered, however. At a Notley luncheon for Douglas, Lancaster and other guests, Vivien filled a conversational gap by turning to Olivier: 'Larry, why don't you fuck me any more?' An embarrassed silence was only relieved when the actor George Sanders raised his wine glass and asked with his patented world-weariness, 'Oh, Vivien, stop! In a moment, Benita [his wife] will be asking the same question, and then we're all in for trouble!' In a further bid for Olivier's attention, Vivien turned to Kirk Douglas, becoming (as he later said) 'very seductive, with Olivier sitting right there'.

Guest and host then discussed Douglas's plans to produce a Roman epic in Hollywood the following year, based on Howard Fast's novel *Spartacus* – which Olivier wanted to star in and direct. By that September (much to the relief of Douglas, who planned to play Spartacus himself), Olivier had accepted an offer to return to Stratford for the summer of 1959 in another Roman epic, *Coriolanus*. Still, eager for the Hollywood salary, he wrote to Douglas offering to play the smaller but crucial role of the powerful and vindictive Crassus.

As Olivier withdrew from her, Vivien redoubled her efforts to keep him, resorting ever more wildly to hysterical tactics. In addition, her drinking increased dramatically, and there were early signs of alcoholic dementia. Although her doctor, Arthur Conachy, maintained that she was not an alcoholic (a condition which would have precluded shock therapy) he admitted that she had a 'tendency to take considerable and regular amounts of alcohol, particularly in moments of stress [and] she refuses to modify this'. Noël Coward was blunter:

She is obviously in a bad way, drinking far, far too much and attacking everyone right and left. I know she is unhappy inside, but her predicament has been entirely her own fault from the first . . . She is certainly barmy up to a point, but she has been so spoilt and pampered for so many years that the barminess becomes ugly and dull . . . For all her beauty and charm and sweetness, she has let Larry down for years and really tormented him. If he can succeed in breaking away, good luck to him.

Coward's assessment may appear harsh. But he had been Vivien's loyal and affectionate attendant from the earliest days of her emotional instability, and he identified an important component in her condition: that Vivien had become the grand tragic actress of her aspirations. This itself was a kind of illness, the direct result of an admirable ambition unwittingly linked to a pattern of self-sacrifice to her art. Vivien was, in other words, brilliantly ill. At the weekends she often threw tantrums; she vanished for two days, causing rumours of suicide; she requested and received courses of shock therapy, from which she emerged temporarily calmed; she fled to Europe (turning *Duel of Angels* over to her understudy for two weeks that autumn) where she abandoned a car; and she turned up unexpectedly at the homes of friends. The situation became more pathetic with each turn of the plot, and even her most loyal and sympathetic confidantes lost patience with her antics. Her so-called manic depression was never firmly verifiable, and one medical report – Conachy's two and a half pages written in 1961 – is simply not sufficient from which to extrapolate twenty years of 'madness'.

As for Olivier, he compounded the problem by alternately treating her like a child, indulging her moods and simply withdrawing. And when she responded by behaving towards him like a possessive mother, he reacted in a way that prevented him from losing a mother again: he had to leave her before she left him. He was irreversibly out of love, bound by the kind of guilt that can only attend dead passion and a confusion of memories – by 'bonds that can only tighten', as Emlyn Williams said of that year, 'until he suffocated – a sufferer at the end of his tether'. In failing to respond to Vivien's devotion he had missed something fundamental in adult life – the opportunity for complete self-donation not to a career or a role but to another human being. He had benefited from her partnership, her tutelage and her presence as a glamorous ally, but in the end he knew he had – through an excess of passion for himself and his craft – withdrawn from her, in effect emotionally abandoned her. Once he had needed her adoration and her dependence; now he resented it.

Later in 1958, Olivier accepted an offer to appear on television, in an adaptation of Ibsen's *John Gabriel Borkman*, suggested to him by Vivien (whom he attempted to placate by presenting her with a Rolls-Royce on her forty-fifth birthday that November). 'With *Macbeth* off,' he told a reporter, 'I thought well, I am not going to shoot up again in popularity as a film star. So I read [Ibsen]. I think it is a good, strong part. A man whose power is just a little behind him.' But the filming for television went badly. He was hounded by Vivien; there were only two days of rehearsal for the one day of filming; the techniques of the medium were strange to him; and his brother Gerard – who had for five years managed Notley Abbey and its farm – was dying of leukemia. 'Olivier was punctual to the dot and agreeable to all,' according to Michael Meyer, who translated the play and was present for the production,

> but he had made up his mind how he was going to play the part, and when Caspar [Wrede, the director] tried to get more out of him for the last act, Olivier told him: 'This is the performance you're going to get.'

On 28 November, 'Dickie' Olivier, aged fifty-four, died at Notley, and Laurence carried out his brother's wish to be buried at sea. During their adult years there had been little contact between the brothers, but when Gerard needed employment he was given the cottage and a stipend at Notley. There seems to have been little socialising between the two families in those final years (Gerard and his wife Hester had two daughters), but occasionally the brothers shared memories over a drink.

By year's end, the Oliviers both knew their marriage was over, although appearances would be kept up in public for another year. Vivien confided in Coward, who found her completely calm and sweet about it, and inconsolably unhappy that Olivier had effectively left her. Then, still capable of doing exactly as she pleased, Vivien contracted to act the following year in *Look After Lulu* (Coward's adaptation of a Feydeau farce) and arranged for her first British television appearance – in *The Skin of Our Teeth* in three months' time. Meanwhile, Olivier departed for New York to make his American television debut. 'Everything seems to be downbeat with him at the moment,' Noël Coward wrote in his diary, noting Dickie's death and Vivien's dour moods. 'I think he rather self-indulges this, but I am sure he is genuinely lonely and unhappy.'

As often before, Olivier distracted himself with a ceaseless schedule of work. For a fee of $100,000, he rehearsed for two weeks in lower Manhattan for *The Moon and Sixpence*, based on Somerset Maugham's *roman à clef* about Paul Gauguin. Then, over three days and nights between Christmas and New Year, the television taping (one of the first dramatic specials in colour) was completed in Brooklyn. As the stockbroker who abandons civilisation for a simple artist's life in the South Seas, Olivier spoke with a kind of weary longing apposite to his own feelings that year: 'Sometimes, I've thought of an island – lost in a sea – where I could live in some hidden valley, with strange trees, in silence. There – I think – I think I could get what I want . . . I look forward to the day I can live free of all desire and live, without hindrance, for my work.' After broadcast the following 30 October, his performance won the American Emmy as the best by an actor that year.

Glad of his escape from the home-front traumas, Olivier also missed Joan, who had her own London stage commitments; they wrote and occasionally telephoned, but marriage was still hypothetical. From New York, he proceeded directly to Hollywood for the filming of *Spartacus*, which began on 27 January 1959 and added $250,000 to his income. But the production was chaotic from the start. Each major cast member (including Jean Simmons, Charles Laughton, Peter Ustinov and Tony Curtis) had been sent a script favouring his particular role, and the resulting confusion of temperaments during rehearsals led to (among other transitions) a change of director – from Anthony Mann to Stanley Kubrick (Kirk Douglas's director on the earlier *Paths of Glory*).

Olivier, arriving before the first day of shooting, applied pressure for his own role to become more important, as Peter Ustinov remembered: 'It was always amusing to watch him at work in the wings, in the process of getting his own way. When discovered, he would give you a mischievous wink and what had begun as an artifice ended as a performance, simply because he was being watched.' Typically, Olivier insisted on riding the horse appointed for one scene, and when thrown he leaped back on, shrugging off a bruised hip with the comment, 'Must be a Method horse.' He also relished the bold seduction scene written by Dalton Trumbo for Olivier (as Crassus) and Tony Curtis (as his innocent slave Antoninus):

Crassus: Do you eat oysters?

Antoninus: When I have them.

Crassus: Do you eat snails?

Antoninus: No, Master.

Crassus: Do you consider the eating of oysters to be moral, and the eating of snails to be immoral?

Antoninus: I – I don't think so.

Crassus: Of course not. It's a matter of appetite, isn't it? And appetite has nothing to do with morals, has it?

Antoninus: No, Master.

Crassus: Therefore, no appetite is immoral, is it? It's merely different.

Antoninus: Yes, Master.

Crassus: My appetite includes both oysters and snails.

Hollywood censors, however, intervened and ordered the scene cut that year – and so it was, until the 1991 restoration of the complete and original *Spartacus*, one of Olivier's smoothest throwaway performances.

During production, Olivier – anticipating the possibility of divorce and its attendant publicity and expense (he was, after all, still paying alimony to Jill Esmond) – lived frugally in a rented cottage with his old friend Roger Furse, rarely entertaining and rememorising the role of Coriolanus for Stratford that summer. As the filming lengthened to the end of May, his mood darkened. Talli Wyler, among others, recalled that he was miserably unhappy, and that the thought of remarriage did not automatically bring happiness. 'My life,' he said later of this time, 'has been an equal meting out of horror of what I'm going through and guilt for what I plan to go through . . . And then [I] say, Oh, thank Christ, for the next three hours I'll be Coriolanus, nothing like me, not one of my problems. . . . Or, if [the character] hates himself as I hate myself, then we have a partnership.' He was, he added, 'contorted with embarrassment' at being himself. The source of this self-loathing may well have been a twofold guilt: for his homosexual conduct and for his treatment of Vivien.

There was an ironic aptness in the Crassus–Antoninus dialogue in *Spartacus*, for that spring Olivier (as if taking his cue from the Hollywood censors) seemed to know that such a scene would never play in his own life. Quietly but firmly, threatened by the implications of a deep and abiding connection that was also dangerously unconventional – and persuaded by Joan, who was understandably cool about it and more vocal in her opposition even than Vivien – Olivier terminated his ten-year intimacy with Danny Kaye. Invitations from the Kayes were simply ignored, telephone calls went unreturned. The public image of Sir Laurence Olivier, after all, was that of the knight of the realm, the dignified actor-manager, the representative of England's great theatrical tradition; but privately, he was – and he knew it – not so grandly mythic a figure but a man dependent on those he considered his cultural superiors; he was also a genial companion and more emotionally needy than he admitted even to himself. Danny Kaye, on the other hand, projected an image of perpetual adolescence. He too had a wife, but whereas the Oliviers were locked in a collusion of guilt, insecurity and remorse, the Kayes seemed to have reached an accommodation, or at least a private compromise. To Olivier, Kaye both represented and radiated an attitude of spontaneous pleasure – and it was perhaps this most of all that he both admired and with which he feared to be associated.

Privately, Kaye had been a sensitive confidant who demanded little of Olivier beyond his presence. Like Vivien, he bristled with wit, charm and sexual energy; unlike her, he was willing to settle for a place on the fringe of Olivier's life. During the 1950s, the Kaye–Olivier relationship was not only physically intimate but also mutually supportive. Now, however, Kaye was what Olivier had initially perceived Joan to be – a sprightly, buoyant companion – and she may well have known this; hence the complexity of her jealousy and dread. As Vivien had also realised, she could compete with another woman, but not with a man.

Noël Coward had been Olivier's devoted mentor, but he had shone with a sophistication Olivier could only admire, never entirely emulate. Kaye was also polished and quick, but he was at heart always Danny Kaminsky, the antic Jewish boy from Brooklyn who quickly formed a bond with the son of an Anglican priest. With Kaye, Olivier was perhaps most himself, vulnerable, relaxed, unconcerned with style and status (as Vivien had required him to be), and Kaye therefore gained Olivier's trust and earned his self-disclosure in a way Vivien never had. Appreciating Olivier's genius, Kaye settled for private truth and public subterfuge, aware that social disgrace would certainly have attended widespread knowledge of their relationship. Vivien as well had only the remnants of her image as Lady Olivier; her truth was very different, but it too could not be revealed.

Olivier had so devoted himself to himself – to the pursuit of 'being

England' – that in fact something was lacking. Striving for the widest variety of identities, he had run the risk of being no one, and consequently he often felt he had failed to locate the contours of his own adult character. 'I don't like myself,' he repeated throughout his life like an antiphon. 'I'm not a nice person . . . I can't wait to be this other person for three hours.' The depth of his self-rejection may have been, in the final analysis, a poignant longing to discover just who he was. And so his self-loathing and the contortions of embarrassment indicated a deeper kind of guilt – a primal sense of need, the emptiness that derives not from what one has done but from what is missed. None of this could have been discussed with Vivien, and certainly not with Joan Plowright. And now Danny Kaye, too, was outside the circle of his confidence, and again there was only the sustenance of work.

Back in London in June, Olivier prepared simultaneously to revive *Coriolanus* for a 7 July opening at Stratford and to film *The Entertainer*. That summer he lived in hotels at Stratford or the resort of Morecambe on the Lancashire coast, attempting to establish that his break with Vivien was indeed definitive. Yet her friend Godfrey Winn recalled a particularly moving moment when, visiting Notley, she shortened a walk with her guest through the gardens: 'We must stay near the house. Larry has promised to telephone as soon as the curtain is down.' The call never came. As for Joan Plowright, she had left Roger Gage; she and Olivier were now living together as they reprised their stage roles for Tony Richardson's film that summer. Joan was not especially pleased that the Oliviers continued to tell the press that divorce was out of the question.

Olivier was equally adamant in matters professional. Twenty-eight-year-old Peter Hall, directing at Stratford, remained very late one evening arguing with Olivier about the pride of Coriolanus, whom Olivier saw as an essentially tragic figure; he wanted, therefore, to omit the lines referring to the mock modesty and refusal of praise – these were, Olivier insisted, attractive to Elizabethans but no longer intelligible for a modern audience. But Hall insisted the character was indeed so proud he could never ask for (much less accept) love, which would mean for him a loss of self. 'All right,' Olivier said at last, 'since you believe in it so passionately, I'll do it your way. But you're wrong.' The glory of the performance, as it happened, lay in the nuances brought to the role as Olivier took full cognisance of Hall's counsel. His Coriolanus was unanimously acclaimed as one of his greatest achievements, not least for the character's desperate exhaustion and for his memorable, astounding death-scene. After leaping up a steep staircase, Olivier shrieked his final lines from a platform twelve feet above stage level. He then threw himself, as if diving into a pool, turned in mid-air and was caught by the ankles so that he dangled upside down, facing the audience. He managed this dangerous stunt without incident until early October, when he tore a knee cartilage and was replaced by his twenty-three-year-old understudy, Albert Finney.

The accident did not interrupt the filming of *The Entertainer*, for which he was driven every day first to Shepperton Studios, then over 150 miles from Stratford to Morecambe. At one point during a four-day break from *Coriolanus*, he managed London meetings for two plays he presented that season (*The Shifting Heart* and *One More River*), both at the Duke of York's Theatre, both failures and his last solo ventures as producer. (In 1960, he co-produced two final disasters, *Over the Bridge* and *A Lodging for the Bride*; with their closing Laurence Olivier Productions became inoperative.) That autumn, he also attended several performances of *Look After Lulu* (at the Royal Court, ironically enough), in which Vivien delighted audiences and Noël Coward himself: 'She is desperately unhappy inside although very good and gay outwardly.' Several times, she coerced Olivier into taking her to dinner or a midnight charity benefit. He was performing two demanding roles, travelling almost daily from Stratford to Morecambe in an ambulance so that he could sleep on the way, and Vivien was prevailing on him to squire her around town. He was very near collapse.

On 10 July 1959, John D. Wood estate agents formally listed Notley Abbey for sale, and a prominent advertisement appeared in the 13 August edition of *Country Life*. Although the Oliviers had agreed to the sale together, this had an immediate impact of finality on Vivien. When he visited the Royal Court not long after, there was a terrific quarrel between them during an interval, and as Olivier departed she pursued him from her dressing room, clutching at his coat tearfully as he attempted to descend the stairs towards an exit. Typically, she completed her comic performance impeccably, but the event altered their stance with the press. 'Our marriage is going through ups and downs,' Olivier told an Associated Press reporter. 'Vivien and I have our problems.' To an enquiry about separation, she now replied equivocally: 'I won't say yes and I won't say no.'

With *Coriolanus* and *The Entertainer* concluded by December,

60. *Right* As George Hurstwood, with Jennifer Jones as *Carrie* (1950). *National Film Archive, London*

61. *Middle right* With Danny Kaye at a Hollywood party; at right, Shelley Winters. *Courtesy of the Academy of Motion Picture Arts and Sciences*

62. *Below* Sir Laurence and Lady Olivier at Durham Cottage, 1950. *Tom Blau/ Camera Press*

63. *Bottom right* As Mark Antony in *Antony and Cleopatra* (1951). *Culver Pictures*

64. *Left* The Oliviers as *Caesar and Cleopatra* (1951). *Culver Pictures*

65. *Middle left* With Maxine Audley (centre, facing camera) and cast members of the two *Cleopatras* (1951). *From the collection of Maxine Audley*

66. *Bottom left* During filming of *The Beggar's Opera* (1952). *National Film Archive, London.*

67. *Below* Peter Finch. *Courtesy of the Academy of Motion Picture Arts and Sciences*

68. *Top right* As Macheath, with Dorothy Tutin as Polly in *The Beggar's Opera* (1952). *From the collection of Felix Barker*

69. *Top far right* With Claire Bloom, in the film of *Richard III*. *National Film Archive, London*

70. *Right* The Oliviers as the Macbeths (Stratford-upon-Avon, 1955). *Angus McBean/Harvard Theatre Collection*

71. *Far right* As *Titus Andronicus*, with Vivien as Lavinia (Stratford-upon-Avon, 1955). *Angus McBean/Harvard Theatre Collection*

72. *Below right* With Marilyn Monroe, meeting the press before filming *The Prince and the Showgirl* (1956). *National Film Archive, London*

73. *Below far right* As Archie Rice, in *The Entertainer* (1957).

74. *Top* With Joan Plowright as Jean in the film of *The Entertainer* (1959). *National Film Archive, London*

75. *Above left* In his death scene as Coriolanus (Stratford-upon-Avon, 1959). *Angus McBean/ Harvard Theatre Collection*

76. *Above* As Becket, with Anthony Quinn as Henry II (New York, 1960). *Culver Pictures*

77. *Left* With Sarah Miles, in the film *Term of Trial* (1962). *National Film Archive, London*

Olivier and Joan slipped quietly away for a Paris holiday. He then departed alone for a few final shots on *Spartacus* in Hollywood and at Christmas visited the nearby ranch of Jean Simmons and her husband Stewart Granger. Their apparent happiness so impressed him that he decided he must marry Joan – which was ironic, as Simmons recalled, since at that time she had already decided to divorce Granger.

'My baronial period is just about over,' he had said that summer when Notley was put up for sale. 'I wonder what comes next.' As 1960 began, Olivier still had no clear idea; he was, in fact, in a state of almost paralytic indecision about his personal life when an offer to direct on Broadway helped to forestall any momentous choice. In the first week of January, he travelled from Los Angeles to New York to prepare for the opening of a verse play by his old friend Benn W. Levy, who had written Olivier's first movie role. The eventual fate of this play demonstrated how quickly the baronial period was indeed over.

CHAPTER THIRTEEN

1960–1963

It all seems far too easy.

Thomas Becket, in Jean Anouilh's *Becket*

On 8 January 1960, Olivier invited the leading actors in *The Tumbler* – Charlton Heston, Hermione Baddeley and Rosemary Harris – to his suite at the Algonquin Hotel. (The leading players were to have been Trevor Howard and Brenda de Banzie, but Olivier would not accede to Howard's demand for sole above-the-title billing.) There they read through the script, a gloomy and overwritten verse play about an embittered, married English farmer whose infatuation with a lovely young woman eventually drives him to suicide. In choosing this work (written by Levy many years earlier for his wife Constance Cummings), Olivier's standard of judgement had evidently not much improved, but he may have believed that a verse play with a grittier, more tragic tone than *Venus Observed* would suit Broadway's taste. Besides, he needed the money and appreciated the chance to prolong his absence from London.

The play's weaknesses were immediately evident to Heston, who had accepted the role only for the chance to work with Olivier. Cuts by Levy did not help much, but Olivier was fervent that it should succeed. By the second week, he had introduced a painstaking approach to blocking the actors' moves: scale models of the two sets had been constructed – a tiny barn and a parlour – around which he pushed five dolls, suiting the actions to the words and asking the cast to write down the positions in their scripts. Every entrance, exit, cross and seating pattern was thus foreseen. Asked if this approach merely transformed people into puppets, Olivier had a ready reply, his first extensive statement on the director's function:

The actor must be disciplined, trained so that he automatically carries out the director's orders. I expect my actors to do exactly what I tell them to do and do it quickly, so I can see my own mistakes immediately if I have gone wrong. I believe the director alone knows where the action should rise and where it should fall. He provides a point of view on the shape, meaning and rhythm of the play, when to slow the tempo, when to speed it. When to use a pause. I'm not against spontaneity, but these improvisations have to be worked out within a framework set by the director.

In fact his method was as helpful to his cast as to himself (even in this ultimately disappointing play), for he taught what he had learned: that the actor must take command of the stage, must capture a parcel of space on it and mark it as his own.

This aggressive attitude towards stage presence was something he advised his friends to adopt. Not long after, John Mills confided his fear of performing onstage (in *Ross*) after an eight-year gap, and told Olivier he would probably turn down an offer to act on Broadway. But Olivier changed Mills's mind. Go on to the stage, he told him, fifteen minutes before the play begins, and from behind the curtain, whisper to the audience: 'You are about to see the greatest fucking performance of your entire theatregoing lives – a great actor at work. I've given some miraculous performances in the past, but tonight I shall excel them all. You lucky people – you'll find it impossible to take your eyes off me!' (Later, actor Robert Lang recalled he was often told by Olivier to avoid an area onstage where another actor had been particularly good moments before: 'It's too hot. The audience has used up this spot. Try somewhere else.')

On 4 February, *The Tumbler* opened in Boston even as rehearsals continued, but the critical reaction was disastrous. Everyone was fairly depressed, recalled Rosemary Harris, but Olivier buoyed their spirits up by performing a hilarious striptease. This was inspired by an innocent enough gesture of Charlton Heston, who arrived at a cast meeting, peeled off his heavy white cableknit sweater and tossed it aside onto a chair. Moments later, while giving his notes to the actors, Olivier removed his jacket. Continuing to discuss the play, he then took off his tie. A few moments later, he sat down and pulled off one shoe, then the second – then came his socks, and finally he unbuttoned his trousers and slipped out of them. By this time, his cast was convulsed with laughter.

The director also cheered up his cast, as Heston recalled, with vast quantities of champagne and lobster, and Levy continued to rewrite and cut. Olivier then yielded to the producer's demand that Hermione Baddeley, a gifted comic actress, be replaced by the more serious Martha Scott; they all struggled on bravely, and the production limped into New York on Wednesday, 24 February. The first disastrous notices came in while the cast party was in progress at Sardi's restaurant that evening.

An hour later, Heston was sitting alone with Olivier and a bottle of brandy. 'Well,' Heston said philosophically, 'I guess you learn to dismiss the bad notices.' Olivier grasped Heston's shoulder and replied, 'Laddie, it's much more important and much harder, but you've got to learn to dismiss the good ones!' On Saturday, after five performances, the play closed. Ten days later – just as Vivien was leaving London for the New York run of *Duel of Angels* – Olivier was back in England, removing the last of their possessions from Notley Abbey, which had just been sold to a Canadian television executive for £30,000. The purchaser recalled that Vivien was near tears.

Meanwhile, Joan encouraged Olivier's forays into the unknown territory of contemporary theatre by recommending he act with her in Ionesco's absurdist satire *Rhinoceros*, directed by Orson Welles. Forever after, Welles complained that Olivier behaved terribly, virtually upstaging him as director. Never an easy-going or predictable director, Welles seemed to Olivier bombastic and temperamental, and this provoked his ill-advised strategy of direct interference. 'He took every actor aside,' according to Welles,

> and [said] that I was misdirecting them. Instead of making it hard for me to direct him, he made it almost impossible for me to direct the cast. He got them off in little groups and had little quiet rehearsals having nothing to do with me.

Finally, repeating his treatment of Gielgud at Stratford in 1955, Olivier asked Welles to leave the theatre several days before the 28 April premiere – and took over direction himself. As the reluctant clerk who retains his humanity while everyone around him turns into a rhino, Olivier reduced himself to an abject, pathetic anti-hero, and the role was considered so bizarre an addition to his gallery that ticket-buyers crowded the Royal Court for over a hundred performances.

With Vivien in New York, Olivier had the flat in Eaton Square to himself; Joan's flat in Ovington Square, too, was only a short distance from the Royal Court. Although he at last drafted a letter to Vivien requesting a discussion of divorce terms, he was not yet entirely committed to the idea of marrying Joan. (Coward, among others, urged him not to take any precipitous action.) Olivier was apparently undecided for some time, and he subjected Joan to some tactless comparisons. At a restaurant one night he removed her white gloves. 'Why did you do that?' she asked. 'Because they were dirty,' he replied, 'and Vivien would never have worn dirty gloves.'

Vivien would, however, resort to untidier tactics. On receiving his letter (in which he wrote 'I am bored with the legend of the Oliviers'), she became so hysterical that the meddlesome Robert Helpmann dictated a press release for her in New York, where he was directing her in *Duel of Angels*: 'Lady Olivier wishes to say that Sir Laurence has asked for a divorce in order to marry Miss Joan Plowright. She will naturally do whatever he wishes.' In addition to the sly ambiguity of 'she', this announcement, indicating to the American press only the compliance of an injured party, threw the issue askew in England – as Vivien and Helpmann doubtless intended. Publication of her cooperation endangered the granting of a divorce since English law considered her statement possible collusion with the petitioner.

In London, the press at once swung into action, camping in Ovington and Eaton Squares and outside the Royal Court. The day after Olivier's fifty-third birthday, Joan withdrew from *Rhinoceros*, and the play closed on 4 June, only to reopen at the Strand Theatre four nights later with Maggie Smith in her role. At the same time, *Duel of Angels* had its last New York performance and Vivien returned to London, where she was met by *her* new love (or, at least, the man who was providing some of love's elements), actor John Merivale; he was her co-star in *Duel* in New York and had known her as far back as the Old Vic in 1937 and the New York *Romeo and Juliet*. Far from seeming haggard and psychologically frail, Vivien appeared confident and optimistic, telling Merivale she had no intention of dissolving her marriage. To journalist David Lewin, who asked if she would modify anything in her past life, Vivien replied (in Merivale's presence): 'I would want to be an actress and marry Larry. I would want everything again – except the last few months.' Not long after arriving, Vivien asked Rachel Kempson to 'please ask Larry just to have an affair with Joan – I won't mind – if only he won't leave me'.

Her unhappiness was not entirely ignored, for Olivier was certainly susceptible to guilt over the end of their marriage. To David Fairweather's wife Virginia (who had become Olivier's personal publicist), he confided an enormous burden of anguish, and said that if anyone were to seem the villain, it must be him.*

Olivier knew he had taken advantage of Vivien's love, had exploited her as a useful public consort, had nourished his own ego with her unalloyed devotion. 'He almost wept, remembering her unshakeable trust in him, and his gratitude for how she had refined his social and intellectual life,' Virginia Fairweather recalled. Later, Olivier had to justify his actions: the situation had become, he said, 'like someone holding out a hand to save another in a lifeboat and saying, "I can't – if I pull you on, you'll pull me in." That's the way I felt with Vivien.'

That June, Noël Coward found Vivien quite in control of herself except when she drank, and he rightly assessed the core of her problems to be indulgence of both self and alcohol.

> I suspect there is far less genuine mental instability about it than most people seem to think [and] that all this disgraceful carry-on is really a *vino veritas* condition! She has always been spoilt and when she fails to get her own way she takes to the bottle and goes berserk.

Sympathetic but frank, Coward maintained close contact with Vivien throughout the year, noting her simultaneous hankering for Olivier and abandonment to the arms of Merivale, who was content with whatever arrangement she required; that became, as it happened, life-time companionship. But Vivien was very tough with Merivale, according to John Gielgud, because she was frankly in love with Olivier until the end of her life. It was his photograph on her night table, his old love letters in her desk. When Olivier learned about Merivale, he was predictably relieved, and in a letter dated 16 August he wished them every happiness. Much would Merivale need the blessing, for over the next seven years (until her death in 1967) Vivien's emotional and physical decline was inexorable.

Events continued to unfold quickly. After the closing of *Rhinoceros*, Olivier was eager to be rid of the prying London press and the importu-

---

* Olivier's autobiography is remarkable for its repetition of the words 'guilt' and 'guilty'; see *Confessions*, e.g. pp. 25, 39, 100–1, 185, 218, 226, 261, 295, 311. The epigraph of the book is a variant on the ritual of sacramental penance in confession: 'Bless me, Reader, for I have sinned. Since my last confession, which was more than fifty years ago, I have committed the following sins . . .' and three hundred pages later he concludes: 'For these and all my other sins, which I cannot now remember, I firmly purpose amendment of my life and humbly ask pardon of God and of you, Reader, counsel, penance and absolution.'

nate Vivien, and he asked his agent for work in America again, where Joan was contracted by producer David Merrick for Shelagh Delaney's play *A Taste of Honey* the coming autumn. As it happened, Merrick was also producing Jean Anouilh's *Becket* and negotiations were swiftly completed for Olivier to play the twelfth-century archbishop in conflict with his friend Henry II. By September, Olivier and Joan were happily settled again at the Algonquin. Soon after their arrival in New York, Roger Gage (in a London court) cited Laurence Kerr Olivier as co-respondent in his divorce suit against Joan Plowright, on grounds of adultery. No response was immediately forthcoming, nor was it expected; the cases simply moved forward, and time was the determinant in adjudicating the *de facto* dissolution of a marriage.

Meanwhile, the first week of October in New York could not have gone better. On 3 October, the film of *The Entertainer* opened and Olivier was greatly acclaimed for his performance. On 4 October Joan opened in *A Taste of Honey*, for which she later received both the Tony and the Drama Critics' Circle awards as best dramatic actress of the year. On 5 October there was the first performance of *Becket* at the St James's; Olivier received even better notices than the play, and a spring tour was planned. ('One always knows that this Becket will be faithful to his duty,' wrote one critic, '[but] Olivier plays with admirable scope. The courtier is limned with elegance and spirit; the man of God has dedicated simplicity and sad, consoling wisdom.') On 6 October, *Spartacus* had its world premiere in New York and was soon screened round the country.

From the first rehearsal for *Becket*, Olivier had been troubled by the torn cartilage sustained the previous year during *Coriolanus*, but Margaret Hall (who played the Queen) remembered that he insisted on kneeling throughout Becket's long third-act prayer, and Anthony Quinn, King Henry to his Becket, recalled the experience of performing with Olivier as like being onstage with a cageful of lions. On opening night, while the two actors were listening to another player deliver a short speech, Olivier suddenly started tugging at the costume of Quinn, who tried to ignore the gesture until Olivier finally leaned over and whispered, 'Tony, where the fuck can you get good English beer in New York?' This was not so much amusing as disorienting to Quinn, who was also put off by Olivier's turning aside onstage to perform (out of the audience's view) tongue-loosening exercises.

Quinn also had the impression that Olivier had odd opinions about certain things. India's Prime Minister Nehru had invited Quinn to lunch at the Carlyle Hotel because there was some discussion about the actor playing him in a film. When Olivier learned of this, he was annoyed: why hadn't he been invited too? Quinn arranged for him to be included, and as they waited outside Nehru's hotel suite Olivier turned and asked a bodyguard, 'Do you think Nehru will have yoghurt for lunch?' Surprised, Quinn asked what he meant. 'Well, I hear that Indians eat a lot of yoghurt,' Olivier replied innocently, 'and I just wondered.'

Olivier and Joan enjoyed a singularly untroubled and successful season in New York. As for their future, she pressed him for a decision – even more intensely after 2 December, when in London Roger Gage was granted a decree of divorce on the grounds of her adultery with Sir Laurence Kerr Olivier; the same day, Vivien was granted her decree of divorce, on identical grounds. Dressed in a severe, almost Dantesque outfit of red and black, she appeared before Judge Ifor Lloyd of the Probate, Divorce and Admiralty Division. 'Until 1952,' she said calmly, beginning her testimony, 'the marriage was very happy. Then I noticed a change in my husband's attitude. He told me he was interested in someone else [Dorothy Tutin].' The decrees were to become absolute the following March, at which time Olivier and Joan would be free to marry.*

For their eventual return to England, they planned to make their main home in Brighton, where Olivier in early 1960 had purchased a Regency terrace house facing the Channel (this ultimately required almost two years' refurbishment).

With the new year 1961 came a letter from the ex-Mayor of Chichester, Leslie Evershed-Martin, one of the developers of contact lenses in the British Isles, a man with a canny business sense and a keen interest in the arts. Watching Huw Weldon's television interview with Tyrone Guthrie in January 1959, Evershed-Martin imagined that Chichester, very near the English Channel and only about fifteen miles from Brighton, could have a summer festival theatre similar to that

---

* In accordance with the law, Vivien had been asked to provide a written declaration about her own conduct, in which she admitted two instances of adultery with an unnamed other or others. Her barrister contended that, following her discussion of these actions with Olivier, reconciliations constituted his forgiveness; a similar situation prevailed in the case of Gage. Thus he and Vivien were adjudged the offended parties and granted the divorces. Olivier bore everyone's court expenses.

which Guthrie had built in Stratford, Ontario. The demolition of London theatres, the need for the arts in the provinces, the attractiveness of Chichester's parks and fields – these considerations led Evershed-Martin to approach Guthrie directly. They discussed prospective candidates for artistic director – John Gielgud, Peter Hall and Peter Brook among them – until Guthrie told Evershed-Martin he had just received a long letter from Olivier, complaining about the wretched state of Broadway theatre, due to crass commercialism. Olivier had also said he would soon return to England and settle in Brighton.

Thus it happened that on 11 January 1961, at the Algonquin Hotel, Olivier received a letter from Evershed-Martin offering him the position of the first Festival Director for Chichester:

> I feel [Evershed-Martin wrote] that this is going to be a great opportunity for someone who has inspiration, and who is dedicated to the Theatre, to contribute something new, extremely valuable and exciting to British drama. I believe you will agree that if we lag behind Canada, America and the rest of Europe, we shall be betraying our heritage and giving ammunition to those who would like to say that Britain is becoming decadent.

He added that local citizens had already pledged £42,000 and that Olivier would be welcome to direct and act in plays he himself selected. With promises of creative freedom from elaborate committees, Evershed-Martin requested an early response: he hoped to open the theatre during the summer of 1962.

Two weeks later (on 25 January 1961), Olivier replied briefly, simply referring the matter to Cecil Tennant, his agent at MCA.*

Privately, as he later admitted to Evershed-Martin, the offer could not have come at a better time. For one thing, Olivier had not been successful at the St James's, and he was still eager to prove himself as an actor-manager. Second, he was still smarting from his failure to finance the film of *Macbeth*. Third, there was at last the real prospect of a National Theatre, and Chichester could be both a seedbed for its talent and, perhaps as well, a place from which he might move on to the National.

---

* Tennant had been managing director of the Frank Joyce–Myron Selznick talent agency which had been acquired by MCA (Music Corporation of America), the worldwide talent representation company whose London office was headed by Olivier's old friend Laurence Evans and by Robin Fox. After a series of mergers and divestitures, the resulting conglomerate eventually became known as International Creative Management (ICM).

As correspondence continued, Olivier asked if he could make contributions to the design of the thrust stage and the entire theatre; in a lengthy letter dated 17 February, for example, he suggested modifications in the cantilevered structure of the stage lip, removable sections for traps, cross-surface plans for pushing flats and props, and the placement of central pillars – all of which were based on his painstaking study not only of Guthrie's Stratford (Ontario) prototype but also of stagecraft from Elizabethan times to the twentieth century. He also liked the idea of a stage surrounded on three sides by the audience (a plan he had once seen improvised by Father Heald at All Saints and had later discovered by accident in 1937, during the Elsinore downpour). 'The purpose of such a shape,' he wrote, 'is to provide greater concentration on the action . . . The star will be the theatre, the stage the unifying feature.'

On 3 March, Olivier stated his final condition for acceptance of the job: that the choice of plays and all artistic decisions be his alone. Evershed-Martin and his colleagues acceded to this, and there remained only the matter of Olivier's fee. When they offered him £5000 for the first year, Olivier immediately and generously insisted that he wished to be part of a 'first great adventure' and suggested he receive only £3000 – an idea that received ready acceptance since Evershed-Martin took no salary from the enterprise and the players were to receive almost nothing. On 14 March, Olivier's appointment was confirmed, and the press was informed within the week. 1 May 1961 was the date set for laying the foundations of the Chichester Festival Theatre, which left only a year before the first performances.

Meanwhile, there were important developments in America. David Merrick planned to take *Becket* on tour to Boston, Philadelphia, Detroit and Toronto, but after almost two hundred performances Olivier was weary of the martyr's two-dimensional pieties: the part he should have chosen, he had soon realised, was the spiky and acidulous King Henry II, gloriously human in all his greed and lusty bravado. And so in February Olivier asked to play the King (Quinn having been contracted for a film); he also negotiated for himself 10 per cent of the gross receipts for the tour. During the final performances of the New York run in March, Olivier prepared the role of Henry and rehearsed with the new Becket, Arthur Kennedy.

At about this time, Vivien arrived in New York and made a last attempt at reconciliation, despite her divorce suit. But Olivier refused to discuss it with her and agreed to meet her only with Joan present. The trio met for a late supper at Sardi's, where Olivier (fearing a scene but wishing to make an end of it with Vivien) held Joan's hand and said they would marry as soon as the divorce was final. Vivien endured this calmly, but she left the restaurant without eating.

The divorces of Olivier and Joan became absolute soon after, and they were free to marry – but not in New York State, where a waiver was required for a certain period after a divorce granted for adultery. Undeterred, Olivier and Joan drove to Connecticut after their performances in *Becket* and *A Taste of Honey* on Thursday, 16 March; they stayed with director Joshua Logan and his wife Nedda that night, and next day stood before Justice of the Peace Edward S. Rimer, Jr. in the town of Wilton and were pronounced man and wife. At once, because they were due onstage that evening, they returned to Manhattan, making their way through the parading St Patrick's Day crowds. Next morning, newspapers in London and New York offered readers smiling photographs of Sir Laurence and his new Lady Olivier.

'Because we were both so aware of it when we married,' Joan said later, 'we didn't want all the legend stuff – he had had it and didn't want it any longer, and I had never had it and didn't like it anyway. It was simply a man and a woman living together. I married a man, not a myth.' But she was not marrying a Brighton tobacconist, after all, and her statement comprised only half the reality: whatever the private simplicities of their life, Olivier was always a public figure, and in marrying him Joan Plowright also united herself with his legendary glamour, influence and fame. Those attributes could not, despite her protestations, have made him less attractive.

For his part, Olivier was effectively forming a new professional alliance in marrying Joan. As he had once joined the respectable social-theatrical set by wedding Jill Esmond, so now he linked himself to a fashionably modern theatre movement with Joan Plowright. He had also chosen – as he had in Jill and Vivien – an aggressive woman quick to take charge. 'Ever since my mother's death,' he said, 'I've been looking for someone like her. Perhaps with Joanie I've found her again.' In later television interviews, too, he spoke of his attraction to Joan in terms of her 'likeness to [his] mother'. Indeed, Olivier saw qualities of maternal endorsement and encouragement similar to those which had initially attracted him to his previous wives, and like her predecessors Joan was leading him to new developments in his career. These women had in a sense led the way for him to follow – Jill professionally, Vivien socially – and each had been apt for earlier stages in his life and career. Now, as a new wave of actor emerged, Joan provided fresh ideas, a blunt, modern and unselfconscious style of life – and the gratification of an intelligent young woman's attention. And in a way – since they planned a family – he had married a mother-figure in order to make her one. But their life would not be as uncomplicated as he wished after the unceasing agitation with Vivien.

While Joan continued with her play in New York, Olivier toured from late March to 8 May, when *Becket* returned to Broadway for a final three weeks. (To his nervous dismay, Vivien was present at a performance that season, sending a message to his dressing room before curtain up and a bouquet of flowers afterwards.)

Onstage as the King, Olivier's performance was even more enthusiastically received than his archbishop – even with his subtle but pointed implications of Henry's sexual attraction to Becket. With exquisite delicacy, Olivier suggested that in depriving the young Becket of a bedfellow and simultaneously appropriating her for himself, Henry desired one who had been close to him, and implied that Henry raised Becket to the rank of archbishop to unsex him. Any doubt of this subtext was erased by Olivier's final stage gesture (new to this production and entirely his invention): before his exit, he turned towards the martyr's tomb, winked and blew a kiss to the man he could not control in life or death. This, some critics grumbled, threw the play (subtitled 'The Honour of God') out of focus; there was no doubt, however, that in acting Henry with civilised humour and angular nonconformism Olivier took Anouilh's play and made it very much his own.

Concurrent with his last weeks of performances that May, Olivier began daily rehearsals as the leading character in a television film based on Graham Greene's novel *The Power and the Glory*. As a weary, doubting Mexican priest in jeopardy during an anti-clerical period, he may have known that he was not well cast and insisted on elaborate make-up and four sets of coloured contact lenses, so that with each change of scene and lighting he at least looked the part of a dissipated Latin who has moved from village to jungle and back again. But he could not master the accent, which altered from Cockney to Middle European to Hispanic, and he could not help appearing monumentally silly in an outsize sombrero. Stuffing cotton wool in his cheeks and fussing with the various contact lenses made his preparation seem almost mechanistic, recalled Dale Wasserman, who wrote the teleplay.

Olivier seemed to realise this, for during the final rehearsal he asked Wasserman to write an additional speech, something to win sympathy for the character. When the writer said that just wasn't consistent with *The Power and the Glory* or the role of the whisky priest, Olivier replied bluntly, 'Fuck the role – let's just do it.' Producer David Susskind yielded, and the result was Olivier's prison prayer-scene – not in Greene's text and not at all consistent with the integrity of the work. It was written on command for Olivier, to be his moment of warm rapport with his audience.

Olivier's practice had always been to find a role slowly, adding to it by a process of creative accretion – but he did not have that opportunity here. He also had a kind of double personality about the play, according to Wasserman. 'He was aware of his own placement in relation to others, and if he thought a scene was written or directed to his detriment he worked to guard his prestige and possession of the scene.' An example of this occurred early in rehearsals: fourteen-year-old Patty Duke was impressing everyone with her polished and highly nuanced performance as an American girl, and she was so affecting in her scene with Olivier that he went to Wasserman and Susskind and said, 'Let's kill the little darling, shall we?' And with that her dialogue was drastically cut so she would not conquer the scene.

But for Susskind and director Marc Daniels, Olivier in any disguise assured success, and so filming began on 30 May, in the NBC Brooklyn television studios. From the control room, however, there was soon a major complaint: an annoying, buzzing hum could be heard on the track of the first take. The air-conditioning equipment was shut down and another take was made, but the noise persisted. Delay followed delay on the tight schedule, but still the sound could not be located. Technicians finally determined that the cause was steel harmonics, a 120-cycle vibration from alternating current in the building. By this time, according to cast member Julie Harris, they were so far behind schedule that they had to film straight through, for twenty-four hours. Olivier's contact lenses had caused an eye irritation, and this further annoyed and exhausted him. But he worked without complaining.

Becket closed at the end of May and the production of *The Power and the Glory* was completed on 4 June, but *A Taste of Honey* was still running successfully and Joan's contract with Merrick was in force. The only legal excuse for her release soon occurred – her pregnancy – and so they happily boarded the *Queen Elizabeth* on 7 June, disembarking at Southampton on the thirteenth. Because the house in Brighton was still not ready for them, they moved into the Royal Crescent Hotel, a few doors away. In London, Olivier read a series of Old Testament excerpts for a set of studio records produced by his old friend Douglas Fairbanks, Jr., and then, on 23 June, he hurried off to Chichester for meetings with Evershed-Martin.

'Olivier was naturally very sticky on some points as we went along. He looked at me many a time as if to say, "Why should you have an opinion? You're not of the theatre!"' For his part, Olivier described his colleague as 'a really good man with a certain smugness [and] a proneness to be high-handed [and] stubborn'. Evershed-Martin quickly learned that Olivier's mercurial temperament, his manner of speech, the lift of an eyebrow, the slow lick of his lips or tossing of the head with an upward glance – all this would later be revealed in the part he was rehearsing. Olivier was set to act in two and direct three plays over the first ten-week season: *The Chances*, a Beaumont and Fletcher play dating from 1638 (rewritten by the Duke of Buckingham) whose last performance had been in 1808; Ford's *The Broken Heart*, dating from 1633 and most recently staged in 1904; and Chekhov's *Uncle Vanya*, in which he had appeared so successfully with the Old Vic in 1945. This would be 'three entirely different styles,' Olivier insisted, 'to show off the amenities of this particular theatre: the first with no sets at all beyond that designed more or less for permanency by the architect; the second as scenically ambitious as it could well be without impinging upon the lines of sight; and the third utterly realistic.' This programmatic idea was more impressive than the eventual reality.

On the first day of December, Olivier drove Joan to the White Haven Nursing Home, Wilbury Road, Hove, where just after one o'clock on the morning of 3 December she gave birth to a boy they named Richard (obliquely derived from 'Dickie', nickname of Olivier's brother Gerard Dacres). Olivier's delight at fatherhood was evident to everyone who saw him, but he had no time for warm, domestic scenes or the daily details of infant care – these he left to Joan and a nanny while, immediately after New Year's Day 1962, he sped off to Ireland, where he had agreed to appear in a film by Peter Glenville, who had directed him in *Becket*.

Earlier, Glenville had shown Olivier the first draft of a screenplay he had written and would direct, based on a novel by James Barlow. *Term of Trial* was a double-edged title, referring to a year in the life of a Midlands schoolteacher and to the courtroom drama that unfolds when a smitten teenage girl reacts to his rejection of her by falsely accusing him of molestation. Gritty and grave, the script was as contemporary in language and situation as Anouilh's was antique. With Joan's encouragement, Olivier had accepted the role of the teacher.

But Joan might have had second thoughts, for during the production of *Term of Trial* Olivier found himself (in light of the script) in an ironic and potentially dangerous situation. As the lovestruck student, twenty-year-old Sarah Miles was appearing in her first picture; pert and intelligent, she was as smitten with Olivier as her character Shirley Taylor was with the teacher Graham Weir. She came to know him as 'an extremely brave man with a certain cunning, and this was perhaps most evident when he missed his lines in a scene and asked me to correct him whenever that happened again'. Appreciating her talent, Olivier at once treated her like a professional equal; and soon after filming began, life went much further than art as Olivier succumbed to a brief affair with his young co-star. Despite marriage and parenthood, Olivier was, according to Miles, 'deeply vulnerable and still suffering from some kind of guilt and sadness over Vivien'. Partially, at least, the reason for this dalliance may have been Olivier's almost obsessive need at fifty-four to convince himself of his virility – again, with a compliant, young, unthreatening apprentice. Additionally, parenthood and its responsibilities had come as something of a shock, for he had to confront both his past failure with Tarquin and his future in a real-life role for which he was completely unprepared. Among gestures of independence, few are as dramatically self-satisfying as a sexual escapade. In any case, Joan must have learned of the affair, for suddenly she arrived with her month-old baby – a journey that could hardly have been inspired by Ireland's winter climate – and her presence interrupted a romance that concluded quietly during location filming in Paris that February.

As a sad, slightly bored and tippling teacher whose wife (played by Simone Signoret) would not allow them to adopt a child, Olivier's Graham Weir is a logical extension of his Archie Rice period. He gave a subdued, almost minimalist performance, reciting lines whose ironic aptness must have been clear to him and Miles:

> Listen, think how young you are. I'm more than twice your age. I have a wife. I love her. You're a young girl in my charge. I was very fond of you because of your sweetness and eagerness. I wanted to help you – as a teacher and as a father, too. You're a beautiful young creature, but I can't allow myself to think of you like that.

The film, rarely seen after a brief release that summer, is one of the best examples of Olivier's immersion in a colourless role he transformed with the tints of his own emotional reality. Tender and protective towards an abused boy in his class, confused with guilt about his weary, contemptuous wife, attracted and yet afraid of a futile passion, Graham Weir remains a character far more compelling than Archie Rice, and one which, perhaps for obvious reasons, Olivier never chose to discuss.

That spring, plans for the summer festival galloped forward as Olivier assembled his casts for rehearsals in London while the Chichester building was completed. His repertory company of established performers – Sybil Thorndike and Lewis Casson, Nicholas Hannen and Athene Seyler, Michael Redgrave, Fay Compton, Joan Greenwood and John Neville – certainly suggested (as much as his choice of classic plays) that he was anticipating the nucleus of a National Theatre.* Directing his casts, Olivier also had to anticipate the arena stage, to invent action compensating for the lack of a traditional proscenium and curtain; he devised ingenious entrances and exits through the audience as well as casually unorthodox methods of introducing and removing props. As Olivier's loyal aide, Chichester's general manager Pieter Rogers, recalled, the text was always the primary focus for Olivier, who urged his actors to find (as he did in his own roles) a single phrase, to isolate it and by a change of rhythm or tone make that phrase illuminate the character's inner world.

When the company moved to Chichester in June, Olivier attempted – both with his staff and with locals – a kind of camaraderie absent in recent years. Lynda Gilby, then sixteen and a general office assistant for the festival, recalled his stylish, almost old-world courtesy that could be friendly and familiar but also vaguely condescending: 'Who is the lovely little fat girl?' he asked as he introduced himself to her. Later, he frequently asked what books she was reading and how her latest diet was proceeding. 'You'll be a smash hit in Africa,' he once told her. 'There they feed them sago pudding to make them fat.' Olivier seemed, she thought, to inject a gentle mockery into everything he said – not in an unpleasant way, because it was somehow self-mockery too. He seemed to know exactly the type of mild flirtation which would

* He also invited Claire Bloom to join the company for *The Chances*, 'but I felt I was wrong for farce. I think he could not forgive me for rejecting the offer, and in any case he never asked me to join the National Theatre later.'

make an awkward young person feel safe, and he was, as always, wholly aware of the effect he had on people.

With his publicist Virginia Fairweather and her husband David, Olivier enjoyed going to the Horse and Groom, a tiny pub near Oaklands Park, frequented mostly by farmers. After a round of drinks, Olivier anonymously engaged one of them in a detailed discussion of pig-breeding, comparing his days at Notley with the farmer's life in Sussex. Next time, news of the great actor's pub visit had circulated but the same farmer greeted Olivier with a disclaimer: 'I told them not to talk daft. After all, I said, you've seen the man in here yourself – he's no fuckin' actor!' Olivier gravely agreed and bought him a pint.

Olivier was much more relaxed at Chichester than he had been at the St James's (where he had frequently rehearsed *Antony and Cleopatra* in a morning coat and striped trousers). During rehearsals for the Chichester premiere, a civic reception was held for the members of the company and (as actor Timothy Bateson remembered) Olivier, who had worn an old shirt and jeans to work, had to borrow a suit from a colleague. His casual style was not due to a sudden rush of humility; rather he was very much under Joan's influence, and there was to be none of the regal air that had typified the Vivien–Durham–Notley days, nothing of the world of Binkie Beaumont, of traditional, distinguished evenings in the West End, no cries of 'Darling!' at the theatre bar to those one scarcely knew. With Joan's application of a more casual lifestyle, the new Olivier would be, as much as possible within the boundaries of his dignity and position, firmly and distinctly theatrical/proletarian. Nothing about him must appear to represent the past or the years with Vivien: there must be a clean break with his old associations, his styles, his entire manner of life – this was the most deliberate characteristic of his marriage enjoined by his new wife. But the effects were mixed: Joyce Howard, the Redgraves, even Noël Coward – were among the old friends who regretted that they saw little of Olivier, for Joan resented socialising with those who had known Vivien.

At 6.56 on the warm evening of 3 July, Olivier's taped voice resounded over the park's external loudspeakers: 'Ladies and gentlemen, the performance will commence in four minutes . . .' A flurry of London critics joined the audience, some of them carrying the late editions of newspapers reporting the London meetings about the imminent announcement of a director for the long-delayed National Theatre.

Olivier was the favoured bet, but his name caused some dissension after that first performance at Chichester. *The Chances*, which he had unearthed among the recondite dramatic literature at the British Museum, was the story of two Spanish blades on a romantic mission in Italy. An intermittently jolly satire on the conventions of Elizabethan drama, it was weighted by a plot of Byzantine complexity and an assortment of stock characters (a betrayed woman, an evil nobleman, an array of zanies with mistaken identities and a crew of sexual roustabouts). 'When you open a theatre or a new company,' as Olivier said often that year, 'you put on a suit of armour and stand there, waiting for people to shoot you.' And shoot they did, for the critics soundly berated *The Chances*.

The Broken Heart, which followed on 9 July, fared worse. The huge and elaborate scenery was a negation of everything Chichester stood for, and Olivier admitted that he was 'trying to be too clever in not wishing to be thought afraid to be recondite'. Its story of vengeance (with murder, suicide, lunacy and broken hearts aplenty) evoked more giggles than frissons in the audience, and even Olivier's frenzied performance as a jealous nobleman went awry; his line 'My agonies are infinite' brought sage nods from critics. Whereas audiences had rather enjoyed the silliness of *The Chances*, *The Broken Heart* pleased no one. With two critical failures and half the 1400 seats unsold as of 10 July, the Chichester season seemed about to join the list of Olivier's fiascos at the St James's. As often, Kenneth Tynan focused the critical consensus, and in typically unorthodox style. Addressing an open letter to Olivier in the *Observer*, he opined that 'all is not well with your dashing hexagonal playhouse, something has clearly gone wrong', and that the cause of the disappointment was Olivier's misconceived directorial style.

A week later, with an anxious cast and a depressed director co-starring, *Uncle Vanya* played to a nearly full audience, swelled by local university students and pensioners. At the final rehearsal, sound effects were mismatched to action, players (among them Michael Redgrave in the title role, and Sybil Thorndike as the nurse) forgot their cues, and this production, too, seemed headed for disaster.

Everyone had miscalculated, but this time happily so. *Uncle Vanya* was brilliantly played and heartily received – although this was not evident until two days later, when the first reviews came in; at the end of the evening, Joan – pregnant and uncomfortable beneath a heavy costume – had been so certain she had heard a hiss in the audience that she burst into tears backstage. Soon *Vanya* was filmed on the Chichester stage with the original cast, and seen many years later its first welcome seems entirely justified – especially in Olivier's unobtrusive staging and his mature, casually despairing portrait of Astrov, 'a fresh creation', as one reviewer wrote, 'a kind of revelation of what is in the part – a memory to cherish'. The critics were as unanimous in their use of superlatives as they had been dismayed by the preceding productions; there were twenty-five additional performances of the play (almost every one to a full house), the season eventually concluded with no loss and the future of Chichester was assured. Olivier's instinct in reviving Chekhov (and including himself in one of his favourite roles) had been unassailably right.

On 31 July, Queen Elizabeth and the Duke of Edinburgh attended the festival, and after the performance of *Vanya* they met the entire company. This was a benediction of their efforts, and it gave the evening a kind of surreal quality. Olivier felt so keenly the obligation to have everything proper and correct that by the time of the Queen's departure and the post-play dinner for the company, in his nervous exhaustion he had drunk too much alcohol.

At the party, Evershed-Martin casually asked which three plays the director had in mind for the 1963 summer season, and when Olivier replied that *Vanya* would certainly be among them, Evershed-Martin argued against a repetition. Olivier shouted his indignation, reminding Evershed-Martin and everyone else nearby that *he* was artistic director of the festival – that he was not working for Evershed-Martin's benefit, that Evershed-Martin was a theatrical ignoramus who simply had access to money, that he should leave such matters to his betters, and, most stingingly, that Evershed-Martin had founded Chichester only to get a knighthood for himself.

The outburst was worthy of Vivien, and revealed something important about Olivier. Offstage and on, in his work as in his relationships, he could have an unpredictable temper. A man and an actor ruled by instinct rather than intellectual processes or interior speculation, he had perpetual access to a wide variety of feelings and emotions that ran just beneath the surface of his placid exterior. All of these reactions provided him with material for his craft. Additionally, Olivier could be a tangle of contradictions. He loved ritual, ceremony, formality and tradition, but at times he relished the *déclassé*, the vulgar joke, the brash and eccentric reaction; there was, in other words, a conflict in him between a man who desired conformity and a wild, passionate creature. Usually his violent outbursts, like his most ardent moments, were reserved for the stage, where everything in his temperament flashed unalloyed. 'The only time I ever really feel alive,' he often said, 'is when I'm acting.'

The party that night ended in shocked silence. 'He had killed the event,' Evershed-Martin said, 'but I greatly admired him for his elaborate apology next morning. He admitted he had been all worked up and had too much [to drink]. And of course, I was wrong – they did *Vanya* again next season, and it was a great success!' (As for Olivier, he went on record taking the blame for the only personal unpleasantness to have marred the first Chichester season.) Perhaps another outburst was averted when Vivien came to the festival that summer. Since the divorce, she had completed a film, redecorated a new home in Sussex, toured Australia in three plays and was living more or less contentedly with John Merivale. When Evershed-Martin was told of Vivien's arrival, he diplomatically intercepted her during the interval and somehow managed to prevent her from approaching Olivier who, also alerted, went into hiding until her departure.

On 9 August, it was announced in London that following a century of argument and a dozen years of government indecision the National Theatre was now officially a corporate reality, under the directorship of Sir Laurence Olivier. This was no surprise to anyone in Chichester, but it was news of international significance. 'Well, are you going to do the National?' Joan had asked him earlier that summer. 'I think I certainly shall,' Olivier had replied quietly. He had known of the board's deliberations and his opinions had been sounded on several matters.

'He wanted that [appointment] most passionately from the start,' according to Virginia Fairweather.

> He knew he hadn't been the first choice for Chichester, but he accepted it precisely as a proving ground for the National. If he made mistakes at Chichester – which he did – well, after all it was only Chichester, and better to err here than in London, to which he looked forward all year.

'I doubt whether the National would ever have finally happened without Larry's power, prestige and glamour at that particular time,' said Peter Hall (head of the Royal Shakespeare Company and subsequently second director of the National). 'He went about the whole thing very cunningly and very rightly, going to Chichester in order to experience the open stage, and he used that experience to start a National Theatre company.'

And so the National Theatre was born at last. Proposed in 1848 by the publisher Effingham Wilson, an intermittently active public fund had been stalled and occasionally revived under pressure from Matthew Arnold, Harley Granville-Barker, George Bernard Shaw, Winston Churchill and others. A site was purchased in 1937 in Kensington, but the war intervened. Later, the London County Council chose land on the South Bank of the Thames and there, in 1951, a cornerstone was laid – only to be moved the following year. By 1962, it was hoped that a building would be ready within three or four years; in fact the National would play at other quarters until 1976 (by which time Olivier was no longer its director).

In starting Chichester and winning the appointment as the National's first executive administrator, Laurence Olivier reached the pinnacle of achievement as actor-manager-director, beyond any of his predecessors in the craft. 'I was the best person for the job,' he said frankly, adding: 'I had had so many failures [at the St James's Theatre] that the governors [of the National] felt it meant I'd learned a great deal. Very few actors had the breadth of experience I had.' Confident of his abilities though he was, he knew he needed a company that would not only take direction but also collaborate creatively towards success. Peter Glenville, among many colleagues, had expected Olivier's appointment as head of the National Theatre. Aware of what he called Olivier's 'greed for achievement' and 'appetite for leadership', Glenville agreed with other directors (Peter Brook, Tony Richardson, Glen Byam Shaw) that the National Theatre had its best possible chance of success in Olivier. Critics, of course, began at once to express fears that at the National he would simply stage British plays best forgotten (like *The Chances* and *The Broken Heart*), that he would make the new institution a museum, or would yield to special-interest groups (such as players from the Royal Court) and overload the repertory with only contemporary works. Advice, counsel and caution were urged; the grave furrowing of literary brows was much in evidence across the land.

Olivier, meanwhile, was determined to keep the critics guessing, and part of his strategy was to accept the leading role in a new work to be directed by Tony Richardson called *Semi-Detached*, by a young ex-teacher named David Turner. Scheduled for a November opening in Edinburgh prior to a London premiere the following month, the play was a satire on British suburban life: Fred Midway (Olivier) is an ambitious, pretentious and intellectually lightweight insurance supervisor who aspires to higher rungs on the social ladder.

He memorised his role during a three-week holiday with Richard and Joan (now five months pregnant) in September at Eze-Plage, on the French Riviera. While there, they accepted an invitation from Prince Rainier and his wife Princess Grace of Monaco, the former American film actress Grace Kelly. After a lavish dinner, Rainier began to nod, and Olivier attempted to cover the embarrassing moment by asking Grace if she had seen his film *The Prince and the Showgirl*. He suddenly realised this might seem like an affront, so he corrected himself and began to discuss the original play, *The Sleeping Prince* – a topic even less appropriate at that moment. Finally, he turned to Grace, who never affected any stuffy formality and was greatly enjoying the comedy. Olivier smiled, winked and asked, 'Well, did you ever play Detroit?'

In October, the Oliviers' new home at 4 Royal Crescent, Brighton, was at last ready for occupancy; he had paid £20,000 for it and spent half as much more on improvements. One of several four-storey grey brick houses in a terrace midway between Palace Pier and Black Rock, it had twelve rooms and directly overlooked the Channel. While Joan and a housekeeper settled in, Olivier began a busy round of rehearsals for *Semi-Detached*, meetings in London for the inauguration of the National's first season in 1963, and continuing plans for the second season at Chichester.

From the 19 November premiere in Edinburgh, it was clear that Turner's play was in trouble – and so was Olivier, who could do little to leaven a regional farce on keeping up with the Joneses. Fred Midway was perhaps his most antipathetic non-classical role, an utterly charmless and pallid character, and his two wigs, droopy moustache and idiosyncratic (and inconsistent) thick Midlands accent amused no critics and very few spectators. 'It is a dull and silly little play,' wrote Bernard Levin in the *Daily Mail* after the 5 December London opening.

> Every now and then our greatest actor turns a neat bit of business, but that is about all. And if this is the kind of play the director of the National Theatre thinks worth putting on, I can only say that it were better that a Foundation Stone be hanged about his neck and he be cast into the uttermost depths of the sea.

'Oh, what a bad judge he is,' Noël Coward noted in his diary. 'To do this play was a major mistake.' Olivier agreed: 'I was miserable doing it. They hated me – the critics, the audiences. I could feel it coming over me every night . . . it was thirteen weeks of sheer torture.'

The unpleasantness and the demands of his schedule provoked, during December, a period of rather heavy drinking he knew might be dangerous, and so as a New Year's resolution Olivier gave up alcohol from 1 January 1963 for an entire year. Although he was never dependent on drink and was certainly never an alcoholic, he had an enormous capacity for whisky. (A typical social event – and there was one almost every day during these years – ordinarily meant several drinks, a bottle of wine and numerous brandies.) Acting each night, attending meetings daily, dashing from Brighton to Chichester to London in a constant round of varied duties – this demanding schedule required the utmost stamina. And so Olivier modified his diet, abstained from alcohol and each morning donned a tracksuit and ran two miles along the Brighton promenade.

There was of course another incentive for this attention to his health: he was married to a young wife and was responsible for a family, augmented on 10 January 1963 by the birth of a daughter they named Tamsin Agnes Margaret (the first name a variant of Thomasina, the second after his mother). As generous and attentive to his new family as his professional duties permitted, Olivier shone with pride and often spoke about them to colleagues. This was, he may have vaguely felt, an opportunity to compensate for his neglect of Tarquin; and although his age now made him more of a grandfatherly figure to his children, there was no doubt of his concern and devotion.

The early months of 1963 were crowded with administrative meetings and auditions for the National Theatre. These tasks were despatched in perhaps the most unglamorous spaces ever assigned for artistic offices. With no theatre, the National was to take over the Old Vic until the new buildings were completed on the South Bank, and the offices and rehearsal space were housed in three long, ramshackle workmen's huts several hundred yards away in Aquinas Street – located down a back alley near the riverbank, on a derelict site once bombed flat during the Blitz. At one end was a large room used for rehearsals and auditions, and off a long passage were small offices and a makeshift 'board room'. Icy in winter, torrid in summer and foul-smelling year-round, the huts were unhealthy, cramped and difficult for visitors to find. The place resembled a coastal aerodrome command station somewhere in the south of England during World War II, and here Olivier was commanding officer in a dingy atmosphere of great expectancy, good will and cooperation. Actor Ronald Pickup described the atmosphere as 'slightly rumpled and messy, improvised and knotty. There were warm and encouraging moments within this family, but also tensions, rows, the slammings of doors.'

One of the first important collaborators to sign into Aquinas Street was none other than Kenneth Tynan, who had assumed the role of wise father to the country's theatrical life. By 1963 he was drama critic for the *Observer* and was acknowledged as one of the wittiest, most incisive writers in English, a man who had read widely in private and was dangerously epigrammatic in print – and therefore was admired and feared by those over whom he exercised journalistic power. Twenty years Olivier's junior, he was an Oxford-educated essayist and dandy who routinely wore mauve or lilac suits to the theatre, a congenital stutterer who would demolish a performance (as he often had Vivien's) and then wonder why he was not invited to dinner by the wounded party.

A chain-smoker who ultimately died of emphysema at fifty-three, Tynan was more than anything the Ultimate Fan. An actor's fame was almost an aphrodisiac to him – but not quite, for privately Tynan was equally eccentric, an overgrown boy with the kind of sexual obsessions that remarkably often pepper his critiques. He devised the long-running soft-core pornographic revue *Oh! Calcutta!* and (as his biography amply details) he freely indulged the milder forms of sado-masochism: with ironic aptness for a critic who attacked so viciously, Tynan's preferred sport was the spanking of willing women. He was also fascinated by homosexuality, which he denied so often and vigorously that many were convinced of his secret experimentation.

Tynan's engaging literary style, his impressive knowledge of theatre lore and his fearless rapier attacks led many to mistake his cleverness for genius. Olivier, who throughout his life felt keenly his own lack of advanced education, was among Tynan's great admirers even when angered by a review (of Vivien, for example), but when Tynan wrote to him offering to leave the *Observer* and join the National Theatre administration, Olivier was at first inclined to turn him down. It was Joan who suggested that it would be better to have the critic ('the little fucker', as Olivier more than once called him) in their own camp. And so within two weeks, press representative Virginia Fairweather announced that Kenneth Tynan had been engaged as the National's literary manager (he had preferred the Brechtian title dramaturg, but there Olivier demurred). He would share all non-directorial responsibilities, including the selection of plays, casting, publicity and long-range planning, and eventually Tynan was involved in every detail, down to the design of the National Theatre's stationery.

Tynan greatly admired Olivier's achievements, his status, his glamour and international appeal. But John Osborne, for one, considered Tynan's influence disastrous, marked by a mere sense of the stylish that Olivier mistook for intelligent modernity. Peter Hall, too, judged that Olivier nursed a sensitive inferiority complex about his own intellect despite his acute professional instincts and prodigious gifts. 'Those great eyebrows descended like shutters when he felt he was confronted by an intellectual, because he felt he wasn't. When he went to the National, he decided to buy the biggest brain-box he could find, so he bought Ken.' And in so doing, Olivier made a tactical error, for Tynan was a slick manipulator, largely motivated by his own obsession with stardom and given to a kind of court intrigue worthy of a Renaissance prince. Wreathed in cigarette smoke, he glided along the shabby corridors of Aquinas Street fomenting intrigue. And because he was intimidated by mere education, Olivier was inclined to submit his own creative intuition to Tynan's.

Yet the partnership was ultimately legendary in its spiky and uneven inventiveness, its wary mutual admiration and its controversial and occasionally odd fecundity. Unsure of the new wave of drama and (because of past mistakes) even of his own ability to select plays wisely, Olivier relied on Tynan's literary judgment to select a repertory both classical and contemporary, British and foreign, so that the National would be a library-museum of great world drama. Eclecticism was evident from the day the 1963–64 season was announced: from Chichester there would be *Uncle Vanya* and *Saint Joan*, and to these would be added *Hamlet* and *Othello*; Farquhar's *The Recruiting Officer*; Harold Brighouse's *Hobson's Choice*; Max Frisch's *Andorra*; a double bill of Beckett's *Play* and Sophocles' *Philoctetes*; and Ibsen's *The Master Builder*.

Equally significant were the actors chosen: Olivier, eschewing both competition with Hall's Royal Shakespeare Company and any charge of being behind the times, avoided engaging the older rank of established British players and opted for a younger generation; here Joan's influence was felt most significantly. At the same time, Olivier coveted his own primacy. Gielgud never performed with him at the National and was not even invited to play there until 1967; Richardson was not at the National at all during Olivier's tenure; only a few women trained in an earlier generation – Edith Evans and Peggy Ashcroft, for example – played there (and not often), and there was no man of anything like his own stature in the company. (Michael Redgrave, the only other knight in the company, came to the National via the Chichester troupe but left in 1964.) 'When he's had the Gielguds, the Scofields, the Finneys, he never played with them,' as Tony Richardson reflected a few years later. 'It's never been on equal terms, and Larry finished up with relatively minor actors merely surrounding him.'

Olivier's commitment to the idea of an ensemble was not always wholehearted, according to William Gaskill, whom he engaged along with John Dexter as directors, and this was partly due to the influence of Tynan, who wanted to engage stars. When he could not, there was a double effect, for while Olivier did not set out to make himself the centre of the National's acting universe, this became the case and many British actors were offended by being summarily ignored. They would have brought their own popularity and influence, and this Tynan found unacceptable. His regime with Olivier, whom he admired to the point of adulation, effectively gave the impression that while there was no star status at the National, Olivier's always gleamed brightly.

Gaskill was one of many who believed the Olivier–Tynan collaboration did not produce first-class results, and that Tynan's influence was much to blame. Osborne, Dexter and Gaskill agreed with critics who felt that Olivier should have acted more, that the reign of an opinionated literary doyen like Tynan impeded the stated ideals of the National. In fact, many in the company felt that except for his performances and inspired direction (of nine plays over the course of his entire tenure) Laurence Olivier was more of a benign figurehead than a powerful influence. In this regard, he was fair game for one far more autocratic than himself, for Tynan was both trenchant and despotic. Neither endured fools gladly, but Olivier never felt obliged to rid the planet of them.

On a personal level, their relationship was not easy to categorise. At times it seemed as if Tynan wanted and tried to dominate Olivier, and often colleagues heard the director defer with the comment, 'Whatever you say, Kenboy.' Rather like schoolgirls, each complained about the other to third parties, but whenever this reached Tynan and angered him, Olivier's 'girlish' quality (as Elia Kazan called it), his ability to tease and play the coquette, eventually won him over.

Ever mischievous, Olivier frequently adopted an almost seductive pose, using his physicality as a satisfying and effective way of winning people. When he wanted to bring Gaskill over from the Royal Court to the National, his technique was to treat him like a woman – he called it 'The Wooing of Billy Gaskill' and used every trick of the flirt. But precisely because he was a man of such great virility he could assume femininity whenever he wanted, and this was a major part of his fascination and skill. Thus everything he used onstage to win an audience he also employed with consummate skill offstage. (Anthony Quinn, among others, had noted this trait during rehearsals and the run of *Becket*.)

Unpredictable, often secretive and slightly bizarre, the Olivier–Tynan relationship, not surprisingly, incited widespread rumours that they were, at least for a time, lovers; in fact, this was considered common knowledge in London theatrical circles. According to John Gielgud, Vivien was convinced of the affair, and Gielgud himself agreed that Tynan seemed to have a crush on Olivier. Being in love, of course, does not automatically effect its expression, but while both men coveted the respectable images of sexual conventionality, Tynan loved to play the *enfant terrible*, and Olivier found his outrageous manner and conversation amusing, much as he had Danny Kaye's. Sexual intimacy with Tynan might well have been consistent with their mutual admiration, and many National Theatre colleagues then and later believed the increasingly exclusive relationship had frankly erotic overtones, that for once Olivier's flirtatiousness and seductiveness went too far and that Tynan, aware of both his own influence and Olivier's eagerness to be modern, finally waged a successful campaign of sexual conquest. Women he could spank; Olivier Tynan had to cosset. Whatever may have transpired privately – and an overtly homosexual affair cannot definitively be established – Tynan's threat a few years later to publish a book about their relationship caused Olivier to become violently upset beyond what would have been warranted by a simply professional memoir. There remain, too, Tynan's often curiously sexual comments on Olivier's performances. 'You cannot make love by instalments,' he wrote in one typical passage, 'and Olivier's relationship with his audience is that of a skilled but dominating lover.' The allusion is vintage Tynan.

On his fifty-sixth birthday that May, Olivier was honoured with a quiet teatime celebration in the rehearsal hall at Aquinas Street;

limping with gout, he declined more elaborate festivities and preferred to spend the day at work, rehearsing *Vanya* for Chichester and the National and meeting with the boards of both. (Joan opened the summer festival at Chichester on 24 June as Shaw's Saint Joan; Olivier appeared there only as Astrov that second season.) Otherwise, he and Tynan held open auditions for the National throughout spring and summer. In many cases, these were a formality, for Olivier had an intuitive sense of an actor's potential for their repertory, based not only on appearance but even on a brief conversation. As he told Rosemary Harris, he knew if someone had talent merely by listening to a voice on the telephone.

Olivier was certainly aware of being the most public figure in the history of the theatre itself, different from every predecessor by virtue of constant media exposure and the glamour he wore so naturally. Movie star and classical actor, knight errant on behalf of the Empire and now also a man of the contemporary stage – all these combined to make him a documented public commodity. As such, he was determined simultaneously to justify that pre-eminence and to earn approval by creating a National Theatre composed largely of rising young talent.

In addition, he entered fully into the spirit of theatrical experimentation to which previously he would have been averse. Gaskill directed him in the small but crucial role of Captain Brazen in *The Recruiting Officer* that first season, and although Olivier disliked improvisation at rehearsal, his willingness to explore on the spot impressed everyone. But perhaps to compensate for a method of preparation he found alien, Olivier's performance at rehearsals seemed an overplayed caricature to Gaskill, Dexter and even the adoring Tynan. They approached him late one afternoon and offered their criticisms, and although surprised, Olivier listened attentively, noted the criticism and modified his performance. (As for spontaneity, Olivier was forthright: 'I don't like improvisation in rehearsal. As soon as a director says, "Try this, try that," I think, "Listen, chum, I can do that at home."')

On 24 June the second Chichester season opened with Joan as Shaw's *Saint Joan*; a week later, Olivier played in the revival of *Vanya*, with Rosemary Harris now in the role of Ilyena (to the critics' unanimous delight). At the same time, he was memorising the supporting role of Captain Brazen and – at Tynan's urging – he had agreed to play Othello for the four hundredth anniversary of Shakespeare's birth the following spring. As if this were not pressing enough, he negotiated the purchase of a second home, a four-bedroom, seventeenth-century cottage in rural Sussex for which he paid £8750; the price was justified by his savings from film roles, for his National Theatre salary was just over a hundred pounds a week. As with all his homes, this one required a lengthy period of refurbishing and modernising. To maintain the physical stamina necessary for this punishing schedule, Olivier began weight-lifting thrice weekly at a London gymnasium in addition to his daily run.

There was also the constant round of administrative meetings, many concerning the forthcoming South Bank theatre for the National. Denys Lasdun, chosen that year as architect, recalled that Olivier wished a committee to work on plans and also took the advice of George Devine, Peter Hall and Peter Brook. The meetings, which continued throughout 1964 and after, were often argumentative, but Olivier chaired them patiently, never imposing his personal fancies. Lasdun also remembered that Olivier championed a design that was most dangerous for actors. In the typical post-Elizabethan theatre, the actor confronts his audience but is removed from them, but Olivier always thought a more exciting prospect was not to confront but to appear to embrace the audience and have them embrace him. An open thrust stage as at Chichester, therefore, would give the feeling that player and audience are in the same space and nothing is hidden. A great deal more would be asked of actors, and this appealed to Olivier.

When Olivier offered *Uncle Vanya* at Chichester, he had to be thinking constantly of his audience, because it was a production with so much movement – and with the audience on his right, left and to the front. He loved the idea of the danger and the risk this presented for actors, but his first concern was that every member of the audience should be able to see and hear and be comfortable. And so the main stage at the National (eventually called the Olivier Theatre) was a thrust stage. But as was argued by Tynan and others, they would not be doing justice to drama if they ruled out those plays which live properly in a proscenium: thus the more traditional Lyttelton Theatre, named for Oliver Lyttelton, Lord Chandos, chairman of the National Theatre board from 1962 to 1971. (Eventually the South Bank complex also housed a smaller, flexible, gallery-like theatre, the Cottesloe).

At the same time as these architectural meetings progressed, Olivier instituted various technical, acting and stagecraft classes for his players. These he frequently visited, commenting once that some absent members would do well to avail themselves of the opportunities.

*

The National Theatre at the Old Vic gave its first performance on 22 October 1963 and that night Olivier presented every member of the company with a bottle of champagne. Peter O'Toole – who had just completed his film role as Henry II in *Becket* and had recently been raised to stardom by *Lawrence of Arabia* – tore his way through a five-hour *Hamlet*. Chosen to represent the new generation, O'Toole (Tynan's suggestion) admired and resented Olivier, who thought his excessive drinking inappropriate and often fixed on him (thus O'Toole) 'that grey-eyed myopic stare that can turn you to stone'. O'Toole had wanted the play cut (as is the tradition); he also wanted to appear bearded – like every other man in the cast – and with his own hair. On opening night, O'Toole performed the entire role, clean-shaven and with his hair dyed white. 'Such,' the actor said, 'is the power of Olivier.'

A happier collaboration prevailed with Rosemary Harris as Ophelia, with whom Olivier had had a warm and uncomplicated friendship since *The Tumbler*. Harris recalled Olivier preparing her to play the mad scene as if it were virtually a cameo appearance by Vivien in one of her altered states. Rehearsing her privately, he walked slowly round the stage: 'I've lived through this many, many times,' he said quietly. 'When someone acts like this, you want to kill them one moment and caress them the next.'

As usual, Olivier was in complete control, working especially on *Hamlet* with lighting manager Leonard Tucker and stressing an accepted norm of stagecraft, that inadequately lighted actors are often inaudible to certain spectators. 'Bring [the light] up, dear boy,' he said to Tucker at a late rehearsal, 'I can't see them.' Ten minutes later Olivier returned: 'Darling boy, I still can't see them.' Later still he was back ('in a rage worthy of Richard III', as Tucker recalled): 'Bring the fucking lights up! If you could fucking see them, you might fucking hear them!'

The first production received mixed notices, for the Old Vic was an inadequate theatre for the rather heavily decorated and designed production; on opening night, stage machines failed to operate. Rosemary Harris's Ophelia and Michael Redgrave's Claudius were highly praised, but O'Toole was generally assessed as too rebellious and angry a prince, lacking real poetic reflection. Olivier took the production out of the repertory after nine weeks, but the season was saved by the success of the Shaw and Chekhov plays imported from Chichester: the National Theatre, despite backstage tensions and the resentments of actors and directors both present and absent, had begun a forward-reaching era under Olivier's earnest patronage.

But he could not entirely escape the past. That year, Tarquin wrote to his father for advice on preparing the manuscript of a book on his Far East travels. Claiming he had no time to reply, Olivier asked his private secretary Renée Gilmore to answer the letter with brusque good wishes. *The Eye of the Day*, published in 1964, was nevertheless dedicated to both the author's parents.

But one day (very much to Joan's annoyance) Olivier visited Vivien in her Sussex home. Her housekeeper recalled that Lady Olivier – as Vivien still called herself – prepared a lavish luncheon and opened Olivier's favourite wine. The couple then walked round the lake on her property. Olivier, unwilling to lead her to false expectations, was friendly but somewhat aloof, and the afternoon was cut short by a telephone call from Joan, urging him to see to other business. He departed at once, Vivien watching his car recede along the driveway. 'That is the man I am going to marry,' she had said thirty years earlier, seeing him act before they had met. 'And what do you think,' she told John Gielgud the day after Olivier's visit, 'I am still hopelessly in love.'

CHAPTER FOURTEEN

1964–1967

There comes a moment . . . when imagination gives
out and reality leaps forth. It is frightful!

Edgar, in Strindberg's *Dance of Death*

Of the great Shakespearean roles still unattempted by Laurence
Olivier by 1964, Othello remained the most daunting; until then,
he had seen the Moor as merely a foil for the more incandescent Iago,
a role he had thoroughly enjoyed in 1938 at the Old Vic. Now, a
quarter of a century later on the same stage, he would at last play a
character he saw as seething even more with pride than jealousy. He
also seemed to want to prove something, members of the company
often felt – that he was the greatest actor in their midst. One of the
tactics to guarantee that designation was Olivier's choice of his Iago –
Frank Finlay, who had played only one Shakespearean role before (the
gravedigger in *Hamlet*); unassuming as well as inexperienced, Finlay
would not steal the show.

When he met director John Dexter and the cast for the first read-
through on 3 February, Olivier gave a finished performance, as cast
member Edward Petherbridge remembered. 'He tossed a hand gren-
ade,' wrote Tynan in a diary account of the production, 'a fantastic
full-volume display that scorched one's ears. Like the cast, I was awed.'
It was, to be sure, a polished performance: every gesture, every turn
of the head and glance indicated that each movement had an inner
counterpart. For the deep vocal volume, Olivier had expanded his rib-
cage by trebling his weight-lifting, and he had exercised his voice,
lowering it a full octave for the role – just as he had filed two of his
front teeth for Archie Rice. (Fabia Drake, his old acquaintance since
the All Saints *Twelfth Night* half a century earlier, told him she was
glad he never played Abelard.) 'I had to be black,' Olivier insisted.

282

78. *Right* With Joan, at the christening of their daughter Tamsin (1963). *Globe Photos*

79. *Below* Kenneth Tynan. *Culver Pictures*

80. *Below right* As Othello, with Maggie Smith as Desdemona (1964). *National Film Archive, London*

81. *Bottom* The Oliviers returning from the National Theatre's visit to Moscow (1965). *Globe Photos*

82. *Bottom right* With Noël Coward, during the filming of *Bunny Lake is Missing* (1965). *National Film Archive, London*

This page
83. *Above* During a break in filming
Khartoum (1965). *National Film Archive,
London*

84. *Above right* Clowning on the set of *The
Dance of Death* (1969). *National Film
Archive, London*

85. *Below* With Joan in the film of *Three
Sisters* (1970). *National Film Archive,
London*

86. *Below right* As Shylock, with Joan as
Portia in *The Merchant of Venice* (National
Theatre, 1970). *Anthony Crickmay*

Opposite page
87. *Top left* As James Tyrone, with
Constance Cummings as Mary, in *Long
Day's Journey into Night* (National Theatre,
1971). *Zoë Dominic*

88. *Top right* As the Duke of Wellington in
the film *Lady Caroline Lamb* (1972).
National Film Archive, London

89. *Right* In the film *Love Among the Ruins*
(1974), with Katharine Hepburn. *National
Film Archive, London*

90. *Far right* As the sadistic Dr Szell in the
film *Marathon Man* (1975). *National Film
Archive, London*

91. *Bottom far right* In the film *The Betsy*
(1977), as the avaricious Hardemann.
National Film Archive, London

92. *Above* On location during the filming of *A Little Romance* (1978). *National Film Archive, London*

93. *Left* Still doing his own stunts, in *A Little Romance*. *National Film Archive, London*

94. *Below* As Lord Marchmain, in *Brideshead Revisited* (1979). *National Film Archive, London*

I had to feel black down to my soul. I had to look out from a black man's world . . . External characteristics to me are a shelter – a refuge from having nothing to feel, from finding yourself standing on the stage with just lines to say, without a helpful indication of how to treat them or how to move. I construct my portrait from the outside with little techniques, ideas, images – and once the portrait becomes real, it starts travelling inwards.

The sheer physical efforts that winter took a toll: for the first time, Olivier at fifty-six was stricken with a serious viral infection that kept him at home for over three weeks, sabotaging the plans for a four-city tour of *Othello* before its April premiere in London. Joan, meanwhile, was continuing in several roles at the National, and it was natural that staff and actors submitted requests and asked her 'what Sir would like us to do about . . .' She often assumed her husband's responsibilities, and no one considered her suggestions arbitrary.

Finally, after a preliminary week in Birmingham, *Othello* opened at the Old Vic on 21 April 1964. Olivier spent the morning at the gymnasium, despatched company business, and had an early luncheon of steak and half a bottle of red wine (the teetotalling ceased at Christmas 1963). Then he answered letters and telephone calls and rested for three hours – this was his schedule whenever he played the Moor that season. At five he began the arduous, nearly three-hour process of applying the make-up he had designed: he shaved the hair from his chest, arms and legs, then applied Max Factor number 2880, a black liquid stain, over his entire body. When that had dried, a lighter brown was added, then a third coat to give a mahogany sheen. He and his dresser then used yards of chiffon to polish his skin until he shone (pancake powder would run under perspiration). Then he painted his fingernails with a pale-blue varnish, coated the inside of his mouth with gentian violet, put on a tightly curled black wig, and with a pinkish hue polished his palms and the soles of his feet; four hours later, after the performance, almost two hours were required to remove the make-up. This radically detailed surface was the extreme example of Olivier's external approach to a role – the bits and pieces of an appearance meticulously calculated and entirely controlled by him.

Olivier stepped onstage to a collective gasp from the audience. Moving like a panther (and sounding more like a West Indian from Notting Hill Gate than a Moor, some critics complained), contorting his muscles and rolling his eyes, he spoke feverishly in a calypso rhythm. In that first entrance, he held a rose, smelling its fragrance and brandishing it like a gentle prod, an inspired device to suggest the alien who is primed for failure – a man who so lingers over the recitation of his past unhappiness that Iago's wicked innuendoes seem almost to gratify his own proudly negative expectations.

With but a few dissenting opinions, Olivier received the most exuberant reviews of his career:

'He has scaled the last unconquered Everest and planted his standard firmly, triumphantly on top.'

'He triumphs in a performance that is a combination of great physical and bravura acting and considerable thought.'

'It is a performance full of grace, terror and insolence. I shall dream of its mysteries for years to come.'

'Olivier struck deeper chords than I have ever heard from him. The sheer variety and range of the actor's art made it an experience in the theatre altogether unforgettable.'

'The power, passion and verisimilitude of Sir Laurence's performance will be spoken of with wonder for a long time to come.'

Within days, every ticket for the season's remaining performances of *Othello* had been sold and the personal columns of newspapers offered high prices for a seat. On the days he was playing Othello, William Gaskill recalled, nothing else mattered. 'He was more absorbed than ever in his craft, and everything focused on that performance. Even at other times he wasn't particularly interested in other actors, but now it was magnified.'

This was not merely a matter of ego: married to a much younger woman and surrounded by a company whose average age was thirty-two, Olivier was more than ever conscious of his seniority. 'I don't really approve of all these awards for actors unless I'm receiving them,' he said when Michael Redgrave and Joan received acting awards from the *Evening Standard*. The jest, Redgrave felt, had an underlying truth, for he had observed both Olivier's humility and ruthlessness for his own position as the pre-eminent actor of his time. Redgrave, Olivier's contemporary and the only other knight in the company, had played four major roles with the National. It was therefore a shock to many when Olivier essentially dismissed him after a few memory lapses during performances of *The Master Builder* that June. Unknown to anyone (including the actor himself), the missed cues were insidious symptoms of the Parkinson's Disease that was diagnosed nine years later and eventually took Redgrave's life in 1985, but Olivier and several members of the company wrongly assumed he was drinking to excess. 'You're losing your mind,' he said bluntly one afternoon, and added that he would assume the role of Solness himself if Redgrave felt no longer capable. Shocked and saddened by this callousness, Redgrave withdrew from the company, preserving his dignity by telling colleagues (and maintaining in his autobiography) that he himself decided the part was too demanding. But to his wife Rachel Kempson, he confided his indignation: 'I admire him so much,' Redgrave said, 'that it's agony to me when he thinks I'm no good and wants to play my part.'

The reasons for this uncharacteristic harshness are not difficult to fathom, for in addition to his jealousy of his own position Olivier privately condemned Redgrave, a devoted husband and father who was also, it was widely known, actively homosexual. Harbouring profound confusion and guilt over his own life, Olivier's intolerance extended to his press representative Virginia Fairweather, who although married had lately discovered her homosexual nature and was dismissed from her position by Olivier in 1968 on vague charges of incompetence.

That year, Olivier insisted on maintaining a schedule that would have exhausted a twenty-year-old. He awoke early in Brighton and after exercise arrived by train at Waterloo around ten-thirty. There followed meetings with Tynan, rehearsals, interviews and, on average three times a week, an evening performance and visits to his gym. When he was not acting, Olivier often remained in London to see National Theatre productions that had difficulties during rehearsals – Peter Shaffer's *The Royal Hunt of the Sun* and the revival of Coward's *Hay Fever*. In one week, he played Captain Brazen and then Othello and Solness twice each, and during the summer he acted the Moor sixteen times in Chichester's airless, torrid theatre. Finally, in September, he took Joan and the two children for a Majorcan holiday, but this rest – urged by her doctors – did not alleviate a problematic pregnancy, and in late October she suffered a miscarriage. (She did not appear onstage again for almost three years.)

Back in London, Olivier continued his gruelling performances as Othello and directed a revival of Arthur Miller's *The Crucible*, which in January opened to appreciative notices from both the critics and the visiting playwright. Since they had last met, Miller had been divorced from Marilyn Monroe (who committed suicide in August 1962), and he had written a play about their marriage called *After the Fall*. He and others found Olivier as charming as ever, but apparently exhausted. Much of this was due to his self-imposed schedule (although he did decide that year to make the summer season of 1965 at Chichester his last as artistic director); but there was also inexorable, intensified friction among the team of administrators.

Most obvious was the growing influence on Olivier of Tynan, who continued to press for star directors and successfully negotiated to import Franco Zeffirelli to direct *Much Ado About Nothing* and Jacques Charon (from the Comédie française) for Feydeau's *A Flea in Her Ear*. When he could not realise his hope of having Anna Magnani appear as Brecht's *Mother Courage*, Tynan sought to fill the repertory with other international celebrities, many of them from the movies (in this he was stymied mostly by the stars' incompatible schedules and the National's insistently low pay). Gaskill and Dexter found Tynan's star-struck approach offensive and counterproductive, and when plans for the coming season were discussed at Olivier's home in Brighton, Gaskill spoke up. He understood Larry's reliance on Tynan's advice for the choice of plays, he said, but he did not think it was appropriate for Tynan to dictate the casts. To this Olivier at once reacted angrily and left the room. After he had conferred with Joan for half an hour, he returned and calmly told Gaskill that Tynan must be involved in every aspect of the National Theatre. Gaskill, unwilling to fight such a closed system, soon accepted an offer to return to the Royal Court, where he followed George Devine as artistic director.

In these matters, Joan's influence must not be underestimated. When Olivier met her, she had represented the new era of actors, from whose taste and methods Olivier often felt alien. But pleasing her was crucial for him: in acknowledging her nurturing and embracing influence and fulfilling her expectations he again achieved, as yet without the domestic melodramas, exactly what Vivien at her best had once provided. Joan had urged the engagement of Tynan in the first place – not only to defuse possible criticism of the National, but because she genuinely admired some of his innovative ideas about the theatre. And while Olivier never forgot Tynan's earlier unrelenting diatribes against Vivien, this hardly bothered Joan; the critic and the wife – each for distinct reasons – were joined in resenting the fact that Vivien was never very far from Olivier's concern and his expressed memories.

On 8 January 1965, Tarquin Olivier (then twenty-eight) married Riddelle Gibson at St Mary's, Cadogan Square. The press turned out in force as Olivier, for his son's sake, agreed to escort Jill. Vivien too, who had always had a closer bond with Tarquin than his father, insisted on attending the ceremony – much to the dismay of Olivier, who protested to John Merivale that he could not appear with three wives. He need not have worried, for when she learned that Vivien was going Joan refused to attend. As Merivale recalled, Olivier was shaken with anxiety throughout the day, overcome with awkwardness in the presence of his son and two ex-wives.

In addition to his chronic guilt about his failed relationships, Olivier's embarrassment was not unrelated to his fear of being deficient, of being replaced personally or professionally, and to his concomitant impulse constantly to prove himself. This attitude was frequently demonstrated even before much less experienced actors – like twenty-seven-year-old Anthony Hopkins, who auditioned for the National that spring. Hopkins had prepared scenes from Chekhov, Shaw and Shakespeare, and when he said the last was an excerpt from *Othello*, Olivier barked, 'You've got a bloody nerve!' Hopkins was asked to begin, and as he did so, Olivier asked for a cigarette: 'I'm terribly sorry,' he said flatly to Hopkins. 'I'm so nervous in case you're better than me.' After the recitation, Olivier expressed his approval, invited Hopkins to join the company and said, 'I don't think I'll lose any sleep tonight, but you're awfully good.'

That spring, Olivier accepted an offer from Otto Preminger to play a police inspector in the film *Bunny Lake is Missing*, about a schoolgirl kidnapped by her uncle, who is jealous of his sister's affection for her own child. There was nothing in John and Penelope Mortimer's screenplay a score of other middle-aged English actors could not have managed, but Olivier needed to replenish his bank account and relished the chance to joke off-camera with Noël Coward, who was cast as a perverse old landlord with a collection of macabre items from the time of de Sade. (Olivier found Preminger 'a real bully who never let up . . . a heavy-handed egotist [whom] Noël Coward and I didn't like much'.)

This six-week assignment was followed by an arduous and swift filming of his *Othello* at Shepperton Studios, directed by his colleague from the Old Vic in the time of Lilian Baylis, Stuart Burge (who had also filmed the Chichester *Uncle Vanya* for television the previous year). Burge was distressed at the hasty three-week schedule imposed for blocking, rehearsals and production, and the result was perhaps too overtly theatrical in close-up: Olivier seemed to be acting in an empty theatre. It remains, however, a permanent record of one of his most controversial performances, no matter how quickly made.

The hurry was occasioned by an important engagement late that summer, for the National Theatre had been invited to be the first Western theatrical company to play in Russia. On 5 September, Olivier playfully donned a chief steward's hat and jacket and greeted sixty-four members of his company boarding a flight for Moscow, where they performed three plays a total of eighteen times in two weeks. Later, Olivier exchanged the flight attendant's uniform for a regulation Communist worker's suit and peasant cap.

All the plays were offered in English without translation, and after the first performance of *Othello* the audience rushed to the footlights, stamping their feet, clapping wildly, hurling bouquets of flowers and demanding curtain calls for thirty-five minutes. East–West relations momentarily thawed as Olivier spoke to the crowd in carefully rehearsed Russian: 'Comrades, it was our great dream to play in Moscow. Thank you for making that dream come so wonderfully true.'

Performances of Harold Brighouse's *Hobson's Choice* followed, and then the National's premiere of Congreve's *Love for Love* (which would be part of the following season's repertory in London). Olivier took the role of the gossip Tattle, playing him as a faded, effeminate dandy, romping and delving into the mannerisms of camp with undisguised glee. As with his Stratford Malvolio and his Captain Brazen in *The Recruiting Officer*, Olivier obviously relished the opportunity for clearly gay characterisations. Two weeks after they had arrived in Moscow, the company flew to Berlin and presented two plays at that city's Festival; by 1 October they were back at the Old Vic.

Two strange things had occurred during performances of *Othello* before the end of 1965. Once (and only once) Olivier was somehow able to weep onstage at the appropriate moment – an effect he otherwise could never achieve in his career. Calling a member of the company backstage after the performance, he was almost dancing with delight: 'Did you see? Did you see what happened? I did it! I cried!' And on an even more memorable occasion, when Maggie Smith (his Desdemona) came to his dressing room to congratulate him on a singularly impressive performance, he replied with a combination of mild anger and confusion: he knew he had been exceptional, but he did not know why, nor had he the remotest idea how to repeat it. She recalled that his expression and tone were almost unbearably sad, as if he had stumbled on a great treasure only to have suddenly lost it.

The moment must have been poignant for Olivier, filled with a sense of his fragile and unpredictable talent. For all his careful control over a performance and his painstaking preparation of every external detail, there was after all an element of mystery. And in the case of Laurence Olivier (who knew he was a great performer), this was a tragic moment that augured profound inner turmoil. Not long after that evening, he was overcome with an almost paralysing stagefright, the first sign of which had afflicted him momentarily during a performance of *The Master Builder* (ironically the play in which Redgrave's forgetfulness incurred his criticism). At first he felt completely breathless, and then there was a constriction of the throat, mouth and tongue – and a fear that the whole world was closing in on him. Eventually this affected his Othello, and one night onstage he whispered to Frank Finlay, 'Don't leave the stage, move downstage where I can see you – or I'll run – and whatever you do, don't look me in the eyes, look over my shoulder.' He was only able to continue this performance because he recalled that Noël Coward, Binkie Beaumont and other colleagues were in the audience and he feared embarrassing them. Later, Olivier said he had to face the decision in 1965 and 1966, when the anxiety attacks were at their fiercest, whether to abandon his career or weather the storm.

That stagefright should visit him so powerfully at this point is not at all surprising, for it was a natural manifestation of his many fears – of ageing, of losing his powers, his control and his status. The insecurity that haunts performers – driving them continually to perfect a craft, to gratify others, to receive the all-embracing endorsement of as many people as possible – overwhelmed Olivier at almost every performance for three years. Would his past guarantee his future, his skills endure? By autumn 1965, Joan wanted another child and spoke of an even larger family thereafter: could Olivier, at fifty-eight, sire healthy issue, or offspring at all? The actor's anxiety is, at root, a kind of spiritual vertigo, a fear of impotence with all its ramifications that can produce a variety of psychosomatic symptoms: for Olivier, the apprehension often took the form of colitis, which owes as much to stress as to unwise eating habits. And of anxiety his life had its full complement.

Film roles were naturally a different matter, with their short takes and opportunities for immediate remedies in case of accident. In December (for eight days and a fee of £250,000), he worked on *Khartoum*, an expensive desert epic cashing in on the recent success of *Lawrence of Arabia*. Playing opposite Charlton Heston's General Gordon, Olivier was the Mahdi, a fanatical Arab who led 200,000 Dervishes against their Turkish-Egyptian rulers in 1883. Producer Julian Blaustein had hoped to film their scenes on location in the Middle

Eastern desert, but Olivier, who had only just learned that Joan was pregnant, would not leave England; the director then exploited the tricks of modern cinema and shot Olivier's scenes at Pinewood. And so he reapplied his arduous, dark Othello make-up, augmenting the size of his lips, cheeks, eyelids and nose and assuming a careful Sudanese accent. A portrait of frightening, undiluted zealotry, Olivier's Moslem sliced his words with steely perversity and seemed to command heaven and earth – but according to Heston, he was anxious about forgetting his lines. 'Let's do just one more rehearsal, can't we, laddie?' he asked several times before takes. 'I want to be sure I have this right.'

Despite his almost constant stagefright and his doctor's recommendation that he take a holiday, Olivier made continuing demands on himself, never missing an administrative meeting, a conference with Tynan, a performance or a directing assignment. In early 1966 he agreed to direct the National's revival of *Juno and the Paycock* for an April premiere and to be interviewed by Tynan on BBC television. Eager to be considered *au courant*, Olivier also consented to join a protest against the censorship of the Royal Court production of Edward Bond's *Saved*, which had run afoul of the Lord Chamberlain.

On 7 February 1966, he appeared at a magistrate's hearing as a witness on behalf of the English Stage Company. William Gaskill, by then artistic director of the ESC, had produced the play, and was indicted for not implementing the censor's pre-production demands – mostly to excise a scene in which a baby is stoned to death in a pram – but by the time of the final decision the play had run its controversial course. (*Saved* was defended by many notables, among them the Earl of Harewood, cousin of the Queen and founder of the Edinburgh Festival.) Olivier's support, strongly urged by Tynan and Joan, contributed to the dismantling of the Chamberlain's censorship office a few years later.

On 27 July, after several painful weeks during which both Joan and her unborn baby were in jeopardy, the birth was induced. While Joan lay in a perilous state, the child was christened – at once, for her survival, too, was uncertain – and given the names Julianne Rose Henrietta Katherine; she was thenceforth always called Julie-Kate. The cost of private care for a month was enormous, and Olivier was grateful for his income from *Khartoum* and the tax-free sum of 125,000 Danish crowns (£6250) that accompanied the Sonning Prize for his contributions to European culture. With five Oliviers plus staff, it was time to think of enlarging the residence at Royal Crescent, and in January 1967 he bought the adjacent house and contracted for the work necessary to join the two.

On 21 February, Olivier acted for the first time the role of the spiteful, bitter captain Edgar, locked into a lifelong battle of wits with his equally strident and vindictive wife Alice in Strindberg's dour play *The Dance of Death* – a performance many critics considered the finest of his later years (and one soon preserved in a colour film). 'I've been married a bit myself and [the play] seems to me realistic,' he said later. 'There isn't a line that I haven't said to one of my wives' – an astonishingly frank remark in light of the character's prevalent tone: 'Perhaps you and I were sent here to torment each other,' Edgar says typically and sneeringly to his wife.

Opposite Geraldine McEwan (as a pinched shrike of a wife, regally icy but pathetic in her emotional vacuity), Olivier strutted, guffawed, chortled, fumed, bellowed, preened, shouted, agonised with heart spasms and wept for the loss of a love that was only illusion. Towards the end of the three-hour play, alone onstage, he collapsed in great heaving sobs, lamenting at last that his emptiness had made him 'Lonely – lonely, oh, – lonely!' This was a portrait of no simple villain but of a man recognisable in his hideous hatred, yet somehow deserving compassion. And as 1967 unfolded, Olivier himself could certainly claim the sympathy of friends, for tensions and griefs accumulated without interval.

First was the brouhaha over Rolf Hochhuth's *Soldiers*, which Tynan insisted would place the National Theatre on the map as an international company fearlessly offering controversial political plays (it was also championed by Joan). But there was a problem: *Soldiers* – which blamed Churchill for the plane crash that killed the Polish General Sikorski during World War II and accused him of criminal inhumanity in the bombing of Dresden – was simply not very good, as even Olivier recognised. 'I don't like the bloody thing,' he told his wife. 'But I expect it'll get near to grounds for divorce if you think I'm frightened of doing new stuff. You'll despise me, won't you?' His remark was worthy of *The Dance of Death*. (Hochhuth's first play was similarly controversial. *The Representative* – called *The Deputy* in America – charged Pope Pius XII with criminal non-intervention in not acting to save Jews from the Holocaust.)

And so, in a joint effort to please his literary manager and his wife, and to demonstrate (as he had in the case for *Saved*) that he was a man of the day, Olivier defended *Soldiers* when the National's board, led by Churchill's former Cabinet colleague Lord Chandos, rejected it as offensive to the great hero and indeed to English wartime history. 'I maintain that this play is a far finer piece of work . . . than *The Crucible* . . . [and] far more important,' Olivier claimed, completely reversing his private opinion and parroting a statement prepared by Tynan. At the same time, the latter claimed that the distinguished historian Hugh Trevor-Roper had admitted the possible truth of the play's claim; Trevor-Roper's subsequent denial did nothing to endorse Tynan's integrity or Olivier's faith in him. Additionally, Hochhuth weakly claimed there were secret documents locked in a Swiss vault (but unavailable to the public until the year 2017) that proved his charge against Churchill – an assertion that impressed no one. The National board understandably believed Olivier to be far too much under Tynan's influence, and this shook their faith in his judgment. This placed him in an impossible situation: desiring freedom in the theatre and wanting to maintain his autonomy as director of the National, Olivier was divided on three issues – those of patriotism, of the play's worth, and of his relationships with Tynan and Joan.

After Hochhuth revised some scenes without weakening his thesis, the Lord Chamberlain announced that the play could not be seen in Britain without the permission of Churchill's family, a proviso that was, predictably, unmet. After major changes to English censorship laws in 1968, *Soldiers* was finally staged, but it closed when the pilot of Sikorski's plane, who had survived the crash, issued a writ for libel. The fate of the work was less important than the ructions it caused at the National Theatre, for Tynan – with his own position in jeopardy – urged Olivier to resign his post. This was going too far, and Olivier stood his ground. 'Tynan thought he could manipulate people,' as Peter Hall reflected later, 'but he couldn't because people simply compared notes about his manipulations. He had tried to run the National like a Renaissance court, with himself as secretary of state or chief cardinal to Olivier as Pope. In gliding around like a not very Machiavellian Machiavelli, Tynan was really not very helpful to Larry.'

With this sorry episode Tynan's influence as literary manager went into swift decline. 'The significant thing is that Ken, who started all the fuss about putting the play on, didn't resign himself,' said Gaskill, who certainly never hesitated to defend and to stage controversial works. Over this episode, as Gaskill, Hall and others felt, the Olivier –Tynan relationship revealed its full complexity.

Olivier stood, then, at the centre of a political issue out of proportion to the merits of the play, and a curious dilemma resulted in which there were neither villains nor victors. Chandos, unwaveringly loyal to the memory of Churchill, genuinely liked Olivier but neither admired nor trusted Tynan; furious when it was clear that Tynan had lied about the support for the play's veracity, Chandos dug in and invoked the Lord Chamberlain's aid. Olivier then said he would enlist the help of his wife to guarantee a truce of six months. Tynan could argue, with some justification, that he was simply doing what Olivier had engaged him for – keeping pace with the times and expanding the repertory in daring new ways.

At the same time Olivier supported both Tynan and Joan and tried to wear two hats simultaneously – that of Her Majesty's staunch subject and that of the new-wave artistic director. If he failed in any way it was not, as Chandos believed, simply because of blind faith in Tynan but rather that Olivier felt compelled to prove himself to a much younger colleague and a much younger wife. Keeping his own ego largely in check, he was caught between unwavering enemies, and it caused him anguish for the rest of his life; in his memoirs he devoted a twenty-six-page appendix to setting forth some of the facts (and correspondence) in the case.

Behind the entire issue lies one subtler than theatrical politics, having to do perhaps with the unacknowledged motivations of both Kenneth Tynan and Joan Plowright, each of whom made the hilarious claim that *Soldiers* somehow made Churchill more sympathetic. 'My wife, who is thirty-six and is a very sensible girl,' said Olivier, 'cannot understand the objections. The play does not diminish Churchill to her; it rather increased her admiration for him.' Since Joan had none of the characteristics of a mindless fanatic, it is difficult to know just how she arrived at this odd view, nor did she ever elucidate. In fact Joan and Tynan in some ways may have regarded Olivier as a surrogate Churchill – a stuffy, hallowed representative of an earlier generation, whose reputation they were called to challenge. The issue, in other words, would have appealed to her highly competitive spirit, from which even (and especially) Olivier was not immune. Similar sentiments, more deeply interwoven with an erotic affinity based on the exertion of power, animated Tynan. Both allies, then, became accidental adversaries, each acting sincerely but not wholly out of regard for Olivier's function. Even good people, as Aeschylus wrote, are inclined to envy a friend's success.

*

As he performed, directed, auditioned and negotiated delicate administrative manoeuvres that spring, Olivier began to feel unwell – continual lower-back pain at first and then abdominal discomfort. These symptoms he dismissed as signs of tension and exhaustion, and at the end of April he flew to Canada for two days to participate in the opening of the Montreal Expo World Festival, at which the National had been invited to perform later that year. On 2 May, Olivier returned in greater discomfort, and three weeks later (on his sixtieth birthday, while directing a new cast in rehearsals for Chekhov's *Three Sisters*) a doctor was called. After a preliminary examination, a biopsy revealed a first-stage cancer of the prostate gland. There was no question that Olivier's ordinary activities would have to be immediately curtailed and decisions made about a course of treatment.

In 1967, the standard procedure against cancer of the prostate was radical surgery, followed by a course of drugs with unpleasant side effects. The treatment routinely left patients impotent, and Olivier was especially anxious to find an alternative. One was available – an experimental course of hyperbaric oxygen radiation therapy. Doctors at St Thomas's Hospital (A. W. Badenoch, consulting with Kenneth E. Shuttleworth) advised this treatment, which Olivier could undergo on an out-patient basis, thrice weekly for three weeks.

When he told Virginia Fairweather of his revised acting and directing schedule, she asked what excuse should be given to the company and the press. Olivier replied that the truth of the matter must be told at once: he wanted to encourage others similarly afflicted, as he hoped to be the successful guinea pig for this new kind of treatment. On 16 June the National Theatre announced his illness and course of therapy, adding that some of Olivier's duties would have to be temporarily curtailed.

The treatment to which Olivier submitted that June was relatively painless but slightly Orwellian and more than a little frightening. He was sealed in an opaque chamber just a little larger than a coffin; inside there was space only for a speakerphone and an oxygen tube, and he remained immobilised while enormous cylindrical objects swung round him, aiming blasts of radiation at the precise site of disease. While his attitude to the public, the press and his acquaintances was blithe and cheerful, privately Olivier was not so sanguine. 'I remember his reaction when he first learned of the cancer,' Joan said later. 'It wasn't shock. He felt something like this was his due – it was something that had been meted out to him. It just came a bit before he expected.'

Referring to 'the cancer which I have been guilty of having', Olivier interpreted the illness as somehow a punishment for wrongdoing. This is not an uncommon reaction, but in his case he also suspected that his illness was a sign of weakness, and that he was disappointing colleagues and audiences if he failed to appear at work and onstage. So far as the treatment permitted, therefore, he continued to work: this was his way of taking a stand against the disease itself. In addition, he simply had to go on with his life. 'Acting, after all,' he said later that year, 'is a kind of masochistic form of exhibitionism that was born in me, and I don't seem to be able to stop.' Nor could he be dissuaded, despite the inevitable side effects, from attending rehearsals for *Three Sisters*, where he reacted ambivalently to the news that Anthony Hopkins, who had stepped into *The Dance of Death* in his absence, had thereby leapt to fame. He was also unwilling to cut back on directing. A doctor attended his visit to the Old Vic for the Chekhov rehearsal and after the permitted hour and a half prodded Olivier to depart. This injunction was ignored, and an hour later the doctor insisted. 'My dear sir,' Olivier said grandly, 'you and I are both professionals. I have been to your theatre, now you are in mine, and I have not yet finished my job.'

But his efforts could not be sustained. On 20 June he fell ill at Brighton and was rushed back to London with pneumonia, wryly complaining during admission to hospital that he had gone there to be cured of a cancer he knew he had, only to be given pneumonia he did not want. Joan realised at once that a sudden hospitalisation after out-patient treatment would only seem ominous to journalists, and so she announced a press conference. Giving them a detailed report and answering every question forthrightly, she defused rumours and asked reporters to stress that Olivier must remain at St Thomas's until the pneumonia had been routed and the next round of treatment concluded – a ploy designed to keep him resting once she showed him the news accounts.

While Douglas Fairbanks, Jr., was visiting Olivier in his hospital room on the evening of Saturday, 8 July, a telephone call was put through from John Merivale. Alone in her flat at 54 Eaton Square, Vivien had died; the coroner certified the cause of death as chronic pulmonary tuberculosis. 'There was a long, sad moment,' Fairbanks recalled, 'and then he said, "Poor, dear little Vivien." It seemed to me that their life together was running like a film through his mind.'

Especially since 1963, Vivien's life had been unsettled and unhappy. With Merivale she had travelled to India; she had appeared in the American film *Ship of Fools* as an anxiously ageing and faded matron, and she acted twice on Broadway, once becoming so deranged backstage that she was taken forcibly to London for treatment. But an odd kind of calm had come over her in the months before her death. She spoke of returning to the stage and even entertained a few friends, and on 27 June Coward had found her 'pale but lovely, and smoking, which she shouldn't have been doing'.

No one had expected Vivien to die quite so suddenly and Olivier, still in the throes of his own confrontation with mortality, was visibly shaken. She was fifty-three years old, and though frail she had seemed somehow indestructible by sheer force of her indomitable will. Olivier never denied the excitement Vivien had so long infused into his life, nor the social, cultural and intellectual education she had provided. In almost every way, she had raised him – except with respect to his superior talent, which she always acknowledged. She had met Olivier at a time in their lives when they both seemed almost desperate for the redemption they thought love could provide, and although they seemed to relish an image they and millions accepted as true, that image had at last played them false. Their passion for one another had been so fierce it had become part of the myth, but finally it could sustain neither the inevitable encroachment of reality nor the best effects of precisely what they had offered each other – a certain freedom from their prior limitations.

'It is,' Olivier wrote later, 'inhuman, immoral, to love a thing more than people, work, intellect, art, my dead.' His dead – his precious dead, as he stressed – were always pre-eminently his mother and Vivien. That July night, he left his hospital bed at once and went directly to Eaton Square. 'I stood and prayed for forgiveness for all the evils that had sprung up between us . . . [for] it has always been impossible for me not to believe that I was somehow the cause of Vivien's disturbances.'

To the end of her life, still insisting she was rightfully Lady Olivier, Vivien kept his photograph at her bedside, with his old letters that she read and reread. A few friends told her she was obsessive and unrealistic, living in an illusory past; it was the only issue over which she never argued. She simply smiled at the speaker as if to dismiss the statement as unimaginably juvenile or at least imperceptive. Among her bequests were some treasured items of jewellery and art from her former life at Durham Cottage and Notley Abbey, which were to be delivered with all haste from Vivien Mary, The Lady Olivier, to Sir Laurence, ever her knight, her best beloved, her Larry-boy.

CHAPTER FIFTEEN

⚏

1967–1974

They are waiting for me to go . . . but I am not
going to die.

Antonio, in Eduardo de Filippo's *Saturday, Sunday, Monday*

At Vivien's funeral – a Catholic service at St Mary's, Cadogan Square
– Olivier was a grim attendant. Ignoring the press, he tried to
comfort her mother Gertrude, her daughter Suzanne and her first
husband Leigh Holman, but it was Olivier himself who required solace.
And more tragic news awaited him the following morning: Cecil Tennant had been killed in a car accident on the way home from the funeral.
Olivier's business partner in LOP and a longtime friend, Tennant had
been an agent at MCA until that company had ceased to represent
artists in 1961. Since then, he had advised Olivier unofficially.

Among the practical aspects of life requiring immediate decisions
late that summer, therefore, was the choice of an agent. Not surprisingly, he turned to his close friend Laurence Evans, who had represented Vivien during the last years of her life. One of London's most
respected agents, Evans had a long and impressive client list (among
them John Gielgud, Ralph Richardson, John Mills, Ingrid Bergman,
Rex Harrison, Alec Guinness, Peter Hall and Wendy Hiller) not only
through his articulate negotiating skills but because of his reputation
for unassailable integrity and candour. His friendship with Olivier had
flourished for almost forty years, since the days of *Too Many Crooks*;
he had served as general manager at the Old Vic during Olivier's first
wartime seasons and then as production manager on *Henry V*; and
henceforth Olivier would benefit from his professional counsel. Above
all, he treasured and relied on the buoyant humour and affectionate
constancy offered by Laurence Evans and his wife Mary, much admired

for her discretion and understanding; to the end of his life they were his two most devoted friends.

From the first week, Laurence Evans was kept busy with his new client, who was being offered a number of film roles in addition to his National Theatre engagements, and for whom Evans at once negotiated substantial fees. Olivier's nominal salary with the National was the same as that of the other players: he received forty-two pounds for each performance. His motion picture fees, however, were another matter, and from 1967 to 1971 Olivier (who played only minor roles in seven films apart from *The Dance of Death*) received a total of more than £300,000 for what amounted to less than eight weeks of actual movie work in four years. With three children, two homes and high British tax rates, this was a comfortable but not princely emolument, which explains why, in 1972 and 1973, he accepted an offer of over $700,000 to appear in several American television commercials for Polaroid cameras (with the stipulation that they never be broadcast in the United Kingdom).

On 30 September 1967, a troupe from the National Theatre departed for a Canadian tour, entertaining 85,000 people in forty-eight performances in which Olivier assumed three roles: the small part of the servant Étienne in the Feydeau farce *A Flea in Her Ear*, a comic cameo with bowler and short tight jacket reminiscent of Chaplin; Tattle (in *Love for Love*) and Edgar (in *The Dance of Death*). In Vancouver, Edmonton and Winnipeg, Olivier drew remarkable stamina from his diminished reserves, but by the time they reached Montreal he was visibly weary and seemed suddenly ten years older. Always annoyed by backstage talking among players and crew during a performance, he usually corrected people with a gentle, private reproof, but on the tour he grew loudly furious over such misconduct. Next day he would apologise for the outburst, but his closest associates – Diana Boddington, for one, who had been stage manager for him since the wartime years at the Old Vic – were concerned, for he was constantly edgy and depressed.

His unpleasant disposition was caused primarily by his cancer therapy and its attendant anxiety, but that winter he accepted an offer for a brief but crucial role in *The Shoes of the Fisherman*, based on Morris West's bestseller. The film, an intelligent epic about a Russian priest (Anthony Quinn) who becomes Pope and leads the Church into a new age, was produced that winter in Rome, where Olivier earned

$200,000 for eleven working days. As the politically astute Soviet premier who frees a priest from prison, Olivier conveyed a Cold War sternness filtered through a canny insight about the choice between doom and brotherhood. Offering a toast with an expansively casual grace, emphasising thick guttural h's and staring unblinkingly and wisely at narrow-minded colleagues, his performance used a minimum of technique for a maximum of seriocomic effect.

When not required on the set at Cinecittà that January 1968, Olivier dashed to a nearby soundstage, where Franco Zeffirelli was filming *Romeo and Juliet*. Asking if there were any way he might be included, Olivier was delighted when Zeffirelli asked him to read a voice-over prologue. Olivier also dubbed the voice of Lord Montague (covering for Antonio Pierfederici's heavy accent) and then – with almost a child's alacrity to be involved, to ransack the actor's grab-bag – he insisted on dubbing a variety of small parts and even crowd noises. These voice cameos Olivier despatched without pay or credit, simply for the pleasure of being involved in the project.

As Laurence Evans let it be known that Olivier was available for limited film work, the offers fairly tumbled in over the next two years. First was his four-and-a-half-minute turn as an adulterous, boozing Sir John French in Richard Attenborough's World War I satire *Oh! What a Lovely War*. In the celebratory *Battle of Britain*, he was far more serious as Air Marshal Sir Hugh Dowding, whose strategy in 1940 enabled the Royal Air Force to withstand the Luftwaffe. In half a dozen scenes totalling less than five minutes, Olivier created a man of rueful duty, patriotic but disgusted with war and saying with a kind of grim finality, 'Our young men will have to shoot down their young men at the rate of four to one.' There followed two roles: a minute-long walk-on as the sadistic schoolmaster Creakle in an American television production of *David Copperfield* and the army doctor Chebutikin, a shaggy old man trying to recapture his lost youth, in the National's film of *Three Sisters*, which he directed at Shepperton – his first time behind the camera since *The Prince and the Showgirl*.*

These and other film roles in the last twenty years of his life – only a few of them memorable – he said he accepted for the money. 'I worry

---

* Olivier also made a test for the role of *The Godfather*. 'He had a sneer on his mouth with happiness in his eye,' recalled actor Robert Duvall, who watched him film the scene and heard his perfectly enunciated Italian accent. But when Olivier fell ill the role went to Marlon Brando.

about my children and the future, dying and leaving nothing, and my wife with three hulking kids.' He did not add another reason, that despite his general frugality he had the odd luxury ('a Daimler – very nice, I love it'). But there were other considerations: films allowed him to work at his craft, to protest (with Edgar in *The Dance of Death*) 'I'm not dead yet!' When asked in 1970 if his various illnesses encouraged him to retire, he was adamant: 'They'll have to kick me out. I don't want to dig in my garden or play golf.' This same spirit of endurance also prevented him from exploiting discomfort, nor did he ever seek concessions for his age. On the contrary, as his energies gradually lagged and memorisation became difficult, he redoubled his efforts, refusing stuntmen or doubles and rehearsing more avidly. 'Get out of my way!' he shouted to an actor he was directing in *Love's Labour's Lost* in 1968. 'Here's how it's done!' And with that he climbed a ten-foot stage tree and hurled himself to the floor.

But there were setbacks. After a day trying to ignore his abdominal discomfort, Olivier was flown on 23 February to London from Edinburgh (where he was playing Edgar) for an emergency appendectomy. The sequel was again a round of pneumonia that left him severely weakened. His recurrent sieges of pulmonary infections and his prior history of smoking combined to afflict him with chronic obstructive pulmonary disease causing constant shortness of breath.

On his return to the depressing office in Aquinas Street, he might have wished he had remained at St Thomas's Hospital. Peter Brook, with whom Olivier's collaborations had hitherto been cordial, was preparing a stark modern production of Seneca's *Oedipus*, starring John Gielgud. With his celebrated production of Peter Weiss's *Marat/Sade* behind him and committed to the sociopolitical objectives of the Theatre of Cruelty (mostly towards the audience), Brook had, with Tynan's support, fuelled a number of controversies. During rehearsals, Brook had asked his cast to imagine all kinds of horror and violence, and he asked them for primal screams, animal imitations and improvisations drawn from their own memories – a routine to which all complied with varying enthusiasm except Gielgud, whom Brook approached. Could he think of nothing terrifying? 'Actually, Peter, there is,' the actor replied. 'We open in two weeks.'

The event was an embarrassment for Olivier as the increasingly beleaguered director of the National Theatre. He had always been frank in his admission that his approach to the theatre was instinctual rather than intellectual. 'I'm one of the least educated men you ever met,' he told a critic. 'I've never read anything except scripts, and outside of that I'm an ignoramus.' This was perhaps a neat way to defuse the onslaught of academic objections, but a lifetime of studying Sophocles, Shakespeare, Sheridan, Chekhov, Ibsen and Shaw (and more recently Osborne, Ionesco and Anouilh) was an education in itself. Trusting his instincts, Olivier loudly objected to the finale of Brook's *Oedipus*, in which an enormous golden phallus was unveiled while actors danced round it singing 'God Save the Queen' (and later invited the audience also to dance onstage). Adolescent indulgence, Olivier considered it, not merely in bad taste but anti-theatrical. Tynan, as so often, held the trump card to ensure the theatrical shock he wanted: Brook would no doubt complain to the press if Olivier continued to object. And with that threat Olivier capitulated, accepting 'the punch that started my undoing', as he called it later. *Oedipus* was indifferently received and there were ironic newspaper and magazine articles hinting that perhaps Sir Laurence ought to forgo management for acting.

That autumn he co-directed Joan in Natalia Ginzburg's *The Advertisement* (leaving most of the rehearsals to Donald MacKechnie) and staged *Love's Labour's Lost*, the last of only three Shakespearean plays he ever directed. Then (on 30 January 1969), he assumed the small comic role of the wily divorce lawyer in Somerset Maugham's *Home and Beauty*. Withholding no effort, he designed another fantastic false nose, augmented his lips with rubber padding, donned an unruly wig and pince-nez, and affected an exotic East-End-Jewish accent. His ten-minute scene bordered on *kitsch*, but the play withstood his antics and no one in the audience could have known he was still suffering from severe stagefright, at least partially caused by his difficulty with the lines. 'I'm such a slow study these days,' he lamented that year. 'A single scene takes me three weeks. My wife can memorise twenty-three pages in a night, and when I was young I learned Romeo in two days.'

'I found him in the wings at the prompt table,' recalled cast member Robert Stephens, 'desperately repeating the lines over the book. I said, "Come on, we've got to go on!" and he looked up and said, "This is no profession for an adult person."' But the 'masochistic form of exhibitionism', as he had termed it, still dominated – and a good thing, for remarkably there were even greater performances to come, and this single comic scene emboldened him to repeat *The Dance of Death* in April. Ominously, he suffered a momentary blackout onstage but insisted this was due to exhaustion. He then dashed to New York on a twenty-four-hour jaunt, to collect a special Tony award for the National Theatre and his contributions to it. His hosts were the producer Alexander H. Cohen and his wife, the writer Hildy Parks, who looked after him with friendly attention. Returning, Olivier was pale and in acute discomfort, and soon he submitted to the unpleasant rigours of a haemorrhoidectomy.

Lewis Casson died at ninety-three that May, and on hearing the news Olivier went at once to comfort Sybil. From this time, his friendships – marked by more frequent visits and a new, unrestrained openness in his affections – became ever more important to Olivier. 'Acting's a beastly profession in many ways,' he told a journalist.

> I don't mean the competitiveness, the out-of-work risks, the cruel bad luck and the intoxicating good luck (which is worse), the jealousies, the tensions, and the wear and tear – not that. All that's an occupational hazard in many other walks of life. But in the theatre it is exceptionally hard to keep friendships.

On 16 January 1970, he accompanied the National Theatre troupe to Los Angeles to promote the productions of *Three Sisters* and Farquhar's *The Beaux' Stratagem*, but Olivier was not in the casts, and after meeting the press he returned to London for rehearsals of *The Merchant of Venice*. To direct, he had invited Jonathan Miller, the gifted young doctor-turned-actor-turned-director whose productions of plays classic and contemporary were highly regarded in England and America. Miller accepted with the proviso that *Merchant* be staged in a nineteenth-century setting, and Olivier was so excited by this idea that he decided to play Shylock himself.

As rehearsals began, Miller found that Olivier wanted to be treated like any cast member: 'He never pulled rank, and although he was obviously full of little suggestions and helpful bits, he was never intrusive.' Any specific contribution he had to make regarding the direction, according to Miller, was so that another actor could be seen more prominently, and he never looked for a scene to be played for his own advantage. But although Olivier had a remarkably collegial attitude to direction, the nature of his performance, he thought, should be entirely his own. Basing his characterisation on George Arliss's famous film of *Disraeli*, Olivier fashioned an elaborate make-up with a prominent hooked nose, Hassidic curls, a beard and false teeth. He also rehearsed what he thought was a typically Jewish way of speaking English. 'This would have been very vulgar,' Miller said years later. 'And being

Jewish myself I could say to him, "Larry, you know this is rather a cliché – not all of us sound and look that way."'

In Jonathan Miller, Olivier had a director who was not only perceptive but fearless in criticism, and so his acting in *The Merchant of Venice* turned out to be a major stage of growth in his art. If Olivier wanted to proceed with a stereotype, Miller said, he could go ahead and do so – but he advised against it and suggested alternatives.

> Slowly [Olivier admitted] he made me see myself as others saw me. I'd made a mountain out of mannerisms and had ended up impersonating myself – a habit old actors fall into very easily. Miller opened my eyes . . . Here was I, the one actor who had always prided himself on his originality, and here was a young director telling me I was as original as yesterday's newspaper . . . It was a lesson I well learned.

Except for a row of false teeth, Olivier gradually exchanged the exaggerated make-up for gestures and intonations suggested by Miller. This made for a slightly confusing if finally rewarding documentation of the production, according to Anthony Crickmay, official photographer for *The Merchant of Venice*. Daily he was told, 'Olivier's changing his make-up, you'll have to take more photographs at the rehearsal tonight.'

Miller gave Olivier many significant points to develop Shylock. First he suggested that Olivier break into a gleeful little dance (as Hitler did at Compiègne when France capitulated) on hearing the news of Antonio's lost ships. Then Miller gave him the idea for the heartbreaking offstage cry that synthesised both role and play. The result was an entirely fresh perspective on the character – not the stereotypical villain but a despised and hardened sophisticate – and this might not have happened but for the coincidence of the director's inspired frankness and the actor's fundamental humility. The respect and acquiescence towards one whose erudition he much admired resulted in an unqualified triumph.

There were no anxieties during rehearsals, according to Miller, and certainly nothing to indicate the awfulness of what happened immediately after the first night. From the wings, the director observed Olivier almost paralysed with stagefright, the perspiration flowing heavily, his breathing irregular. His eyes went blank, and there was a dreadful silence backstage among those watching, for it seemed Olivier might not continue. But he did, and from that second performance on, he obtained a generous prescription for the tranquilliser Valium, which was then thought to be mild enough for repeated use without danger of addiction. The panic attacks, common enough in older (and some-times even younger) actors but singularly acute in Olivier's case, were another obstacle for him to overcome, and more threatening than any stunt or swordplay. But he refused to yield to almost a decade of stagefright and illness, and in continuing to struggle with anxiety he overcame it.

That June, after several years of rumour, a life peerage was conferred on Olivier in the Queen's Birthday Honours; the actual ceremony of investiture occurred nine months later. 'I've been working fifty years for this,' the new baron, The Right Honourable The Lord Olivier said, and to Richard Burton he confided that for a very long time he had been 'determined to be the first actor-peer'. That was now another goal achieved, and immediately after the announcement, he sent a letter to everyone at the National, asking that the honour not alter the way he was personally addressed; most continued to call him 'Sir'. He still had to cope with the demands of the National Theatre office, of course, and one of the least pleasant weeks of his career was spent that June as host to the Swedish director Ingmar Bergman, whom Tynan had cajoled into staging *Hedda Gabler*. Tynan briefly welcomed Bergman to a company dinner but then departed, leaving the overworked Olivier to squire the guest to receptions and rehearsals. '[Olivier] wanted my idea for the play,' Bergman complained later, 'and then he wanted to take over and stage it himself, in my choreography.' More to the point, Bergman was eager to return home for a film commitment and con-sidered *Hedda Gabler* a boring play from which he cut a quarter of the text.

A bout of pleurisy that summer landed Olivier back in St Thomas's Hospital, and he developed a severe thrombosis in his right leg, which became painfully and dangerously swollen. The blood clot kept him confined to bed for six weeks, after which his doctors insisted he not act for a year and radically reduce his official activities. This had the predictable effect of disturbing the National's board, who depended on Olivier's regular appearances as they continued to be embroiled in ongoing controversies about the South Bank building schedule, public funding, box-office receipts and the vagaries of balancing popular, classical and controversial plays in the schedule. 'Now that I have been told I cannot act for a year, I am screaming!' he said that autumn. But his inactivity did not last for as long as the doctors had predicted, and by year's end he signed to work for five days on the film *Nicholas and Alexandra* in the small role of Count Witte, the administrative genius who gave Russia its first constitution and advised the last Czar.

Olivier himself needed all the political acumen he could muster to deal with the first business of 1971. Tynan had championed a play by Fernando Arrabal called *The Architect and the Emperor of Assyria*, for which the word 'absurdist' might have been invented. 'I think it's a load of rubbish,' Olivier told Anthony Hopkins, one of the play's two actors, 'but Ken is very keen on it and I'm sure you babies [Hopkins and his co-star Jim Dale] will have a good time.' Without script and with direction conveyed through a translator, Hopkins and Dale had to fight onstage, gradually strip, cover themselves with parachute silks, meditate on a fork-lift, build an elephant from Brazilian tree-bark, recite lengthy nonsensical speeches and at last succumb to apparent cannibalism. When asked how he intended to stage the grisly finale, director Victor Garcia stormed away, muttering angrily in various languages that Olivier had no imagination.

'I can't fucking sleep,' Olivier complained to Hopkins as the February premiere approached. 'What is this little shit Arrabal doing?' When Hopkins replied that he had not the remotest idea of the play's theme or controlling idea, that there were no real rehearsals and that he felt like killing the director, Olivier added, 'Wait until I get there [at that day's rehearsal] and then you can kill him!' Garcia was not present for the rehearsal that day (the actors were to improvise their performances for 'human authenticity'), and the translator mentioned something about *Chinois*. 'He loves the Chinese,' Olivier said to Hopkins. 'He's going to have a Chinaman in the play driving a fork-lift truck.'

Garcia had ordered Hopkins to appear almost nude for much of the play, and at the final undress rehearsal the actor waded through a four-page speech of stunning incoherence while pulling bark off a tree. Two and a half hours later, a listless Olivier prepared to depart but was told that he had seen only the first act. This provoked his rage against Tynan.

As Olivier expected, the production did not benefit the dwindling fortunes of the 1970–71 season at the National Theatre, where 'there was a prevailing atmosphere of a camp divided', as Christopher Plummer described it. Critics complained of bad ensemble acting, poor recruitment of young actors and mediocre productions, and audiences (as Samuel Goldwyn once said) stayed away in droves. Olivier's illnesses forced postponements and recastings, and a summer season at the New Theatre – once the site of his triumphs – was a failure, his staging of Giraudoux's *Amphitryon 38* prime among them ('relentlessly mediocre', complained one critic in a typical dismissal). Comparison of box-office receipts showed the differential: in the first four years of Olivier's tenure, the National had presented twenty-eight plays, of which twenty-two had been undiluted hits; the same number was offered in the second four years, but only half could be called successful. Curious productions of obscure plays were overloading the repertory, pleasing neither critics nor public.

To ease the burden on Olivier, John Dexter and Michael Blakemore were appointed associate directors, and to aid the budget a long-planned production of the lavish musical *Guys and Dolls* was scrapped; Olivier had hoped to play Nathan Detroit in it, and he and a large cast had already taken extensive singing and dancing lessons. In its place, Tynan wisely suggested Eugene O'Neill's tragic drama *Long Day's Journey Into Night*, to which the National had English stage rights – a single-set, five-character play with a dazzling lead for Olivier as the failed actor and frustrated husband and father James Tyrone. (Because of the enormous demands on his memory and stamina, there would be an unusually long rehearsal period.) Tynan also promoted three other eventually successful productions for 1972: Tom Stoppard's new play *Jumpers*, a revival of Hecht and MacArthur's *The Front Page* and Jonathan Miller's production of *The School for Scandal*.

Before work began on *Long Day's Journey*, Olivier gave his only speech in the House of Lords, on 20 July 1971. Peter Plouviez, an administrator (and later general secretary) of the actors' union Equity, had asked for Olivier's support in opposing the Heath government's efforts to curb the power of trade unions, so that actors could continue to maintain a closed shop. Plouviez found Olivier ill and in obvious pain, wearing a neck brace because of a whiplash injury and incipient arthritis, and carpet slippers because of his painful leg. But as usual he rose to the occasion; his address failed to alter the legislation, but this can hardly be attributed to Olivier's notoriously baroque and almost incomprehensible diction: 'I must beg to suggest to your Lordships that it would be most contrary to the chivalry for which your Lordships' House is so famous to withhold your gallantry and refuse to indulge the coyest maiden of sixty-four.'

But Olivier had nothing like an eager girl's energy or enthusiasm as rehearsals began for *Long Day's Journey* that autumn. For one thing, he thought the play too long and dreary; for another, he did not relish playing a failed and cranky ex-actor. Still limping slightly and wearing the neck collar, he logged the text into memory and then, with director Michael Blakemore and the cast – Constance Cummings as Mary, Ronald Pickup as Edmund and Denis Quilley as Jamie – he set to the task of rehearsing O'Neill's agonised exchanges. They sat round a table for three weeks before the start of proper blocking, but even at that early stage Olivier's performance was sculpted and shaped, and he had the American accent to perfection. He was in fact tending to dominate, and Blakemore quietly suggested that he tone down the first three acts in preparation for the volcanic fourth.

Typically, Olivier at first prepared an elaborate facial makeover. But this time he needed no directorial counsel to forgo his cosmetic alterations, and even before dress rehearsals he put aside any semblance of a false nose, modified teeth or jawline – even a moustache was absent. He transformed himself, recalled Constance Cummings, by finding the character somehow there within – not by going to outside detail first.

This coincidence of actor and role naturally led Olivier to elaborate the man's frugality and love of risk, traits he synthesised in one brilliant bit of business. Where O'Neill's text indicates that Tyrone extinguishes a light, Olivier pushed the part and himself farther, asking Blakemore and designer Michael Annals to arrange the scene so that he could climb precariously onto a table to unscrew a single bulb. As he stepped back off the table at rehearsals, his colleagues watched, terrified. But Olivier forced his body to do what he wanted. The moment was entirely in character, the bravado of the once agile actor Tyrone. But it bespoke Olivier, too, who was showing off, as if to say, 'I am sixty-four, but I can still do these things.'

And he did even more. In addition to five hours of daily rehearsals that autumn, there were also office duties, which he despatched in the mornings and during breaks, wearing Tyrone's suit so it would appear slightly shabby by opening night. 'Every minute we stopped rehearsal he was back in his office,' Constance Cummings recalled, 'and eventually this was an almost intolerable burden to him, being actor, producer, director, general manager – responsible for everything, actually.' By early December there were fears he might not after all have the stamina for the premiere on the twenty-first.

No one need have worried, for the National Theatre's reputation was suddenly and brightly restored that Christmas with the perfect ensemble playing of *Long Day's Journey into Night*, led by Olivier's performance as the guilt-ridden, baffled and finally pathetic old actor incapable of relating to his family. Counterpoising forbearance with moral outrage, his Tyrone was a jumble of contradictions, by turns loving and arrogant, concerned and selfish. Never had he been required to weep so much in a role; never had his stifled sobs and averted gazes been so moving, or the briefest pauses so finely gauged.

This constant capacity to renew himself was nothing short of astonishing, and indeed Olivier had accomplished just that, first moving from his kingly roles to the Archie Rice/Graham Weir phase and then on to this completely realised portrait of an American loner. Tyrone was precisely the kind of man Olivier had avoided becoming, an obsessive tightwad out of touch with himself and his past, a ragged, ageing schoolboy blustering vainly through a torrent of illusions about his glorious Irish-Catholic heritage yet grieving fully over the loss of his wife to morphine addiction. 'It's what I call one of my autobiographical jobs,' he said at the time. 'That chap wasn't a stranger to me at all. I didn't have to invent for his eccentricities. I knew them all.' As did his family, for his daughter Tamsin wrote him a note after seeing his performance: 'Darling Daddy, now we know why you have been so strict about turning off lights at home. It's because you were practising for your play.' Olivier incarnated not only Tyrone's exaggerated frugality, but the paradoxical sudden display of largesse as well. ('To women he was very liberal with the champagne, especially in the wee hours,' recalled Olivier's friend the novelist Edna O'Brien, 'while in the early morning the puritan in him would count the damage evidenced by the empty bottles.') The role clung to him, in fact. Tom Pate, house manager at the National, said that Olivier found it difficult to come out of character during the play: when he rang to ask about the evening's box-office receipts, he would speak in Tyrone's American accent.

Playing the role that winter, dashing from meetings at the Old Vic to performances at the New Theatre, Olivier could often be found dozing between acts (and even between scenes), and several nights each week he elected to remain in London at a flat he had taken in Roebuck House, Victoria. Yet after every performance he invited Cummings, Pickup and Quilley to his dressing room for a shot of Jack Daniels (the American whiskey, entirely in character for Tyrone). Despite fatigue, Olivier seemed back at the top of his form.

But he was not, and he knew it. The performances drained him, and the details of running the National were increasingly unrewarding. That autumn of 1971, he told colleagues he was trying to persuade Joan to take over the artistic direction of the National – an idea she said was ridiculous, as she had neither the training nor the temperament for the position. Since 1968, Joan had appeared in only six roles in repertory (and co-directed one unexceptional new play), and although she would become ever more active and successful on stage and screen in coming years, she was at that time a busy mother whose name was not widely known outside London. But despite Joan's ostensible modesty, many thought she actively importuned her husband to put forth her name as his successor. In a long conversation with Peter Hall at Brighton in June 1973, for example, she protested that she hoped to do more than act: she wanted to direct and to manage. He left this meeting convinced that she very much wanted the position of artistic director. She had a great deal of influence over the National Theatre company for years, according to producer Derek Grainger, a family friend soon to collaborate on several projects with Olivier, and that influence extended to the choice of plays, players and directors. But of course Olivier had not the power to confer the directorship on her, and no great echo resounded when her name was casually dropped in official circles.

Olivier's proposal of her name was not the only indication that he knew his eventual retirement from administration was more or less imminent. Sir Max (later Lord) Rayne, an influential businessman and property tycoon, was appointed chairman of the board after Lord Chandos's death in 1972, and at once Olivier – somewhat half-heartedly – offered a *pro forma* resignation. Rayne replied that Olivier should stay on at least until the South Bank Arts Centre opened – scheduled for 1974 but not to take place until 1976. Meanwhile (prior to *Long Day's Journey*), following the failure of four National productions, Olivier was wary: 'Four flops in a row,' he said to Tynan. 'Now they'll have to ask me to go.' Tynan observed that throughout 1971 Olivier 'ruminates and reminisces as the hatchet-men gather in the shadows. And always, at the back of his mind, is the unspoken thought which Danton utters [in Büchner's *Danton's Death*, which opened on 3 August]: "They'll never dare."'

All institutions are susceptible to an atmosphere in which people avoid assuming unpleasant responsibilities, out of a fear of being thought either too bold or too cowardly and a jealous guarding of their own reputations. During the next year there followed at the National

Theatre an array of petty and sometimes downright hypocritical moves that bruised everyone, Olivier most of all. In the thick of it he was not always his own best advocate, whereas, for various reasons, Tynan was. An illegitimate child who bore his mother's name, Tynan frequently attached himself to creative and famous father-figures he respected (Orson Welles among them), but no one had Olivier's claim on him, and no one was so willing an intellectual subordinate as the first peer of the stage. But because of Olivier's refusal to allow him to direct plays and because of either a real or imagined withdrawal of emotional and professional support, Tynan felt estranged from Olivier's paternal affection. Although he certainly cherished his own influential position at the National, he decided to return to full-time writing. Additionally, he did not want to be 'one of a dozen planets circling round a dying sun', as he bluntly put it.

But as Olivier more or less sincerely considered resigning or at least sharing power with several directors like Blakemore, he was unaware of further developments. The National board member Lord Goodman had, while Olivier was hospitalised with thrombosis in August, approached Peter Hall, then forty-one, late director of the Royal Shakespeare Company and an internationally successful director of both theatre and opera. If the position of artistic director became available, Goodman asked, would he be interested? Definitely, Hall replied; but he would only join first as Olivier's assistant and with his blessing. In some secrecy – Olivier above all was not to know – the discussions continued, and by the end of 1971 there were private negotiations for Hall's contract as director of the National Theatre. At the same time Tynan was arguing for Blakemore to be appointed Olivier's associate and heir, to take over the National only when Olivier himself chose to announce his retirement. Blakemore, forty-three, had directed numerous plays before staging four at the National and being appointed associate director. Tynan put this proposal to Rayne, who summarily dismissed it on the absurd pretext that he did not know Blakemore; and on 2 February Olivier again half-heartedly told Rayne he was thinking of resigning. As developments became more knotty and underhand – and as Olivier, Tynan and their colleagues at the National were ever more systematically ignored by Rayne and the board – Tynan's major objection was proved correct: by refusing to nominate a successor himself, Olivier played directly into the board's hands. 'Some days he was resigning and some days he was staying,' Peter Hall remembered.

In the meantime, things were not in a good state. He wasn't really able to run the place . . . The thing dragged on and on, all very secret, for six months, and when Lord Rayne finally told Larry I was prepared to succeed him on the understanding he would open the National on the South Bank, I think he welcomed it and hated it.

The issue was very nearly at crisis point when Olivier flew to Rome for a week in mid-March 1972 to appear briefly as a drily detached Duke of Wellington in Robert Bolt's film *Lady Caroline Lamb*, for which he received £20,000 for five days' work and performed a bedroom scene with the title character, played by none other than Bolt's wife Sarah Miles. Olivier knew exactly how he wanted to do the part when he arrived, Bolt recalled, and although he listened to direction, his mind was made up. 'We had a hundred extras in one of his short scenes, and Olivier greeted each one with total courtesy. There was something of visiting royalty about him.'

During the filming, Olivier was definitely anxious about a possible coup at the National. In his absence, Peter Hall approached his own agent, who happened to be Laurence Evans: 'What shall I do?' Hall asked, informing Evans for the first time about the offer and requiring secrecy of him – which of course put Evans in an impossible situation regarding Olivier. Accordingly, Evans at once telephoned Binkie Beaumont, who was on the National board, and registered his profound displeasure at the intrigue. If the board did not inform Olivier immediately and include him in the process of change, Evans insisted, he would go to Olivier himself.

This turned out to be unnecessary. On his return to London, Olivier was summoned to Rayne, who told him flat out that the board wanted Peter Hall to succeed him as artistic director. Angry to the end of his life over this unilateral announcement, Olivier found himself in a position similar to that caused by Lord Esher's notorious letter of 1948 when he, Richardson and Burrell were dismissed from the Old Vic. Rayne demanded public silence from Olivier for the duration of Hall's contract negotiations, and he obeyed – but only for the moment. Meanwhile Tynan, on holiday in France, received a call: someone on the board had leaked to the *Observer* that Peter Hall was to be Olivier's successor. Joining Olivier in outrage that they had not been consulted, Tynan still privately blamed the unhappy outcome on Olivier's waffling as much as the board's lack of ethics.

As it happened, Olivier confused the matter even further on 12 April by announcing to the assembled National Theatre company that Hall's appointment was by no means certain, that he would stay on as artistic director and that no one would lose their job during Olivier's tenure. This meeting Tynan cagily described to an eagerly awaiting London press. Within a week the board simply announced that discussions were concluded, and that Hall would join the National as director-designate in 1973, to succeed as director only after Olivier had led the company to the South Bank complex in early 1974. The proscenium stage auditorium would be named the Lyttelton in honour of the first chairman and his family, and, the press announcement concluded, the main amphitheatre would be named the Olivier Theatre 'to celebrate Laurence Olivier's outstanding contribution to the National Theatre'. But Olivier – perhaps suspecting that his influence would immediately wither – at once insisted that on arrival in spring 1973 Hall and he be billed as co-directors.*

Publicly genial, in private Olivier revealed his rage. Richard Attenborough found him shattered with hurt that season, the sense of rejection bowing him as if he was under a great weight. With her gift for curt precision, Joan said later that Olivier 'was absolutely pole-axed' by the events of that year.

'The *putsch* was achieved,' according to Jonathan Miller, 'in an appallingly offensive manner. Olivier put a brave public face on it, but we talked about it several years later and he was still seething with rage. He should have been directly involved in the change of administration, and he knew it.' Robert Bolt was blunter: 'The whole business was a moral outrage.' And Peter Hall, who genuinely liked and admired Olivier, was put in an embarrassing position.

For all the noble achievements of his tenure at the National, Olivier had alienated many colleagues. He had not exactly turned the limelight on himself – of the seventy-nine productions in his time he acted in twelve and directed eight – but he was fundamentally a one-man regime. And the next generation of talent (Anthony Hopkins, Derek Jacobi, Ronald Pickup, Denis Quilley, among others) were rather kept in their place, told they were not yet ready for the great classical roles. All were potential successors (and enjoyed significant careers later), but during Olivier's time they were accidentally reduced to the level of

---

* Olivier's account in *Confessions of an Actor* is one of proper fury, but he seriously erred in dates and time spans. He was not given, in 1972, six months to terminate his directorship, for example (p. 295); in fact he did not formally retire from this position until the autumn of 1973.

perpetual supporting players, courtiers round the great *roi soleil* him-self. The truth is that Laurence Olivier never really guided others as Noël Coward, John Gielgud and Tyrone Guthrie had guided him.

'The observed of all observers' (as Ophelia calls the distracted Ham-let), Olivier had to bear the burden of fame and adulation; accustomed to the admiring gazes of others, he expended considerable energy simply absorbing them. Such is often the price of success in any pro-fession; with performers the risks are magnified. Dependent on the approval of others, almost as frightened of offending as of losing his own gifts, Olivier became the ultimate actor, his vulnerabilities and his ego matching his apparently limitless talent. And from this complex sprang a concomitant need to control, to supersede, to appear better and nobler than any other player. 'Of course he was a great actor,' Hall reflected later, 'but I do not think he was a genius administrator.' Hall was on the mark. Olivier had admitted his failures as a manager at the St James's, and his successes at the National were perhaps out of all proportion to his natural abilities. Coping with appalling political circumstances, wavering financial support and uncertain budgets, wretched compensation (and, since 1967, health to match), Olivier actually fared amazingly well in his position. His glamour and occasional appearances, Tynan's counsel and the sheer good fortune of having colleagues like Gaskill, Dexter and Blakemore were certainly factors contributing to the significant achievements of his reign – an era far more successful, in the long run, than his six years at the helm of the Old Vic. But it may reasonably be asked just how much can be required of a man: had he better skills as literary judge, business executive or manager, he may not have been a great and intuitive actor.

Olivier's craftsmanlike intelligence was extremely shrewd, and he had a perfectly pitched sense of what was right on the stage, but many who worked with him had the equivocal feelings one has for a powerful leader – 'one who, in his case,' as Miller said,

> through the force of his personality and the greatness of his talent could take on the subjective role of a father. The result was that many of us felt both enormous sentiments of love, of longing to be approved by him, and patricidal feelings at the same time. On a day he said 'That's very good' about something and smiled, a glow would extend over one's life for the next three weeks. At the same time, we knew he could be selfish, scheming and treacherous – but on a grand scale,

and never with vulgarity. He was fearful, and this led him to be envious and sometimes imperial.

Indeed, to hear 'Dear Boy', or 'Precious friend' in a delicate conversation with Olivier could be to feel more than a hint of sarcasm. But none of these contradictions justified the treatment meted to Olivier by the board of the institution to which he had completely dedicated himself.

At exactly this awkward and wounding time, as he turned sixty-five, Olivier received his highest single fee to date ($200,000) for appearing opposite Michael Caine in the film of Anthony Shaffer's thriller play *Sleuth*, directed by Joseph L. Mankiewicz that spring and early summer at Pinewood. At the outset there was trouble, for Olivier could not remember even four lines of dialogue. Otherwise there was no mental dysfunction apparent, and there was considerable dismay until the cause of short-term memory loss was determined to be the quantities of Valium which Olivier had been taking for almost two years. 'For God's sake, stop the pills!' Caine implored during rehearsals; Olivier did, and within days all was well.

His co-star was a genial and welcome ally. ('You can call me Lord Olivier the first day,' he told Caine. 'It's to be Larry after that.') 'I wouldn't have liked to take him on in the theatre,' Caine observed later, 'but after a few days working together I said, "Look, Larry, there's no way I can override you, but I'm not going to back off, either."' Olivier agreed that was a fine approach – and the next day, proving he could match the energy of his thirty-nine-year-old acting partner, attacked a highly dramatic confrontational scene 'like a whirl-wind', Caine said.

> He overwhelmed me! It was frightening the way he bore down on me – and just kept coming! He was like a force of nature. Suddenly he was this other person, this young performer showing his mettle, and I realised that was what all the risks and danger were about. But I also had to stop the scene and barter a few minutes to pull myself together. From that moment on I decided I had to fight him to a draw and not yield, rather than let him have a runaway victory with the picture.

This tension, of course, gave the film a bite and a suspense quite beyond Shaffer's ingeniously concocted plot. *Sleuth* energised Olivier (and earned him an Oscar nomination), and after a family holiday on Corfu he pitched himself happily into the studio taping of *Long Day's Journey into Night* and the narration of a twenty-six-part television epic, *The World at War*, on which he worked intermittently through early 1973.

But Olivier was still divided in his feelings about retirement during the supposed time of shared responsibilities, as Peter Hall's diary for 1973 records. In early January, Olivier was exhausted and ready to step down, but on the twenty-second he was not sure that he would leave as arranged the following autumn. Nine days later he changed his mind again, but throughout February he vacillated. 'It's very difficult to know what motivates Larry's vacillations,' Hall recorded on 26 February. 'Certainly in some cases – and this is one of them – a Machiavellian love of intrigue. He loves being naughty.'

Olivier's mischievous fluctuation was perhaps mostly based on fear. 'He was an artist, and temperamental as all artists are,' recalled John Goodwin, formerly Olivier's press associate at the Old Vic and later head of publicity and publications for the Royal Shakespeare Company and then the National.

> He feared that Hall, from a rival company [the RSC], was a personal rival, and it was painful for him to see someone coming to take over just at the moment he'd been waiting and dreaming for. But of course it turned out not to be the moment: there were those awful delays in completing the South Bank buildings, and the longer the delay, the more ill and unfit for administration Olivier became.

To this no one was more sympathetic than Hall himself: 'Talk about the British disease of procrastination! That is what wounded us all, what hurt and confused Larry.' And it aroused in Olivier a virtual paranoia about the intentions of everyone from the board to the architect and builders to administrators new and old to the least experienced player in the company. By spring 1973, Olivier gazed warily at everyone around him; it was no wonder that three times that year he changed his mind about playing King Lear.

Finally, Olivier decided to announce that he would resign from the directorship of the National Theatre on 31 October in favour of Hall. But there was still, Hall noted, a curious duality in Olivier's decision: he wished to be seen to be leaving of his own free will, but he also wanted to attract sympathy by appearing to have been pitchforked out of the company. On 13 March, a press conference was called and Olivier made his announcement, simultaneously revealing that Tynan had decided to withdraw from the National during the coming season.

It was indeed a time of endings, none more poignant for Olivier than the death of his old friend and staunch ally Noël Coward at the age of seventy-four that March. It was Coward who had given him the role that helped him so much in 1930, and although their contact had been only sporadic in recent years, Olivier always knew he was never really far away. 'Noëlie' had often come to the National, had supported Larry's every career step and achievement, had sustained him during the darkest days with Vivien, and although he did not seem to like Joan (he thought her bossy and ambitious) he was pleased for Olivier's apparent happiness and enjoyment of his role as father. Whatever the vagaries of the early years, however complex their friendship might have been, there had never been any shadow of guilt or remorse, nor was there anything but the profoundest mutual respect and tender affection. Few theatrical friendships in either Coward's or Olivier's life endured so long and so lovingly; few were so misunderstood by their other friends. When Olivier spoke at Coward's memorial service at St Martin-in-the-Fields, Trafalgar Square, on 24 May, his remarks were punctuated with evident emotion. Because their different schedules placed Olivier and Joan in danger of becoming (in his words) 'like ships that only pass in the night', he was relying more and more on his friends for support. And he felt keenly the loss of one so precious as Coward.

During the summer of 1973, Olivier committed *The Merchant of Venice* to television tape. 'It's a comedy,' he advised the audience in an odd on-camera introduction, 'brimming with different flavours and ingredients, a fairy-tale simplicity. It overflows with bright and dark jewels.'

In July, the Oliviers visited Zeffirelli in Positano, Italy, to discuss his production of Eduardo de Filippo's comedy *Saturday, Sunday, Monday* for them that coming autumn at the National. Zeffirelli came with them back to Brighton, bringing with him truffles, which he knew Olivier loved.

> Without thinking, I referred to them by the Italian word *tartufi*, and Larry instantly picked up on the obvious connotation with Molière's [Tartuffe], the eponymous religious hypocrite of the famous play. Without hesitation, Larry launched into an Italian extravaganza, a sort of Commedia dell'Arte in which all the characters, beginning with the anti-hero Tartuffi, were taken from Italian cooking . . . The story centred around a pretty maiden called Tagliatella with her

maid, Pastatina. Sweet little Tagliatella was the daughter of old man Panettone and oh, what trouble they had with their lovesick servants – Risotto, Tortellino and Spaghetto. Further complications were provided by a Neapolitan doctor, Maccherone, and the priest Don Raviolo . . . I proposed the arrival of three foreign suitors: Le Comte de Foie Gras, Lord Salmon and Prince Kaviar – which Larry seized upon with relish, because he could now add three strong foreign accents to the mix.

Another time, Zeffirelli witnessed an equally amusing moment with a more ominous subtext. Olivier was a prodigious drinker, 'much to Joan's irritation', Zeffirelli observed. This became, one evening, the cue for a new role – 'the poet of the whisky bottle'.

'Shall I have just a little of this splendid amber fluid, this nectar of the gods? But who could say no to the tiniest splash, the smallest tear?' Olivier knelt before Joan: 'My lady, will you grant me the smallest taste, a mere nothing?' He lifted a bottle of soda water: 'But what is this? The tiniest little fizz, a sparkle to add to my golden glass.' Finally, Joan (whose permission Olivier seemed to need) relented – but moments later there was a loud crash outside, and Zeffirelli's servant rushed in to say Olivier had fallen and was dying. 'Nonsense,' Joan said, not interrupting her game of cards. 'He's just found a new role.' Although Olivier was playing the fall to full melodramatic advantage, he had in fact cut his leg badly.

The Oliviers then spent a quiet summer at their new country home in Ashurst, Sussex, where they tended the garden and enjoyed the swimming pool, and where Olivier – happily slathered with mud – carefully planted hedges and cleaned out the goldfish pond. The pleasant weeks of indolence ended dramatically when, on their return to Brighton in late September, Olivier encountered a burglar who fled through an upper window after punching him in the face. Reluctantly, he contracted the addition of expensive alarms at Royal Crescent.

By that time, Olivier had begun rehearsals in the brief but comically effective role of the Italian grandfather Antonio, master haberdasher and genius prankster in Eduardo de Filippo's *Saturday, Sunday, Monday*; the premiere on 31 October coincided with his last day as director of the National Theatre. At the same time, he was rising at seven each morning to spend four hours learning a twenty-minute speech for his role as a raging Trotskyite revolutionary in *The Party*, by Trevor Griffiths, and he had decided to direct a spring production of J.B. Priestley's *Eden End*, starring Joan.

Olivier undertook the role of Tagg in *The Party* on her recommendation. A verbose exploration of the English leftist response to contemporary French political turbulence, it was perhaps most noteworthy for its introduction of street language to the precincts of the National Theatre. 'This is the first time the word "cunt" has ever been uttered on the stage of the National,' he told Griffiths. 'You're not serious?' the playwright countered. 'Well,' Olivier continued, 'at least as part of the play.'

Olivier had his long, tutorial speech word-perfect at the first rehearsal on 5 November, but thereafter he frequently lost lines – as any actor would, having to cope with such aridities as: '. . . a revolutionary perspective in the possibility of a socialist society and the creation of socialist man – and we must face the combined weight of imperialist expansion, massing behind the most sophisticated technology of destruction and the active opposition of bourgeoisified proletariats . . .'

'When he loses the words,' wrote company member Clive Merrison in his November rehearsal diary, 'he goes purple in the face, hits his brow with a crack, pulls his knees up to his chest, eyebrows squashing together till his eyes disappear. He seems in terrible pain. Can't bear that his memory is not as sharp as it was.' In the case of *The Party*, Olivier should perhaps have been more patient with himself.

He continued in repertory as the Old World grandfather and the New Wave revolutionary, but as 1974 began he felt suddenly fatigued and uncharacteristically old, as he confided to several friends. He was looking forward to his farewell in *The Party* on 21 March, to his withdrawal from the National Theatre company and the beginning of a long holiday. He did not, however, intend this to be his last theatrical performance – although in fact it was to be so. After the curtain call that night, Peter Hall met him backstage. 'He turned and looked at me, horrified. For about a hundredth of a second I saw the natural reaction: "What are *you* doing here? Get off the bloody stage." It was then replaced by the actor's mask, looking surprised, amazed.' Hall led Olivier before the audience: 'I ask you to be upstanding,' he said, and there was a loud and prolonged ovation. Olivier replied in a brief but elaborately filigreed speech, his syntax worthy of Milton. He knelt down and kissed the stage, his sovereign, his great lover, and then – in the theatre where he had heard just such applause for his Hamlet, Henry V, Macbeth and Coriolanus almost forty years earlier – the curtain of the Old Vic slowly descended.

In the unglamorous rehearsal hall, champagne corks popped and Olivier was presented with a farewell gift, an ice-making machine for his home bar. A piano was rolled in and robust, sentimental melodies filled the room – 'Nellie Dean' and 'Mother Kelly's Doorstep' – until Olivier suggested a medley of Noël Coward songs. He crooned 'I'll See You Again' and 'Some Day I'll Find You', and then – yes, the company swore later, Olivier was swallowing hard, stifling a sob – he got through 'If Love Were All', lingering over Coward's gentle self-deprecation:

> But I believe that since my life began
> The most I've had is just
> A talent to amuse.

CHAPTER SIXTEEN

1974–1980

Lady Pitts: What's the matter with you?
Sir Joseph: Death, my dear. The first natural thing
that has happened to me in half a century.

James Bridie, *Daphne Laureola*

The termination of Laurence Olivier's ten-year reign as director of
the National Theatre was formally marked on the evening of 4
April 1974 after the premiere of *Eden End*, a play about a family
gathering and the return of an actress daughter fleeing a broken marriage. Undertaken as a showcase for Joan and to honour J.B. Priestley's
eightieth birthday, it was imbued by Olivier with a Chekhovian wistful-
ness paralleling his own mood that season. A slight work, it nonetheless
received his usual attention to every detail, and he even tracked Priestley down in a Yorkshire pub to ask whether a woman in provincial
England would have used lipstick or extra rouge in 1912. After the first
night, Peter Hall and the National company presented him with a silver
model of the forthcoming Olivier Theatre, under construction at the
South Bank Arts Centre.

But Olivier was not idle for long. George Cukor, who had directed
Katharine Hepburn in nine films, sent her a teleplay called *Love Among
the Ruins*, by James Costigan. Realising the male lead was perfect for
Olivier, Hepburn sent Cukor to London with the script. Olivier read
it and Cukor cagily asked, 'Larry, what would you think of Kate as
your leading lady?' An inspired idea, Olivier replied. ('I don't know
what we'd have done if Larry had turned it down!' Hepburn said later.)
Set in 1911, *Love Among the Ruins* concerns a once-great actress
(Hepburn) who asks a famous lawyer (Olivier) to defend her in a
false charge of breach of promise, filed by a young adventurer. As it
happened, the elderly couple had met many years before and had a

brief romance – a fact which, to his dismay, she has forgotten. In a trial both touching and funny, he wins the suit on her behalf, and there follows the predictable romantic finale.

Gossamer-thin, the story – which swept the American Emmy awards the following year – depended entirely on Hepburn and Olivier (then sixty-five and sixty-seven), who elevated the film beyond its material. 'I was working with two bums, Hepburn and Olivier,' Cukor quipped, 'but in spite of them I did all right.' So did Olivier, who performed with comic agility, leaping up and down staircases, gazing with fearful hesitation at his long lost love, and conveying a kind of entreating emotion with unstudied humility.

When the filming at Pinewood was complete that July, the Oliviers again visited Zeffirelli in Italy. But their relaxation was punctuated by disturbing omens, for Olivier noticed strange physical changes. One afternoon, without warning, his back ached dreadfully, and then his legs almost buckled under him. He rested and appeared better next morning, although he had a slight fever, and while relaxing in a bath he noticed red patches on his elbows and knees – something in his diet, he assumed. But soon the skin eruptions spread to his neck, forehead and eyelids.

By the time he was back in Brighton that September, the rashes were so severe that he consulted the dermatologist Dr Pat Hall-Smith. During the examination Olivier could scarcely raise his arms above his shoulders, and rising from bed or a chair was painfully difficult. On 8 October, when he went backstage to congratulate Joan after she re-opened at the Queen's Theatre in a revival of *Saturday, Sunday, Monday*, Olivier refused to pose for photographs: there were large red lesions all over his face and every step was an effort.

Throughout this time, Olivier affected a brave but somewhat unrealistic attitude, convinced that he was having an allergic reaction – although to what he could not hazard a guess. But Hall-Smith, suspecting a collagen vascular disease akin to muscular dystrophy, referred Olivier to Dr Joanna Sheldon, a respected diagnostician. After laboratory tests, a muscle biopsy, and a thorough examination of the ulcerations on his legs, the alarming weakness of his neck muscles and the exquisite pain in his hands, Sheldon informed Olivier that he was suffering from acute dermatomyositis, a grave connective tissue disease. Atrophy and loss of muscle use are the usual results – sometimes permanent, although infrequently with remission – but the entire body can be so dramatically affected that not only mobility but also swallowing and breathing are compromised. Even when responsive to treatment, the disease usually recurs and is often fatal following progressive muscle deterioration, malnutrition and respiratory failure.

A rare disease, dermatomyositis and its causes were not well defined in 1974. Between five and nine people per million develop it in the United States, where exhaustive studies were conducted in 1989. The results, published in *The Journal of Rheumatology*, confirmed three contributing factors significant in the emergence of the condition, each of which correlated with Olivier's case: a previous malignancy (his prostate cancer), habitual heavy muscular exertion (his thrice-weekly weight-lifting) and recent emotional stress (the last eighteen months at the National Theatre).

By mid-October Olivier was in the Royal Sussex County Hospital, Brighton, for aggressive treatment – eighty milligrams daily of the corticosteroid Prednisone to counteract his system's massive inflammation. The side effects were particularly unpleasant: swelling of the legs, a puffy face, severe thirst and, most upsetting, mood changes and hallucinations. Eventually Olivier was totally paralysed and inarticulate, fed through a nasogastric tube and with no energy to respond even to the gentlest touch. When at last his respiration became dangerously compromised, death seemed very near indeed. 'It was really a kind of total nervous breakdown,' Joan said a few years later. 'It was as though he had given up, and there didn't appear very much reason to fight.'

He was confined to the hospital for sixteen weeks and then began a course of intensive physiotherapy. Like a stroke victim, Olivier had to relearn the simplest movements; it was painfully exhausting and humiliating for so active and proud a man to find he could not walk, feed himself, sit or stand by sheer force of will. Anyone would find such a condition alarming and burdensome, but for the independent and ever-active Olivier it was intolerable. Yet he endured both disease and therapy with a stoic calm, and although he slowly recovered there were permanent residual effects. Worst of all was the acute pain caused by the slightest touch on his skin. Fearful of advancing age and its attendant loss of powers, Olivier now faced an illness that excluded him from the most basic human contact, even a handshake.

In his memoirs, Olivier referred to his lifetime problem of premature ejaculation. Doubtless in the belief that he was confessing all with a modern star's frankness, this candid detail (like his reference to the time he tried 'fucking [his] love [for Vivien] back into existence') revealed perhaps more than he intended. For the truth of the matter was that, after the first rush of endorsing passion from Vivien, Olivier had throughout his adult life placed no great premium on physical intimacy precisely because he was so rarely emotionally accessible to anyone. This of course had been Vivien's constant complaint – that intimacy and companionship (not to say sex) were clearly subordinate to his career. And his mistresses attested that Olivier was an uninvolved lover, his manner perfunctory, almost ritualistic. Premature ejaculation (like the manifestations of transient frigidity in women) often betokens not real passion but in fact its opposite – a subconscious revulsion towards sex as something to be got through, sometimes even withstood, at best an attempt at affection and at worst an exertion of power which a man would really prefer to express otherwise. Olivier's detachment was perhaps unsurprising in a man who had become a genius at role-playing – especially as the exponent of men larger than life in their nobilities, their needs and their cruelties.

Actors often wonder, as they assume one personality after another, just which might be their own; library shelves groan under the weight of theatrical autobiographies redolent of self-doubt, of performers confused about their identities. Having devoted a lifetime to the convincing assumption of different manly personae, Olivier had in a way become a man ever more remote even from himself, and his life – so envied in so many ways – now had a strangely apt medical condition.

His emotional history in fact reveals a pattern of timidity, insecurity and withdrawal he constantly sought to overcome onstage. After an awkward boyhood, the shock of his mother's death and the confrontation of his 'sissy' self in school years, he became an apprentice actor – but he remained long ill at ease in real society, notwithstanding, for example, the loving tutelage of Noël Coward. Subsequently, marriage to Jill Esmond had confirmed neither his masculine attractiveness nor his social acceptability, and only the surprise and ardour of his relationship with Vivien Leigh made possible a 'baronial period' – an era in which he still never felt entirely comfortable. Then, from the 1960s, Olivier was surrounded mostly by younger colleagues who regarded him with something like reverence. This pattern created a fantastic accident, the canonisation of artifice. 'He says he's not quite sure when he's acting and when he's not,' Joan remarked, 'and I can't always tell. It's a bit eerie, really.'

Had he not fallen ill and been forced to relinquish forever the theatre – his one great love – Olivier would perhaps have never perceived that there was a gaping emptiness in his life, an absence of constancy and continuity in his relationships. Sovereign, independent, supreme and unwittingly isolated, he had used work as a refuge, assuming a genius for versatility as a way of searching for his elusive identity. In this regard, his two pivotal roles were Henry V and Archie Rice, the heroic lord mustering the troops and the cowardly man failing his family – and this pair synthesised his personality and informed his relationships. Alternately a grandiloquent speaker and (as Coward called him) a 'doctor of four letters', Olivier was throughout his life poised between extremes of self-awareness. This at least partially explains, too, why three other royals – Oedipus, Richard and Hamlet – were so compelling, for in them were all the explosions of anger, rage and cruelty he never allowed himself to confront in real life and to integrate within his own personality: rage at his mother's death and his father's remoteness and remarriage; anger at his bisexual inclinations; calculated proprietariness about his primacy onstage which, he intuited, removed him from so much ordinary human communion. Thus it was that the inability to be physically touched – caused by the dermatomyositis – became almost a sign of the defensive spiritual habit of a lifetime.

The shy, spindly child abandoned by the death of one parent and by the virtual rejection of the other explored throughout his life a myriad of identities. Acting had given him purpose and direction. But it had also confused him, for his primary reality was the thoughts, words, actions of characters, and because he was the quintessential actor, Olivier believed that art was his life: 'Real people are artists,' he had said in 1942. 'Ordinary people aren't.' That was, of course, the enthusiast speaking, the uncritical schoolboy still lurking in the Air Arm uniform. Human relations and emotions, access to wonder and mystery, the tangle of possibilities: all this was available to him only through plays he saw, studied, acted in. But little of that human depth was filtered through this artifice, and every intimate relationship was marked by loss, deception, frustration or deliberate termination. Gradually estranged from trust and intimacy, he depended only on the current disguise, the next role, the freshly designed face. 'In my heart of hearts,' he admitted late in life, 'I only know that I am far from sure when I am acting and when I am not, or, should I more frankly put it, when I am lying and when I am not . . . I suppose to some degree I am liberated only when acting.'

And herein lies the fundamental poignant paradox of the creative man's destiny, for perhaps only if he has not dealt with all this in life can he give it in art; only because so much was dimly perceived and unexorcised could so much passion be brought to his craft. 'I believe in the theatre,' he said, 'because it is the most ready and acceptable glamoriser of thought . . . An actor must be a great understander, either by intuition, observation or both – and that puts him on the level with a doctor, a priest or a philosopher.' Born a commoner, Olivier had become an aristocrat by fame, a sub-royal by acclaim, and eventually a lord in fact; now at last he would find authentic nobility in the annealing process of pain and the attendance of devotion rather than adulation. Need would betoken not weakness but strength.

The neediness he had long experienced was now at last to be winnowed, challenged, exploited for more than mere professional accomplishment. Henceforth, there was a real shift in his character, marked by the change in his approach to role-playing and to life. Prior to this devastating illness, his needs were expressed in his art, as he moved from outward details to inward discovery, his personality shaped by the roles. After his recovery, his needs were expressed in his life, as he moved from fresh internal perceptions outwards, his own character shaping the roles – and more than the roles, shaping his life and relationships. He never again acted on the stage. But now there was indeed a fresh beginning, the emergence of a real, hitherto suppressed component in his personality. He laid aside the elaborate make-up of great roles and began to be – fully and with true grandeur – only himself.

That year, his mysterious, habitual resilience rallied him, and just as he had conquered prostate cancer, pneumonia and blood clots, he slowly rebounded. When a portion of the medication was reduced and replaced by an immunosuppressive agent (Imuran), the adverse psychological and emotional side effects diminished, but he suffered reactions to this drug too; and since he was forced to take some combinations of these drugs for the rest of his life, he suffered chronic weakness and an alarming tendency to bruise and to bleed easily. He spent the first half of 1975 in recovery, submitting to physical therapy, hydrotherapy and vigorous massages as well as a constant adjustment of his medication. 'We all thought he would never work again,' Laurence Evans recalled, 'so we put out the fiction that when he was better he would direct opera, which had been a lifelong interest. We gave him tapes and scores, and he bravely spoke of directing at Covent Garden.' From February until the summer, Olivier was mostly at home in Brighton or at the country house in Ashurst, Sussex (an amalgam of cottages called the Malthouse, after its original function). His once rich baritone voice was now only a high, thin whisper; he had lost thirty pounds, he walked slowly and tired easily, and his few visitors were shocked at the alarmingly reduced scale of the man who had always projected limitless energy.

But he set himself goals in his pool: not content with mere paddling or passive exercise, Olivier tried a few laps in April, and one evening not long after his sixty-eighth birthday his astonished nurse found him swimming ten lengths. He was soon trimming the hedges, joining the gardener in planting a topiary in the shape of Chekhov's Three Sisters, telephoning Laurence Evans to talk about movie work – and generally undertaking a most strenuous recuperation, although every task was painful. Never pleading for sympathy and rarely complaining, he insisted he would return to as full a life as possible.

Joan's brother David Plowright, managing director of Granada Television, had thoughtfully suggested that when he recovered Olivier might consider coming up to the studios in Manchester and producing a few plays for television. And so, during that spring and summer of 1975, Olivier seized the chance much before anyone expected. He met several times weekly with the Granada producer Derek Granger, and soon they had decided on half a dozen plays to be produced over the next two years.

Then, at the end of July, he announced he wanted to go to London to see John Schlesinger's production of Shaw's *Heartbreak House*. Olivier's gait was still tentative and his voice was strained and pinched; but Peter Hall found him alert, humorous, with a mind dancing from subject to subject. Olivier also requested a tour of the National's buildings-in-progress: 'It must have taken great courage on Larry's part,' according to Hall, 'to come and see everybody after a year, his appearance so different, feeling so frail, and being the man outside this wonderful place that he has created.' His courage had practical manifestations, too, for he had decided to be no merely nominal producer of television plays. Olivier made two quick journeys to America to sell the idea of 'Best Plays of the Year' to networks and to woo movie and stage stars to join him; he pored over costume and set designs, met with composers, learned the latest television camera techniques, began to hold acting auditions and spent many hours cutting the play texts and planning shots for the small screen. Stage performing was a thing of the past, but Laurence Olivier had no time for nostalgic pining. He intended once again to be a man of his era, and if younger people made a financial killing (and even an occasional artistic success) in television, he could too.*

With Antonio in *Saturday, Sunday, Monday* (one of the plays and roles he chose for Granada), he could say, 'They are waiting for me to go, but I am not going to die!' Quite the contrary: 'I have to act to breathe. I can only stop if He up there smites me.' That turned out to be a groundless fear.

In September, John Schlesinger (an associate director at the National as well as a film director) and the American producer Robert Evans rang Olivier to ask if he would consider playing the supporting role of the Nazi arch-villain Dr Szell in their forthcoming production of the thriller *Marathon Man*. Olivier refused, Schlesinger recalled, but eventually he did come to lunch, protesting he would have only coffee.

> He was terribly enfeebled, and hearing his very high old man's voice I realised it would be impossible for him to work with us. But he wanted to know the story, so I went through it with him. His eyes sparkled at the prospect of playing this monstrous villain, and he became very theatrical and a bit camp, insisting how much fun it would be to act this wicked man. And there, right before my eyes, I saw the old actor coming to life, making a recovery!

To everyone's surprise, Olivier was able to pass the medical insurance examination for the film, and production was scheduled to begin late that autumn in New York. But before signing the contract with Paramount for *Marathon Man*, Olivier played a small role as Sherlock Holmes's nemesis Professor Moriarty in *The Seven-per-cent Solution* (on which he worked two days, for $75,000). 'I wanted to be sure,' he said at the time, 'that I would not burst into tears and run crying off the set, or that I would not be able to memorise one line. I was grateful to be in that movie – to take little tiny baby steps.' In his scene, Olivier looks dreadful, but he played to perfection the wily Moriarty, all hypocritical befuddlement. He then proudly signed on for *Marathon Man* and flew to New York in November after admitting that his stage-acting

---

* Laurence Evans negotiated for Olivier to receive an annual salary of £25,000 as producer of the plays, an additional £12,500 as an American distribution fee, and acting and producing fees totalling almost half a million dollars. For eight brief BBC radio narrations between 1969 and 1977 (honouring entertainment personalities), he received the token sum total of £115.

days were indeed over: 'That demands a particular energy I don't have any more, whereas films and the telly require concentration for shorter periods of time.'

Olivier was travelling alone (Joan was acting onstage in London), but he was welcomed by old New York friends. On Thanksgiving Day, 27 November, Garson Kanin and Ruth Gordon feared that supper at Sardi's and attendance at a Broadway musical revue might exhaust him, but afterwards Olivier took them and the cast on to the 21 Club for drinks. There were also visits to Douglas Fairbanks, Jr., Lillian Hellman and Irene Selznick, among others – and Bette Midler made a great impression on Olivier, who loved her brassy bawdiness and satiric vulgarity. For Olivier, America had produced nothing so reminiscent of British music hall as Midler.

Filming *Marathon Man* outdoors on West Forty-Seventh Street, Olivier had to cope with gathering crowds, the autumn chill and the normal delays and retakes of movie-making. Lotta Palfi-Andor, the German actress who played a woman who recognises Szell in public, recalled that between takes Olivier sat quietly in the Gotham Book Mart, breathing with difficulty, feeling unwell and eager to have someone nearby. But when they had to go outside for filming, he was transformed, she remembered. He simply sprang to life, to everyone's amazement.

With Schlesinger, Olivier was like a grateful apprentice. 'When I had to tell him he was really overdoing it with some lines, I said, "Larry, could we – perhaps – make that line more intimate?" And he replied, "You mean cut the ham fat, dear boy? You know, a lot of people don't tell me these things because I have this reputation of being so perfect I don't need direction – but I do, I do, just like the next man."' As the production moved to Los Angeles (so that Olivier would not have to endure the winter in New York) he was, as Schlesinger put it, 'an old lion recovering more and more each day'.

Marathon Man remains most terrifying during Olivier's few scenes, playing an expert torturer still capable of monstrous evil, everyone's nightmare of an ice-cruel sadistic dentist. Trying to pry information from the hero (Dustin Hoffman), he repeatedly asks a code question, 'Is it safe?' – each time in a different tone and with differing emphases. This sequence caused the only moment of awkwardness between Olivier and Hoffman. In an intense effort for realism, the younger actor had ingested various mood-altering substances to appear exhausted, dazed and in pain, 'But that gave us trouble with the close-ups and we had a lot of retakes', Schlesinger remembered – a situation that inspired Olivier's exasperated comment, 'Oh, gracious, why doesn't the dear boy just act?!' As for his own performance, only his attempt at a German accent failed, emerging part Irish, part Hispanic; production was delayed when much of Olivier's dialogue had to be redone.

In Los Angeles, Olivier preferred to stay with his American movie agent Ben Benjamin (Laurence Evans's colleague). At work and in social situations, his skin was still so sensitive he had to remind people not even to shake his hand, and until Schlesinger asked for him on the set he sat alone, almost doubled over with pain.

Returning to England early in 1976, Olivier worked daily preparing the television plays, and despite continuing weakness, he stood on the roof of a Manchester office building on a cold late-winter morning to direct the background for the credit sequence – the Granada Television tower and the sunset over Salford, on which the words 'Laurence Olivier Presents' would be superimposed. He worked as he had at the Old Vic in the 1940s, as manager of LOP in the 1950s and at the National thereafter – taking control of everything, selecting the credit music (from Handel), supervising the graphics, meeting with his old friend Beatrice Dawson (who had designed costumes for his films and whom he engaged for the series), ignoring his own comfort and treating illness like a performance challenge, a duel to be won.

In March 1976, when the Lyttelton – the first of the National's three new theatres – opened at last on the South Bank, Olivier was absent from the celebrity gathering. This was not because of pique, however: he was in Tunisia for a week, appearing in the small role of Nicodemus for the television mini-series *Jesus of Nazareth*. Director Franco Zeffirelli was alarmed at his pallor and weakness, and when they gathered to see the rushes, Olivier pointed out how much he had suffered for each shot. 'Of course,' he added with a theatrical sigh, 'nothing compared to the sufferings of Our Lord.' Anthony Quinn (who played Caiaphas) recalled that Olivier's legs were quite painful and deformed, and sometimes it was impossible for him to walk. At a restaurant one evening, Olivier confided how lonely and unhappy he felt, despite all the work offers, and Quinn was surprised that he was travelling alone in so frail a condition.

Olivier felt no better back in Manchester in April, but he went gamely on, appearing as the effete designer Harry Kane in Harold Pinter's *The Collection*, his first television production. Olivier selected the one-hour play for its verbal obliqueness and its difference from standard video fare, as his co-star Helen Mirren recalled. Still the quintessential actor-manager, he liked being in charge of everything from camera setups to dubbing.

To everyone he was more warmly cordial, more grateful for professional cooperation and personal kindness than he had ever been in his life. There was no air of the grand old man of the theatre about him; he was simply a journeyman glad of a job and a welcome from colleagues. When Natalie Wood and her husband Robert Wagner arrived in London on 19 May to appear with him as Maggie and Brick in a television version of Tennessee Williams's *Cat on a Hot Tin Roof*, Olivier met them at Heathrow at six in the morning, honoured them later at a formal dinner and generally acted as expansively as Big Daddy, the role he chose for himself in that play. But according to Maureen Stapleton (Big Mama in the production), memory lapses made rehearsals a trial for him; a veteran of several Williams dramas, she was asked by Olivier to coach him in the fine points of a Southern accent.

Towards the end of these rehearsals he flew to Amsterdam to play a cameo role as a Dutch doctor in the film *A Bridge Too Far* (for which he received $200,000 for six days of work), returning via Paris to dub unclear lines for *Marathon Man*. Back in Manchester for the shooting of *Cat*, he had constant trouble with the dialogue; the finished performance, however, was relaxed and flawless, his Southern inflections perfectly tailored to the character's blustering. As the dying family tyrant who rages about 'pleasure with women – I'm gonna find a woman and cover her in minks, strip her naked and smother her in diamonds', he was triumphantly perverse.

After a summer holiday with his family in California (where they rented Carol Burnett's Malibu beach house), Olivier returned to London more than ever eager to work, still mostly ignoring his intractable pain. It was ironic that films and television, the media he had once held in such frank contempt, were now his refuge, providing 'a reason for keeping on', as he said. But Olivier also relished the collegial atmosphere of his work; in the theatre, after all, one can be solitary all day, act with others briefly at night, then disperse. But now he spent the daytime with casts and crews, and he was so eager for companionship that he prolonged the bond by inviting actors and directors to drinks and dinner. With old friends like Laurence and Mary Evans and new friends like Robert Wagner and Natalie Wood, open displays of friendly affection became precious for him as never before, however physically painful on his skin, however long stifled beneath the persona of the theatre's great man. It was as if the disease had become an object lesson he had well learned, bestowing an appreciation of the grace of human contact. He learned a new kind of strength in accepting ministration.

In October, the Olivier Theatre at the National was at last opened. The staff tried to involve him in the events and activities of that month, recalled John Goodwin, but without success. Resistant as much because of his mixed emotions as because of frailty, Olivier was notably absent until the formal opening, which was attended by the Queen. For that celebration, he prepared with dogged determination. Asked to speak briefly from the stage he had once longed to act on, he now had to content himself with a written speech, meticulously copied onto small cards. But when he learned that Peter Hall was to speak from memory, he told Diana Boddington (his stage manager since 1944), 'I've got to do it that way, too. I'll bloody well memorise.' On the morning of 25 October, a stooped, nearly bald figure slipped into the Olivier Theatre and asked the workers please to take seats for a couple of moments. And there, in the presence of Boddington and a few startled others, Lord Olivier rehearsed his brief speech of thanks.

As the gala formal opening ceremonies began that evening, it was uncertain whether Olivier's stamina would enable him to attend, much less step onto the stage. 'I felt like a ghost,' he said a few weeks later about that evening, but there was nothing spectral about his behaviour. He insisted that Joan help him into their hired lavender limousine, and braving a torrential downpour he joined the crowd awaiting the Queen's arrival. Alternately flushed and livid from the after-effects of steroids, Olivier seemed desperately frail and distracted, but he rose to the occasion, standing onstage while the applause continued for a full five minutes after his slightly breathless remarks.

Olivier's speech preceded a revival of Goldoni's *Il Campiello* (a critical and popular disaster, as it happened), but as Peter Hall noted, it was difficult for any play to follow the appearance of the National's first artistic director. Thereafter, Olivier attended the theatre named for him only two or three times – never very cheerfully – and once when Michael Caine met him in the foyer and jokingly asked if Olivier had to pay for tickets, he replied angrily: 'Yes, I fucking *do* have to pay!' ('I'm reputed to have the language of a below-decks sailor,' he admitted at the time. 'I'm not very proud of it but it's a habit, I'm afraid.')

Back in Manchester, he directed for Granada Television Stanley Houghton's *Hindle Wakes*, in which his old friend and mentor Sybil

Thorndike had starred in 1912. She had died that June, and during production Olivier told warm anecdotes about her – as he did of other fellow-actors whose deaths greatly affected him that year: Edith Evans, Margaret Leighton, Roger Livesey and his old flame from the 1925 *Henry VIII*, Angela Baddeley.

The new year 1977 began with three appearances in the teleplays he produced: as the weary, whiskied Doc to Joanne Woodward's Lola in William Inge's *Come Back, Little Sheba;** as Sir Joseph Pitts, a minor character opposite Joan as his wife in *Daphne Laureola* (offered to honour Edith Evans, the star of his 1949 production); and as the old haberdasher passing through *Saturday, Sunday, Monday*, for which – despite the Neapolitan wisps of hair and the Italianate gestures – Olivier could still not master any accent other than American. The conclusion of the last coincided with his birthday in May.

That summer, before she began rehearsals for the lead in another Eduardo de Filippo comedy set to open that autumn (*Filumena*), Joan departed for an Italian holiday. Olivier, however, had been approached by the American film director Daniel Petrie, who convinced him to accept the role of a vulgar automobile tycoon in *The Betsy*, to be produced in Detroit, Newport (Rhode Island) and Los Angeles that July and August. (His fee for eight weeks was his highest to date, $400,000.)

The director's twenty-three-year-old son Donald Petrie (who also later became a film-maker) was Olivier's driver during the production. Despite the agony in his hands, the constant bruises caused by the residual effects of dermatomyositis and the recurrence of a clot in his leg, Olivier usually asked Donald Petrie or his father (or both) to dinner, working on his American accent while relishing a steak and a bottle of wine – and often reminiscing about Vivien. Early in production, he marked the tenth anniversary of her death, and speaking of her he seemed to need reassurance that he had not been a bad boy, as Daniel Petrie recalled. Saddened by his own memories, Olivier spoke of her as if she were still alive, still the Glory Girl of his life.

As filming progressed, it was fortunate that Olivier was to play many of his scenes in a wheelchair. But not the flashbacks to the character's forties: 'Just when we needed him to walk,' according to the director, 'his leg gave him trouble. He slept when he could between scenes, and when I went to awaken him he roused himself with great difficulty, struggling to stand and proceeding slowly for his mark. But when I

---

* The Granada deal guaranteed NBC at least two American plays.

called "Action!" it was as if a switch had been thrown – magic! – he was alive, fully in character, the energy was there!'

From this point in his life, Olivier actively sought companionship and avoided solitude – a common trait among the elderly, but especially poignant in his case. The Petries, among others, knew he invariably wanted to prolong the evening, to order another glass of Chivas regardless of the late hour and an early call next morning. And unlike the social splendour of the days with Vivien, he forsook the demands of formal etiquette in favour of easy relaxation and ordinary entertainments. When Donald Petrie asked what diversion he might enjoy in Los Angeles, Olivier replied, 'More than anything else, I'm dying to see *Star Wars*. That little Carrie Fisher is a darling – she just acted with me in *Come Back, Little Sheba*.' Meanwhile, to his own performance as the tyrannical industrial emperor in *The Betsy* he brought a spirit that came perilously close to high camp. He had regained much of his vocal timbre and gave a menacingly comic tone to lines like, 'Joke with me, young man, and I'll break ya in half!' Amid the glamorised vulgarities of the story, he offered a Grosse Pointe Godfather who refuses to yield power even when old and frail.

Olivier himself was just as stubborn, and although the filming exhausted him he returned to London and begged Evans for another assignment. As it happened, producer Robert Fryer and director Franklin Schaffner had sent a script based on Ira Levin's novel *The Boys from Brazil*, in which there was a role ideal for Olivier after his menacing villain in *Marathon Man*: the Viennese Jewish Nazi-hunter modelled on Simon Wiesenthal who tracks down the notorious Dr Mengele (played against type by Gregory Peck). The picture, for which Olivier received $725,000, was to be filmed that autumn in Vienna, but just before departure – on the eve of Joan's opening night in *Filumena* (which was to occupy her for almost two years) – Olivier collapsed at home in Brighton and was admitted to the hospital in acute pain with an attack of kidney stones.

Released from hospital in December, he felt dreadfully ill and looked wretched, recalled Laurence Evans, who accompanied him for the first day's shooting in Vienna. But after a lifetime of constant activity, Olivier knew nothing else to do. Additionally, he was a lonely man who for the last years was living more and more separately from his wife, her work and her friendships.

And so, frailer than ever, he pitched himself into *The Boys from Brazil*, his gaunt and pained expressions giving added poignancy to the role. Throughout production, he was appallingly unwell, according to Fryer, but there was never a complaint and he was always letter perfect. The final climactic scene – a hand-to-hand combat with Peck – seemed certain to be beyond him: wounded by Mengele's gunshot, Lieberman was to turn, stagger and collapse near a couch.

'You can drop here, Larry, on the sofa,' Schaffner said. 'But wouldn't it be better,' Olivier replied, 'if I wheel around and then fall against the couch, perhaps on the hand-rest, and then fall off the couch onto the floor?' Schaffner, fearing for Olivier, said that was unnecessary. 'But it would be better, Frank,' Olivier insisted. 'I can do it. Don't worry, I can do it.' After rehearsals and several takes for various camera angles, Olivier finished the scene of the fierce wrestling match with Peck, who tried not to grasp his partner's hands, nor to put too much of his weight on Olivier's sensitive skin. 'Nice faking,' Peck said supportively, helping him to his feet. 'Just like Tristan and Isolde,' whispered Olivier in mock flirtation. And when Schaffner tried to ease his scenes, Olivier said, 'Nonsense, you're worrying too much about me.'

Olivier's Viennese accent was coached by Marcella Markham, an actress who had often helped colleagues with diction and dialects. He insisted on her presence throughout production – not only in the studio, where he turned to her for approval and advice after each scene, but also for dinner and at production meetings. As filming continued into early 1978, it seemed to Markham that Laurence Olivier was in love with her. He made no importunate advances, but he ordered champagne lunches for the two of them under the pretext of working on his accent, and at these times he spoke of the grand passion he had once had with Vivien, and how he identified champagne with their life together. To Markham he seemed a man famished for affection.

Her suspicions about Olivier's feelings were confirmed when the production moved to London in February 1978. He arrived at her home one afternoon with a gardenia, at the bottom of which he had placed a small box from Harrod's and a note describing the enclosed gift as token of his love and gratitude. The box contained a diamond-studded ring in the shape of a four-leaf clover, a gift far more extravagant than he had given to anyone since the time of Vivien. He showed her a photo of himself, taken not long before, and pointed to his unhappy expression in it. 'Were it not for you, my dear,' he whispered, 'I would still feel this way.'

This was a difficult situation for Markham, who did not return his romantic sentiments, and when she told him of her imminent engagement, Olivier was visibly angry. 'Well,' he said, 'it'll all be over in a few years – sex, the relationship, everything. It doesn't last – why do you bother?' Markham had the impression he was suffering a loneliness more lacerating than any illness. He loved his children deeply and often spoke proudly of them, she recalled, but after all they were so very much younger and had lives of their own, and he felt a terrific distance from their experience. And as Laurence Evans and others confirmed, he was indeed lonely, which is why he was thrilled when his sixteen-year-old son Richard came to stay with him in Vienna during his school holidays, which coincided with filming *The Boys from Brazil*.

No one was surprised as Olivier continued to accept movie roles in 1978 – first as a dotty old codger encouraging teenage love in George Roy Hill's *A Little Romance*, filmed that summer in Paris, Venice and Verona. Off-camera, he had to have his legs constantly massaged because of the recurring thrombosis, but he insisted on doing his own stunts – a downhill race on a bicycle, for example, which had everyone breathless – and at the end of a strenuous day's shooting he was always ready for drinks and a night on the town. On such occasions Olivier regaled his colleagues with a fund of bawdy stories, flirted with waitresses and continued to reminisce about life with Vivien.

Then, from September 1978 to February 1979, Olivier accepted an offer of almost a million dollars for the part of Professor van Helsing in John Badham's *Dracula*, filmed in Cornwall and near London, with Frank Langella in the role of the perennial Transylvanian nuisance. 'They criticise me in the papers, asking "Why's he doing such muck?"' he said at the time.

> I'll tell you why: to pay for three children in school, for a family, and their future. But nothing is beneath me if it pays well. I've earned the right to damn well grab whatever I can in the time I've got left. Thank God for the movies. I get a fortune for doing it, which is absolutely what I'm after because I've always overspent in my life.*

Without Marcella Markham, Olivier's Dutch accent was almost as unfortunate as the screenplay ('Vot in de name uff Gott do you tink iss heppenink?'), but he put himself through several punishing scenes, always insisting, Badham remembered, that if any physical exertion were required he intended to do it. Nevertheless, his shooting schedule

---

* That he made the films to support his family Joan later claimed was 'a pure excuse . . . He didn't really care at the end. He just wanted to work.'

had to be arranged so that he worked for only a few hours in the middle of the day, as that was all he could accomplish.

At the weekend, Olivier occasionally visited Laurence and Mary Evans or stayed in a Cornwall guest-house, and when Badham asked why he did not go to Brighton, Olivier quietly replied, 'No, dear boy, Brighton is death.' He was referring not to the city, where he was always comfortable, but to life at home. He and Joan had indeed become, as he had said, like ships simply passing in the night. Later that year, citing the financial pressure of taxes, medical expenses and school fees, he put his house in Royal Crescent on the market, and soon the Oliviers – at Joan's suggestion – moved to a house in St Leonard's Terrace, Chelsea, only a few steps from Durham Cottage.

On 29 March 1979, Olivier, with the Evanses, flew to Los Angeles. Over the years he had received eleven Academy Award nominations (most recently for *Marathon Man* and *The Boys from Brazil*), a special Oscar for *Henry V* and the best actor award for *Hamlet*. At the fifty-first annual celebration on 9 April Cary Grant presented him with an honorary statuette 'for the full body of his work, for the unique achievements of his entire career and his lifetime of contributions to the art of film'. After more than twenty clips of his various roles were screened for the assembled gathering and a worldwide audience exceeding one billion, Olivier slowly walked onto the stage of the Dorothy Chandler Pavilion, his face swollen from steroid injections and bearded for his forthcoming role as Zeus in the hilariously nonsensical *Clash of the Titans*. 'Oh, dear friends,' he began his carefully written and rehearsed speech, laced with his usual byzantine syntax.

> Am I supposed to speak after that? Cary, my dear old friend for many a year – from the earliest years of either of us working in this country [they had met perhaps twice] – thank you for that beautiful citation and the trouble you have taken to make it and for all the warm generosities in it. Mr President and Governors of the Academy, Committee Members, fellows, my very noble and approved good masters [these last seven words were from *Othello*], my colleagues, my friends, my fellow-students. In the great wealth, the great firmament of your nation's generosities, this particular choice may perhaps be found by future generations a trifle eccentric, but the mere fact of it – the prodigal, pure, human kindness of it – must be seen as a beautiful star in that firmament which shines upon me at this moment, dazzling me a little, but filling me with warmth and the

extraordinary elation, the euphoria that happens to so many of us at the first breath of the majestic glow of a new tomorrow. From the top of this moment, in the solace, in the kindly emotion that is charging my soul and my heart at this moment, I thank you for this great gift which lends me such a very splendid part in this, your glorious occasion. Thank you.

As Olivier admitted, his everyday speech was never so formal as the diction he adopted on ceremonial occasions. But his florid rhetoric (and equally turgid writing style) were attempts to present that part of himself that was expected to portray royal status, and perhaps also to compensate for his insecurities as an undereducated man. Speaking as he thought appropriate for a peer, he was personally more comfortable and more natural with simpler, racier language, and it is significant that, once robed and sworn as Baron Olivier, he visited the House of Lords only once. The son of a clergyman, Olivier was at heart always (like his father) an aristocrat *manqué*, the pretender whose dream of the peerage was finally realised and then revealed to him as specious and unrewarding: the real Olivier said 'Call me Larry,' and he meant it.

During that same visit, he also received a lifetime achievement award from Filmex, the Los Angeles Film Festival. There were large and small private parties in his honour (offered by, among others, Robert Wagner and Natalie Wood, George Cukor, Elia Kazan, and Paul Newman and Joanne Woodward) and for two weeks Olivier shone in the adulation of his American colleagues. Back in England, he received $300,000 for a week's work on the mythological epic *Titans*, essentially a special-effects showcase. Nervous and irascible, he fell to intimidating everyone – as if he did not really want to be there, as his co-star Claire Bloom remembered. Considering only the quality of the script, she was probably quite right.

That season, Olivier also spoke irritably and publicly against Kenneth Tynan, who had announced that he intended to write a biography of him. Aware that Tynan meant to disclose hitherto unrevealed information – most significantly about Jill, Vivien and his own friendship with Olivier – he not only refused to cooperate but urged friends and colleagues to decline interviews. Tynan (already battling the emphysema that would soon kill him) abandoned the project and Olivier, hoping to deflect any such subsequent book, agreed at last to write his own memoirs. As it happened, this took him two years, and *Confessions of an Actor* (published in 1982) was a masterpiece of improvisation and invention, with many factual errors and glaring omissions. 'He tells you everything in it,' said Tarquin Olivier perceptively, 'and reveals absolutely nothing.' But Olivier had a defence: 'I've had so much to hide in my life I suppose I was bound to be nervous with interviewers. There was always a romance or something going on that I was anxious not to be questioned about.'

On his seventy-second birthday, Olivier dined with the Evanses at a Charlotte Street restaurant, where he wondered aloud whether his third marriage had been a mistake. He wanted to be with his children as much as possible, but there was now an unofficial separation from Joan: when necessary, Olivier was tended by nurses, and he and his wife seemed mostly to occupy their two homes separately, making social and public appearances together only for propriety's sake.

On 2 July he invited Mary Evans to join him in the royal box for the tennis tournament at Wimbledon; later her husband joined them for dinner at Wilton's restaurant. Convinced that there was now an irreparable rupture in his marriage and that Joan's affections lay elsewhere, Olivier – not for the first time – spoke of divorce. The Evanses dissuaded him, arguing that he consider his age and illness as well as the effects of the adverse publicity on his children. For the time being, Olivier agreed – but several months later he sent for his lawyer, Laurence Harbottle, and dictated instructions: The Lord Olivier wished to terminate his marriage.

Somehow this reached the press, and the Oliviers tried to cover up the matter: he claimed to have jokingly threatened a divorce 'if you play at the National'. Olivier's sentiments did not alter, despite the constant flow of uxorious remarks for the benefit of journalists. 'Though Larry and I do seem to be working in different countries some of the time,' Joan said, 'we at least manage uninterrupted weekends with the children.' Inevitably, such times would become less frequent, and as Olivier told the Evanses this was all the more reason for him to distract himself from an unhappy private life by making films, no matter how unattractive.

He did not have to wait long, for the most absurd project of his career was soon to begin. The right-wing Korean evangelist Reverend Sun Myung Moon, eager to promote a film extolling his country's fight against Communism, convinced Japanese backers to finance a picture based on General MacArthur's campaigns. Olivier was paid one million dollars that summer to spend four weeks in Seoul, where amid suffocating humidity he wore the heaviest make-up of his career to simulate the general's appearance (plastic lips and jaw prevented him from eating lunch). When not before the camera, recalled the film's director Terence Young (his friend from the days of

Henry V), Olivier lay on a cot, virtually immobile with pain and exhaustion. Shooting took place in 120-degree heat, and he seemed almost moribund, but when needed he dropped fifty years and stepped forward without a complaint. Final scenes were photographed in Rome that autumn, and soon after *Inchon* (with a budget of $23 million) was taken over by the 'Moonies', who edited it with the unskilled abandon of schoolchildren and several years later released a film unrecognisable to Young and incomprehensible to audiences.

From this fiasco Olivier recovered almost at once, appearing in December as Lord Marchmain in the television adaptation of Evelyn Waugh's novel *Brideshead Revisited*. In the role of a patriarch who had abandoned his wife and children but who returns to die at the family estate (filmed at Castle Howard, Yorkshire), Olivier gave what he called a preview scene of his own end – a long confession and a yearning for forgotten faith. Gasping for breath, his eyes blazing with guilt and remorse, Lord Marchmain emerges as one of Olivier's last two great achievements. 'Free as air,' he mutters to Phoebe Nicholls (as his daughter Cordelia),

> that's what they say death is. I was free once – and now they bring me my air in an iron barrel. I committed a crime in the name of freedom. Cordelia, what became of our chapel? I built it for your mother. When I went away, I left her praying in the chapel. It was hers. The place for her. I never came back to disturb her prayers. They said we were fighting [the World War] for freedom. I had my victory. Was that a crime?

And when Cordelia says she thinks Marchmain's neglect of his family was indeed a crime, Olivier's gaze is slowly infused with horror – a pain (as Emily Dickinson wrote) that had 'an element of blank'. Perhaps the most compelling scene of the twelve-hour series was his simulacrum of dying moments later, unable to speak and finally marking himself with the sign of the cross. In the weight of Olivier's own arms, in the stillness of his features and his imperceptible breathing there was conveyed an icon of faith deeper than mere culture, of hope revived in death.

But this was only a brief respite between disasters, and in January 1980 he was back in Los Angeles, accompanied by the Evanses, who saw that he was comfortably settled at L'Ermitage Hotel. The project at hand was another variation on his now hallowed Old Jewish Gentleman role, as Neil Diamond's father in *The Jazz Singer*, a remake of the Al Jolson story (for which Olivier was paid another million dollars). En route, he stopped at Joan's behest in Boston, where Franco Zeffirelli had left the American production of *Filumena* and hurried off to a Rio holiday. Olivier assumed nominal direction of the comedy during the pre-New York previews, jetting back and forth from the Hollywood production and, to combat the rumours about their marriage, appearing at Joan's Broadway opening on 3 February. (The play that had run for two years in London closed in New York after four weeks.)

Joan chose to return to England instead of accompanying her husband back to Los Angeles, where *The Jazz Singer* was anything but a harmonious enterprise. Director Sidney J. Furie, who often used half a dozen cameras for a single scene and shot almost a quarter of a million feet of film, had pushed the picture disastrously over budget, Olivier was being handed daily script changes, and there was general hysteria on the set. 'Larry was ready to abandon the entire job,' Evans recalled, 'and one day when some new pages arrived just before shooting, he read them and said more or less jokingly, "I can't read this piss!"' The film was only saved when Evans had the idea that director Richard Fleischer (a friend but not a client) should take over, and after some delay almost the entire film was remade, beginning on 17 March – much of it necessitated, as Fleischer at once recognised, by Olivier's shameless mugging. 'Eventually he lost patience with me and himself,' Fleischer recalled, 'and he said quietly, "Why don't I just quit? Why does an old man like me insist on acting?"'

Constant contact with the Evanses by telephone and with Marcella Markham, who had returned as dialogue coach, buoyed his spirits. Tired, lonely and desperate for company, he prolonged evenings with crew members and relied on the attentions of friends like Markham, Natalie Wood and Robert Wagner (who over a long weekend spirited him away for a Las Vegas holiday). For the remainder of filming, his mood lightened and his old good humour revived. To a young actress who complained she was not taken seriously because she was a blonde, Olivier replied with feigned innocence, 'But my dear, it was your decision!' And when arriving at a restaurant as the importuned guest of an actor he resented, Olivier sniffed, gazed round and muttered to Markham, 'I imagine this is the sort of place where they sing "Happy Birthday".'

On 6 March, at a London meeting of the family's advisors and lawyers, Joan had asked their son Richard to announce on her behalf what had already become public knowledge: thenceforth, she would neither attend award functions for her husband nor accompany him on trips.

CHAPTER SEVENTEEN

1980–1989

Old men forget . . .
But he'll remember with advantages
What feats he did . . .

Henry V

For a week in April 1980, Olivier, his secretary Shirley Luke and
Laurence and Mary Evans went to Venice for the filming of a few
delayed scenes of *Brideshead Revisited*. On the way home, while
visiting David Niven on the French Riviera, he was afflicted with a
sudden fever and a minor but painful urinary tract infection. Preferring
his own doctor, he returned at once to London and was put to bed with
a course of antibiotics.

While recuperating, he began to work in earnest on his contracted
autobiography. Publisher George Weidenfeld had arranged for Mark
Amory (literary editor of the *Spectator*) to collaborate as ghost, but
after several months of almost daily meetings, Olivier visited the
Waltons on Ischia, where he decided to write the book alone. Amory
was dismissed, and every word of *Confessions of an Actor* came from
Olivier.

In summer 1981 (after receiving from the Queen the nation's highest
honour, the Order of Merit), he felt sufficiently confident about the
progress of *Confessions* to take time out for acting in the television
drama *A Voyage Round My Father*, John Mortimer's autobiographical
account of his relationship with his blind barrister-father. When production began at Mortimer's own home in Buckinghamshire, Olivier
was dreadfully unwell, his circulation poor and his memory unreliable.
By early afternoons he was so tired and confused that often the day's
shooting had to be suspended, according to director Alvin Rakoff.
Everyone on the project thought it was doomed, for the more he forgot

his cues the less he could take guidance. But he knew he was failing, and became very upset. 'Finally,' as Rakoff recalled, 'he became so ill-tempered, frustrated and embarrassed he asked me to clear everybody from the room, and then we agreed to use huge blackboards off-camera with his lines. Yet despite all the difficulties, he was astonishing, and he never failed to look like a blind man.' Perhaps because of the hardships he had unintentionally caused during production, Olivier was cheerfully cooperative during postproduction as he had to record and re-record his lines to correct the errors during filming.

Several of his last roles (Lord Marchmain, Clifford Mortimer and King Lear) reflected the great transformation of Laurence Olivier's character in his final years. His external achievements were established and unassailable; only his inner and emotional life had wanted tending. Great acting, considered the sole mechanism by which he realised and expressed himself, had for decades combined with the burden of fame to generate a certain remoteness in his personality – a condition his unrelenting illnesses might have aggravated. But as he had told a journalist, 'Your mind expands as your body shrinks, and you adjust to it, giving in age what you couldn't give in youth.'

And so instead of the tragic decline of Olivier there was in fact a remarkable ascent. Abandoning his noble status, 'Sir' became 'Larry', discovering that the same gentle actions and slight expressions required for television and film close-ups bound him, in real life, to his friends and nourished his affections. False noses, disguises, titles, public dignities, beautiful consorts – these ceased to have value for him. He was achieving through a gradual *rallentando* what he had not realised earlier through ceaseless effort, finding strength in weakness, accepting help from friends and colleagues. His abilities were failing, but by giving in age what he could not in youth – the open acknowledgment that he depended on the affection of others – he became a living example of the truth that a life lived is more valuable than the creation of any artwork.

In this regard, his portrayal of the eccentric Clifford Mortimer is one of his most deeply felt characterisations – very close to a stencil of Olivier himself. Bravely affecting indifference to pain and grief, joking about sex, pontificating on everything from gardening to the law, raging about fools, directing everyone's attention as he wishes, the character was uncannily fused to himself, and his laboured breathing was a sign of both Clifford Mortimer's illness and Olivier's valour during production. By carefully timed pauses and an almost detached stillness, this portrait remains sharply moving: 'Why do you bother?' demands his son's wife-to-be in his and his family's presence. 'Why do you bother with all this gardening when you can't see it? Why do you all walk about pretending he's not blind?' Olivier as Mortimer rises painfully and approaches the girl, then finds her by reaching out and gently patting her shoulder, his voice strained and dry, utterly without self-pity: 'Would you take me down to the west copse? I'd like a report on the magnolia. Would you do that – be my eyes?' *A Voyage Round My Father* has not a moment of pretence; craft is here at its deepest level of emotional truth.

In early 1982 Olivier spent four days in Vienna, filming a cameo part in the television mini-series *Wagner* as a minister of court during the time of the composer. For the first time since Olivier's film of *Richard III*, he was professionally rejoined with John Gielgud and Ralph Richardson, who gave similar star turns, and the press was provided with a battery of fictitious accounts of a sentimental reunion while the trio staged an elaborate affectation of lifelong friendship.

There was calculation, too, when Olivier travelled to New York that autumn to promote *Confessions of an Actor*. Dining with his American publisher Michael Korda and Milton Goldman (Laurence Evans's New York colleague at ICM), Olivier was determined that his public appearances on behalf of the book would be at his own discretion, and to that end he acted the part of a slightly dotty Englishman visiting America for the first time. What exactly was a baked potato? he asked the waiter at Gallagher's. And hash browns? Lyonnaise? Cottage fries? He then ordered all eight varieties of potatoes on the menu – and Vivien's favourite flavour of ice cream. Korda soon realised that Olivier simply did not want to embark on a lengthy publicity tour, and so he assumed the role of a man who could not possibly appear in public.

That journey interrupted the filming for television of his *King Lear* at the Granada studios in Manchester, which he had planned for years and prepared since the previous winter, slowly memorising the text and seeking the right gestures for every line. Dorothy Tutin (who played Goneril) recalled that when rehearsals began in May 1982 Olivier seemed 'to carry the loneliness of a lost little boy – and in a way this helped his amazing performance'. Exploiting his own fragile health and shortness of breath for the aged, confused Lear, Olivier described the old king's descent into madness as a kind of spiritual epiphany. Withstanding the full force of wind and rain machines, he and Lear became one reality in a production designed as an impressionistic hallucination, a dream image where timber structures, horses and storm-swept heaths loom out of swirling mists. Over and within it all, Olivier's mature vulnerability shines through, a performance suffused with humanising tenderness, which he knew surpassed his stage acting of the role in 1946. Indeed, he seemed inspired from moment to moment as if he had become like Lear himself, as he wrote soon after.

> I wear an invisible theatrical crown which I like, am very attached to and will not give up. Just as I was determined to eliminate [memories of Henry] Irving and let the spotlight rest on me . . . so I was rehearsing my own madness and death in *King Lear* [who is] . . . just a selfish, irascible old bastard – so am I. It's an absolutely straight part for me. My family would agree with that statement.

First on his schedule that spring was the filming, in a Bristol studio (interrupted for a day's cameo work on *The Bounty*, as an admiral in the trial scene), of an American-financed television two-hander, *Mr Halpern and Mr Johnson*, directed by Alvin Rakoff and co-starring none other than Jackie Gleason.* After Dr Heather Cooper (at Rakoff's request) weaned Olivier off steroids and an array of other drugs he took at the time, he became daily stronger during the two-week production. Rakoff also convinced him to benefit from the autocue, a device positioned just off-camera that relieved him of the burden of memorisation; Olivier was to rely on it for all his subsequent film and television performances. The hefty American comic television star and the hallowed British peer began somewhat warily in their roles as a recent widower (Olivier) who meets the man with whom his wife had a long and intimate friendship. But soon Olivier and Gleason discovered they had very much in common – a love of good whisky, wine and risqué humour, as Alvin Rakoff recalled. 'There were filthy stories aplenty and raucous, loud laughter – much to the shock of the blue-rinsed ladies. Sometimes one had to ask Olivier to lower his voice, because he was booming really very dirty jokes to the farthest corner of the restaurant.'

Freed from dependence on his many medications, Olivier was healthier on *Mr Halpern and Mr Johnson* than on any project for years,

---

* From 1981 to 1983, Olivier received a total of almost five million dollars for six major film and television appearances, three fleeting cameos, two extended interviews and the foreign rights pertaining to them. Most of these sums were lost to taxes.

and the unlikely chemistry of his friendship with Gleason buoyed him. After one difficult dialogue scene had been concluded, Gleason (uncharacteristically) hugged Olivier affectionately – and Olivier (equally atypically) responded, at first with mild surprise and then gratitude. 'It was a very touching moment between these two very different old pros,' Rakoff added, 'and when we finished the show after just two weeks of shooting, Larry said to me wistfully, "Oh, I was just beginning really to like Jackie."' As the production team disbanded, Rakoff received a handwritten note from Olivier, thanking him for the greatest pleasure in his recent life. He was, he added, looking forward to another part as soon as possible, so that a new generation of television viewers might at least remember him as a bit player. Rakoff replied later that year with *A Talent for Murder*, another television film made in four days, with Angela Lansbury – which turned out to be a disappointment for them all, with unsatisfying roles and the sort of dialogue in which people constantly say things like, 'Why? Why? It all seems so senseless!' Olivier also despatched a quick television cameo as a Roman patrician enduring *The Last Days of Pompeii*.

Inevitably, awards and honours accumulated: the Albert Medal from Prince Philip, half a dozen Emmy awards (from America's National Academy of Television Arts and Sciences), *Evening Standard* and Variety Club awards, honorary degrees, a Hollywood Golden Globe press award and the re-naming of the Society of West End Theatre Awards (London's most prestigious entertainment honour) as the Olivier Awards. On 25 April 1983 he was honoured at a tribute by the Film Society of Lincoln Center, in New York (where Olivier's speech was an even more filigreed reworking of his 1979 Oscar statement), and the next evening he was guest of honour at a White House dinner, where President and Mrs Reagan invited thirty guests for dinner and a screening of *King Lear*.

That autumn, despite two sojourns in hospital for recurrent thrombosis and pleurisy during the preceding three months, Olivier (accompanied by his son Richard) travelled to a château near Limoges, where he filmed the role of an old English painter in a television adaptation of John Fowles's *The Ebony Tower*. Bearded, balding, gnarled and cantankerous, Olivier filled the part perfectly, and although nervous and insecure he was deftly directed by Robert Knights and encouraged by the cast, to whom he confided that he neither knew nor cared very much about painting or art history despite the education Vivien had tried to instil. This led him to reminisce about his life at Notley Abbey as he told the director and cast of waking more than once there to find Vivien's place beside him empty. He searched the gardens, he said, expecting to find that she had hanged herself.

Poignant memories were evoked, too, at the news, brought to him in France on 10 October, that Ralph Richardson had died. Olivier shared with his fellow players a cascade of anecdotes stretching back almost sixty years, for although he could no longer commit one line of dialogue accurately to memory, he recalled in vivid and colourful detail his time with Richardson at the Birmingham Rep, their antics while playing in *The Taming of the Shrew*, the long, boozy nights barrelling in their cars down Piccadilly. He described their controversial *Othello* and the passionate kiss, and he described hilariously how they seemed to compete for the number of aircraft they demolished during wartime, and how Ralphie 'nearly killed me one night' in Paris.

'Well, after all, you can't have any sort of art without danger!' Olivier said, echoing words from the script he was then filming. Whereas Richardson had only recently told a friend he had 'no idea what the real Laurence is like', the two actors had an intersecting history that included virtually every rise and turn in modern British theatre. 'I'm probably the next to go,' Olivier said. Back in London, he wept at Richardson's memorial service at Westminster Abbey on 17 November, as he did when reading a lesson at the remembrance for David Niven, a spirited companion since the time of *Wuthering Heights* and throughout the Hollywood traumas with Vivien.

These deaths upset him keenly, Mary Evans remembered, and Olivier spent a good deal of time reminiscing that season. He was then hit by another painful ailment: a loop of fibrous tissue had threatened to strangulate a ureter, and so in December a delicate kidney operation was performed at St Thomas's Hospital. Bad kidneys or not, he welcomed a visit from Robert Wagner, whose wife Natalie Wood had recently died in a boating accident. In his hospital room, they drank a bottle of Jack Daniels just as at Manchester, recalled Wagner.

> I had come to cheer him, but he consoled me. He was so lonely in so many respects. But when he put his arms around you he enabled you to touch him in his loneliness. Then he was simply Larry – no title, no fame.

Indeed, as Michael Caine described him, Olivier was 'just one of the lads'.

95. *Right* With Neil Diamond, during filming of *The Jazz Singer* (1979). *National Film Archive, London*

96. *Below* Joan and Richard, opening night of *Filumena* in New York (1980). *Darleen Rubin*

97. *Middle right* The Oliviers at the cast party for *Filumena* (1980). *Darleen Rubin*

98. *Bottom right* As the blind barrister Clifford Mortimer, with Alan Bates, in *A Voyage Round My Father* (1981). *National Film Archive, London*

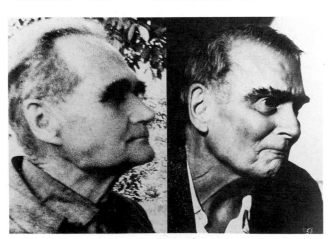

99. *Top left* With Jackie Gleason, in *Mr Halpern and Mr Johnson* (1982). *National Film Archive, London*

100. *Above* As King Lear on television, 1982. *Granada TV*

101. *Above left* With director Robert Knights, during filming of *The Ebony Tower* (1984). *From the collection of Robert Knights*

102. *Left* Rudolf Hess and Olivier's impersonation of him in *Wild Geese II* (1984).

103. *Right* With Mary Evans, visiting New York (1985). *From the collection of Laurence Evans*

104. *Below right* At Chichester in 1985 for the unveiling of the Olivier sculpture by Lawrence Holofcener (far left). *From the collection of Lawrence Holofcener*

105. *Bottom* Lord and Lady Olivier, with Julie-Kate, Tamsin and Richard (1985). *Camera Press/R.Open*

106. *Right* Arriving in Los
Angeles, assisted by Mary
Evans (1985). *From the
collection of Laurence Evans*

107. *Below* With his friend
and agent Laurence Evans, in
Olivier's garden on his
eightieth birthday, 22
May,1987. *From the collection
of Laurence Evans*

But his illnesses did not alter the family arrangement, and so the Evanses accompanied him to New York for a star gala at Radio City Music Hall the following February. There, Olivier received a prolonged and tumultuous ovation simply for appearing onstage. 'Let's telephone Joanie!' he said proudly, but when the call was put through the maid reported, 'Lady Olivier says she is at dinner.' There was a long stillness in the room before Olivier turned to his friends and said quietly, 'Joan expected me to die when I was seventy. Unfortunately I didn't.' As his friend Angela Fox commented of these years, 'His aloneness was huge, like his talent.'

By Christmas 1984, Olivier was back at home in Sussex, gamely swimming in his heated pool, for which he had provided a protective covering so he could swim all year round. He also decided to answer the critics who had complained about the lack of serious professional commentary in *Confessions of an Actor*, and so he sat for taped interviews which were collated into a rambling, chatty book entitled *On Acting*, published in 1986. More anecdotal than informative, the book (compiled by actor Gawn Grainger) is remarkably honest about his shortcomings as a film actor, but it also reveals a mean-spirited streak that derived from Olivier's professional avarice. Of Gielgud, for instance, he wrote: 'John is a very sweet man who is forever saying terrible things about me' – a complaint of hilarious and pathetic inaccuracy, for throughout their careers Olivier was ungenerous towards and critical of Gielgud, who was consistently courteous and laudatory. Olivier may have had his own unpleasant trait in mind when he overstated his self-perception on American television in 1980: 'I'm not a very nice man – I just don't like me,' an assessment that recurs frequently in *Confessions of an Actor* and many interviews. Such abjection invariably brought forth fierce protests, of course, but throughout his latter years, Olivier admitted his envy of other actors. 'Cary Grant!' he said to Alvin Rakoff with considerable awe not long after Grant's death. 'Now that was real success. I never had anything like his greatness.'

The diminution of his powers certainly contributed to Olivier's conviction that he no longer had much to offer a film, although producers were still eager to include his bankable name in the credits. Euan Lloyd, who produced *Wild Geese II* in 1984, was pleased when Olivier accepted the role of Rudolf Hess in a story about a plot to smuggle him out of Spandau prison. Olivier listened to recordings of Hess's voice, for he felt it was vital to find the right tone, and he studied photos carefully.

Hess's son Wolf Rudiger said afterwards that the likeness was uncannily accurate. And although he had great trouble with dialogue, he laboured for hours on his one long speech, and when he finally managed it (as co-star Edward Fox recalled), the entire cast and crew were hushed and there were many tears.

Within a period of eighteen months, Olivier also acted cameos as William III in *Peter the Great*, as the head of British Secret Service in *Jigsaw Man*, and, most bizarrely of all, as a hologram in the musical *Time*. With an income totalling two million dollars for the ten days of work on these projects, he was able to sell the house in St Leonard's Terrace and move his family to a more lavish one in Mulberry Walk, Chelsea – a grand home with a thirty-foot reception room, five bedrooms, a study, a staff flat and a south-facing garden. The new house was largely occupied by Joan and the children, as Olivier spent most weeks in Sussex, where his room overlooked his beloved gardens and a glorious expanse of Sussex countryside. Hidden at the end of a long, rocky driveway, the Oliviers had modified and supplemented the original malthouse, and by 1985 it was a peaceful setting where he could dictate anecdotes to Gawn Grainger, invite friends for champagne lunches and surprise his guests by swimming ten or twenty laps in his heated pool each day. But very often, even while he was lunching with friends, insupportable fatigue overcame him and he had to ask his nurse to put him to bed.

The last four years of his life were an unpredictable mixture of pleasant moments with a few close friends and times of appalling pain and the gradual erosion of all memory but the most remote. Able to detail the fine points of life aboard the *Berengaria* in 1930 or the geography of Birmingham after the First World War, Olivier most of all tended to speak long and lovingly (and sometimes guiltily) of his life with Vivien. Conversely, the director of a recent film or the events of a few hours earlier were all but lost to him. There were also the effects of impaired circulation and long-term steroid dependence – occasional blackouts and intermittent muscular dysfunction, despite his valorous efforts at normal activity.

At times he was remarkably well for weeks, as at the twenty-fifth wedding anniversary celebration for Laurence and Mary Evans in March 1985. With a large crowd of friends and clients attending, Evans and Olivier sang old standards and kept the party in high spirits. 'Lol Evans and I have been doing this double act on and off for years,' Olivier told a reporter next day, 'and I felt so good that nothing would stop me!' In August he travelled to Edinburgh, where Richard was directing short plays on the Festival fringe and where he patiently met both press and public while turning the spotlight clearly on his son.

But he was also prone to dizzy spells and thus dangerous falls, and once cut his leg so badly that emergency treatment was needed to halt excessive bleeding; later, while filming the small role of Harry Burrard, an antique music-hall entertainer *à la* Archie Rice in the television series *Lost Empires*, he fell from the stage of the Buxton Opera House, Derbyshire, badly lacerating his left elbow. ('He's just pleased it wasn't his drinking arm,' his secretary told the press.) The performance itself almost cruelly reveals Olivier's frailty as he walks in evident pain and with short breath, ridiculously costumed and berouged like a demented Pierrot as Harry is hooted off the stage by bored spectators.

Also in March 1985 he went again with the Evanses to Los Angeles, where he presented the best picture Oscar. After being introduced by Jack Lemmon, he thanked the audience briefly and simply, his words a refreshing corrective to the evening's hype and his own previous hyperboles: 'Thank you for such a perfectly wonderful reception. I hope I won't let the occasion down too bad.' He then forgot to read the five nominees before quickly announcing '*Amadeus*!' and this caused him such embarrassment that he left Hollywood the next evening. Two days later, on 23 March, he learned of the death of Michael Redgrave after more than a decade's struggle with Parkinson's Disease, and interrupted a luncheon to wire his condolences to Rachel.

Olivier was by this time most comfortable in the circle of the past, and in Los Angeles he insisted on visiting Vivien's friend and companion Sunny Lash. During lunch at the Bel-Air Hotel, she recalled, he wanted to talk mostly about Vivien, still requiring assurance that he had not been a 'bad boy' for leaving her. He worked, he said, for the sake of his family, and added quietly that no, his wife did not travel with him. He also saw Constance Cummings (then visiting in Hollywood), but she had the sense that when they spoke of that year's events he had suddenly withdrawn to a world of his own. When she asked him a question about the Old Vic during wartime, however, suddenly the doors were open and he was bright and alert.

Such little lapses could have extreme results, however, as on 5 May 1985, when he attended the dedication at Chichester of Lawrence Holofcener's bronze bas-relief depicting twenty-eight Olivier roles. That week, he had repeatedly been referring to Joan as 'Vivien', and finally he had apparently overstretched her patience and she departed for a

Majorcan holiday. Still, Lord and Lady Olivier graciously performed their roles for the public, even filming interviews together for a twenty-fifth wedding anniversary programme in 1986 (for which they were paid £20,000), walking politely round the garden he loved so much at home.

But above all (and unrealistically now) he longed to work, as Laurence Evans recalled.

> He rang my London office daily to ask, 'Have you got anything for me?' And I replied, 'Not today, Larry – maybe tomorrow.' Then he would say, 'I can get on the train and come up, you know, if you have a job for me.' But of course by 1986 that was impossible.

Proudly, Olivier attended the naming of a British Rail engine for him at Euston station that June, and he quit his bed after a bout with pleurisy during the summer of 1986 to see Tamsin's acting debut at Chichester, where she was understudying and had a brief walk-on. Hospitalised again with kidney trouble in late July, he turned one afternoon to Mary Evans and said quietly, 'My courage – it's gone.' But it had not, and on 4 August he was back at home, eager to reply to get-well cards and letters.

That year Laurence Olivier composed his will. There were cash bequests to nurses, secretaries, in-laws and a few cousins, and from his personal effects he left mementoes to ten friends, among them the Evanses, Peggy Ashcroft, John Mills, Rachel Kempson Redgrave, Pieter Rogers and Meriel Richardson. An early prompt-copy of *Hamlet* he bequeathed to John Gielgud, and to the National Theatre and the Garrick Club he left portraits of himself. He also set up a trust for his children, but to Joan he left only their jointly held furniture and furnishings – no art, nor silver or gold objects, china, historic pieces, antique books or theatrical mementoes. She was to be allowed the Malthouse in her widowhood or until she decided to vacate it (the home in Mulberry Walk was jointly owned), but in either case it would be included in the rest of his estate, finally valued at just over one million pounds, which was to be administered by four trustees. Asked during the anniversary garden party that year to name the most important things in his life apart from acting, he replied, 'Women, Shakespeare and gardening.' But when the microphone was turned on and the interviewer repeated the question, Olivier replied with cheerful dignity, 'My wife and my children.'

'People expect him to go on forever, but he really doesn't want to,' Laurence Evans told the press when Olivier conceded that film or television work were beyond his powers in 1987. But that May he did perform a half-hour radio play by Peter Barnes (*No End to Dreaming*) about a Polish-American who recounts to his psychiatrist a boyhood dream. It was an apt memory-piece for Olivier, who by this time spoke mostly of his parents, of Barry Jackson, Noël Coward, Tyrone Guthrie and Ralph Richardson – the entire supporting cast of his life seemed to fill his rooms. They were all visiting him, he often announced to visitors with quiet gratitude, and when he sometimes complained to friends like Mary Evans that Vivien was late for luncheon, he smiled with resignation and shrugged: he was accustomed to her delays – she was probably shopping and would soon arrive. They must have another drop of champagne while they waited for her. Memories crowded his letters, too; in a note to a cousin who still lived in a Kensington house that had been in their family for generations, he recalled weekend visits there when he came down from St Edward's. His 'precious Mummy' had died when he was twelve, he wrote, and were it not for his Auntie Margaret he would have been very bereft indeed.

In May, his eightieth birthday was marked by a gala at the National Theatre, and this, too, seemed like a living album. John Mortimer wrote a revue typifying and satirising acting styles of Shakespeare, and there were little variety acts interspersed. From a box-seat Olivier watched with apparent indifference until the finale, when Julie-Kate popped out of a huge cake to wish him happy birthday. At this he laughed and cheered, and then his eyes filled with tears when the evening concluded with a tribute from Peggy Ashcroft, his classmate at the Central School and later his Juliet. She donned Lilian Baylis's cap and gown and moved slowly towards Olivier's seat. 'You did very well, Larry,' she said, speaking for Baylis, for herself and for millions. 'Awe and wonder – that's what you gave us, awe and wonder.' When escorted to the stage, he accepted a thunderous ovation and was reluctant to leave, raising his right hand in acknowledgment and gesturing as if cupping butterflies. The audience would have happily stayed for an hour, and he would gladly have stayed with them.

Shortly afterwards, there was an odd disturbance at the stage door. Olivier wanted to leave the theatre, but Joan indicated a crowd of fans and photographers: 'If you go out there, you'll be mobbed. Do you want to be mobbed?' But Olivier insisted, 'I just want a breath of fresh air.' Someone indicated an exterior veranda above the stage door, and moments later the crowd spotted him there, standing like a victorious Romeo on his beloved's balcony, waving to them all as the cheers ascended.

Inevitably, there were fewer and fewer activities in 1987 and 1988. Olivier measured time from the ground floor of his Sussex home, marking the seasons in his garden from his cluttered desk or, more often now, from his bed. Attended by nurses and encouraged by his children, he tried to make a commercial tape of Shakespeare's sonnets, but his voice was strained and breathless and the project was abandoned. Occasionally he astounded everyone, as at the Evanses' 1987 Christmas party. When someone began a round of carols after luncheon, Olivier raised his voice above the others with a choirboy's fervour, leading everyone in a chorus: 'Oh, come, all ye faithful, joyful and triumphant . . .' And so he seemed to be.

At last there was the final performance. On 17 October 1988 he was feeling well enough to appear for one day as a wheelchair-bound old soldier, photographed outside Darrenth Park Hospital, Kent; this was a cameo in Derek Jarman's film *War Requiem*, a non-narrative collage of images set to Benjamin Britten's mass. Producer Don Boyd recalled Olivier's pleasure at the sudden rush of energy he managed, chattering away about his work with William Walton on recording the score for *Henry V*. That same day, he recorded with great empathy Wilfred Owen's poem 'Strange Meeting', heard over the film's early moments:

> . . . Whatever hope is yours,
> Was my life also; I went hunting wild
> After the wildest beauty in the world . . .
> For by my glee might many men have laughed . . .
> Courage was mine, and I had mystery,
> Wisdom was mine, and I had mastery.

The following February he wrote to Boyd that he would be delighted with more work like this, if it could be found for him. Most of all, he concluded, he was grateful for his kindness. The note, written slowly in pencil in his weak hand and then overlaid by him in ink, was signed 'Larry Olivier'. But *War Requiem* was to be his last artistic testimony. In addition to directing thirty-eight plays, six films and six television shows, he had performed 121 stage roles and appeared in fifty-eight films, fifteen television and forty-two radio programmes. 'I suppose I should be tired,' he told Laurence Evans.

The crystalline memory essential for this remarkable career had all but deserted him by early 1989, and then he took a terrible fall during the night of 18 March. Despite the risks there was no alternative but surgery to replace his shattered hip. Mary and Laurence Evans sat by their telephone awaiting news from his hospital room, and a call came the next night. To their amazement it was Olivier, asking them to visit next day – and to bring champagne. Back home in early April, he tried valiantly to negotiate limping with canes and a walking frame, but the pain was too severe. His sister Sybille had died peacefully on 10 April at eighty-seven, but the news never quite seemed to register with him. He barely acknowledged his eighty-second birthday on 22 May.

In June, while Joan was filming in America, he often asked to be driven over to the Evanses' for luncheon or tea, and late in the afternoons he happily accepted a glass of champagne. Sitting contentedly in the warmth of their home and friendship, he recalled funny stories about the Old Vic, about Sam Goldwyn, about a day in the choir at All Saints or onstage at the New Theatre.

By 1 July, Olivier was no longer able to leave his bed at the Malthouse, but his remarkable pluck had not entirely abandoned him. When he was too weak to lift a glass, his nurse assisted, accidentally spilling some juice onto his cheek. As it trickled towards his ear, he winked and then – referring to the play-within-a-play in Shakespeare, when the Player King receives an infusion of poison in his ear – he slowly turned and said, 'My dear, we are not doing fucking *Hamlet*!'

For most of Saturday the eighth he was unconscious. That evening, Olivier's kidneys began to fail, and when the doctors said the end was near, Richard telephone Laurence and Mary Evans, who arrived at the Malthouse on Sunday afternoon. Mary went to sit by the bedside while her husband conferred with Richard, his wife and his sisters. For the flicker of a moment, Olivier responded to Mary, smiling faintly and taking her hand. Then Laurence Evans entered. 'Well, my dear friend,' Evans began, and he offered their familiar greeting, summoning a memory precious to them both for sixty years: 'What have you been doing since *Too Many Crooks*?' But there was no reply, only deep, irregular breathing. Joan, who had been in Los Angeles filming her brilliant comic portrayal of a Slavic shrew in *I Love You to Death*, was on her way home after Evans had telephoned her director on Saturday, informing him of the situation. She arrived at the Malthouse on Monday afternoon.

It had been unseasonably cool throughout southern England during the previous weeks, and without Olivier's supervision the garden seemed in a state of mutiny, withering, untended and doomed never again to flourish. But during the weekend there was a brief shower, and in the sunlight blossoms opened by the hour. Early on Tuesday, 11 July 1989, a priest was called. During the prayers, Olivier's respiration became more laboured, but he was beyond pain.

The scene resembled the last moments of the once displaced and defiant but ultimately faithful Lord Marchmain in *Brideshead Revisited*. But this was no chilly Yorkshire castle, and with Laurence Olivier there was at last neither practised grandeur, settled pose nor fearful effort. After a morning haze, the sun broke through brilliantly at midday, arching a long shaft of light across his beloved garden and into the quiet room. For a moment he seemed to whisper, and then there was stillness. Through the open windows came the gentle sounds and welcome scents of summer in full flower at last, and a warm breeze gathered across the Sussex downs.

BIBLIOGRAPHY

Barker, Felix, *Laurence Olivier*. Tunbridge Wells: Spellmount, 1984
—— *The Oliviers*. Philadelphia and New York: J.B. Lippincott, 1953
Beaton, Cecil, *The Happy Years: Diaries 1944–1948*. London: Weidenfeld and Nicolson, 1972
Behlmer, Rudy, ed., *Memo from David O. Selznick*. Los Angeles: Samuel French, 1989
Benedetti, Jean, *Stanislavski: A Biography*. London: Methuen, 1988
Berg, A. Scott, *Goldwyn*. New York: Knopf, 1989
Bergan, Ronald, *The Great Theatres of London*. London: Multimedia/ Admiral, 1987
Billington, Michael, *Peggy Ashcroft*. London: John Murray, 1988
Blakelock, Denys, *Finding My Way*. London: Hollis and Carter, 1958
—— *Round the Next Corner*. London: Victor Gollancz, 1967
Bloom, Claire, Limelight *and After*. New York: Harper and Row, 1982
Brady, Frank, *Citizen Welles*. New York: Scribner's, 1989
Bragg, Melvyn, *Laurence Olivier*. London: Hutchinson, 1984
Briers, Richard, *Coward and Company*. London: Robson, 1987
Brown, John Russell, ed., *Focus on* Macbeth. London: Routledge and Kegan Paul, 1982
Buckley, Richard, ed., *Self-Portrait with Friends: The Selected Diaries of Cecil Beaton*. New York: New York Times Books, 1979
Burton, Hal, ed., *Great Acting*. New York: Bonanza Books, 1967
Callow, Simon, *Charles Laughton: A Difficult Actor*. London: Methuen, 1987
Casson, John, *Sybil and Lewis: A Memoir*. London: Collins, 1972
Castle, H.G., *Fire Over England*. London: Leo Cooper/Secker and Warburg, 1982
Chambers, E.K., *The Elizabethan Stage*. Oxford: Clarendon, 1923
—— *William Shakespeare: A Study of Facts and Problems* (2 vols). Oxford: Clarendon, 1930
Clark, Sandra, ed., *Hutchinson Shakespeare Dictionary*. London: Hutchinson, 1986
Clinch, Minty, *Burt Lancaster*. London: Arthur Barker, 1984
Cocroft, Thoda, *Great Names*. Chicago: Dartnell Press, 1941
Cole, Marion, *Fogie: The Life of Elsie Fogerty*. London: Peter Davies, 1967

Cottrell, John, *Laurence Olivier*. Englewood Cliffs: Prentice-Hall, 1975

Coward, Noël, *The Lyrics of Noël Coward*. London: Heinemann, 1965

—— *Present Laughter*. Garden City: Doubleday, 1937

Craig, Edith and St John, Christopher, *Ellen Terry's Memoirs*. New York: Putnam's, 1932

Cross, Brenda, ed., *The Film* Hamlet. London: Saturn Press, 1948

Cushing, Peter, *Peter Cushing: An Autobiography*. London: Weidenfeld and Nicolson, 1986

Dalakas, Marinos C., ed., *Polymyositis and Dermatomyositis*. Boston: Butterworth, 1988

Daniels, Robert L., *Laurence Olivier: Theater and Cinema*. New York: A.S. Barnes, 1980

Dark, Sidney, *Mackay of All Saints*. London: Centenary Press, 1937

Darlow, Michael and Hodson, Gillian, *Terence Rattigan: The Man and His Work*. London: Quartet, 1979

Dent, Alan, *Preludes and Studies*. London: Macmillan, 1942

Douglas, Kirk, *The Ragman's Son*. New York: Simon and Schuster, 1988

Drake, Fabia, *Blind Fortune*. London: William Kimber, 1978

Dundy, Elaine, *Finch, Bloody Finch*. New York: Holt, Rinehart and Winston, 1980

Edwards, Anne, *Vivien Leigh*. New York: Simon and Schuster, 1977

Elsom, John, *Post-War British Theatre*. London: Routledge and Kegan Paul, 1976

Ensor, R.C.K., *England 1870–1914*. Oxford: Clarendon, 1936

Evershed-Martin, Leslie, *The Impossible Theatre*. London and Chichester: Phillimore, 1971

—— *The Miracle Theatre*. Newton Abbot and London: David and Charles, 1987

Fairbanks, Douglas, Jr, *Salad Days*. New York: Doubleday, 1988

Fairfield, Sheila, *The Streets of London*. London: Macmillan, 1983

Fairweather, Virginia, *Olivier: An Informal Portrait*. New York: Coward-McCann, 1969 (originally published as *Cry God for Larry*. London: Calder and Boyars, 1969)

Falk, Quentin, *Anthony Hopkins: Too Good to Waste*. London: Columbus Books, 1989

Faulkner, Trader, *Peter Finch: A Biography*. New York: Taplinger, 1979

Findlater, Richard, *At the Royal Court*. London: Amber Lane Press, 1981

—— *The Player Kings*. London: Weidenfeld and Nicolson, 1971

Fisher, Clive, *Gielgud Stories*. London: Futura, 1988

Fontaine, Joan, *No Bed of Roses*. New York: William Morrow, 1978

Forbes, Bryan, *Dame Edith Evans*. Boston: Little, Brown, 1977

Forsyth, James, *Tyrone Guthrie*. London: Hamish Hamilton, 1976

Fox, Angela, *Completely Foxed*. London: Collins, 1989

BIBLIOGRAPHY

Galloway, Peter and Rawll, Christopher, *Good and Faithful Servants: The Vicars of All Saints' Church, Margaret Street*. Worthing: Churchman Publishing, 1988

Gaskill, William, *A Sense of Direction: Life at the Royal Court*. London: Faber and Faber, 1988

Gielgud, John (with John Miller and John Powell), *An Actor and His Time*. New York: Clarkson N. Potter, 1986

Gielgud, John, *Backward Glances* (containing his previously published *Times for Reflection* and *Distinguished Company*). London: Hodder and Stoughton, 1989

Goodwin, John, ed., *The Complete Guide to Britain's National Theatre*. London: Heinemann, 1977

—— *A Short Guide to Shakespeare's Plays*. London: Heinemann, 1989

Goodwin, Tim, *Britain's Royal National Theatre: The First 25 Years*. London: Nick Hern/Walker, 1988

Gordon, Ruth, *An Open Book*. New York: Doubleday, 1980

Gottfried, Martin, *Jed Harris: The Curse of Genius*. Boston: Little, Brown, 1984

Granger, Stewart, *Sparks Fly Upward*. New York: Putnam's, 1981

Guthrie, Tyrone, *A Life in the Theatre*. New York: McGraw-Hill, 1959

Haill, Lynn, ed., *Olivier at Work: The National Years*. London: Nick Hern/Walker, 1989

Hall, Peter, *Diaries*. New York: Harper and Row, 1984

Hamilton, Ronald, *Now I Remember*. London: The Hogarth Press, 1983

Harris, Radie, *Radie's World*. New York: Putnam's, 1975

Harrison, Rex, *Rex*. New York: William Morrow, 1975

Hay, Peter, *Theatrical Anecdotes*. London and Oxford: Oxford University Press, 1987

Hayman, Ronald, *Playback*. London: Davis-Poynter, 1973

Heston, Charlton, *The Actor's Life: Journals 1956–1976*. New York: Pocket Books, 1979

Hill, R.D., *A History of St Edward's School 1863–1963*. Oxford: St Edward's School Society, 1962

Hirsch, Foster, *Laurence Olivier on Screen*. New York: Da Capo, 1984

Holden, Anthony, *Olivier*. New York: Athenaeum, 1988

Huggett, Richard, *Binkie Beaumont: Eminence Grise of the West End Theatre*. London: Hodder and Stoughton, 1989

Jenkins, Alan, *The Twenties*. London: Heinemann, 1974

Kanin, Garson, *Hollywood*. New York: Viking, 1974

Kazan, Elia, *A Life*. New York: Knopf, 1988

Kemp, Thomas C., *Birmingham Repertory Theatre*. Birmingham: Cornish Bros., 1948

Kiernan, Thomas, *Sir Larry*. New York: Times Books, 1981

Kitchin, Laurence, *Mid-Century Drama*. London: Faber and Faber, 1960

Korda, Michael, *Charmed Lives*. New York: Random House, 1979

Landstone, Charles, *Off-Stage*. London: Elek Books, 1953

Lasky, Jesse L.(with Pat Silver), *Love Scene*. New York: Thomas Y. Crowell, 1978

Leaming, Barbara, *Orson Welles*. New York: Viking, 1983

Lesley, Cole, *The Life of Noël Coward*. London: Jonathan Cape, 1976

Lewis, Roger, *Stage People*. London: Weidenfeld and Nicolson, 1989

Loney, Glenn, *20th Century Theatre* (2 vols). New York: Facts on File Publications, 1983

McBean, Angus, *Vivien Leigh: A Love Affair in Camera*. Oxford: Phaidon, 1989

MacDermott, Norman, *Everymania*. London: Society for Theatre Research, 1975

McLeish, Kenneth, *Longman Guide to Shakespeare's Characters*. London: Longman, 1985

Madsen, Axel, *William Wyler*. New York: Thomas Y. Crowell, 1973

Manvell, Roger, *Shakespeare and the Film*. London: J.M. Dent and Sons, 1971

Marker, L.L. and E.J., *Ingmar Bergman: Four Decades in the Theatre*. Cambridge: The University Press, 1982

Marx, Arthur, *Goldwyn: A Biography of the Man Behind the Myth*. New York: Norton, 1976

Massey, Raymond, *A Hundred Different Lives*. Toronto: McClelland and Stewart, 1979

Matthews, Bache, *A History of the Birmingham Repertory Theatre*. London: Chatto and Windus, 1924

Meyer, Michael, *Not Prince Hamlet*. London: Secker and Warburg, 1989

Miller, Arthur, *Timebends*. New York: Grove Press, 1987

Miller, Jonathan, *Subsequent Performances*. London: Faber and Faber, 1986

Mills, John, *Up in the Clouds, Gentlemen, Please*. New Haven: Ticknor and Fields, 1981

Montagu, Ivor, *With Eisenstein in Hollywood*. Berlin: Seven Seas, 1968

Montgomery, John, *The Twenties*. London: George Allen and Unwin, 1957

Morley, Margaret, *The Films of Laurence Olivier*. Secaucus: Citadel, 1977

Morley, Sheridan, *Gladys Cooper*. London: Heinemann, 1979

—— *The Great Stage Stars*. London: Angus and Robertson, 1986

—— *The Other Side of the Moon: The Life of David Niven*. New York: Harper and Row, 1985

—— *A Talent to Amuse: A Biography of Noël Coward*. Boston: Little, Brown, 1969

—— *Tales from the Hollywood Raj*. New York: Viking, 1983

Mortimer, John, *Character Parts*. London: Penguin, 1987

—— *In Character*. London: Penguin, 1984

Niven, David, *Bring on the Empty Horses*. New York: Putnam's, 1975

Norton, Graham, *London Before the Blitz*. London: Macdonald, 1970

O'Connor, Garry, *Darlings of the Gods*. London: Hodder and Stoughton, 1984

—— *Olivier: In Celebration*. New York: Dodd, Mead, 1987

—— *Ralph Richardson: An Actor's Life*. New York: Limelight, 1985

Olivier, Laurence, *Confessions of an Actor*. New York: Simon and Schuster, 1982

—— Henry V, *by William Shakespeare*. London: Lorrimer, 1984

—— *On Acting*. New York: Touchstone/Simon and Schuster, 1986

Payn, Graham and Morley, Sheridan, eds., *The Noël Coward Diaries*. Boston: Little, Brown, 1982

Priestley, J.B., *Particular Pleasures*. London: Heinemann, 1975

Purser, Ann, *Looking Back at Popular Entertainment 1901–1939*. East Ardsley (Wakefield, Yorkshire): EP Publishing, 1978

Redgrave, Michael, *In My Mind's Eye*. New York: Viking, 1983

Roberts, Peter, *The Best of* Plays and Players, *1953–1968*. London: Methuen, 1988

Sanderson, Michael, *From Irving to Olivier*. London: The Athlone Press, 1984

Spoto, Donald, *The Dark Side of Genius: The Life of Alfred Hitchcock*. Boston: Little, Brown, 1983

Sprigge, Elizabeth, *Sybil Thorndike Casson*. London: Victor Gollancz, 1971

Tanitch, Robert, *Olivier: The Complete Career*. New York: Abbeville, 1985

Trewin, J.C., *The Birmingham Repertory Theatre*. London: Barrie and Rockliff, 1963

—— *Peter Brook – A Biography*. London: Macdonald, 1971

Tynan, Kathleen, *The Life of Kenneth Tynan*. London: Weidenfeld and Nicolson, 1987

Tynan, Kenneth, Othello: *The National Theatre Production*. New York: Stein and Day, 1966

—— *Profiles*. London: Nick Hern/Walker, 1989

—— The Recruiting Officer: *The National Theatre Production*. London: Rupert Hart-Davis, 1965

—— *The Sound of Two Hands Clapping*. New York: Holt, Rinehart and Winston, 1975

—— *A View of the English Stage*. London: Methuen, 1975

Ustinov, Peter, *Dear Me*. Boston: Atlantic Monthly Press, 1977

Vickers, Hugo, *Vivien Leigh*. Boston: Little, Brown, 1988

Walker, Alexander, *Vivien Leigh*. London: Weidenfeld and Nicolson, 1987

Walton, Susanna, *William Walton: Behind the Façade*. Oxford: The University Press, 1988

Wapshott, Nicholas, *Peter O'Toole*. London: New English Library, 1983

Weinreb, Ben and Hibbert, Christopher, *The London Encyclopaedia*. London: Macmillan, 1983

Wiley, Mason and Bona, Damien, *Inside Oscar*. New York: Ballantine, 1987

Williams, Harcourt, ed., *Vic-Wells: The Work of Lilian Baylis*. London: Cobden-Sanderson, 1938

Williamson, Audrey, *Old Vic Drama*. London: Rockliff, 1948

Winn, Godfrey, *The Positive Hour*. London: Michael Joseph, 1970

Young, Stark, *Theatre Practice*. New York: Scribner's, 1926

Zeffirelli, Franco, *Zeffirelli*. London: Weidenfeld and Nicolson, 1986

Zierold, Norman, *Garbo*. New York: Stein and Day, 1969

NOTES

For brevity, details of *interviews* conducted for this book are supplied only at the first citation; unless otherwise stated, subsequent quotations from the same source derive from the identical interview with that source.

CHAPTER ONE

4 Recollections of Sybil Thorndike, quoted in Logan Gourlay, ed., *Olivier* (New York: Stein and Day, 1974), p. 23.

4 He was very . . . *The Church in Dorking and District* (1912), cited in 'Lord Olivier Slept Here', *Dorking Advertiser*, 7 March 1980.

4 The modern English . . . Charles Wyndham, quoted in Percy Hutchison, *Masquerade* (London, 1936), p. 58.

5 Creed sat lightly . . . R.C.K. Ensor, *England 1870–1914* (Oxford: Clarendon, 1936), pp. 526–7.

6 genteel poverty . . . LO, in Curtis Bill Pepper, 'Talking with Olivier', *New York Times Magazine*, 25 March 1979, p. 56.

6 feeling of . . . 'Olivier: The Terry Coleman Interview', *Guardian*, 8 April 1970.

7 I was the . . . LO, in *Time*, 29 December 1975, p. 59.

7 Regarding the beating of LO as a boy, cf. John Mortimer, *In Character* (London: Penguin, 1984), pp. 59–60.

7 my heaven, my . . . Laurence Olivier, *Confessions of an Actor* (New York: Simon and Schuster, 1982), p. 18. Henceforth: LO, *CA*.

7 Mummy was just . . . Sybille Olivier Day, in Richard Meryman, 'First Lord of the Stage,' *Life*, 8 December 1972, p. 65.

7 Regarding LO's terror of his father, cf. Hal Burton, ed. *Great Acting* (New York: Bonanza, 1967), p. 12.

8 I was frightened . . . Melvyn Bragg,

Laurence Olivier (London: Hutchinson, 1984), p. 20.

10 Regarding Father Mackay, cf. Sidney Dark, *Mackay of All Saints* (London: The Centenary Press, 1937), p. 116.

11 I was a . . . LO, in 'Olivier', *The Observer*, 2 February 1969.

11 Recollections of Laurence Naismith, BBC-TV tribute to Laurence Olivier, 1984.

11 The distinction between . . . *Suggestions for the Consideration of Teachers and Others Concerned in the Work of Public Elementary Schools* (London: The Board of Education, 1914), Circular 873, p. 13.

11 Distinct articulation must . . . *Ibid.*, Circular 808, p.7.

11 Shakespeare is perhaps . . . *Ibid.*, p. 20.

12 We embarked on . . . Dark, *op. cit.*, pp. 127–8.

12 After the performance . . . Evelyn Light to DS, 15 January 1990.

12 Who is she . . . LO, in Burton, *op. cit.*, p. 11.

13 Regarding the Church Pastoral Aid Society, cf. 'E.F.S.', *Our Stage and Its Critics* (London, 1910), p. 158.

13 to organise the . . . Annual Report of the Actors' Church Union, 1899.

13 Regarding the Actors' Church Union, cf. Michael Sanderson, *From Irving to Olivier* (London: The Athlone Press, 1984), p. 148.

13 the atmosphere of . . . Annual Report of the Actors' Church Union, 1914–1915.

14 Stress should be . . . *Suggestions for the Consideration of Teachers*

(London: The Board of Education, 1905), p. 104.

15 She had all . . . Henry Ehrlich, 'Sir Says', *Look*, 27 January 1970, p. 24.

15 Regarding John Freebairn-Smith, cf. Robert Tanitch, *Olivier: The Complete Career* (New York: Abbeville, 1985), p. 18.

16 Goodbye, my darling . . . Sybille Olivier Day, in *Life, art. cit.*

CHAPTER TWO

17 I don't think . . . LO, to Barbara Walters, NBC-TV *Today* show, quoted in *Sunday Times*, 15 July 1973.

18 Bless me, Reader . . . LO, *CA*, p. 9.

18 very very sad . . . Elizabeth Sprigge, *Sybil Thorndike Casson* (London: Victor Gollancz, 1971), p. 134.

18 The Yeats poem is from *The Wind Among the Reeds* (1899); cf. Richard J. Finneran, ed., *W.B. Yeats: The Poems* (New York: Macmillan, 1983).

19 an idea of . . . Edith Craig and Christopher St John, *Ellen Terry's Memoirs* (New York: Putnam's, 1932), p. 53.

19 a perfect little . . . Sybil Thorndike, quoted in Gourlay, *op. cit.*, p. 24.

20 Recollections of Richard F. Wyatt to DS, 11 January 1990.

20 Recollections of J.D. Newhouse to DS, 17 January 1990.

20 I was ostracised . . . LO, *CA*, p. 32.

20 In any case . . . LO to Melvyn Bragg, London Weekend Television/South Bank Show Special (produced and directed by Bob Bee), 1982.

20 Recollections of Carew Wallace to DS, 15 January 1990.

21 Up the great . . . H.F.B. Mackay, 'Stratford', in the All Saints parish newspaper, May 1922.

21 Katharine has fire . . . *The Times*, 29 April 1922.

21 The boy who . . . *Daily Telegraph*, 29 April 1922.

21 boldly and vigorously . . . *Birmingham Post*, 29 April 1922.

21 as delightful a . . .

Stratford-upon-Avon Herald, 5 May 1922.

22 open stage production . . . R.D. Hill, *A History of St Edward's School* (Oxford: St Edward's School Society, 1962), p. 198.

22 this wretched part . . . LO, *CA*, p. 34.

22 The boy who . . . quoted in Garry O'Connor, *Olivier: In Celebration* (New York: Dodd, Mead, 1987), p. 89.

22 by far the . . . Hill, *op. cit.*, pp. 198–9.

22 Don't be such . . . LO, *CA*, p. 15; cf. also Burton, *op. cit.*, p. 12.

24 son of a . . . Laurence Irving, *Precarious Crust* (London, 1971), p. 182.

24 poor unfortunate child . . . Mrs Patrick Campbell, *My Life and Some Letters* (New York: Dodd, Mead, 1922), p. 33.

25 healthy and natural . . . from the gala performance programme of the Central School of Speech and Drama, 10 November 1981, n.p.

25 Recollections of John Gielgud to DS, 4 November 1989.

25 Recollections of Peggy Ashcroft to DS, 24 January 1990.

25 Regarding society ladies at the Central School of Speech and Drama, cf. Norman MacDermott, *Everymania* (London: Society for Theatre Research, 1975), p.9.

26 When you say . . . quoted in LO, *CA*, p. 37; cf. also LO in the foreword to Marion Cole, *Fogie: The Life of Elsie Fogerty* (London: Peter Davies, 1967), p. ix.

26 I lacked for . . . Richard Meryman, 'Actor for the Ages', *Life*, December 1982, p. 142.

26 But he was . . . Evelyn Ascherson, in BBC-TV tribute to LO, 1984.

27 Recollections of George Coulouris, in Michael Billington, *Peggy Ashcroft* (London: John Murray, 1988), p. 19.

27 Recollections of Athene Seyler on BBC-TV tribute to LO, 1984.

28 an invisible wall . . . quoted in Felix Barker, *The Oliviers* (Philadelphia: Lippincott, 1953), p. 37.

32 They used to . . . Sybil Thorndike, in Gourlay, *op. cit.*, p. 25.

CHAPTER THREE

33 to enlarge and . . . Barry V. Jackson, intr. to Bache Matthews, *A History of the Birmingham Repertory Theatre* (London: Chatto and Windus, 1924), p. xiv.
34 all genuine artists . . . *Ibid.*, p. 170.
34 Recollections of Gwen Ffrangçon-Davies to DS, 14 November 1989.
34 Recollections of Denys Blakelock, *Finding My Way* (London: Hollis and Carter, 1958), p. 31.
35 a cocky young . . . Garry O'Connor, *Ralph Richardson* (New York: Limelight, 1985), p. 53.
35 I want to . . . Ralph Richardson, 'Chimes at Midnight', *Sunday Times*, 21 October 1973.
35 Laurence, never – never . . . *Ibid.*
36 The versatility I . . . LO to Melvyn Bragg, LWT, 1982.
37 Review of *Bird in Hand* by R. Crompton Rhodes, *Birmingham Post*, 5 September 1927.
39 Larry looked down . . . Denys Blakelock, 'Larry the Lamb', *art. cit.* 9.
39 We thought he . . . Burton, *op. cit.*, p. 13.
40 The smooth naturalness . . . Raymond Massey, *A Hundred Different Lives* (Toronto: McClelland and Stewart, 1979), pp. 69–70.
41 Of course I . . . Burton, *op. cit.*, p. 15.
44 tedious nobilities . . . *The Times*, 31 January 1929.
44 [Olivier] is overwhelmed . . . Charles Morgan, '*Beau Geste* to the Stage', *New York Times*, 17 February 1929, ix, p.2.
45 Recollections of Alexander Clark to DS, 30 May 1990.
45 with an alarming . . . J. Brooks Atkinson, 'The Play', *New York Times*, 12 September 1929, p. 35.
46 engaging and straightaway . . . John Mason Brown in *New York Evening Post*, 12 September 1929.
46 I suggested you . . . Denys Blakelock, *Round the Next Corner*, p. 56.

48 If his future . . . *The Bioscope*, 6 August 1930, p. 27.
48 Recollections of Laurence Evans to DS, 5 January 1990.
49 Recollections of Noël Coward, notes on *Private Lives*, in *Plays: Two* (London: Eyre Methuen, 1979), n.p.

CHAPTER FOUR

50 What an entrance . . . Richard Briers, *Coward and Company* (London: Futura, 1987), p. 27.
50 From the desk . . . *Ibid.*, p. 37.
50 I've always said . . . *Ibid.*, p. 22.
51 Noël Coward, in . . . Kenneth Harris, 'Olivier', *Observer*, 9 February 1969; cf. also Sheridan Morley, *A Talent to Amuse: A Biography of Noël Coward* (Boston: Little, Brown, 1969), p. 147; cf. also LO in Burton, *op. cit.*, p. 15.
51 Noël adored Larry . . . Cole Lesley, *The Life of Noël Coward* (London: Jonathan Cape, 1976), pp. 137–8.
51 expect married life . . . Jill Esmond, 'What I Think of Marriage', *Daily Herald*, 22 May 1930.
52 the same unspoken . . . LO, *CA*, pp. 81–2.
52 Larry never really . . . Burton, *op. cit.*, p. 169.
53 nearly passionate involvement . . . LO, *CA*, pp. 85–6.
53 swathed in luxury . . . Noël Coward, *Present Laughter* (Garden City: Doubleday, 1937), p. 337.
54 Larry managed, with . . . Coward, *Present Laughter*, p. 338.
54 precious little to . . . LO, *CA*, p. 83.
54 If I did . . . Charles Castle, *Noël* (London: W.H. Allen, 1972), p. 115.
55 DIVIDED, WITH MAJORITY . . . Rudy Behlmer, ed., *Memo from David O. Selznick* (Hollywood: Samuel French, 1989), p. 32.
56 He has no . . . Sheridan Morley, *Tales from the Hollywood Raj* (New York: Viking, 1983), p. 80.
56 I went for . . . LO, *On Acting* (New York: Touchstone/Simon and Schuster, 1986), p. 251.

57 Recollections of Douglas Fairbanks, Jr., to DS, 29 March 1990.

58 It was a . . . Charles Champlin, 'Olivier Better Than Ever', *Los Angeles Times*, 19 January 1976.

59 Recollections of Helen Hayes, in Arthur Marx, *Goldwyn: A Biography of the Man Behind the Myth* (New York: Norton, 1976), p. 265.

60 Listening to the . . . LO, *On Acting*, p. 141.

63 Recollections of LO at Central School in Laurence Kitchin, *Mid-Century Drama* (London: Faber and Faber, 1960), p. 50.

63 He has such . . . LO, *CA*, p. 95.

CHAPTER FIVE

64 Regarding Mamoulian, cf. Sheridan Morley, *Tales from the Hollywood Raj* (New York: Viking, 1983), p. 89.

65 Oh, well . . . *CA*, p. 93.

65 Regarding LO and Greta Garbo, cf. Norman Zierold, *Garbo* (New York: Stein and Day, 1969), p. 67.

65 Although he had . . . DeWitt Bodeen, 'Laurence Olivier', *Films in Review*, vol. 30, no. 10 (December 1979) p. 580.

65 wasn't really surprised . . . *Ibid.*

66 secrets and friends . . . quoted in John Cottrell, *Laurence Olivier* (Englewood Cliffs: Prentice-Hall, 1975), p. 64.

67 not acting . . . Florence Fisher Parry, in the *Pittsburgh Press*, cited in Tanitch, *op. cit.*, p. 45.

67 an extraordinarily searching . . . Brooks Atkinson, 'Style and Pace in Jed Harris's Staging of Mordaunt Shairp's *The Green Bay Tree* – Tragedy of Character and Environment', *New York Times*, 29 October 1933, II, p. 1.

69 Recollections of Constance Cummings to DS, 9 November 1989.

73 Recollections of Greer Garson on BBC-TV tribute to LO, 1984.

74 lively impudence . . . *The Times*, 31 May 1935, p. 14.

74 vitality and charm . . . *Ibid.* (re: Oxford preview), 14 May 1935, p. 14.

74 I'm washed up . . . quoted by Emlyn Williams in O'Connor, *Olivier: A Celebration*, p. 155.

74 as lost as . . . *Ibid.*, p. 158.

75 Though she had taken . . . John Gielgud, *Backward Glances* (London: Hodder and Stoughton, 1989), p. 23.

76 beautiful poise . . . *CA*, p. 100.

76 When I suggested . . . John Gielgud to DS, 4 November 1989.

78 knock their bloody . . . *CA*, p. 34.

78 I will show them . . . Burton, p. 13.

78 inexpertness . . . gabbling . . . *Sunday Times*, 20 October 1935.

78 temperamentally ill . . . *The Times*, 18 October 1935.

78 I have seen . . . St John Ervine in *Observer*, 18 October 1935.

79 He didn't have . . . Alec Guinness to DS, 19 January 1990.

79 almost sprang . . . J.C. Trewin on BBC-TV tribute to LO, 1984.

79 Mr Olivier was . . . *New York Times*, 18 October 1935, p. 27.

79 inclined to be . . . John Gielgud (with John Miller and John Powell), *An Actor and His Time* (New York: Clarkson N. Potter, 1986), p. 178.

80 John had . . . Ronald Hayman, *Playback* (London: Davis-Poynter, 1973), pp. 156–7.

80 rivals rather than . . . John Gielgud in *Today*, 12 July 1989, p. 1.

80 brilliant . . . W.A. Darlington, *Sunday Telegraph*, 29 November 1935.

80 sparkling . . . Charles Morgan, *New York Times*, 29 December 1935, IX, p. 1.

80 quick and lusty vitality . . . Alan Dent, *Preludes and Studies* (London: Macmillan, 1942), p. 83.

80 extraordinary power . . . Morgan, *ut supra*.

82 ambition . . . LO, 1987 Granada Television interview for his eightieth birthday; produced by Derek Granger and Roy Roberts, directed by Eugene Ferguson.

82 and so we went . . . Vivien Leigh to David Lewin, *Daily Express*, 17 August 1960.

82 Regarding VL and Alexander Korda, cf. Hugo Vickers, *Vivien Leigh*

(Boston: Little, Brown, 1988), p. 57.

82 Some day . . . Anne Edwards, *Vivien Leigh* (New York: Pocket Books, 1978), p. 56.

82 intensely ambitious . . . Fabia Drake, *Blind Fortune* (London: William Kimber, 1978), p. 82.

CHAPTER SIX

83 I was trying . . . Richard Findlater, *The Player Kings* (London: Weidenfeld and Nicolson, 1971), p. 211.

86 Recollections of Michael Korda to DS, 3 April 1990.

87 [Olivier] liked . . . Michael Redgrave in Gourlay, *op. cit.*, p. 68.

87 Recollections of Alexander Knox to DS, 2 November 1989.

88 a cheap and decent . . . 'The Old Vic: A Short History', from the programme of the Old Vic Theatre, autumn 1989.

89 I knew I was . . . Findlater, *op. cit.*, p. 213.

90 but because she . . . *Ibid.*

90 She's an absolute . . . Sybil Thorndike, on the audio cassette 'The Old Vic: Story of a Theatre'. London: Soundfact series, no. WHC007.

90 Are you pure . . . *Five Seasons of the Old Vic* (London: Saturn Press, 1950), p. 3.

90 Now, boys and . . . quoted on the cassette 'The Old Vic: Story of a Theatre'. *ut supra.*

91 Of course, you . . . Laurence Olivier, 'Over the Water', in Harcourt Williams, ed., *Vic-Wells: The Work of Lilian Baylis* (London: Cobden-Sanderson, 1938), p. 28.

91 I adored her . . . *Ibid.*

91 The theatre still . . . Peter Roberts, ed., *Lilian Baylis Centenary Festival, 1974* (souvenir programme), p. 29.

91 Dear boy . . . *Ibid.*

91 On the Oedipal reading of *Hamlet*, Jones's famous essay was originally presented in 1923 in *Essays in Applied Psychology*. It was later republished as a book under the latter title (New York: Norton, 1949).

92 My dears . . . James Forsyth, *Tyrone Guthrie* (London: Hamish Hamilton, 1976), p. 155.

92 He moved with . . . Tyrone Guthrie, *A Life in the Theatre* (New York: McGraw-Hill, 1959), p. 187.

93 unfortunately, the sword . . . Stuart Burge to DS, 16 November 1989.

94 Ladies and gentlemen . . . Michael Redgrave, *In My Mind's I* (New York: Viking, 1983), p. 108.

94 I was looking . . . *OA*, p. 91.

94 only now and then . . . quoted in Findlater, *op. cit.*, p. 213.

95 Oswald Frewen's diary entry for 28 June 1937, cited in Vickers, *op. cit.*, p. 77.

95 in complete control . . . *OA*, pp. 100, 96.

96 You are England . . . 'Shakespeare and Laurence Olivier', *Theatre World*, vol. xvi, no. 1 (1967), p. 68; cf. also Findlater, *op. cit.*, p. 213.

96 transfigure the raw . . . Simon Callow, *Charles Laughton: A Difficult Actor* (London: Methuen, 1989), p. 138.

98 Recollections of Basil Dean, *Mind's Eye* (London: Hutchinson, 1973), p. 251.

98 Regarding VL's collapse, cf. Rex Harrison, *Rex* (New York: William Morrow, 1975), p. 51.

99 This has got . . . Forsyth, *op. cit.*, p. 159

99 It was the . . . J.C. Trewin in BBC-TV tribute to LO, 1984.

99 we could not . . . *CA*, p. 101.

101 an almost claustrophobic . . . quoted in Vickers, *op. cit.*, p. 87.

102 He taught Larry . . . Basil Langton to DS, May 11, 1990.

102 You hear Macbeth's . . . Findlater, *op. cit.*, p. 214.

102 I 'made up' . . . *OA*, p. 108.

103 closed in by . . . Audrey Williamson, *op. cit.*, p. 93.

104 the magnificence of . . . Garry O'Connor, *Ralph Richardson*, p. 89.

104 It's inescapable . . . *Ibid.* p. 88; cf. also Barker, p. 166; Forsyth, p. 165; and Olivier in *Theatre World*, art. cit. 72.

105 Bold . . . quoted by Mark Amory in *The Independent*, 12 July 1989.

108 the nearest thing . . . James Agate, in Findlater, *op. cit.*, p. 215.
109 Idyllic . . . *CA*, p. 104.

CHAPTER SEVEN

112 a little pickup . . . A. Scott Berg, *Goldwyn* (New York: Knopf, 1989), p. 325.
112 Why, you amateur . . . *Ibid.*
112 How do you want . . . quoted by Billy Wilder in *William Wyler*, a television documentary.
113 Willy, if this . . . LWT South Bank tribute to LO, 1982 (Melvyn Bragg); cf. also *OA*, p. 259.
113 What do you . . . *OA*, pp. 258–9.
113 He knew . . . *OA*, p. 260.
113 I haven't yet . . . Bosley Crowther, 'Mr Olivier Comes Clean', *New York Times*, 26 March 1939.
115 I want you . . . Rudy Behlmer, ed., *Memo from David O. Selznick* (New York: Viking, 1972), p. 186.
115 Recollections of Sunny Alexander Lash to DS, 8 March 1990.
117 They seemed to . . . Douglas Fairbanks, Jr., *Salad Days*, p. 344.
118 Regarding LO on his father, cf. *CA*, p. 29.
119 I could never love . . . quoted by Rachel Kempson in *Vivien Leigh: Scarlett and Beyond*, written and produced by Gene Feldman and Suzette Winter/A Wombat Production for Turner Pictures, Inc., 1990.
121 partly because . . . Lord Lothian's cable reply to the British press is reprinted, e.g., in Sheridan Morley, *The Other Side of the Moon: The Life of David Niven* (New York: Harper and Row, 1985), p. 103.
122 Couldn't you . . . Joan Fontaine, *No Bed of Roses* (New York: William Morrow, 1978), p. 116.
122 but he is . . . Sheridan Morley, *Gladys Cooper* (London: Heinemann, 1979), p. 184.
122 his pauses . . . Behlmer, p. 292.
124 Evidence was given . . . Court record

noted in the *Daily Telegraph*, 30 January 1940.
124 darling Greer . . . *OA*, p. 262.
124 Acting for film . . . Crowther, *art. cit.*
125 the last time . . . Garson Kanin, *Hollywood* (New York: Viking, 1974), pp. 99–102.
128 to pop on . . . Thoda Cocroft, *Great Names* (Chicago: Dartnell Press, 1941), p. 243.
130 a personal triumph . . . Russell McLauchlin, *Detroit News*, 20 April 1940.
131 Recollections of Joan Shepard to DS, 13 July 1990.
131 may well be . . . quoted in Barker, p. 215.

CHAPTER EIGHT

133 I have quite . . . Morley, *Gladys Cooper*, p. 195.
135 Recollections of Joseph Laitin to DS, 16 April 1990.
137 Not a good . . . Forsyth, p. 183.
138 I think I . . . *CA*, p. 120.
138 Olivier couldn't fly . . . Richard Huggett, *Binkie Beaumont: Eminence Grise of the West End Theatre* (London: Hodder and Stoughton, 1989), p. 275.
139 The trouble . . . O'Connor, *Ralph Richardson*, p. 105.
139 ordinary people . . . Hayman, *Playback*, p. 163.
142 the *éminence grise* . . . Terence Young to DS, 16 January 1990.
143 I was ambitious . . . Susanna Walton, *William Walton: Behind the Façade* (Oxford: The University Press, 1988), p. 94.
144 he exuded . . . Lasky, p. 147.
144 A famous instance . . . Walton, p. 94.
145 Shakespeare in a way . . . LO, 'The Making of *Henry V*', in Andrew Sinclair, ed., *Henry V* (London: Lorrimer, 1984), n.p.
147 It had long . . . Ivor Montagu, *With Eisenstein in Hollywood* (Berlin: Seven Seas, 1968), p. 90.
148 Larry was . . . Laurence Evans to DS, 3 January 1990.
151 relentlessly energetic . . . John

Gielgud in *Vivien Leigh: Scarlett and Beyond, op. cit.*

151 Recollections of Rachel Kempson Redgrave to DS, 15 October 1989.

152 Well, if you . . . widely cited, e.g., *OA*, pp. 121–2.

153 Recollections of Diana Boddington to DS, 15 January 1990.

153 Sit down, darlings . . . John Mills, BBC-TV tribute to LO, 1984; cf. also Gourlay, p. 10; Mills, *Up in the Clouds, Gentlemen, Please* (New Haven: Ticknor and Fields, 1981), p. 194.

155 Do you really . . . O'Connor, *Ralph Richardson*, p. 118.

155 things begin to . . . LO, on the Dick Cavett television show (ABC-TV), 1980.

156 I explained . . . quoted by LO in 'The Great Sir Laurence', *Life*, 1 May 1964, p. 98.

156 There was something . . . *Ibid.*, pp. 24–5.

156 a Laurence Olivier play . . . quoted by Bronson Albery to Basil Langton, thence to DS, 11 May 1990.

157 It was absolutely . . . *OA*, p. 200.

CHAPTER NINE

161 Regarding the Old Vic tour, cf. Elizabeth Sprigge, *Sybil Thorndike Casson* (London: Victor Gollancz, 1971), pp. 253–4; and John Casson, *Lewis and Sybil: A Memoir* (London: Collins, 1972), pp. 228–9.

161 Recollections of R.B. Appleton to DS, 25 October 1989.

162 Regarding the dinner in Paris: recollections of Virginia Fairweather to DS, 25 November 1989.

162 I hate him . . . O'Connor, *Ralph Richardson*, p. 128.

163 He had a streak . . . Harry Andrews in Garry O'Connor, *Olivier: In Celebration* (New York: Dodd, Mead, 1987), p. 66.

163 Make-up is a strange . . . *OA*, p. 125.

164 You're very, very . . . Richardson to Melvyn Bragg, LWT South Bank tribute to LO, 1982.

164 painstaking and perfectionist . . . Gourlay, pp. 109–10.

164 I tried to prove . . . LO, in an eightieth birthday interview (1987), produced for Granada TV by Derek Granger and Roy Roberts, directed by Eugene Ferguson.

164 I like to think . . . *OA*, pp. 30, 90–1.

169 A crazy quarrel . . . Garson Kanin, quoted in Garry O'Connor, *Darlings of the Gods* (London: Hodder and Stoughton, 1984), p. 33.

170 Recollections of Frances Tannehill to DS, 30 May 1990.

170 The Old Vic . . . Lewis Nichols in the *New York Times*, 21 May 1946, p. 19.

172 Notley was like . . . Laurence Evans to DS, 3 January 1990.

172 Recollections of Terence Morgan and Georgina Jumel to DS, 10 November 1989.

173 Larry's performance as . . . Graham Payn and Sheridan Morley, eds., *The Noël Coward Diaries* (Boston: Little, Brown, 1982), p. 65.

175 I thought the . . . United Press release, cited in the *New York Post*, 3 December 1946. Cf. also *New York Times*, 26 November 1946, p. 35 and *Los Angeles Times*, 4 December 1946.

175 Recollections of Terence Young to DS, 16 January 1990.

175 I should have been . . . O'Connor, *Ralph Richardson*, p. 141.

176 I've done every . . . Holden, p. 213.

176 Larry's imitations have . . . Richard Buckley, ed., *Self-Portrait with Friends: The Selected Diaries of Cecil Beaton* (New York: New York Times Books, 1979), pp. 187–8.

177 Larry always had . . . John Mills on BBC-TV tribute to LO, 1984.

177 Recollections of Jean Simmons to DS, 12 March 1990.

177 For days on . . . Brenda Cross, ed., *The Film 'Hamlet'* (London: Saturn Press, 1948), p. 48.

178 an essay . . . Cross, pp. 12, 15.

180 Recollections of Sally Ann Howes to DS, 26 December 1989.

180 a face of furious . . . quoted in Vickers, p. 174.

CHAPTER TEN

182 We want to . . . O'Connor, *Darlings*, p. 42.

183 When a man is . . . Filmed speech in Melbourne, included in the BBC-TV tribute to LO, 1984.

184 the glitter of . . . *CA*, p. 169.

184 I lost you . . . *Ibid.*, p. 158.

194 We never converse . . . Vickers, p. 199.

195 She'd have crawled . . . Elia Kazan, *A Life* (New York: Knopf, 1988), p. 387.

200 It is unfortunate . . . Stephen Watts, 'Enter the Oliviers (Diffidently)', *New York Times* magazine, 16 December 1951, p. 46.

202 Recollections of Felix Barker to DS, 18 November 1989.

203 piercing, candid blankness . . . His 1951 review reprinted in Kenneth Tynan, *A View of the English Stage* (London: Methuen, 1984), pp. 107–10.

203 dissatisfaction with self . . . Watts, *art. cit.*

203 Recollections of Elaine Dundy to DS, 20 March 1990.

204 Press reports on VL, e.g., *Daily Graphic*, 8 October 1951.

204 Recollections of Alec McCowen to DS, 17 November 1989.

205 I want to . . . *Ibid.*

CHAPTER ELEVEN

213 Peter Ustinov's recollections in O'Connor, *Olivier: In Celebration*, p. 83.

214 calm and sweet . . . Payn and Morley, p. 215.

214 Is it as funny . . . Gourlay, p. 133.

215 so much talent . . . Milton Shulman in the *Evening Standard*, 6 November 1953.

215 I would like to . . . Virginia Fairweather, *Olivier: An Informal Portrait* (New York: Coward-McCann), p. 22.

217 Recollections of Claire Bloom to DS, 29 May 1990.

219 Great actresses have . . . quoted by LO to Laurence Evans, thence to DS, 3 January 1990.

220 Darling John . . . quoted by Maxine Audley to DS, 17 November 1989.

221 The best Macbeth . . . Harold Hobson, 'Nonpareil', *Sunday Times*, 12 June 1955.

222 shook hands with . . . Kenneth Tynan, *Macbeth* review, reprinted in *A View of the English Stage*, p. 157.

222 Both she and . . . John Gielgud to DS, 4 November 1989.

222 a sort of . . . Payne and Morley, p. 278.

222 *Macbeth* is a domestic . . . In *World Theatre*, XVI/1 (1967), p. 63.

223 [The Oliviers] are trapped . . . Payn and Morley, p. 278.

CHAPTER TWELVE

226 travesty on England . . . Arthur Miller, *Timebends* (New York: Grove Press, 1987), p. 416.

227 Do you suppose . . . *Ibid.*, p. 417.

227 the entire West End . . . Richard Findlater, *At the Royal Court* (London: Amber Lane Press, 1981), p. 19.

229 thoroughly ill-mannered . . . *Daily Express*, 22 May 1980.

230 Recollections of Susan Strasberg to DS, 23 April 1990.

231 He was a top . . . Joan Plowright, 'My Larry', *TV Times*, vol. 137, no. 52 (23 December 1989 – 5 January 1990), p. 127.

231 The music hall . . . John Osborne, *The Entertainer* (London: Faber and Faber, 1961), introductory note.

231 I had reached . . . Findlater, *At the Royal Court*, p. 40.

233 It's really me . . . Cf., e.g., Gourlay, p. 174 and William Gaskill, *A Sense of Direction: Life at the Royal Court* (London: Faber and Faber, 1988), p. 72.

233 It's what I . . . *Time*, 29 December 1975, p. 59; cf. also Meryman, *art. cit.*, p. 146.

235 He already has . . . quoted by Maxine Audley to DS, 17 November 1989.

236 ghastly stories . . . Payn and Morley, p. 358.

236 I just can't . . . Radie Harris, *Radie's World* (New York: Putnam's, 1975), p. 233.

236 mistake after mistake . . . Burton, p. 16.

237 In a sky-high . . . *CA*, p. 222.

239 He got down . . . Plowright, *art. cit.* 127.

239 She was part . . . Tony Richardson on BBC-TV tribute to LO, 1984.

239 It was rather . . . Sue Fox, 'A Hard Act to Follow', *Sunday Times*, 2 October 1983, p. 10.

239 but we learned . . . *Ibid.*, p. 9; and Linda Christmas, 'Acting is Not Enough', *Plays and Players*, no. 346 (July 1982), p. 12.

240 I do not think . . . *Daily Telegraph*, 27 November 1957.

240 I am surprised . . . *Ibid.*, 3 December 1957.

241 All this talk . . . Basil Langton to DS, 11 May 1990; cf. also Dick Williams, 'Olivier's Return Magnet for Mimes', *Los Angeles Mirror-News*, 10 March 1959, p. 7.

241 What they call . . . Maurice Zolotow, 'The Olivier Method', *New York Times*, 7 February 1960, section II, p. 1.

241 a versatile performance . . . *New York Times*, 13 February 1958, p. 22.

242 I personally don't . . . Payn and Morley, p. 379.

243 Larry, why don't . . . Terence Young to DS, 16 January 1990.

243 very seductive . . . Kirk Douglas, *The Ragman's Son* (New York: Simon and Schuster, 1988), p. 291.

243 tendency to take . . . Dr Arthur Conachy, notes on the psychiatric condition of Vivien Leigh dated 20 June 1961.

244 She is obviously . . . Payn and Morley, pp. 392–3.

244 bonds that can . . . quoted in O'Connor, *Olivier: In Celebration*, p. 161.

245 With *Macbeth* off . . . David Lewin, 'The Big Step I'm Taking', *Daily Express*, 18 November 1958.

245 Olivier was punctual . . . Michael Meyer, *Not Prince Hamlet* (London: Secker and Warburg, 1989), p. 161.

246 It was always . . . Peter Ustinov,

Dear Me (Boston: Atlantic Monthly Press, 1977), p. 300.

247 Recollections of Talli Wyler to DS, 19 July 1990.

247 My life has . . . Curtis Bill Pepper, *art. cit.*, p. 57.

247 contorted with embarrassment . . . Alfred Bester, 'Sir Larry', *Holiday*, February 1960.

249 We must stay . . . Winn, p. 393.

249 All right . . . quoted in Peter Hall, 'Olivier: Exit the Emperor', *New York Times*, 23 July 1989, sec. II, p. 26.

250 She is desperately . . . Payn and Morley, p. 420.

250 Our marriage is . . . Associated Press release (cf., e.g., *Los Angeles Times*), 2 December 1959.

251 My baronial period . . . quoted in O'Connor, *Olivier: In Celebration*, p. 68.

CHAPTER THIRTEEN

252 Recollections of Charlton Heston to DS, 6 March 1990.

253 The actor must . . . Zolotow, *art. cit.*, p. 3.

253 You are about . . . John Mills in Gourlay, p. 11; cf. also Mills, p. 247.

253 It's too hot . . . *Olivier at Work*, p. 48.

253 Recollections of Rosemary Harris to DS, 20 June 1990.

253 For rehearsal details, cf. Charlton Heston, *The Actor's Life: Journals 1956–1976* (New York: Pocket Books, 1979), p. 112.

254 Regarding sale of Notley Abbey, cf. *Daily Mail*, 1 March 1960.

254 He took . . . Barbara Leaming, *Orson Welles*, p. 456.

255 Why did you . . . quoted by Elaine Dundy to DS, 20 March 1990.

255 I am bored . . . quoted in David Lewin, 'Sex, Guilt and Olivier', *Daily Mail*, 18 October 1982, p. 7.

255 Lady Olivier . . . widely published; cf., e.g., *Daily Mail*, 23 May 1960.

255 I would want . . . *Daily Express*, 15 August 1960.

255 please ask Larry . . . Rachel Kempson Redgrave to DS, 15 November 1989.

256 He almost wept . . . Virginia
Fairweather to DS, 25 November 1989.
256 like someone holding . . . LO, on
BBC-TV tribute, 1984.
256 I suspect . . . Payn and Morley, p. 441.
257 One always knows . . . Howard
Taubman in the *New York Times*, 6
October 1960, p. 50.
257 Tony, where the . . . Quinn, in Larry
King with Peter Occhiogrosso, 'Tell it to the
King', *Playboy*, April 1988.
258 Until 1952 . . . quoted in UPI news
service; cf., e.g., 'Vivien Leigh Wins
Divorce from Sir Laurence Olivier', *Los
Angeles Examiner*, 3 December 1960.
258 Recollections of Leslie
Evershed-Martin to DS, 20 November
1989.
259 I feel that . . . Leslie
Evershed-Martin to LO, 11 January
1961.
260 The purpose of . . . LO, quoted in Leslie
Evershed-Martin, *The Impossible Theatre*
(London and Chichester: Phillimore,
1971), p. 82.
261 Because we were both . . . Joan
Plowright, *art. cit.*, p. 130.
261 Ever since my . . . Meryman, *art. cit.*
146; cf. also Harold Hobson in *Los
Angeles Times*, 24 November 1963;
also quoted by Laurence Evans to
DS, 3 January 1990.
261 likeness to . . . Melvyn Bragg,
Laurence Olivier, p.24.
263 Recollections of Dale Wasserman to
DS, 12 November 1990.
263 Recollections of Julie Harris to DS,
30 July 1990.
265 an extremely brave . . . Sarah Miles
to DS, 28 November 1989.
266 Recollections of Lynda Gilby to DS,
16 June 1990.
268 When you open . . . quoted often by
LO; e.g., to Rosemary Harris, thence
to DS.
268 trying to be . . . LO, in
Evershed-Martin, p. xiv.
269 a fresh creation . . . *The Tatler*, 4
December 1963.
270 The only time . . . quoted by e.g.
Peter Evans in the *Daily Express*,
7 August 1963.

270 Well, are you going . . . quoted by
Virginia Fairweather to DS,
15 November 1989.
270 I doubt whether . . . Peter Hall on
BBC-TV tribute to LO, 1984; also Hall
to DS, 25 January 1990.
272 Well, did you . . . cited in e.g. 'Lady
Olivier Pours', in Earl Wilson's
column, *New York Post*, 20 February
1980, p. 32.
272 It is a dull . . . *Daily Mail*, 6
December 1962.
273 Oh, what a . . . Payn and Morley, p. 519.
273 I was miserable . . . To Peter Evans,
Daily Express, 7 August 1963.
274 Recollections of Ronald Pickup to DS,
20 November 1989.
274 the little fucker . . . Simon Callow,
Charles Laughton, p. 218.
275 Recollections of John Osborne in
Gourlay, p. 152.
276 When he's had . . . *Ibid.*, p. 165.
276 girlish . . . Kenneth Tynan in *The
Sound of Two Hands Clapping*
(New York: Holt, Rinehart and
Winston, 1975), p. 130.
277 You cannot make . . . Kenneth Tynan,
*Othello: The National Theatre
Production* (New York: Stein and Day);
reprinted in his *Profiles* (London: Nick
Hern/Walker, 1989), p. 205.
278 Recollections of William Gaskill to
DS, 23 January 1990.
279 Recollections of Denys Lasdun to DS,
9 November 1989.
280 that grey-eyed . . . Tynan, *The Sound of
Two Hands Clapping*, p. 130.
280 Bring [the light] . . . Leonard Tucker
in *Olivier at Work*, p. 24.

CHAPTER FOURTEEN

282 Recollections of Edward Petherbridge
in *Plays and Players*, *art. cit.*, p. 8.
282 He tossed a . . . Tynan, *Othello: The
National Theatre Production*,
reprinted in *Profiles*, pp. 207–8.
282 I had to be . . . *OA*, p. 153.
284 He has scaled . . . *Daily Mail*, 22
April 1964.
284 He triumphs in . . . *The Herald*, 22
April 1964.

284 It is a performance . . . *Daily Express*, 22 April 1964.
284 Olivier struck deeper . . . *The Guardian*, 23 April 1964.
284 The power . . . *Sunday Times*, 26 April 1964.
285 I admire him . . . Rachel Kempson Redgrave to DS, 15 November 1989.
287 You've got a . . . Quentin Falk, *Anthony Hopkins: Too Good to Waste* (London: Columbus Books, 1989), p. 30.
287 a real bully . . . *Ibid.*, p. 325.
288 Did you see . . . quoted by Alec McCowen to DS, 17 November 1989.
289 Don't leave . . . LO, on BBC-TV tribute, 1984.
290 Let's do just . . . Charlton Heston to DS, 6 March 1990.
291 I've been married . . . Thomas Quinn Curtis, 'Olivier Rewrites Doctor's Script', *New York Times*, 1 February 1967, p. 28.
291 There isn't a . . . Meyer, p. 229.
291 I don't like . . . quoted in Kathleen Tynan, *The Life of Kenneth Tynan* (London: Methuen, 1988), p. 253.
292 I maintain that . . . *CA*, p. 319.
294 I remember his . . . Meryman, *art. cit.*, p. 69.
294 the cancer which . . . 'Sir Laurence Olivier: His Ills and his Wills', *Los Angeles Times*, 5 November 1967, Calendar – 1.
295 Acting, after all . . . *Theatre Crafts*, vol. 2, no. 3 (May-June 1968) 10–11.
295 My dear sir . . . Fairweather, p. 169.
295 News reports on LO's illness, cf. *Daily Mail*, 21 June 1967; *Daily Express*, 20 June 1967; *New York Post*, 21 June 1967.
295 There was a . . . Douglas Fairbanks, Jr., to DS, 29 March 1990.
296 pale but lovely . . . Payn and Morley, p. 651.
296 It is inhuman . . . *CA*, p. 185.
296 I stood and . . . *CA*, pp. 274–5.

CHAPTER FIFTEEN

299 Recollections of Franco Zeffirelli in *Zeffirelli* (London: Weidenfeld and Nicolson, 1986), p. 229.
299 I worry about . . . Terry Coleman, *art. cit.*, p. 45.
300 They'll have to . . . Margaret Harford, 'Olivier Only has Time to Build Stage', *Los Angeles Times*, 21 January 1970.
300 Get out of . . . quoted by Edward Fox to DS, 4 January 1990.
300 Actually, Peter . . . quoted in Peter Hay, *Theatrical Anecdotes* (New York and Oxford: The University Press, 1987), p. 242.
301 I'm one of . . . Kenneth Harris, 'Olivier', *The Observer Review*, 2 February 1969.
301 the punch that . . . *CA*, p. 271.
301 I'm such a slow . . . Robert Musel, 'Join us, Richard, I'm going to be interviewed', *TV Guide*, 11 October 1969, p. 16.
301 I found him . . . Haill, *op. cit.*, p. 46.
302 Acting's a beastly . . . Harris, *art. cit.*
302 Recollections of Jonathan Miller to DS, 27 December 1989.
304 I've been working . . . LO, in *The Observer*, 14 June 1970.
304 determined to be . . . Melvyn Bragg, *Richard Burton, A Life* (Boston: Little, Brown, 1988), p. 340.
304 [Olivier] wanted my . . . L.L. and E.J. Marker, *Ingmar Bergman: Four Decades in the Theatre* (Cambridge: The University Press, 1982), p. 225; cf. also Meyer, p. 213.
304 Now that I . . . Ronald Hastings, 'Olivier Not to Act for Twelve Months', *Daily Telegraph*, 30 September 1970.
305 I think it's . . . Falk, p. 57.
306 relentlessly mediocre . . . Irving Wardle, in *New York Times*, 25 June 1971, p. 18.
306 I must beg . . . *CA*, pp. 339–40.
307 Every minute we . . . Constance Cummings to DS, 9 November 1989.
308 Darling Daddy . . . Meryman, *art. cit.*

308 To women he was . . . *Sunday Telegraph*, 16 July 1989.

309 Regarding Joan's ambitions, cf. Peter Hall's *Diaries* (New York: Harper and Row, 1984), p. 46.

309 Four flops . . . Kathleen Tynan, p. 303.

309 ruminates and reminisces . . . *Ibid*, pp. 303–4.

310 one of a . . . *Ibid*, p. 302.

311 We had a . . . Robert Bolt to DS, 28 November 1989.

312 was absolutely pole-axed . . . Peter Lewis, 'Why Olivier was Sacked – Twice', *Sunday Telegraph*, 16 July 1989.

313 Recollections of Peter Hall to DS, 25 January 1990.

314 You can call . . . Michael Caine to DS, 23 January 1990.

315 It's very difficult . . . Hall *Diaries*, pp. 30ff.

316 like ships that . . . Victor Davis, 'Life can be a Giggle', *Daily Express*, 7 November 1973.

316 Without thinking . . . Zeffirelli, pp. 258–9.

318 This is the first . . . Haill, p. 68.

318 When he loses . . . Clive Merrison, 'Building the Party', *Plays and Players*, no. 366 (March 1984), p. 27.

318 He turned and . . . Hall *Diaries*, p. 86.

319 But I believe . . . Lyrics from 'If Love Were All', from *Bitter Sweet*, in Noël Coward, *The Lyrics of Noël Coward* (London: Heinemann, 1965), p. 73.

CHAPTER SIXTEEN

320 I don't know . . . Katharine Hepburn to DS, 9 April 1990.

321 I was working . . . George Cukor, on the liner notes to the CBS/Fox video laserdisc of the 1975 telefilm *Love Among the Ruins*. Released by ABC Video, 1990.

322 For 1989 data on dermatomyositis, cf. Michael G. Lyon, Daniel A. Bloch, Brooke Hollak and James F. Fries,

'Predisposing Factors in Polymyositis-Dermatomyositis: Results of a Nationwide Survey', *Journal of Rheumatology*, vol. 16, no. 9 (September 1989), pp. 1218–24.

322 It was really . . . Joan Plowright to Melvyn Bragg, South Bank/LWT, 1982.

322 fucking [his] love . . . *CA*, p. 220.

323 He says he's . . . Michiko Kakutani, 'Distinct, Separate, Yet One', *New York Times*, 27 February 1980, p. 23.

324 In my heart . . . Milton Shulman, 'Olivier Reveals All – Almost', *New Standard*, 5 October 1982; cf. also Peter Cowie, 'Olivier, at 75, Returns to *Lear*', *New York Times*, 1 May 1983, p. 25.

325 I believe in the theatre . . . O'Connor, *Darlings of the Gods*, p. 60; also, cf. LO's address to the Old Vic School, 24 January 1947.

326 It must have . . . *Ibid.*, p. 189.

327 I have to act . . . Barker, *Laurence Olivier*, p. 10.

327 Recollections of John Schlesinger to DS, 24 April 1990.

327 I wanted to . . . Mel Gussow, 'Olivier, Prince of Players, Recalls his Slings and Arrows', *New York Times*, 10 December 1975, p. 57.

328 That demands a . . . *Evening Standard*, 21 November 1975.

328 Recollections of Lotta Palfi-Andor to DS, 1 May 1990.

329 Recollections of Ben Benjamin to DS, 26 April 1990.

329 Of course, nothing . . . Zeffirelli, p. 285.

329 Recollections of Anthony Quinn to DS, 1 November 1990.

329 Recollections of *The Collection*: Helen Mirren to DS, 14 May 1990.

330 Recollections of Maureen Stapleton to DS, 20 March 1990.

331 Regarding LO's lack of interest in the opening ceremonies: recollections of John Goodwin to DS, 27 November 1989.

331 I've got to . . . quoted by Diana Boddington to DS, 15 January 1990.
331 I felt like . . . *Sunday Times*, 28 November 1976, p. 73.
331 Yes, I fucking *do* . . . quoted by Michael Caine to DS, 23 January 1990.
331 I'm reputed to . . . Arthur Unger, 'Hello, New York Calling Mr Lord Olivier', *Christian Science Monitor*, 3 December 1976, p. 34.
332 Recollections of Daniel Petrie to DS, 22 March 1990.
333 Recollections of Donald Petrie to DS, 25 April 1990.
334 Recollections of Robert Fryer to DS, 28 April 1990.
334 You can drop . . . Bernard Drew, 'Lord Laurence Olivier as Nazi Hunter', *American Film*, vol. III, no. 9 (July-August 1978), p. 54; cf. also Donald Zec, 'King Larry', *Daily Mirror*, 16 March 1979.
334 Recollections of Marcella Markham to DS, 12 June 1990.
335 Recollections of George Roy Hill to DS, 30 March 1990.
335 They criticise me . . . Pepper, *art.cit.* Cf. also Rex Reed, 'Olivier: After the Accolades, "Money"', *New York Sunday News*, 21 October 1979, p. 22. Reprinted in Brian Pendreigh, 'Oscar Winner's Four Decades in Film History', *The Scotsman*, 12 July 1989.
335 a pure excuse . . . quoted in Simon Garfield, 'Family Drama with Olivier in the Wings', *Independent on Sunday*, 25 November 1990, p. 4.
335 Recollections of John Badham to DS, 23 February 1990.
338 I've had so much . . . Roderick Mann, 'Lord Olivier: Of Lies and Acting', *Los Angeles Times*, 19 October 1980; also in the *Sunday Express*, same date.

338 Though Larry and I . . . *Cosmopolitan*, May 1980.
340 Eventually he lost . . Richard Fleischer to DS, 23 March 1990.

CHAPTER SEVENTEEN

341 Recollections of Mark Amory to DS, 8 November 1989.
341 Recollections of Alvin Rakoff to DS, 19 November 1989.
342 Your mind expands . . . Curtis Bill Pepper, *art. cit.*
343 Recollections of Michael Korda to DS, 3 April 1990.
343 Recollections of Dorothy Tutin to DS, 10 January 1990.
344 I wear an . . . *OA*, pp. 144, 339.
344 just a selfish . . . Peter Cowie, 'Olivier, at 75, Returns to *Lear*', *New York Times*, 1 May 1983, p. 25.
346 Recollections of Robert Knights to DS, 19 June 1990.
346 no idea what . . . Meyer, p. 261.
346 I'm probably the . . . O'Connor, *Ralph Richardson*, p. 241.
347 His aloneness was . . . Angela Fox to DS, 26 December 1989; cf. also her book, *Completely Foxed* (London: Collins, 1989), p. 177.
347 John is a . . . *OA*, p. 192.
347 I'm not a . . . On the 'Barbara Walters Special', ABC-TV, 17 June 1980.
347 Recollections of Euan Lloyd to DS, 11 January 1990.
348 Recollections of Edward Fox to DS, 4 January 1990.
348 Lol Evans . . . *Evening Standard*, 5 March 1985.
349 He's just pleased . . . *Daily Mail*, 14 November 1985, p. 19.
351 If you go . . . Antony Sher, 'Stars Upstaged from the Stalls at Birthday Party', *The Independent*, 12 July 1989.
353 My dear, we . . . Janet Sinclair, R.N., to Donald McKechnie, at LO's memorial service, 20 October 1989.

Index